İstanbul

"All you've got to do is decide to go and the hardest part is over.

So go!"

TONY WHEELER, COFOUNDER – LONELY PLANET

THIS EDITION WRITTEN AND RESEARCHED BY

Virginia Maxwell

Contents

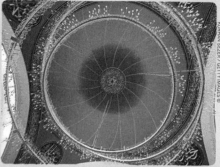

(left) **Mezes p30**
Traditional small dishes
....
(above) **Şakirin Mosque p151** Modern mosque in Üsküdar
....
(right) **Topkapı Palace p57** Famous palace with a colourful history
....

Beşiktaş, Ortaköy & Kuruçeşme
p141

Western Districts
p106

Beyoğlu
p116

Bazaar District
p86

Sultanahmet & Around
p48

Kadıköy
p148

Welcome to İstanbul

This magical meeting place of East and West has more top-drawer attractions than it has minarets (and that's a lot).

Living History

İstanbul's strategic location has attracted many marauding armies over the centuries. The Greeks, Persians, Romans and Venetians took turns ruling before the Ottomans stormed into town and decided to stay – physical reminders of their various tenures are found littered across the city. And the fact that the city straddles two continents wasn't its only drawcard. This was the final stage on the legendary Silk Roads that linked Asia and Europe, and many of the merchants who came here liked it so much that they, too, decided to stay.

Art & Architecture

The conquering armies of ancient times tended to ransack the city rather than endow it with artistic treasures, but that changed with the Byzantines, who adorned their churches and palaces with mosaics and frescoes. Miraculously, many of these are still here to admire. Their successors, the Ottomans, were quick to launch an ambitious building program after their emphatic arrival. The magnificently decorated imperial mosques that followed are architectural triumphs that together form one of the world's great skylines. And in recent years, local banks and business dynasties have reprised the Ottomans' grand ambitions and endowed an impressive array of galleries, museums and festivals.

Culinary Heritage

'But what about the food?' we hear you say. We're happy to report that the city's cuisine is as diverse as its heritage, and delicious to boot. Locals take their eating and drinking seriously – the restaurants here are the best in the country. You can eat edgy fusion creations, aromatic Asian dishes or Italian classics if you so choose, but most visitors prefer to sample the succulent kebaps, flavoursome mezes and freshly caught fish that are the city's signature dishes, washing them down with the national drink, rakı (grape spirit infused with aniseed), or a glass or two of locally produced wine or beer.

Local Life

Some ancient cities are the sum of their monuments, but İstanbul factors a lot more into the equation. Chief among its manifold attractions are the locals, who have an infectious love of life and generosity of spirit. This vibrant, inclusive and expanding community is full of people who work and party hard, treasure family and friendships, and have no problem melding tradition and modernity in their everyday lives. Joining them in their favourite haunts – *çay bahçesis* (tea gardens), *kahvehanı* (coffeehouses), *meyhanes* (Turkish taverns) and *kebapçıs* (kebap restaurants) – will be a highlight of your visit.

Why I Love İstanbul

By Virginia Maxwell, Author

Why do I love this city? Let me count the ways. I love the locals, who have an endless supply of hospitality, good humour and insightful conversation at their disposal. I love the fact that when I walk down a city street, layers of history unfold before me. I love listening to the sound of the *müezzins* duelling from their minarets and I love seeing the sun set over the world's most beautiful skyline. I love the restaurants, the bars and the tea gardens. But most of all, I love the fact that in İstanbul, an extraordinary cultural experience lies around every corner.

For more about our author, see p256.

İstanbul's
Top 10

Aya Sofya *(p50)*

1 History resonates when you visit this majestic Byzantine basilica. Built by order of the emperor Justinian in the 6th century AD, its soaring dome, huge nave and glittering gold mosaics contribute to its reputation as one of the world's most beautiful buildings, and its long and fascinating history as church, mosque and museum make it the city's most revealing time capsule. Looted by marauding Crusaders in the 13th century, stormed by Ottoman invaders during the Conquest in 1453 and visited by millions of tourists since becoming a museum, it is Turkey's greatest treasure.

⊙ *Sultanahmet & Around*

Topkapı Palace *(p57)*

2 The secrets of the seraglio will be revealed during your visit to this opulent Ottoman palace complex occupying the promontory of İstanbul's Old City. A series of mad, sad and downright bad sultans lived here with their concubines and courtiers between 1465 and 1830, and extravagant relics of their centuries of folly, intrigue, excess, patronage, diplomacy and war are everywhere you look. Highlights include the huge Harem (private quarters), impressive Imperial Council Chamber, object-laden Imperial Treasury and picturesque Marble Terrace.

⊙ *Sultanahmet & Around*

TETRA IMAGES / GETTY IMAGES ©

KEITH LEVIT / DESIGN PICS / GETTY IMAGES ©

Bosphorus Ferry Trip (p155)

3 Climbing aboard one of the city's famous flotilla of ferries is the quintessential İstanbul experience. The trip between Asia and Europe on a commuter ferry is hard to beat, but the Bosphorus tourist ferries that travel the length of the great strait from Eminönü to the mouth of the Black Sea are even better, offering passengers views of palaces, parks and ornate timber mansions on both the Asian and European shores. It doesn't matter whether you opt for a long or short cruise – either is sure to be memorable.

🏃 *Day Trips*

Shopping in the Bazaars (p102)

4 The chaotic and colourful Grand Bazaar is the best-known shopping destination on the Historic Peninsula, but it certainly isn't the only one. After exploring its labyrinthine lanes and hidden caravanserais, follow the steady stream of local shoppers heading downhill into the busy shopping precinct of Tahtakale, which has at its hub the seductively scented Spice Bazaar. From there, head back up towards the Blue Mosque and its attached *arasta* (row of shops by a mosque), where you may well find a lasting memento of your trip. LEFT: GRAND BAZAAR (P88)

🏠 *Bazaar District*

Süleymaniye Mosque (p91)

5 Dominating the Old City's skyline, Süleyman the Magnificent's most notable architectural legacy certainly lives up to its patron's name. The fourth imperial mosque built in İstanbul, the Süleymaniye was designed by Mimar Sinan, the most famous of all Ottoman architects, and was built between 1550 and 1557. Its extensive and largely intact *külliye* (mosque complex) buildings illustrate aspects of daily Ottoman life and are still used by the local community – making this a sight that truly lives up to the tag of 'living history'.

⊙ *Bazaar District*

Kariye Museum *(p108)*

6 Tucked away in the shadow of Theodosius II's monumental land walls, Kariye Museum (Chora Church) is a tiny Byzantine building located in the little-visited Western Districts of the city. It's adorned with mosaics and frescoes that were created in the 14th century and illustrate the lives of Christ and the Virgin Mary. These are among the world's best examples of Byzantine art, rivalled only by mosaics adorning churches in Ravenna, Italy. Put simply, it's impossible to over-praise the exquisite interior here – visiting is sure to be a highlight of your trip.

⊙ *Western Districts*

Wining & Dining in Beyoğlu *(p128)*

7 Breathtaking views of the Bosphorus and Old City from the rooftop terraces of a constellation of glamorous bars are just one of the enticements on offer in bohemian Beyoğlu. Locals come here to carouse in traditional *meyhanes* (taverns), eat kebaps in *ocakbaşıs* (grill houses), sample Modern Turkish cuisine in sophisticated bistros and relax in casual European-style cafes and clubs. It's the eating and entertainment epicentre of the city – don't miss it.

✖ *Beyoğlu*

6

Basilica Cistern *(p71)*

8 When the Byzantine emperors decided to build something, they certainly didn't cut corners! This extraordinary subterranean cistern located opposite Aya Sofya features a wildly atmospheric forest of columns (336 to be exact), vaulted brick ceilings, mysterious carved Medusa-head capitals and ghostly patrols of carp. A testament to the ambitious town planning and engineering expertise of the Byzantines, the cistern has played a starring role in innumerable motion pictures (remember *From Russia with Love*?) and is now one of the city's best-loved tourist attractions.

👁 *Sultanahmet & Around*

Visiting a Hamam *(p42)*

9 In life, there aren't too many opportunities to wander semi-naked through a 16th-century Ottoman monument. Unless you visit İstanbul, that is. The city's world-famous hamams offer a unique opportunity to immerse yourself in history, architecture, warm water and soap suds – all at the same time. A hamam treatment offers a relaxing finale to a day spent pounding the city's pavements, and gives a fascinating insight into the life and customs of Ottoman society. You can surrender to the steam at baths on both sides of the Galata Bridge. RIGHT: CAĞALOĞLU HAMAMI (P85)

🏃 *Hamams & Spas*

Blue Mosque *(p67)*

10 The city's signature building was the grand project of Sultan Ahmet I, who urged its architect and builders on in the construction process before his untimely death in 1617 aged only 27. The mosque's wonderfully curvaceous exterior features a cascade of domes and six tapering minarets. Inside, the huge space is encrusted with thousands of the blue İznik tiles that give the building its unofficial but commonly used name. Beloved of tourists and locals alike, it and Aya Sofya bookend Sultanahmet Park in a truly extraordinary fashion.

👁 *Sultanahmet & Around*

What's New

Hop-On/Hop-Off Bosphorus Tour

In an inspired move, the Dentur Avraysa company has inaugurated a hop-on/hop-off ferry loop leaving from Kabataş and stopping at Beşiktaş, Emirgan (for the Sakıp Sabancı Museum) and the Ottoman-era Küçüksu Kasrı and Beylerbeyi Palace. A great way to spend an afternoon, it's fast becoming a popular alternative to the famous Long Bosphorus Tour leaving from Eminönü. (p155)

Karaköy Renewal

The streets between the Galata Bridge and Tophane are undergoing a rapid and exciting revitalisation, with hipster hang-outs such as Karabatak (p134) and Unter (p134) leading the charge.

Kılıç Ali Paşa Hamamı

A painstaking seven-year restoration of this 16th-century hamam designed by imperial architect Mimar Sinan is finally complete, and the result is truly magnificent. (p140)

İstanbul Naval Museum

The new copper-roofed exhibition hall here was purpose-built to showcase the museum's splendid collection of 19th-century imperial *caïques* (ornately decorated wooden rowboats). (p144)

National Palaces Painting Museum

For an introduction to painting during the Ottoman era, you need go no further than this recently renovated and reopened gallery in the former apartments of the Crown Prince at Dolmabahçe Palace. (p144)

Nublu İstanbul

This music venue in Karaköy's Gravida Hotel is a favourite with the city's bohemian set and is the İstanbul base of high-profile jazz saxophonist and composer İlhan Ersahin. (p137)

Europe–Asia Metro Link

The centrepiece of İstanbul's Marmaray transport system upgrade, this metro tunnel under the Sea of Marmara efficiently links the European and Asian sides of the city. (p205)

Carpet Museum

Turkey is famous for its rugs, and this museum occupying an 18th-century *imaret* (soup kitchen) in Sultanahmet gives the visitor an overview of the history of Anatolian carpet-making. (p75)

Bazaar District Culinary Walk

Dedicated foodies will love the latest addition to the portfolio of walking tours offered by the crew from İstanbul Eats, which explores the culinary backstreets of the Bazaar Quarter. (p153)

Aya İrini

Byzantine architecture buffs will be thrilled to hear that it's now possible to visit the interior of this venerable church in the grounds of Topkapı Palace. (p75)

For more recommendations and reviews, see **lonelyplanet.com/Istanbul**

Need to Know

For more information, see Survival Guide (p201)

Currency

Türk Lirası (Turkish Lira; ₺)

Language

Turkish

Visas

Not required for some (predominantly European) nationalities; most other nationalities can obtain a 90-day visa electronically.

Money

ATMs widespread. Credit cards accepted at most shops, hotels and upmarket restaurants.

Mobile Phones

Most European and Australasian phones work here; some North American phones don't. Check with your provider. Prepaid SIM cards must be registered when purchased.

Time

Eastern European Time (UTC/GMT plus two hours November to March; plus three hours April to October).

Tourist Information

Tourist offices operate in Sultanahmet, Sirkeci, Karaköy and Atatürk International Airport. These offer free maps but are of little help otherwise.

Daily Costs

Budget:
Less than €60

➡ Dorm beds: €11–25

➡ Kebap or pide dinner: €6–7

➡ Beer at a neighbourhood bar: €4

➡ Tram, bus or ferry ride: €01.40

Midrange:
€60–200

➡ Double room: from €80

➡ *Lokanta* (eatery serving ready-made food) lunch: €10

➡ *Meyhane* (tavern) dinner with wine: €35

➡ Taxi from Sultanahmet to Beyoğlu: €6

Top End:
More than €200

➡ Double room: from €200

➡ Restaurant dinner with wine: €50

➡ Cocktail in a rooftop bar: €12

➡ Hamam experience: from €50

Advance Planning

Three months before If you're travelling in spring, autumn or over Christmas, make your hotel booking as far in advance as possible.

Two months before İstanbul's big-ticket festivals and concerts sell out fast. Book your tickets online at Biletix (www.biletix.com).

Two weeks before Ask your hotel to make dinner reservations.

Useful Websites

➡ **Lonely Planet** (www.lonelyplanet.com/istanbul) Destination information, hotel bookings, traveller forum and more.

➡ **Not Only İstanbul** (www.notonlyistanbul.com) Expertly curated guide to the city's art, food and culture.

➡ **Yabangee** (www.yabangee.com) Expats' guide to the city, with loads of events listings.

➡ **Time Out İstanbul** (www.timeoutistanbul.com) Web version of the listings-based magazine.

➡ **Hürriyet Daily News** (www.hurriyetdailynews.com) Website of the secularist daily newspaper.

➡ **Today's Zaman** (www.todayszaman.com) Website of the religiously conservative daily newspaper.

WHEN TO GO

Spring and autumn are the best times to visit, with good weather and many festivals. Summers can be unpleasantly hot and winters bone-chillingly cold.

°C/°F **Temp**
40/104 —
30/86 —
20/68 —
10/50 —
0/32 —
-10/14 —
-20/-4 —

Rainfall Inches/mm
— 5/125
— 4/100
— 3/75
— 2/50
— 1/25
— 0

J F M A M J J A S O N D

Arriving in İstanbul

Atatürk International Airport Metro and tram to Sultanahmet (₺8, 6am to midnight); Havataş bus to Taksim Meydanı (Taksim Sq; ₺10, 4am to 1am); taxi ₺45 to Sultanahmet, ₺55 to Taksim Meydanı.

Sabiha Gökçen International Airport Havataş bus to Taksim Meydanı (₺13, 4am to 1am), from where a funicular (₺4) and tram (₺4) travel to Sultanahmet; Havataş bus to Kadıköy (₺8, 4.15am to 12.45am); taxi ₺130 to Sultanahmet, ₺100 to Taksim Meydanı.

For much more on **arrival**, see p202

Sightseeing Tips

➡ Most major museums are closed on Monday; the exceptions are Topkapı Palace (Tuesday) and the Kariye Museum (Wednesday). Dolmabahçe Palace is closed on both Monday and Thursday.

➡ The Grand Bazaar and Kadıköy Produce Market are closed on Sunday.

➡ Purchasing the Museum Pass İstanbul (p73) can save you a considerable amount of money and will also allow you to cut some queues.

➡ Remember to dress modestly if you plan to visit mosques; females should have a shawl or scarf to cover their heads.

Sleeping

Accommodation choices in İstanbul are as diverse, plentiful and expensive as in most major European cities. They're also in heavy demand during peak tourism periods such as spring, autumn and Christmas, so it's important to book ahead. At these times, prices spike. During winter and at the height of summer, prices can plummet.

Most of the decent budget and midrange choices are in or around Sultanahmet; boutique and top-end options are clustered in Beyoğlu and along the Bosphorus.

In recent years there has been a proliferation of suite, apartment and boutique hotel openings. There's also been a huge growth in the number of apartment-rental services

For much more on **sleeping**, see p170

First Time İstanbul

For more information, see Survival Guide (p201)

Checklist

➡ Check if you need a visa; these should be organised electronically before your arrival (see p211).

➡ Make sure that your passport is valid for at least six months.

➡ Check your airline's baggage restrictions; when packing, make sure that you reserve some of your allowance for holiday purchases.

➡ Arrange travel insurance.

What to Pack

➡ Sturdy walking shoes or sandals – İstanbul's sidewalks are often cobbled and uneven so your feet will need support.

➡ Females will need a scarf or shawl to cover the head and shoulders when visiting mosques; also a bikini to wear in hamams (optional).

➡ Males should bring at least one pair of long pants to wear in mosques.

➡ Electrical adaptor (two round pins).

Top Tips for Your Trip

➡ Plan your itinerary – although İstanbul's public transport system is excellent, criss-crossing the city will eat into your time. Instead, choose just one or two neighbourhoods to explore in a single day. For our suggested itineraries, see p20.

➡ When you have prepared your itinerary, estimate how much museum entries will cost and then compare this figure to the cost of a Museum Pass İstanbul (p73) – you may save money (and time) by purchasing one of these.

➡ Even if you're only here for a few days, it's a good idea to purchase an İstanbulkart (p203) to use on public transport.

What to Wear

İstanbul's weather can be variable, so pack an umbrella and sweater (jumper) or jacket.

Mosque visits involve certain dress conventions. In other situations, you can dress as you would in Europe, North America or Australasia.

Be Forewarned

➡ İstanbul is a generally safe city, but you should employ commonsense when exploring. Be particularly careful near the historic city walls, as these harbor vagrants and people with substance-abuse problems – don't walk here alone or after dark. See p209 for more information.

➡ Single males should be wary if approached by locals and invited to go to a club or bar; see p36 for details.

➡ If a shoeshine guy drops his brush in front of you, ignore it – it's a time-tested scam to con you into paying for his services.

Walking Tours

If you have a guidebook and don't have specialist interests, there's no compelling reason to organise a tour guide. That said, there are a number of companies in the city offering excellent walking tours that give an in-depth introduction to neighbourhoods. These include the history-focused İstanbul Walks (p85) and food-focused İstanbul Eats (p153).

Bargaining

These days the non-negotiable price tag reigns supreme in most of the city's retail outlets and bargaining is becoming a dying art. Most exceptions to this rule can be found in the Grand Bazaar, especially in its carpet shops, where shopkeepers continue to take pride in practising the ancient art of bargaining. For more information, see p40.

Tipping

➡ **Restaurants & Bars** Usually 10% in restaurants, *meyhanes* (taverns) and upmarket bars; not necessary in *lokantas* (eateries serving ready-made food) or fast-food joints.

➡ **Taxis** Round taxi fares up to the nearest lira.

➡ **Hamams** Around 10% for the masseuse/masseur in a hamam, but only if you are happy with their service.

➡ **Meyhanes** At least ₺10 per person for musicians in *meyhanes*.

Grand Bazaar (p88)

MATT MUNRO / LONELY PLANET ©

Etiquette

➡ Be punctual for all appointments.

➡ If you invite someone to dine, it is assumed that you will pay.

➡ Avoid eating and drinking on the street during daylight hours in Ramazan.

➡ Don't blow your nose in public.

➡ Never point the sole of your feet towards a person.

➡ Don't use the OK sign as here it is sign language for calling someone homosexual.

➡ See p27 for mosque etiquette.

City Geography

İstanbul is the world's only city to straddle two continents, separated by the Sea of Marmara. You'll spend most of your time on the European side exploring Sultanahmet's sights and Beyoğlu's restaurants and bars, but a trip to the city's Asian side is recommended for the scenic ferry ride between the two shores and for the fascinating glimpse into local life through a visit to suburbs such as Kadıköy and Üsküdar.

Language

The vast majority of people working in İstanbul's tourist sector speak English. However, it goes almost without saying that locals appreciate visitors making the effort to master a few Turkish phrases. See the Language chapter on p212 for pronunciation guidelines and useful phrases.

Getting Around

For more information, see Transport (p202)

Ferry
The most atmospheric way to travel between the Old City and Beyoğlu to the Asian, Golden Horn or Bosphorus suburbs; services operate from 7am to 10pm (approximately).

Tram
The easiest way to travel between Sultanahmet and Beyoğlu; services operate every five minutes between 6am and midnight.

Metro
The best way to travel from Atatürk International Airport to the Old City and from Taksim Meydanı (Taksim Sq) to suburbs in the north of the city. A new line links the Old City and Asian shore via a tunnel under the Sea of Marmara. Services operate from 6am to midnight.

Bus
Used when travelling along both sides of the Bosphorus and from Eminönü to the Western Districts. Services operate between 6am and 11pm (approximately).

Donkey
Only joking.

Key Phrases

Dentur Avrasya Private ferry company

Dolmuş Shared minibus

Funiküler Funicular

İskele Ferry dock

İstanbul Şehir Hatları The city's main ferry service; government-run

İstanbulkart Rechargeable travel card

Jeton Transport token

Mavi Marmara Private ferry line to/from the Princes' Islands operated by Dentur Avraysa

Otobüs Bus

Otogar Bus station

Teleferic Cable car

Tramvay Tramway

Tünel Literally, 'tunnel'; name for funicular between Karaköy and Tünel Meydanı (Tünel Sq)

Turyol Private ferry company

Key Routes

F1 Funicular between Kabataş and Taksim Meydanı.

M1A Metro line linking Atatürk International Airport with Aksaray near Sultanahmet.

M2 Metro line linking Yenikapı with Hacıosman. Stops at Vezneciler, near the Grand Bazaar; on the new bridge across the Golden Horn (Haliç); and at Şişhane and Taksim Meydanı in Beyoğlu.

Marmaray Newly opened metro line that travels from Kazlıçeşme and Yenikapı to Sirkeci near Eminönü and then under the Sea of Marmara to Üsküdar and Aynlık Çeşme on the Asian shore.

T1 Tram line between Bağcılar/Cevizlibağ and Kabataş via Zeytinburnu (for airport and *otogar* metro connections), Sultanahmet, the Grand Bazaar, Eminönü and Karaköy.

Tünel Funicular between Karaköy and Tünel Meydanı.

TOP TIPS

➡ Purchase an İstanbulkart (p203) to save nearly 50% on the standard ticket price every time you take a ferry, tram, metro, funicular or bus ride, and even more on connecting journeys.

➡ Take the funiculars up to İstiklal Caddesi from Karaköy and Kabataş to save yourself very steep climbs, but consider walking down to explore the fascinating neighbourhoods on İstiklal's southern side.

➡ If travelling from the Grand Bazaar or Süleymaniye Mosque to Beyoğlu, consider taking the metro from Vezneciler rather than the slower tram service.

When to Travel

➡ İstanbul is a busy city, and even though public transport services are frequent, they are often crowded. Try to avoid rush hours (8am to 10am and 4pm to 6pm) if possible.

➡ If you need to get to Taksim Meydanı from the Asian or Bosphorus suburbs after services have finished for the night, you should be able to take a *dolmuş*.

➡ All Bosphorus and Princes' Islands ferry services are jam-packed on weekends; consider exploring on a weekday if possible.

Etiquette

➡ Have your İstanbulkart or *jeton* ready before you go through the ticket turnstile – locals are well-practised at moving through ticket barriers without breaking pace.

➡ If you want to stay stationary on an escalator, stand on the right-hand side; you'll need to walk if you are on the left.

➡ Turks are usually very polite, and will give their seats to older passengers, disabled people, pregnant women or parents carrying babies or toddlers if there are no spare seats available. You should do the same.

➡ Queuing to board public transport is honoured in principle rather than in reality. Be proactive but not pushy.

Tickets & Passes

➡ *Jetons* can be purchased from ticket machines or offices at tram stops, *iskeles* and funicular and metro stations, but it's much cheaper and easier to use an İstanbulkart.

➡ You must have an İstanbulkart to use a bus.

➡ Pay the driver when you take a *dolmuş;* fares vary according to destination and length of trip.

➡ Ticket prices are usually the same on public and private ferry services; İstanbulkarts can be used on some private ferries but not all.

➡ İstanbulkarts cannot be used to pay for Bosphorus ferry tours.

➡ If you have a Museum Pass İstanbul (p73), you will receive a discount on tickets for the Bosphorus ferry tours operated by İstanbul Şehir Hatları.

For much more on **getting around**, see p204

Top Itineraries

Day One

Sultanahmet & Around (p48)

Head to Aya Sofya Meydanı (Square) and work out which of the museums and mosques in the immediate area will be on your visiting list. Don't miss **Aya Sofya**, the **Blue Mosque** and the **Basilica Cistern**.

> **Lunch** Investigate the cheap eateries on Sirkeci's Hocapaşa Sokak (p80).

Sultanahmet & Around (p48)

Diverge from the tourist trail and visit some of Sultanahmet's hidden highlights by following our walking tour (p78. Source some souvenirs in the historic **Arasta Bazaar**.

> **Dinner** Have fish at Balıkçı Sabahattin (p81) or kebaps at Hamdi (p100).

Sultanahmet & Around (p48)

After enjoying an early dinner, make your way to Sirkeci, where you can watch dervishes whirl at **Hocapaşa Cultural Centre**, a converted 15th-century hamam. Alternatively, claim a table at **Derviş Aile Çay Bahçesi** or **Cafe Meşale**, where you can enjoy tea, nargile (water pipe) and a free (but very touristy) whirling-dervish performance.

Day Two

Sultanahmet & Around (p48)

It's time to investigate the lifestyles of the sultans at **Topkapı Palace**. You'll need a half day to explore the palace Harem, marvel at the precious objects in the Treasury and wander through the pavilion-filled grounds.

> **Lunch** Matbah (p82) serves Otto-man food in a pleasant garden setting.

Beyoğlu (p116)

Explore the streets, cafes and boutiques of Galata and Çukurcuma, perhaps popping into Orhan Pamuk's nostalgic **Museum of Innocence**.

> **Dinner** Karaköy (p128) in Beyoğlu is the city's new eating and drinking hotspot.

Sultanahmet (p48) & the Bazaar District (p86)

You've spent a full day sightseeing, so why not relax in the steamy surrounds of an Ottoman-era **hamam** after dinner?

Day Three

Bazaar District (p86)

 Get ready to explore the city's famous Bazaar District. After visiting the most magnificent of all Ottoman mosques, the **Süleymaniye**, make your way to the world-famous **Grand Bazaar** to explore its labyrinthine lanes and hidden caravanserais.

> **Lunch** Grab a cheap eat in or around the Grand Bazaar (p98).

Bazaar District (p86)

After lunch follow the steady stream of local shoppers making their way down the hill to the **Spice Bazaar**. While there, seek out the exquisite **Rüstem Paşa Mosque**, camouflaged in the midst of a busy produce market. As the sun starts to set, walk across the **Galata Bridge** towards the eating and entertainment district of Beyoğlu.

> **Dinner** Asmalımescit (p130) in Beyoğlu has lots of restaurants and taverns.

Beyoğlu (p116)

Enjoy an after-dinner drink and the view at one of Beyoğlu's rooftop bars before winding down at the **Tophane nargile cafes**.

Day Four

The Bosphorus (p155)

 Board the **Long Bosphorus Tour** (Uzun Boğaz Turu) for a one-way trip up the Bosphorus and then make your way back to town by bus, visiting museums and monuments along the way. Alternatively, take the Dentur Avraysa **hop-on/hop-off tour** from Kabataş and visit the Sakıp Sabancı Museum in Emirgan, Küçüksu Kasrı and Beylerbeyi Palace.

> **Lunch** MüzedeChanga (p163) for its terrace and Modern Turkish cuisine.

Beyoğlu (p116)

If you decided to take a 90-minute cruise on a Bosphorus excursion boat rather than the full-day or hop-on/hop-off trip, you can devote the afternoon to investigating Beyoğlu's exciting contemporary-art scene. Don't miss the **İstanbul Modern** museum and the **ARTER** and **SALT** cultural centres.

> **Dinner** Relax in a casual but chic cafe in Cihangir (p133).

Beyoğlu (p116)

Finish your day chilling out to live jazz at longstanding favourite **Nardis Jazz Club** or relative newcomer **Nublu İstanbul**.

If You Like...

Contemporary Art

ARTER Four floors of cutting-edge visual art located on İstiklal Caddesi. (p125)

SALT Beyoğlu Nooks and crannies offer up challenging artworks in this İstiklal Caddesi cultural centre. (p126)

Galeri Manâ One of the many impressive commercial galleries in the city. (p120)

İstanbul Modern The city's pre-eminent art museum, with a huge permanent collection of Turkish artworks and world-class temporary exhibitions. (p119)

Ottoman Mosques

Süleymaniye Mosque Crowning the Old City's third hill, this magnificent and largely intact mosque complex is one of the city's major landmarks. (p91)

Blue Mosque Possesses more minarets and visual pizzazz than any mosque should. (p67)

Atik Valide Mosque A majestic structure sitting astride Üsküdar's highest hill, this is the most impressive of that suburb's many Ottoman mosques. (p151)

Mihrimah Sultan Mosque A tapering minaret and delicate stained-glass windows are just two of this mosque's elegant design features. (p111)

Museums

İstanbul Archaeology Museums Eclectic collection of artefacts from the imperial collections,

Atik Valide Mosque (p151)

including outstanding classical sculptures. (p69)

Museum of Turkish & Islamic Arts An internationally renowned collection of antique carpets, plus exquisite examples of calligraphy. (p74)

Pera Museum A splendid collection of paintings featuring Turkish Orientalist themes, plus a changing program of thematic exhibitions. (p126)

Sakıp Sabancı Museum Blockbuster international exhibitions in a scenic Bosphorus location. (p161)

Music

Babylon An İstanbul institution, with a diverse program of live music and an inclusive atmosphere. (p137)

Salon An intimate venue in the headquarters of the İstanbul Foundation for Culture & Arts (İKSV) building in Şişhane; great for jazz. (p137)

Hasnun Galip Sokak This Beyoğlu side street is known for its concentration of *Türkü evleri*, Kurdish-owned bars where musicians perform *halk meziği* (folk music). (p138)

Nardis Jazz Club The city's oldest and best-loved jazz venue is where aficionados congregate. (p137)

Ferry Trips

Crossing the Continents Flit between Europe and Asia in less than one hour on a ferry from Eminönü or Karaköy to Kadıköy or Üsküdar. (p153)

The Bosphorus One of the city's signature experiences, offering magnificent museums, mansions and meals along its length. (p155)

The Golden Horn Hop on and off the commuter ferry that services the city's Western Districts. (p164)

The Princes' Islands Escape the city and head towards these oases of calm in the Sea of Marmara. (p167)

Views

Topkapı Terraces Sequestered in this palace complex, the Ottoman sultans must have loved the scenic viewpoints from its panoramic terraces. (p57)

Galata Bridge Snapshots of local life and unbeatable 360-degree views await when you walk between Sultanahmet and Beyoğlu. (p94)

Rumeli Hisarı This majestic fortress commands views of the Bosphorus from its crumbling battlements. (p160)

Rooftop Bars Glamorous bars on rooftops across Beyoğlu offer sensational views from their outdoor terraces. (p134)

Byzantine History

Kariye Museum A concentration of Byzantine mosaics unrivalled here or perhaps anywhere in the world. (p108)

Aya Sofya Over 1500 years old and still going strong, this basilica has witnessed history unfold and its interior tells many stories. (p50)

İstanbul Archaeology Museums The city's largest collection of Byzantine artefacts is on display at this excellent museum. (p69)

Great Palace Mosaic Museum A remarkably intact and visually arresting remnant of the Great Palace of Byzantium. (p72)

For more top İstanbul spots, see the following:
➡ Eating (p29)
➡ Drinking & Nightlife (p35)
➡ Shopping (p38)
➡ Hamams & Spas (p42)

Palaces

Topkapı Palace Home to the sultans for centuries, this cluster of ornately decorated pavilions houses treasures galore. (p57)

Dolmabahçe Palace This essay in decorative excess was built alongside the Bosphorus in the 19th century. (p143)

Beylerbeyi Palace Nestled under the Bosphorus Bridge, this 30-room imperial holiday shack is set in pretty gardens. (p160)

Yıldız Şale Originally an imperial hunting lodge, this oft-extended Ottoman guesthouse has hosted royalty galore. (p144)

Markets

Grand Bazaar One of the world's oldest – and most atmospheric – shopping complexes. (p88)

Spice Bazaar Has been supplying locals with spices and sugary treats for nearly 400 years. (p93)

Kadıköy Produce Market The city's most enticing fresh food market is found near the Kadıköy İskelesi (Kadıköy Ferry Dock). (p150)

Çarşamba Pazarı A bustling local street market held every Wednesday in the streets surrounding the Fatih Mosque. (p111)

Month by Month

March

It's cold at the start of the month, but as the weather improves, the tourists begin to arrive and the festival season kicks off. Good hotel deals are on offer early in the month; high-season prices apply from Easter onwards.

☆ Akbank Short Film Festival

Beloved by the black-clad Beyoğlu bohemian set, this arty film-culture event is held at the Akbank Culture & Arts Centre (www.akbanksanat.com).

🎆 Nevruz

Locals celebrate this ancient Middle Eastern spring festival on 21 March with jolly goings-on and jumping over bonfires.

April

Locals are well and truly into the springtime swing of things by April. Highlights include the blooming of tulips across the city and the arrival of fresh kılıç (swordfish) on restaurant menus.

☆ International İstanbul Film Festival

If you're keen to view the best in Turkish film, this is the event (http://film.iksv.org) to attend. Held early in the month in cinemas around town, it programs retrospectives and recent releases from Turkey and abroad.

◎ İstanbul Tulip Festival

The tulip *(lâle)* is one of İstanbul's traditional symbols, and the local government celebrates this fact by planting more than 11 million of them annually. These bloom in early April, enveloping almost every street and park in vivid spring colours.

June

It's summertime and, yes, the living is easy. There's an abundance of sweet cherries and sour green plums in the produce markets and the open-air nightclubs on the Bosphorus start to hit their strides.

☆ İstanbul Music Festival

The city's premier arts festival (http://muzik.iksv.org) includes performances of opera, dance, orchestral concerts and chamber recitals. Acts are often internationally renowned and much of the action takes place in atmosphere-laden Aya İrini.

July

It can be as hot as Hades at this time of year, so many locals decamp to beaches on the Mediterranean coast. Those left in town keep the heat under control with a liberal dose of cool jazz.

ISLAMIC HOLIDAYS & EVENTS

Islamic religious holidays and events are celebrated according to the Muslim lunar Hejira calendar, so their dates change every year. The most important event of the year is the holy month of **Ramazan** (called Ramadan in other countries), when Muslims fast from dawn until dusk and then sit with friends, family and community members to enjoy *iftar* (the meal that breaks the fast). These *iftar* meals are sometimes held in streets or in large tents within the grounds of mosques. A three-day festival called **Ramazan Bayramı** – also known as Şeker (Sugar) Bayramı because it involves lots of candy consumption – celebrates the completion of Ramazan.

The four- or five-day **Kurban Bayramı** is the most significant religious holiday of the year. It celebrates the Biblical and Koranic account of Abraham's near-sacrifice of his son on Mt Moriah.

☆ Efes Pilsen One Love

This two-day music festival (www.oneloveistanbul.com) is organised by the major promoter of rock and pop concerts in Turkey, Pozitif. International headline acts play everything from punk to pop, electronica to disco.

☆ İstanbul Jazz Festival

This festival (http://caz.iksv.org) programs an exhilarating hybrid of conventional jazz, electronica, drum 'n' bass, world music and rock. Venues include Salon in Şişhane, and parks around the city.

September

Autumn ushers in an influx of tourists with its cool breezes, and hotels revert to their high-season rates. Arty types are in seventh heaven when the internationally acclaimed art biennial is launched.

◉ İstanbul Biennial

The city's major visual-arts shindig (http://bienal.iksv.org) takes place from early September to early November in odd-numbered years. An international curator or panel of curators nominates a theme and puts together a cutting-edge program that is then exhibited in a variety of venues around town.

October

The year's final festivals take everyone's minds off the impending arrival of winter. Ruby-red pomegranates come into season and are juiced at stands across the city.

☆ Akbank Jazz Festival

This older sister to the International İstanbul Jazz Festival is a boutique event (www.akbanksanat.com), with a program featuring traditional and avant-garde jazz. Venues are scattered around town.

November

As the year draws to a close, street vendors signal the arrival of cold weather by roasting chestnuts and serving them in paper cones.

◉ İstanbul Design Biennial

A reasonably recent addition to the İstanbul Foundation for Culture & Arts' (İKSV) stellar calendar of festivals, this event (http://istanbuldesignbiennial.iksv.org) sees the city's design community celebrating their profession and critically discussing its future. It's held in even-numbered years.

With Kids

İstanbul is a great destination for a family-friendly break. Children might whinge at the number of mosques and museums but they'll be appeased by the fantastic baklava, lokum (Turkish delight) and dondurma (ice cream), not to mention the castles, underground cisterns and parks.

For Toddlers

Playgrounds & Parks

There are good playgrounds in Gülhane Park (p79) and in the waterside park near the Fındıklı tram stop in Beyoğlu. Open areas such as the Hippodrome (p72) and Yıldız Park (p144) also offer loads of space for toddlers to expend energy.

Ferry Trips

Little kids love ferries, and İstanbul offers loads of opportunities to climb aboard.

For Bigger Kids

Rahmi M Koç Museum

Kids will go crazy when they encounter all of the trains, planes, boats and automobiles on exhibit at this museum (p166) in Hasköy.

Rumeli Hisarı

This huge castle (p160) on the Bosphorus is a hit with most children. Just be sure that your junior knights and princesses are careful when they clamour up the battlements.

Princes' Islands

Your kids will love taking *fayton* (horse-drawn carriage) rides around the islands (p167) or hiring bicycles to get around under their own steam.

Basilica Cistern

It's creepy, and children can explore the walkways suspended over the water (p71). Way cool.

For Teenagers

Cooking Courses

Some teenagers see the kitchen as offering more than a refrigerator just waiting to be raided. Book yourself and your aspiring chef into a cooking class such as the one offered by Cooking Alaturka (p85) in Sultanahmet.

İstanbul Modern

The city's pre-eminent contemporary art gallery (p119) has plenty of exhibits – including lots of multimedia – that will amuse and engage.

Ice Cream

They may try their hardest to appear sophisticated, but teenagers almost inevitably lose their attitude and get excited when they sample the *dondurma* sold at the many Mado ice-cream shops found throughout the city.

Need to Know

➡ Children under 12 receive free or discounted entry to most museums and monuments.

➡ Children under seven travel free on public transport.

➡ Most pavements are cobbled, so strollers aren't very useful.

➡ Disposable nappies and formula are easy to purchase.

➡ Children are almost inevitably made welcome in restaurants, although high chairs and kids' menus are the exception rather than the rule.

Like a Local

İstanbul's 14 million residents enjoy a lifestyle crammed with culture, backdropped by history and underpinned by family and faith. Head off the tourist trails to experience the city as they do.

Keyif

İstanbullus have perfected the art of *keyif* (quiet relaxation), and practise it at every possible opportunity. *Çay bahçesis* (tea gardens) and nargile (water pipe) cafes are *keyif* central, offering patrons pockets of tranquillity off the noisy and crowded streets. Games of *tavla* (backgammon), glasses of tea, nargiles and quiet conversations are the only distractions on offer.

Produce Markets

Street vendors selling fruit and vegetables can be found working pavements around town, and most neighbourhoods have a produce market where stallholders hawk everything from pungent farmhouse cheese to plump olives and freshly caught fish, providing self-caterers with plenty of options.

The İskele

Traffic in İstanbul is nightmarish, so it's sensible to take to the waters rather than the roads wherever possible. The city's famous flotilla of ferries transports thousands of commuters daily. Many of these passengers spend time before or after their journey enjoying a glass of tea or a snack at the *iskele* (ferry dock), making these often ramshackle places wonderful pockets of local life.

The Mosque

İstanbul's magnificent Ottoman mosques may be important tourist destinations, but their primary function is a religious one. Observe these rules when visiting:

➡ Remove your shoes before walking on the mosque's carpet; you can leave shoes on shelves near the mosque door.

➡ Women should always cover their heads and shoulders with a shawl or scarf; both women and men should dress modestly.

➡ Avoid visiting mosques at prayer times (within 30 minutes of when the *ezan*, or call to prayer, sounds from the mosque minaret) and also around Friday lunch, when weekly sermons and group prayers are held.

➡ Speak quietly and don't use flashes on your camera if people are praying (and never photograph people praying).

Street Snacking

Locals love to eat, and do so at regular intervals throughout the day. In busy areas around town (*iskeles,* bazaars, shopping strips) street carts and stands sell a huge variety of quick and cheap eats. The most popular of these are fish sandwiches and döner kebap or *kokoreç* (seasoned grilled intestines) stuffed in bread, but other popular snacks include roasted chestnuts, grilled corn on the cob and *pis pilav* (rice and chickpeas cooked in chicken stock).

Sunday Brunch

A chance for friends and extended families to get together over an inexpensive meal, this growing phenomenon is gaining plenty of local devotees. Popular options include Sütiş (p163) in Emirgan, Kale Cafe & Pastane (p161) in Rumeli Hisarı, Akdeniz Hatay Sofrası (p95) in Aksaray and the House Cafe (p131) in Ortaköy.

For Free

The hippies and backpackers who flocked to İstanbul in the 1960s and 1970s would blow their meagre budgets if they headed this way today. Fortunately, the ever-increasing price of hotel rooms, transport and meals is counterbalanced by the top-drawer sights that can be visited at no cost.

Mosques

Topping the seven hills of the Old City and adorning many of its streets, İstanbul's Ottoman mosques are the jewels in the city's crown. Entry to these architectural wonders is open to everyone regardless of their religion. The *türbes* (tombs) attached to these mosques are often sumptuously decorated with İznik tiles and can also be visited; head to the Aya Sofya Tombs (p72) to see some great examples.

Galleries

The recent trend for İstanbul's banks and business dynasties to endow private art galleries and cultural centres is the best thing to hit the city since the tulip bulb arrived. Most are on or near İstiklal Caddesi in Beyoğlu and charge no entry fees. The Pera Museum (p126) offers free admission every Friday between 6pm and 10pm; on Wednesdays admission is also free for students.

In Sultanahmet, the Marmara University Republican Museum (p74) and the Carpet Museum (p75) offer free entry.

Parks & Gardens

Picnicking and promenading are two favourite local pastimes, so it's fortunate that there are so many wonderful parks and gardens open to the public. Particularly beautiful or historic examples include Gülhane Park (p79) and the Hippodrome (p72) in Sultanahmet; Yıldız Park (p144) in Beşiktaş; and Hıdiv Kasrı (p162) and Emirgan Woods (p161) on the Bosphorus.

Churches

There are a surprising number of still-functioning Christian churches in İstanbul, many of which are of great historical significance. The best known of these is the Patriarchal Church of St George (p112) in Fener, the symbolic headquarters of the Greek Orthodox church.

Byzantine Monuments

Many of the city's Byzantine churches were converted into mosques after the Conquest and still function as such. Other Byzantine monuments that can be visited at no charge include the beautifully restored cistern in the basement of the Nakkaş (p78) carpet store in Sultanahmet and the historic city walls built during the reign of Emperor Theodosius II. The best place to see the latter is at Edirnekapı in the Western Districts.

Mezes (p30)

 # Eating

In İstanbul, meals are events to be celebrated. There's an eating option for every budget, predilection and occasion – all made memorable by the use of fresh seasonal ingredients and a local expertise in grilling meat and fish that has been honed over centuries. When you eat out here, you're sure to finish your meal replete and satisfied.

NEED TO KNOW

Price Ranges

The following symbols indicate the average cost of a main course in the reviewed restaurant or eatery:

€ less than ₺20

€€ ₺20 to ₺30

€€€ more than ₺30

Opening Hours

Standard opening hours for restaurants and cafes:

Breakfast 7.30am to 10.30am

Lunch noon to 2.30pm

Dinner 6.30pm to 10pm

Exceptions are noted in reviews.

Reservations

Thursday, Friday and Saturday nights are busy at all popular restaurants – be sure to book at least a week in advance.

Alcohol

Many simple eateries in İstanbul don't serve alcohol. In our reviews, we have indicated if a place is alcohol-free.

Tipping

➡ In restaurants, bistros and *meyhanes*, a 10% tip is standard if you have been satisfied with the service; tipping in cafes is optional.

➡ There's usually no expectation that customers will tip at *lokantas*, *kebapçıs*, *köftecis* and *pidecis*.

What's on the Menu?

The local cuisine has been refined over centuries and is treated more reverently than any museum collection in the country. That's not to say it's fussy, because what differentiates Turkish food from other national noshes is its rustic and honest base. Here mezes (small tapas-like dishes) are simple, kebaps uncomplicated, salads unstructured and seafood unsauced. Flavours explode in your mouth because ingredients are grown locally and used when they are in season.

MARVELLOUS MEZES

Mezes aren't just a type of dish, they're a whole eating experience. In *meyhanes* (Turkish taverns) waiters heave around enormous trays full of cold meze dishes that customers can choose from – hot meze dishes are usually chosen from the menu.

Mezes are usually vegetable-based, though seafood dishes also feature.

MEAT – THE TURKISH WAY

Overall, the Turks are huge meat eaters. Beef, lamb, mutton, liver and chicken are prepared in a number of ways and eaten at home, in *kebapçıs* (kebap restaurants) and in *köftecis* (meatball restaurants).

The most famous meat dish is the kebap – *şiş* and *döner* – but *köfte*, *saç kavurma* (stir-fried cubed meat dishes) and *güveç* (meat and vegetable stews cooked in a terracotta pot) are just as common.

The most popular sausage in Turkey is the spicy beef *sucuk*. Garlicky *pastırma* (pressed beef preserved in spices) is regularly used as an accompaniment to egg dishes; it's occasionally served with warm hummus (chickpea, tahini and lemon dip) as a meze.

A few İstanbul restaurants serve the central Anatolian dish of *mantı* (Turkish ravioli stuffed with beef mince and topped with yoghurt, garlic, tomato and butter).

FRESH FROM THE SEA

Fish is wonderful here, but can be pricey. In a *balık restoran* (fish restaurant) you should always choose your own fish from the display. The eyes should be clear and the flesh under the gill slits near the eyes should be bright red, not burgundy. After choosing, ask the approximate price. The fish will be weighed, and the price computed at the day's per-kilogram rate. Try to avoid eating *lüfer* (bluefish) when the fish are small (under 24cm in length), as overfishing is endangering the future of this much-loved local species.

VEGETABLES & SALADS

Turks love vegetables, eating them fresh in summer and pickling them for winter (pickled vegetables are called *turşu*). There are two particularly Turkish ways of preparing vegetables: the first is known as *zeytinyağlı* (sautéed in olive oil) and the second *dolma* (stuffed with rice or meat).

Simplicity is the key to a Turkish *salata* (salad), with crunchy fresh ingredients being eaten with gusto as a meze or as an accompaniment to a meat or fish main course.

The most popular summer salad is *çoban salatası* (shepherd's salad), a colourful

Above: Kebap stand (p32)
Right: Food stall at the Grand Bazaar
(p88)

KUDÜS
40 tl

HALEP
TATLI
kk.

BAKLAVA
40 tl

Eating by Neighbourhood

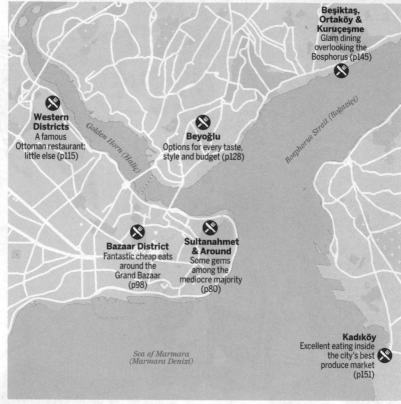

Beşiktaş, Ortaköy & Kuruçeşme
Glam dining overlooking the Bosphorus (p145)

Western Districts
A famous Ottoman restaurant; little else (p115)

Beyoğlu
Options for every taste, style and budget (p128)

Bosphorus Strait (Boğaziçi)

Golden Horn (Haliç)

Bazaar District
Fantastic cheap eats around the Grand Bazaar (p98)

Sultanahmet & Around
Some gems among the mediocre majority (p80)

Sea of Marmara (Marmara Denizi)

Kadıköy
Excellent eating inside the city's best produce market (p151)

mix of chopped tomatoes, cucumber, onion and pepper.

SWEETS

Turks don't usually finish their meal with a dessert, preferring to serve fruit as a finale. Most of them love a midafternoon sugar hit, though, and will often pop into a *muhallebici* (milk pudding shop), *pastane* (patisserie) or *baklavacı* (baklava shop) for a piece of syrup-drenched baklava, a plate of chocolate-crowned profiteroles or a *fırın sütlaç* (rice pudding) tasting of milk, sugar and just a hint of exotic spices.

Other Turkish sweet specialities worth sampling are *dondurma*, the local ice cream; *kadayıf*, dough soaked in syrup and topped with a layer of *kaymak* (clotted cream); *künefe*, layers of *kadayıf* cemented together with sweet cheese, doused in syrup and served hot with a sprinkling of pistachio; and *katmer* (flaky pastry stuffed with pistachio and *kaymak*).

FAST FOOD

The nation's favourite fast food is undoubtedly döner kebap – lamb slow-cooked on an upright revolving skewer and then shaved off before being stuffed into bread. Soggy cold French fries and green chillies are sometimes included; at other times salad and a sprinkling of slightly sour sumac are the accompaniments.

Coming a close second in the popularity stakes is pide, the Turkish version of pizza. It has a canoe-shaped base topped with *peynir* (cheese), *yumurta* (egg) or *kıymalı* (minced meat). A *karaşık* pide has a mixture of toppings. You can sit down to eat these in a *pideci* (Turkish pizza parlour) or ask for your pide *paket* (wrapped to go). *Lahmacun* (Arabic-style pizza) has a thinner crust than pide and is usually topped with chopped lamb, onion and tomato.

Börek (filled pastries) are usually eaten in the morning and are distinguished by their filling, cooking method and shape. They come in square, cigar or snail shapes and are filled with *peynir, ıspanaklı* (spinach), *patates* (potatoes) or *kıymalı*. Bun-shaped *poğaca* are glazed with sugar or stuffed with cheese and olives. *Su böreği,* a melt-in-the-mouth lasagne-like layered pastry laced with white cheese and parsley, is the most popular of all *börek* styles.

Gözleme (thin savoury crêpes stuffed with cheese, spinach or potato) are also great quick snacks.

STREET FOOD

Street vendors pound pavements across İstanbul, pushing carts laden with artfully arranged snacks to satisfy the appetites of commuters. You'll see these vendors next to ferry docks and bus stations, on busy streets and squares, even on the city's bridges.

Some of their snacks are innocuous – freshly baked *simits* (sesame-encrusted bread rings), golden roasted *mısır* (corn on the cob), refreshing chilled and peeled *salatalık* (cucumber) – but others are more confrontational for non-Turkish palates. Those in the latter category include *midye dolma* (stuffed mussels), *çiğ köfte* (raw ground lamb mixed with pounded bulgur, onion, clove, cinnamon, salt and hot black pepper) and *kokoreç* (seasoned lamb or mutton intestines wrapped around a skewer and grilled over charcoal).

VEGETARIANS & VEGANS

Though it's normal for Turks to eat a vegetarian *(vejeteryen)* meal, the concept of vegetarianism is quite foreign. Say you're a vegan and Turks will either look mystified or assume that you're fessing up to some strain of socially aberrant behaviour. There is a sprinkling of vegetarian restaurants in Beyoğlu, a couple of which serve some vegan meals, but the travelling vegetarian certainly can't rely on specialist restaurants.

The meze spread is usually vegetable-based, and meat-free salads, soups, pastas, omelettes and *böreks,* as well as hearty vegetable dishes, are all available. Ask '*Etsiz yemekler var mı?*' (Is there something to eat that has no meat?) to see what's on offer.

SELF-CATERING

İstanbul has many small supermarkets (DIA, Gima, Makro) sprinkled on the streets around Beyoğlu, with giant cousins (such as Migros) in the suburbs. These sell most of the items you will need if you plan to self-cater. Then there is the ubiquitous *bakkal* (corner shop), which stocks bread, milk, basic groceries and usually fruit and vegetables.

The best places to purchase fresh produce are undoubtedly the street markets. In Eminönü, the streets around the Spice Bazaar (Mısır Çarşısı) sell fish, meats, vegetables, fruit, spices, sweets and much more. In Beyoğlu, the Balık Pazarı (Fish Market) off İstiklal Caddesi is a great, if expensive, little market. As well as its fish stalls, it has small shops selling freshly baked bread, greengrocers selling a wide range of fruit and vegetables, and delicatessens *(şarküteri)* selling cheeses, *pastırma,* pickled fish, olives, jams and preserves. Larger produce markets are found six days per week near the *iskele* in Kadıköy; in Fatih and Cankurtaran on Wednesdays; in Kadırga on Thursdays, in Beşiktaş on Saturdays; and in Kasımpaşa (in Piyalepaşa Bulvarı) on Sundays. The best of these is the Kadıköy Produce Market.

COOKING COURSES & TOURS

Ask İstanbullus what makes their city special, and the answer usually comes straight from their stomachs. The local cuisine has a fan club as numerous as it is vociferous, and its members enjoy nothing better than introducing visitors to the foods, eateries and providores of the city. This is a dream destination for everyone who loves to eat, cook and shop for food, particularly as plenty of cooking courses and food-focused walking tours are on offer. These include the following:

Cooking Alaturka (p85) Runs popular classes suitable for all skill levels.

İstanbul Eats (p153) Fantastic foodie walks.

Turkish Flavours (p153) Walking tours and excellent cooking classes held in a private residence on the Asian side of town. If requested, the course can focus on a Sephardic menu.

LOKANTAS

These casual eateries serve *hazır yemek* (ready-made food) kept warm in bainmaries, and usually offer a range of vegetable dishes alongside meat options. The etiquette when eating at one of these places is to check out what's in the bain-marie and tell the waiter or cook behind the counter what you would like to eat. You can order *bir porsiyon* (one portion), a *yarım porsiyon* (half portion) or a plate with a few different choices – you'll be charged by the portion.

Lonely Planet's Top Choices

Klemuri Delicious home-style cooking in bohemian surrounds. (p130)

Antiochia Southeastern dishes that look as good as they taste. (p130)

Zübeyir Ocakbaşı The city's most famous *ocakbaşı* (grill house) for good reason. (p131)

Best by Budget

€

Fatih Damak Pide Everything a neighbourhood *pideci* (pizza place) should be, and then some. (p98)

Siirt Şeref Büryan Kebap Tender slow-cooked lamb from the southeastern city of Siirt. (p98)

€€

Hamdi Restaurant Excellent meat, panoramic views and a bustling atmosphere. (p100)

Lokanta Maya Stylish bistro serving modern versions of traditional Turkish dishes. (p130)

€€€

Asitane Dishes devised for the palace kitchens at Topkapı, Edirne and Dolmabahçe. (p115)

Matbah Palace cuisine served in the shadow of Topkapı's walls. (p82)

Mikla Modern Turkish dishes and views of the Old City, Beyoğlu and the Golden Horn. (p132)

Best Regional Eateries

Antiochia Specialises in dishes from the southeastern city of Antakya (Hatay). (p130)

Klemuri Laz cuisine from the Black Sea region. (p130)

Siirt Şeref Büryan Kebap Tender slow-cooked lamb from the southeastern city of Siirt. (p98)

Akdeniz Hatay Sofrası Flavourful food from the southeast. (p95)

Best Kebaps

Zübeyir Ocakbaşı Locals flock here for the succulent meats cooked over coals. (p131)

Hamdi Restaurant Excellent meat, panoramic views and a bustling atmosphere. (p100)

Gaziantep Burç Ocakbaşı Tasty, expertly grilled meat in the heart of the Grand Bazaar. (p99)

Şehzade Cağ Kebabı Erzurum-style tender lamb kebap. (p82)

Best Lokantas

Hünkar Upmarket choice with top-notch food and service. (p126)

Çiya Sofrası Bain-maries full of unusual dishes from Turkey's southeastern region. (p151)

Erol Lokantası Simple food in the heart of Sultanahmet. (p152)

Best Mezes

Meze by Lemon Tree Fresh, unusual and utterly delicious meze spread. (p132)

Tapasuma Stylish meze bar on the Bosphorus shore. (p163)

Duble Meze Bar Exciting modern take on the traditional *meyhane* (tavern) experience. (p132)

Heyamola Ada Lokantası Delicious mezes on the Princes' Islands. (p169)

Best Cheap Eats

Bereket Döner The neighbourhood is shabby, but the döner is the best in town. (p100)

Aynen Dürüm The pickle spread is even more impressive than the meat. (p99)

Dürümcü Raif Usta Fast but fabulous kebap wraps. (p99)

Pak Pide & Pizza Salonu Hard to find but oh-so-worth-it. (p99)

Dönerci Şahin Usta Much-loved Grand Bazaar döner stand. (p99)

Best Baklava

Develi Baklava Tiny space with a huge (and well-deserved) reputation. (p98)

Karaköy Güllüoğlu The perfect baklava stop at any time of day. (p129)

Best Cafe Food

Aheste House-made cakes, quiches and light dishes. (p129)

Kantın Early and much-loved adaptor of the Slow Food philosophy. (p126)

Gram The İstanbul equivalent of London's Ottolenghi. (p132)

🍷 Drinking & Nightlife

At the end of the working day, İstanbullus love nothing more than heading to a stylish bar, convivial cafe or atmospheric çay bahçesi (tea garden) to catch up with friends and agree on which of the city's many clubs or live-music venues they can kick on to later in the evening.

Nonalcoholic Drinks

Drinking *çay* (tea) is the national pastime. Sugar cubes are the only accompaniment and they're needed to counter the effects of long brewing. No self-respecting Turk would dream of drinking *elma çay*, the sweet 'apple tea' made from chemicals that is offered to many tourists.

Surprisingly, *Türk kahve* (Turkish coffee) isn't widely consumed. A thick and powerful brew, it's drunk in a couple of short sips. If you order a cup, you will be asked how sweet you like it – *çok şekerli* means 'very sweet', *orta şekerli* 'middling', *az şekerli* 'slightly sweet' and *şekersiz* or *sade* 'not at all'.

Freshly squeezed *portakal suyu* (orange juice) and *nar suyu* (pomegranate juice) are extremely popular drinks. In *kebapçıs* (kebap restaurants) patrons often drink *ayran* (a refreshing yoghurt drink made by whipping yoghurt with water and salt) or *şalgam suyu* (sour turnip juice).

If you're here during winter, you should try delicious and unusual *sahlep*, a hot milky drink made from crushed orchid-root extract.

Alcoholic Drinks

Turkey's most beloved tipple is rakı, a grape spirit infused with aniseed. Similar to Greek ouzo, it's served in long thin glasses and is drunk neat or with water, which turns the clear liquid chalky white; if you want to add ice *(buz)*, do so after adding water, as dropping ice straight into rakı kills its flavour.

Bira (beer) is also popular. The local drop, Efes, is a perky pilsener that comes in bottles, in cans and on tap.

Turkey produces its own *şarap* (wine), which has greatly improved over the past decade but is quite expensive due to high government taxes. If you want red wine, ask for *kırmızı şarap*; for white ask for *beyaz şarap*. Labels to look out for include Sarafin (chardonnay, fumé blanc, sauvignon blanc, cabernet sauvignon, shiraz and merlot); Karma (cabernet sauvignon, shiraz and merlot); Kav Tuğra (narince, *kalecik karası* and *öküzgözü*); and DLC (most grape varieties). All are produced by **Doluca** (www.doluca.com). Its major competitor, **Kavaklidere** (www.kavaklidere.com), is known for the wines it puts out under the Pendore, Ancyra and Prestige labels (the Pendore *boğazkere* is particularly good), as well as its eminently quaffable Çankaya white blend.

Together, Doluca and Kavaklidere dominate the market, but producers such as **Vinkara** (www.vinkara.com) and **Kayra** (www.kayrasaraplari.com) are starting to build a reputation for themselves with wines such as Kayra's excellent Buzbağ Reserve *öküzgözü-boğazkere* blend and the vintages it puts out under its Terra and Leona labels (try the Terra *öküzgözü*).

In recent years the Thracian region has become a wine-making hotspot. The vintages that are being released from estates including **Arcadia** (www.arcadiavineyards.com), **Barbare**

NEED TO KNOW

Opening Hours

➡ Opening hours of cafes, *çay bahçesis*, bars and clubs vary wildly; we have included specific hours in our reviews.

➡ Clubs are busiest on Friday and Saturday nights, and the action doesn't really kick off until 1am. Cover charges are levied at many of the clubs on these nights.

➡ Many of the Beyoğlu clubs close from June or July until the end of September. Most of the Bosphorus clubs close for part of winter.

What's On

The monthly *Time Out* and *The Guide* magazines include useful listings sections, and the **Time Out** (www.timeoutistanbul.com/) and **Yabangee** (www.yabangee.com) websites feature events information.

Entry Tips

➡ If you're keen to visit a Bosphorus club, consider booking to have dinner in its restaurant – otherwise you could be looking for a lucky break or a tip of at least ₺100 to get past the door staff.

➡ Long queues are ubiquitous at the popular Beyoğlu clubs after midnight on Fridays and Saturdays; some savvy clubbers arrive earlier to bypass these.

Dress Codes

When İstanbullus go out clubbing they dress to kill. If you don't do the same, you'll be unlikely to get past the door staff at the Bosphorus clubs or into the rooftop bar/clubs in Beyoğlu. What you're wearing won't affect entry at the live-music venues, *meyhanes* (taverns) or grungier clubs.

Nightlife Rip-Offs

Foreigners, especially single foreign males, are sometimes targets for a classic İstanbul rip-off whereby they are approached by a friendly local or group of locals who asks them if they would like to visit a bar or nightclub. Unfortunately, these guys are luring their victims into places run by organised crime groups where drinks and the company of hostesses cost an absolute fortune and where refusing to pay the bill can lead to nasty, often physical confrontations. Be very wary of any such invitations.

(www.barbarewines.com) and **Suvla** (www.suvla.com) are well worth sampling.

Clubbing

The best nightclubs are in Beyoğlu and along the 'Golden Mile' between Ortaköy and Kuruçeşme on the Bosphorus.

Hipsters and bohemians tend to gravitate to the bars and clubs in Beyoğlu's Karaköy, Cihangir, Asmalımescit and Nevizade enclaves. Students hang out on or near Balo Sokak in Beyoğlu or head over to Kadıköy, where they can be found on Kadife Sokak, aka Barlar Sokak (Bar St), or at one of the bars on Moda Caddesi.

Gay & Lesbian İstanbul

Beyoğlu is the hub of the city's gay clubbing scene, and there are a number of venues to choose from. Most welcome both gay and straight clubbers, although the latter will feel vastly outnumbered. The monthly *Time Out İstanbul* magazine has Gay & Lesbian pages listing the top LGBTT venues in town.

Occasional police raids on gay venues occur (homosexuality has an ambiguous legal status – or lack thereof – in Turkey), but the general tenor in Beyoğlu is gay-friendly and inclusive.

Drinking & Nightlife by Neighbourhood

➡ **Sultanahmet & Around** A limited choice of cafes and *çay bahçesis* (tea gardens), but few bars worth considering. (p82)

➡ **Bazaar District** An atmospheric array of *çay bahçesis* and nargile (water pipe) cafes, but no nightlife to speak of. (p101)

➡ **Beyoğlu** The city's entertainment hub, with hundreds of bars, cafes and clubs to choose from. (p134)

➡ **Beşiktaş, Ortaköy & Kuruçeşme** A string of upmarket cafes, bars and clubs alongside the Bosphorus. (p146)

➡ **Kadıköy** A vibrant cafe and bar scene. (p151)

Lonely Planet's Top Choices

Babylon The most famous live-music venue in town. (p137)

MiniMüzikHol Hub of the avant-garde arts scene. (p136)

Mikla Spectacular views and a stylish clientele. (p135)

360 The city's most famous bar for good reason. (p135)

Karabatak İstanbul's best coffee served in hipster surrounds. (p134)

Tophane Nargile Cafes Alcohol-free but atmosphere-rich. (p134)

Best Çay Bahçesis

Erenler Nargile ve Çay Bahçesi Popular hang-out near the Grand Bazaar. (p101)

Pierre Loti Café Favourite weekend destination for couples and families. (p115)

Hazzo Pulo Çay Bahçesi The only old-style tea garden left on İstiklal Caddesi. (p135)

Set Üstü Çay Bahçesi Wonderful views and fresh pots of tea. (p83)

Best Cafes

Mavra Bohemian decor and clientele. (p128)

Karabatak Beloved of coffee connoisseurs throughout the city. (p134)

Dem More than 60 types of tea, perfectly brewed. (p134)

Best Coffeehouses

Fazıl Bey Perfecting the art of coffee-making since 1927. (p152)

Manda Batmaz Popular pit stop off İstiklal Caddesi. (p135)

Best Rooftop Bars & Cafes

Mikla Scenery and style overload (in a good way). (p135)

360 Panoramic view, mixed clientele and weekend club vibe. (p135)

Mimar Sinan Teras Cafe A student hang-out near İstanbul University. (p101)

NuTeras Long-standing favourite overlooking the Golden Horn. (p136)

Leb-i Derya The prototype for the famous portfolio of rooftop bars in Beyoğlu. (p135)

Best Neighbourhood Bars

Unter n the centre of the fashionable Karaköy neighbourhood. (p134) l

Cihangir 21 Popular haunt of Cihangir locals. (p137)

Smyrna Long-standing favourite of arty types. (p137)

Karga Bar The best-loved bar in Kadıköy. (p153)

Best Clubs

MiniMüzikHol The best weekend dance party in town. (p136)

Indigo The city's electronic music temple. (p135)

Kiki DJ action aplenty in Beyoğlu and Ortaköy. (p146)

Best Live-Music Venues

Babylon Eclectic program often featuring big-name international acts. (p137)

Nardis Jazz Club The city's pre-eminent jazz venue. (p137)

Nublu İstanbul Newcomer with serious jazz credentials. (p137)

Munzur Cafe & Bar One of a number of Hasnun Galip Sokak bars showcasing Turkish *halk meziği* (folk music). (p138)

Salon Intimate venue operated by the İstanbul Foundation for Culture & Arts (İKSV). (p137)

Best Gay & Lesbian Venues

Love Dance Point The most Europhile of the local gay venues. (p136)

Tek Yön The city's largest gay dance floor. (p137)

Bigudi The city's only lesbian club. (p136)

Club 17 Jam-packed on weekends with a cross-section of the gay community. (p136)

Grand Bazaar (p88)

MATT MUNRO / LONELY PLANET ©

🛍 Shopping

İstanbullus have perfected the practice of shopping over centuries, and most visitors to the city are quick to follow their lead. Historic bazaars, colourful street markets and an ever-expanding portfolio of modern shopping malls cater to every desire and make sourcing a souvenir or two to take home supremely easy and satisfying.

What to Buy

ANTIQUES

The grand Ottoman-era houses of İstanbul are still surrendering treasures. Head to the antique shops of Çukurcuma or the Horhor Antikacılar Çarşışı (p104) to find something to take home, but note that it is officially illegal to take anything over 100 years old out of the country. In reality, though, officials are only worried about objects from the classical, Byzantine or early Ottoman eras.

BATHWARES

Attractive towels, *peştemals* (bath wraps) and bathrobes made on hand looms in southern Turkey are sold in designer bathware shops around the city. Other popular purchases include olive-oil soaps and hamam sets with soap, shampoo, an exfoliation glove and a hamam bowl.

CARPETS & KILIMS

Asking locals for a recommendation when it comes to rug shops can be something of a knotty subject. The industry is rife with commissions, fakes and dodgy merchandise, so you need to be very careful when making a purchase. Don't fall for the shtick of touts on the street – these guys never, ever work for the truly reputable dealers.

Scam artists abound in the carpet trade. Be extremely wary in all of your negotiations and dealings.

CERAMICS
Turkish ceramics are beautiful and the standard fare fits within most budgets. Many of the tiles you see in the tourist shops have been painted using a silkscreen printing method and this is why they're cheap. Hand-painted bowls, plates and other pieces are more expensive – the best have original designs and are painted without the use of a carbon-paper pattern. Head to the Arasta Bazaar (p83) or Grand Bazaar (p88) to find good examples.

FASHION
The local fashion industry is thriving and there are plenty of chains, department stores and boutiques to investigate. Head to Serdar-ı Ekrem Sokak in Galata, to Cihangir and to Nişantaşı to find the most interesting boutiques.

GLASSWARE
İstanbul produces some unique glasswork, a legacy of the Ottoman Empire's affection for this delicate and intricate art. Paşabahçe (p139) shops around the city sell attractive glassware that is mass produced at its factory on the upper Bosphorus.

INLAID WOOD
Local artisans make jewellery boxes, furniture, and chess and backgammon boards that are inlaid with different-coloured woods, silver or mother-of-pearl. Make sure the piece really does feature inlay. These days alarmingly accurate decals exist. Also, check the silver: is it really silver, or does it look like aluminium or pewter? And what about that mother-of-pearl – is it in fact 'daughter-of-polystyrene'?

JEWELLERY
İstanbul is a wonderful place to buy jewellery, especially pieces made by the city's growing number of artisans making contemporary pieces inspired by local culture. You'll find great examples both around and inside the Grand Bazaar, and in Karaköy, Galata and Nişantaşı.

NEED TO KNOW

Opening Hours
The most common shopping hours are from 9am to 6pm Monday to Saturday, but this is by no means always the case. We have indicated specific hours in most reviews.

Taxes & Refunds
Turkey has a value-added tax (VAT) known as the *katma değer vergisi* (KDV). This means that a tax of between 1% and 60% is included in the price of most goods and services. Rates vary wildly – eg alcohol is taxed at 18% (producers also pay a tax of 50%), whereas food and books are taxed at 8%.

If you buy an item costing more than ₺118 from a shop that participates in the national 'Global Refund: Tax Free Shopping' scheme, you are entitled to a refund of the KDV at your point of departure. At the airports, remember to have customs inspect your purchase(s) and stamp your tax-free form before you go through immigration; you can then collect your refund near the food court in the departure lounge.

TEXTILES
Turkey's southeast region is known for its textiles, and there are examples aplenty on show in the Grand Bazaar (p88). You can also find top-quality cotton, linen and silk there.

Collectors of antique textiles will be in seventh heaven when inspecting the decorative tribal textiles that have made their way here from Central Asia. These are often sold in carpet shops.

TURKISH DELIGHT
Lokum (Turkish delight) makes a great present for those left at home, but is even better to scoff on the spot. It's sold in speciality shops around the city and comes in flavours including *cevizli* (walnut), *fıstıklı* (pistachio), *bademli* (almond) and *roze* (rosewater). Ask for a *çeşitli* (assortment) if you want to sample the various types. The largest concentration of quality outlets is around (but not in) the Spice Bazaar at Eminönü.

SHAWLS

Those keen on buying a shawl should be aware of the difference between a pashmina and a shahtoosh – pashminas use cashmere from Himalayan goats that is blended with silk, whereas shahtooshs are woven from the hair of the Tibetan antelope. Neither bear any resemblance to the cheap faux-pashminas that are sold by stores in the Grand Bazaar, which are made from synthetic fibre. The selling and owning of sha-tooshs is illegal since the Tibetan antelope is now listed as an endangered species.

The Dying Art of Bargaining

The elaborate etiquette of the Ottoman Empire lingers in many day-to-day rituals still observed in its greatest creation, İstanbul. Until recently, the art of bargaining was one of these. Times have changed, though, and these days the non-negotiable price tag reigns supreme in most of the city's retail outlets. Here, as in many former stops along the legendary Silk Road, the days of camel caravans have long gone, supplanted by multinational retailers, sleek supply-chain management and an increasingly homogeneous shopping experience.

Perhaps the only exception to this rule can be found in the city's carpet shops, particularly those located in the Grand Bazaar (p88). Many of these still take pride in practising the ancient art of bargaining.

If you are visiting İstanbul and are keen to buy a carpet or rug in the bazaar, keep the following tips in mind:

➡ The 'official' prices here have almost always been artificially inflated to allow for a bargaining margin – 20% to 30% is the rule of thumb.

➡ Shopping here involves many aspects of Ottoman etiquette – you will drink tea, exchange polite greetings and size up how trustworthy the shopkeeper is. He, in turn, will drink tea, exchange polite greetings and size up how gullible you are.

➡ Never feel pressured to buy something. Tea and conversation are gratis – if you accept them, you don't need to buy anything in exchange.

➡ It's important to do your research. Always shop around to compare quality and pricing.

➡ Before starting to bargain, decide how much you like the carpet or rug, and how much you are prepared to pay for it. It's important that you stick to this – the shopkeepers here are professional bargainers and have loads of practise in talking customers into purchases against their better judgement.

➡ Your first offer should be around 60% of the initial asking price. The shopkeeper will laugh, look offended or profess to be puzzled – this is all part of the ritual.

➡ He will then make a counter offer of 80% to 90%. You should look disappointed, explain that you have done your research and say that you are not prepared to pay that amount. Then you should offer around 70%.

➡ By this stage you and the shopkeeper should have sized each other up. He will cite the price at which he is prepared to sell and if it corresponds with what you were initially happy to pay, you can agree to the deal. If not, you should smile, shake hands and walk away.

The same rules also apply in some textile, jewellery and antique shops in the bazaar, but they don't apply to all. The fashionable stores in Halıcılar Çarşışı Sokak started the trend towards set pricing here a number of years ago and many other shops have followed their lead.

Shopping by Neighbourhood

➡ **Sultanahmet & Around** Top-notch ceramics, rug and bathware stores are found in and around the Arasta Bazaar. (p83)

➡ **Bazaar District** Options galore in the Grand Bazaar, the Spice Bazaar and streets between the two. (p102)

➡ **Beyoğlu** Galata, Cihangir and Çukurcuma are bursting with fashion boutiques, designer homewares stores and antique shops. Karaköy is starting to follow their lead. (p138)

Lonely Planet's Top Choices

Cocoon Striking textiles, rugs and handicrafts from Central Asia. (p83)

Hiç Designer homewares made by local and international artisans. (p138)

Nahıl Felting, lacework, embroidery and all-natural soaps made by economically disadvantaged women in Turkey's rural areas. (p139)

Özlem Tuna Artisan-designed and -made jewellery and homewares. (p84)

Altan Şekerleme Cheap and delicious *lokum* (Turkish delight), *helva* (a sweet made from sesame seeds) and *akide* (hard candy). (p103)

Best for Homewares

Hiç Artisan-made rugs, cushions, furniture and ceramics. (p138)

Özlem Tuna Super-stylish bowls, coffee cups and platters. (p84)

Tulu Colourful range of cushions, bedding and accessories inspired by textiles from Central Asia. (p84)

Paşabahçe Attractive and affordable glassware made in the upper Bosphorus. (p139)

Best for Bathwares

Jennifer's Hamam Towels, robes and wraps produced on old-style shuttled looms. (p84)

Abdulla Natural Products Olive-oil soaps, cotton towels and a large range of *peştemals* (bath wraps). (p102)

Derviş Soaps, towels and wraps to beautify your bathroom. (p103)

Best for Carpets & Kilims

Mehmet Çetinkaya Gallery A showcase of top-quality antique oriental carpets and kilims. (p84)

Cocoon Kilims and saddle bags from Central Asia. (p83)

Dhoku Colourful contemporary kilims. (p103)

A La Turca Çukurcuma antiques shop with piles of rugs to inspect. (p140)

Best for Jewellery

Özlem Tuna Contemporary designs with Turkish accents. (p84)

Ümit Berksoy Artisan jeweller based in the Grand Bazaar. (p102)

Selda Okutan (p139) Avant-garde designer based in Karaköy.

Serhat Geridönmez Byzantine-influenced pieces (and sometimes the real thing) in the Grand Bazaar. (p103)

İstanbul Modern Gift Shop Showcases the work of young İstanbullu designers. (p138)

İKSV Tasarım Mağazası Pieces by the city's up-and-coming artisans. (p138)

Best for Textiles

Muhlis Günbatti Specialises in *suzani* (needlework) fabrics from Uzbekistan. (p103)

Yazmacı Necdet Danış Richly hued bolts of fabric and a range of scarves. (p103)

Mehmet Çetinkaya Gallery Antique pieces in the Arasta Bazaar. (p84)

Mekhann Hand-woven silk from Uzbekistan, plus a range of finely woven shawls. (p103)

Best for Handicrafts

Nahıl Not-for-profit outfit selling hand-made items including embroidery and lace. (p139)

Beyoğlu Olgunlaşma Enstitüsü Felting, embroidery, knitting and lace made by students at the upstairs textiles school. (p139)

Ak Gümüş Central Asian tribal arts, including felt toys and hats. (p103)

Best for Lokum

Altan Şekerleme Selling cheap and delicious Turkish delight since 1865. (p103)

Lokum Gorgeous packaging makes for sophisticated gifts. (p147)

Ali Muhiddin Hacı Bekir Family-run business established in the city more than two centuries ago. (p104)

Hafız Mustafa An İstanbul institution, with branches across the Old City. (p82)

🏃 Hamams & Spas

Succumbing to a soapy scrub in a steamy hamam (bathhouse) is one of the city's quintessential experiences. Not everyone feels comfortable with baring all (or most) of their bodies in public, though. If you include yourself in this group, a number of the city's spas offer private hamam treatments.

Hamams

The concept of the steam bath was passed from the Romans to the Byzantines and then on to the Turks, who named it the hamam. They've even exported the concept throughout the world, hence the term 'Turkish bath'. Until recent decades, many homes in İstanbul didn't have bathroom facilities, and due to Islam's emphasis on personal cleanliness, the community relied on the hundreds of hamams throughout the city, often as part of the *külliye* (mosque complex) of a mosque. Now that most people have bathrooms in İstanbul, hamams are nowhere near as popular, but some carry on due to their roles as local meeting places. Others have become successful tourist attractions.

The city's hamams vary enormously. Some are dank dives where you may come out dirtier than you went in (remember – Turks call cockroaches 'hamam insects'); others are plain and clean, servicing a predominantly local clientele. A small number have built a reputation as gay meeting places (we're talking truly steamy here), and an increasing number are geared exclusively towards tourists. A number of hotels in the city have hamams, too. These include Sirkeci Mansion (p175), Arcadia Blue Hotel (p176), Four Seasons İstanbul at the Bosphorus (p176), Sumahan on the Water (p176) and Vault Karaköy (p177).

We haven't reviewed any gay hamams in this book, as the current socio-political climate makes their legal status ambiguous.

BATH PROCEDURE

Upon entry you are shown to a *camekan* (entrance hall or space) where you will be allocated a dressing cubicle *(halvet)* or locker and given a *peştemal* (bath wrap) and *plastik çarıklar* (plastic sandals) or *takunya* (wooden clogs). Store your clothes and don the *peştemal* and footware. An attendant will then lead you through the *soğukluk* (intermediate section) to the *hararet* (steam room), where you sit and sweat for a while, relaxing and loosening up, perhaps on the *göbektaşı* (central, raised platform atop the heating source).

Soon you will be half-asleep and as soft as putty from the steamy heat. The cheapest bath is the one you do yourself, having brought your own soap, shampoo and towel. But the real Turkish bath experience is to have an attendant wash, scrub and massage you.

If you have opted for the latter, an attendant douses you with warm water and lathers you with a sudsy sponge. Next you are scrubbed with a *kese* (coarse cloth mitten), loosening dirt you never suspected you had. After a massage (these yo-yo between being enjoyable, limp-wristed or mortally dangerous) comes a shampoo and another dousing with warm water, followed by one with cool water.

When the scrubbing is over, relax in the *hararet* or head to the *camekan,* where you can get dressed or have a rest; at some hamams you can order something to eat or drink. The average hamam experience takes around one hour.

Spas

Most of İstanbul's five-star hotels have spas where a hamam exists alongside facilities such as saunas, steam rooms, plunge pools and rain-shower rooms. Hamam treatments in these spas are private, and often incorporate added extras such as facials, foot massages, hair treatments and body wraps. Some also offer remedial massages.

Lonely Planet's Top Choices

Four Seasons Istanbul at the Bosphorus The best of the luxury spas. (p147)

Kılıç Ali Paşa Hamamı Magnificently restored 16th-century hamam in Beyoğlu. (p140)

Ambassador Spa An expert masseur makes this modest place worth considering. (p85)

Ayasofya Hürrem Sultan Hamamı Built by order of Süleyman the Magnificent, and meticulously restored. (p85)

Cağaloğlu Hamamı The most beautiful of the city's Ottoman hamams. (p85)

Çemberlitaş Hamamı An architecturally splendid Ottoman hamam. (p105)

NEED TO KNOW

Opening Hours

Most of the tourist hamams and hotel spas are open from 8am to 11pm or midnight. Local hamams with only one bath have one set of hours for females and another for males; generally they close earlier than the tourist hamams.

Practicalities

Soap, shampoo and towels are provided at all of the hamams we've reviewed. If you're only having a bath, you'll need to pay for the soap and shampoo separately; it's always included in the cost of full treatments. You'll get drenched, so make sure you take a comb, toiletries, make-up and (if you choose to wear underwear during the massage) a dry pair of replacement underpants. There are usually hair-dryers available for customer use.

Modesty

Traditional Turkish baths have separate sections for men and women, or have only one set of facilities and admit men or women at different times.

Bath etiquette requires that men remain covered with a *peştemal* at all times. Women either bare all or wear a bikini or a pair of knickers (Turks tend to do the latter). During the bathing, everyone washes their private parts themselves, without removing the *peştemal* or underclothes.

In tourist areas, there are a couple of hamams with only one bath area that allow foreign men and women to bathe together. In these cases, women should wear a bikini.

Tipping

This is discretionary. Don't feel obliged to tip if your treatment was cursory or substandard.

Explore İstanbul

👁 İSTANBUL'S TOP SIGHTS

Neighbourhoods at a Glance

❶ Sultanahmet & Around (p48)

Many visitors to İstanbul never make it out of Sultanahmet. And while this is a shame, it's hardly surprising. After all, not many cities have such a concentration of historic sights, shopping precincts, hotels and eateries within in easy walking distance. Ideally suited to exploration by foot, the neighbourhood is a showcase of the city's glorious past, crammed with mosques, palaces, churches and houses dating from the Roman, Byzantine and Ottoman periods.

❷ Bazaar District (p86)

This beguiling district is home to the Grand Bazaar and Spice Bazaar. Amid the thousands of shops that surround these centuries-

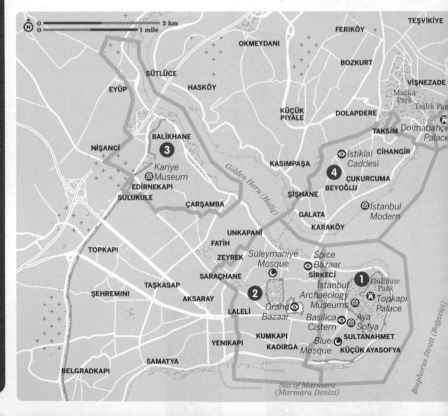

old marketplaces are magnificent Ottoman mosques, historic hamams (bathhouses) and atmospheric *çay bahçesis* (tea gardens) where locals smoke nargiles (water pipes) and play games of *tavla* (backgammon). The streets between the bazaars are a popular stamping ground for İstanbullus, and seem to crackle with a good-humoured and infectious energy.

❸ Western Districts (p106)

A showcase of İstanbul's ethnically diverse and endlessly fascinating history, this neighbourhood to the west of the Historic Peninsula contains synagogues built by the Jews in Balat and churches constructed by the Greeks in Fener. In recent times migrants from the east of Turkey have settled here, attracted by the vibrant Wednesday street market in Fatih and the presence of two important Islamic pilgrimage sites: the tombs of Mehmet the Conqueror and Ebu Eyüp el-Ensari.

❹ Beyoğlu (p116)

The high-octane hub of eating, drinking and entertainment in the city, Beyoğlu is where visitors and locals come in search of good restaurants, bohemian bars, live-music venues, hip hotels and edgy boutiques. Built around the major boulevard of İstiklal Caddesi, it incorporates a mix of bohemian residential districts such as Çukurcuma and Cihangir, bustling entertainment enclaves such as Asmalımescit and historically rich pockets such as Galata and Karaköy that have morphed into hipster central.

❺ Beşiktaş, Ortaköy & Kuruçeşme (p141)

Nineteenth-century French writer Pierre Loti described the stretch of the Bosphorus shore between Beşiktaş and Ortaköy as featuring '...a line of palaces white as snow, placed at the edge of the sea on marble docks'. Fortunately, his description remains as accurate as it is evocative. North of this palace precinct is the famous 'Golden Mile', a string of upmarket nightclubs running between the waterside suburbs of Ortaköy and Kuruçeşme, once humble fishing villages and now pockets of prime real estate.

❻ Kadıköy (p148)

In recent years, locals have been decamping from the European side of town to Asia in ever-increasing numbers, setting up home in the suburbs that are strung south from the Bosphorus Bridge. Of these, bustling Kadıköy is of the most interest to visitors, being the location of İstanbul's best produce market, great eateries, convivial cafes, grunge bars and a progressive vibe.

NEIGHBOURHOODS AT A GLANCE

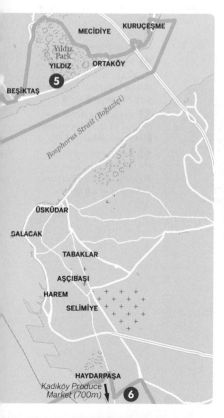

Sultanahmet & Around

SULTANAHMET | KÜÇÜK AYASOFYA | GÜLHANE | SIRKECI | EMINÖNÜ

Neighbourhood Top Five

❶ Standing beneath the magnificent dome of **Aya Sofya** (p50) and imagining what it would have been like to attend a candlelit service in this, the greatest of all Byzantine churches.

❷ Uncovering the secrets of the seraglio in opulent **Topkapı Palace** (p57).

❸ Learning about the fascinating history of the city in the **İstanbul Archaeology Museums** (p69).

❹ Exploring the watery depths of the atmospheric **Basilica Cistern** (p71).

❺ Surrendering to the steam and admiring the historic surrounds in an Ottoman-era **hamam** (p85).

For more detail of this area see Maps p238 and p240 ➡

Explore: Sultanahmet

The fact that there are so many significant monuments and museums in this area means that devising an itinerary is important. To do the neighbourhood justice, you'll need at least three days (four or five would be better).

Plan to visit one of the major museums (Aya Sofya, Topkapı Palace, the İstanbul Archaeology Museums, the Museum of Turkish & Islamic Arts) each day and then add the less time-intensive sights into your daily itineraries. For instance, it makes sense to visit the Archaeology Museums and Gülhane Park together on one day and Aya Sofya, the Blue Mosque and the Basilica Cistern on another.

The ever-present battalions of tour groups tend to visit the museums first thing in the morning or after lunch – you will find that queues are shorter and exhibits less crowded if you visit during lunchtime or later in the afternoon.

This isn't a part of town where many locals live. Restaurants, cafes and shops are geared towards tourists and prices reflect this fact.

Local Life

→**Produce markets** There are weekly street markets in Cankurtaran on Wednesday and in nearby Kadırga on Thursday.

→**Backgammon** Head to Derviş Aile Çay Bahçesi (p82) or Cafe Meşale (p82) to join locals in smoking nargiles (water pipes), drinking tea and playing backgammon.

→**Promenade** On weekends, follow the families who promenade through the Hippodrome (p72) and picnic in Gülhane Park (p79).

Getting There & Away

→**Tram** Efficient tram services link Cevızlibağ and Bağcılar in the city's west with Kabataş in Beyoğlu. From here, a funicular runs up to Taksim Meydanı (Taksim Sq). Trams stop at the Grand Bazaar, Sultanahmet, Gülhane Park and Eminönü en route. Get off the tram at the Sultanahmet stop to visit most of the sights in this chapter.

Lonely Planet's Top Tip

If you are spending a full three days in the city and plan to visit the major museums in Sultanahmet, the Museum Pass İstanbul (p73) will save you money and enable you to jump ticket queues.

✖ Best Places to Eat & Drink

→ Balıkçı Sabahattin (p81)
→ Matbah (p82)
→ Hocapaşa Sokak (p80)
→ Güvenç Konyalı (p82)
→ Set Üstü Çay Bahçesi (p83)

For reviews, see p80.➡

🔒 Best Places to Shop

→ Cocoon (p83)
→ Özlem Tuna (p84)
→ Jennifer's Hamam (p84)
→ Mehmet Çetinkaya Gallery (p84)

For reviews, see p83.➡

⊙ Best Museums

→ Aya Sofya (p50)
→ Topkapı Palace (p57)
→ İstanbul Archaeology Museums (p69)
→ Museum of Turkish & Islamic Arts (p74)

For reviews, see p50.➡

TOP SIGHT
AYA SOFYA

There are many important monuments in İstanbul, but this venerable structure – commissioned by the great Byzantine emperor Justinian, consecrated as a church in 537, converted to a mosque by Mehmet the Conqueror in 1453 and declared a museum by Atatürk in 1935 – surpasses the rest due to its innovative architectural form, rich history, religious importance and extraordinary beauty.

Known as Hagia Sophia in Greek, Sancta Sophia in Latin and the Church of the Divine Wisdom in English, Aya Sofya has a history as long as it is fascinating. It was constructed on the site of Byzantium's acropolis, which was also the site of two earlier churches of the same name, one destroyed by fire and another during the Nika riots of 532.

On entering his commission for the first time, Justinian exclaimed, 'Glory to God that I have been judged worthy of such a work. Oh Solomon! I have outdone you!' Entering the building today, his hubris is understandable. The exterior may be visually underwhelming, but the interior with its magnificent domed roof soaring heavenward is sublimely beautiful.

Enter the building and walk straight ahead through the outer and inner narthexes to reach the **Imperial Door**, which is crowned with a striking mosaic of **Christ as Pantocrator** (Ruler of All). Christ holds a book that carries the inscription 'Peace be With You. I am the Light of the World.' At his feet an emperor (probably Leo VI) prostrates himself. The Virgin Mary is on Christ's left and to his right is the Archangel Gabriel.

DON'T MISS

- Christ as Pantocrator
- Virgin and Christ Child
- Deesis
- Virgin Mary, Emperor John Comnenus II and Empress Eirene
- Constantine the Great, the Virgin Mary and Emperor Justinian

PRACTICALITIES

- Hagia Sophia
- Map p240
- 212-522 1750
- www.ayasofyamuzesi.gov.tr
- Aya Sofya Meydanı 1
- adult/child under 12yr ₺30/free
- 9am-6pm Tue-Sun mid-Apr–Sep, to 4pm Oct–mid-Apr
- Sultanahmet

Through the Imperial Door is the building's main space, famous for its dome, huge nave and gold mosaics. Unfortunately, a huge scaffolding tower erected for restoration works has marred the interior for the past decade.

Nave

Made 'transparent' by its profusion of windows and columned arcades, Aya Sofya's nave is as visually arresting as it is enormous.

The **chandeliers** hanging low above the floor are Ottoman additions. In Byzantine times, rows of glass oil lamps lined the balustrades of the gallery and the walkway at the base of the dome.

The focal point at this level is the **apse**, with its magnificent 9th-century mosaic of the **Virgin and Christ Child**. The *mimber* (pulpit) and the *mihrab* (prayer niche indicating the direction of Mecca) were added during the Ottoman period. The mosaics above the apse once depicted the archangels Gabriel and Michael; today only fragments remain.

The Byzantine emperors were crowned while seated in a throne placed within the **omphalion**, the section of inlaid marble in the main floor.

The large 19th-century **medallions** inscribed with gilt Arabic letters are the work of master calligrapher Mustafa İzzet Efendi, and give the names of God (Allah), Mohammed and the early caliphs Ali and Abu Bakr. Though impressive works of art in their own right, they seem out of place here, detracting from the austere magnificence of the building's interior.

The curious elevated kiosk screened from public view is the **imperial loge** *(hünkar mahfili)*. Sultan Abdül Mecit I had this built in 1848 so he could enter, pray and leave unseen, preserving the imperial mystique. The ornate **library** behind the omphalion was built by Sultan Mahmut I in 1739.

Looking up towards the northeast (to your left if you are facing the apse), you will see three mosaics at the base of the northern tympanum (semicircle) beneath the dome. These are 9th-century portraits of **St Ignatius the Younger**, **St John Chrysostom** and **St Ignatius Theodorus of Antioch**. To their right, on one of the pendentives (concave triangular segments below the dome), is a 14th-century mosaic of the face of a **seraph** (six-winged angel charged with the caretaking of God's throne).

In the side aisle to the northeast of the Imperial Door is a column with a worn copper facing pierced by a hole. Legend has it that the pillar, known as the **Weeping Column**, was blessed by St Gregory the Miracle Worker and that putting one's finger into the hole can lead to ailments being healed if the finger emerges moist.

MOSAICS

In Justinian's day, the great dome, the semidomes, the north and south tympana and the vaults of the narthexes, aisles and galleries were covered in gold mosaics. Remnants exist, but one can only imagine what the interior looked like when overlaid with glittering and gleaming tesserae (small glass tiles incorporating gold leaf). There were no figurative mosaics at this time – these date from after the iconoclastic period, which ended in the early 9th century. When the church was converted into a mosque, the mosaics were considered inappropriate; fortunately most were covered with plaster and not destroyed. Some were uncovered and restored during building works in the mid-19th century, and though once again covered (by paint), they were left in good condition for a final unveiling after the mosque was deconsecrated.

Vikings are said to have left the 'Eric woz here'-type graffiti that is carved into the balustrade in the upstairs south gallery. You'll find it near the Deesis mosaic.

Aya Sofya

TIMELINE

537 Emperor Justinian, depicted in one of the church's famous **mosaics ❶**, presides over the consecration of Byzantium's new basilica, Hagia Sophia (Church of the Holy Wisdom).

557 The huge **dome ❷**, damaged during an earthquake, collapses and is rebuilt.

843 The second Byzantine Iconoclastic period ends and figurative **mosaics ❸** begin to be added to the interior. These include a depiction of the Empress Zoe and her third husband, Emperor Constantine IX Monomakhos.

1204 Soldiers of the Fourth Crusade led by the Doge of Venice, Enrico Dandolo, conquer and ransack Constantinople. Dandolo's **tomb ❹** is eventually erected in the church whose desecration he presided over.

1453 The city falls to the Ottomans; Mehmet II orders that Hagia Sophia be converted to a mosque and renamed Aya Sofya.

1577 Sultan Selim II is buried in a specially designed tomb, which sits alongside the **tombs ❺** of four other Ottoman Sultans in Aya Sofya's grounds.

1847–49 Sultan Abdül Mecit I orders that the building be restored and redecorated; the huge **Ottoman Medallions ❻** in the nave are added.

1935 The mosque is converted into a museum by order of Mustafa Kemal Atatürk, president of the new Turkish Republic.

2009 The face of one of the four **seraphs ❼** is uncovered during major restoration works in the nave.

2012 Restoration of the exterior walls and western upper gallery commences.

TOP TIPS

Bring binoculars if you want to properly view the mosaic portraits in the apse and under the dome.

Ottoman Medallions
These huge medallions are inscribed with gilt Arabic letters giving the names of God (Allah), Mohammed and the early caliphs Ali and Abu Bakr.

Imperial Loge

Omphalion

Imperial Door

Seraph Figures
The four huge seraphs at the base of the dome were originally mosaics, but two (on the western side) were recreated as frescoes after being damaged during the Latin occupation (1204–61).

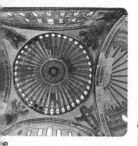

e
...g 56m from ground level, the dome
...iginally covered in gold mosaics but
...ecorated with calligraphy during the
...49 restoration works overseen by
...born architects Gaspard and
...pe Fossati.

P DELISS/GETTY IMAGES©

Ottoman Tombs
The tombs of five Ottoman sultans and their families are located in Aya Sofya's southern corner and can be accessed via Kabasakal Caddesi. One of these occupies the church's original Baptistry.

Christ Enthroned with Empress Zoe and Constantine IX Monomachos
This mosaic portrait in the upper gallery depicts Zoe, one of only three Byzantine women to rule as empress in their own right.

Aya Sofya Tombs

③

④

⑤

Former Baptistry

Astronomer's House & Workshop

①

Exit

Ablutions Fountain

...in
...nce

e of Enrico Dandolo
...netian doge died in 1205, only one year
...e and his Crusaders had stormed the
...19th-century marker in the upper gallery
...es the probable location of his grave.

Constantine the Great, the Virgin Mary and the Emperor Justinian
This 11th-century mosaic shows Constantine (right) offering the Virgin Mary the city of Constantinople. Justinian (left) is offering her Hagia Sophia.

Primary School

DE AGOSTINI / C. SAPPA/GETTY IMAGES©

NRICUS DANDOLO

AYA SOFYA – Ground Floor & Upstairs Galleries

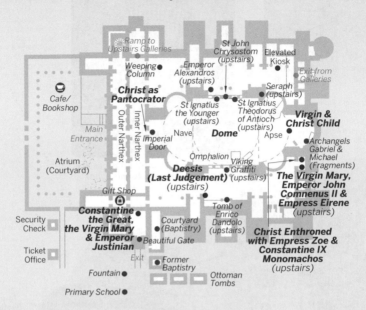

Ramp to Upstairs Galleries

St John Chrysostom (upstairs)

Elevated Kiosk

Exit from Galleries

Weeping Column

Emperor Alexandros (upstairs)

Seraph (upstairs)

Christ as Pantocrator

Cafe/ Bookshop

St Ignatius the Younger (upstairs)

St Ignatius Theodorus of Antioch (upstairs)

Virgin & Christ Child

Main Entrance

Outer Narthex

Inner Narthex

Imperial Door

Nave

Dome

Apse

Archangels Gabriel & Michael (Fragments)

Atrium (Courtyard)

Omphalion

Viking Graffiti (upstairs)

Deesis (Last Judgement) (upstairs)

The Virgin Mary, Emperor John Comnenus II & Empress Eirene (upstairs)

Gift Shop

Tomb of Enrico Dandolo (upstairs)

Security Check

Constantine the Great, the Virgin Mary & Emperor Justinian

Courtyard (Baptistry)

Christ Enthroned with Empress Zoe & Constantine IX Monomachos (upstairs)

Ticket Office

Beautiful Gate

Exit

Former Baptistry

Fountain

Ottoman Tombs

Primary School

Dome

Aya Sofya's dome is 30m in diameter and 56m in height. It's supported by 40 massive ribs constructed of special hollow bricks, and these ribs rest on four huge pillars concealed in the interior walls. On its completion, the Byzantine historian Procopius described it as being 'hung from heaven on a golden chain', and it's easy to see why. The great Ottoman architect Mimar Sinan, who spent his entire professional life trying to design a mosque to match the magnificence and beauty of Aya Sofya, used the same trick of concealing pillars and 'floating' the dome when designing the Süleymaniye Mosque almost 1000 years later.

Upstairs Galleries

To access the galleries, walk up the switchback ramp at the northern end of the inner narthex. When you reach the top, you'll find a large circle of green marble marking the spot where the throne of the empress once stood.

In the south gallery (straight ahead and then left) are the remnants of a magnificent **Deesis** (Last Judgment). This 13th-century mosaic depicts Christ with the Virgin Mary on his left and John the Baptist on his right.

Close by is the **Tomb of Enrico Dandolo**.

Further on, at the eastern (apse) end of the gallery, is an 11th-century mosaic depicting **Christ Enthroned with Empress Zoe and Constantine IX Monomachos**. When this portrait was started, Zoe (r 1042) was 50 years old and newly married (for the first time) to the aged Romanus III Argyrus. Upon Romanus' death in 1034, she had his face excised from the mosaic and replaced it with that of her virile new husband and consort, Michael IV. Michael died eight years later and Zoe, aged 64, wed the eminent senator Constantine IX Monomachos (r 1028–55), whose portrait was added here and remains only because he outlived the empress.

Mosaic detail

THE BUTTRESSES

The original building form designed by Aya Sofya's architects, Anthemios of Tralles and Isidoros of Miletus, has been compromised by the addition of 24 buttresses, added to reinforce the building and its enormous dome. Some date from Byzantine times, others from the Ottoman period; seven buttresses are on the eastern side of the building, four on the southern, four on the northern and five on the western. The remaining four support the structure as weight towers.

To the right of Zoe and Constantine is a 12th-century mosaic depicting the **Virgin Mary, Emperor John Comnenus II and Empress Eirene**. The emperor, who was known as 'John the Good', is on the Virgin's left and the empress, who was known for her charitable works, is to her right; both are giving money to Aya Sofya. Their son **Alexius** is depicted next to Eirene. He died soon after this portrait was made.

In the north gallery, look for the 10th-century mosaic portrait of **Emperor Alexandros**.

Outbuildings

Exit through the **Beautiful Gate**, a magnificent bronze gate dating from the 2nd century BC. This originally adorned a pagan temple in Tarsus and was brought to İstanbul by Emperor Theophilos in 838.

As you leave the building, be sure to look back to admire the 10th-century mosaic of **Constantine the Great, the Virgin Mary and Emperor Justinian** on the lunette of the inner doorway. Constantine (right) is offering the Virgin, who holds the Christ Child, the city of İstanbul; Justinian (left) is offering her Aya Sofya.

The doorway to your left just after the Beautiful Gate leads into a small courtyard that was once part of a 6th-century **Baptistry**. In the 17th century the Baptistry was converted into a tomb for Sultans Mustafa I and İbrahim I. The huge stone basin displayed in the courtyard is the original **font**.

The last Byzantine emperor, Constantine XI, prayed in Aya Sofya just before midnight on 28 May 1453. Hours later he was killed while defending the city walls from the attack being staged by the army of Mehmet II. The city fell to the Ottomans on the 29th, and Mehmet's first act of victory was to make his way to Aya Sofya and declare that it should immediately be converted to a mosque.

To the right after you exit the main building is a recently restored rococo-style *şadırvan* (ablutions fountain) dating from 1740. Next to it is a small *mektebi* (primary school) also dating from 1740. The small structure next to the gate is the *muvakkithane* (place where prayer hours were determined), built in 1853.

The first of Aya Sofya's minarets was added by order of Mehmet the Conqueror. Sinan designed the other three between 1574 and 1576.

After exiting the museum grounds, walk east (left) and then turn left again on Kabasakal Caddesi to visit the Aya Sofya Tombs (p72).

TOP SIGHT
TOPKAPI PALACE

Topkapı is the subject of more colourful stories than most of the world's museums put together. Libidinous sultans, ambitious courtiers, beautiful concubines and scheming eunuchs lived and worked here between the 15th and 19th centuries when it was the court of the Ottoman Empire. Visiting its opulent pavilions, jewel-filled Treasury and sprawling Harem gives a fascinating glimpse into their lives.

Mehmet the Conqueror built the first stage of the palace shortly after the Conquest in 1453, and lived here until his death in 1481. Subsequent sultans lived in this rarefied environment until the 19th century, when they moved to ostentatious European-style palaces such as Dolmabahçe, Çırağan and Yıldız that they built on the shores of the Bosphorus.

Buy your tickets to the palace at the main ticket office just outside the gate to the Second Court.

First Court

Before you enter the **Imperial Gate** (Bab-ı Hümayun; Map p240) of Topkapı, take a look at the ornate structure in the cobbled square just outside. This is the rococo-style **Fountain of Sultan Ahmet III** (Map p240), built in 1728 by the sultan who so favoured tulips. As you pass through the Imperial Gate, you enter the First Court, known as the Court of the Janissaries or the Parade Court. On your left is the Byzantine church of Hagia Eirene, more commonly known as Aya İrini (p75).

DON'T MISS

- Imperial Council Chamber
- Outer Treasury
- Harem
- Audience Chamber
- Treasury
- Marble Terrace

PRACTICALITIES

- Topkapı Sarayı
- Map p238
- 212-512 0480
- www.topkapisarayi. gov.tr
- Babıhümayun Caddesi
- palace adult/child under 12yr ₺30/free, Harem adult/child under 6yr ₺15/free
- 9am-6pm Wed-Mon mid-Apr–Oct, to 4pm Nov–mid-Apr
- Sultanahmet

Topkapı Palace

DAILY LIFE IN THE IMPERIAL COURT

A visit to this opulent palace compound, with its courtyards, harem and pavilions, offers a fascinating glimpse into the lives of the Ottoman sultans. During its heyday, royal wives and children, concubines, eunuchs and servants were among the 4000 people living within Topkapı's walls.

The sultans and their families rarely left the palace grounds, relying on courtiers and diplomats to bring them news of the outside world. Most visitors would go straight to the magnificent **Imperial Council Chamber ❶**, where the sultan's grand vizier and Dîvân (Council) regularly met to discuss affairs of state and receive foreign dignitaries. Many of these visitors brought lavish gifts and tributes to embellish the **Imperial Treasury ❷**.

After receiving any guests and meeting with the Dîvân, the grand vizier would make his way through the ornate **Gate of Felicity ❸** into the Third Court, the palace's residential quarter. Here, he would brief the sultan on the deliberations and decisions of the dîvân in the ornate **Audience Chamber ❹**.

Meanwhile, day-to-day domestic chores and intrigues would be underway in the **Harem ❺** and servants would be preparing feasts in the massive **Palace Kitchens ❻**. Amid all this activity, the **Marble Terrace ❼** was a tranquil retreat where the sultan would come to relax, look out over the city and perhaps regret his sequestered lifestyle.

Harem
The sultan, his mother and the crown prince had sumptuously decorated private apartments in the harem. The most beautiful of these are the Twin Kiosks (pictured), which were used by the crown prince.

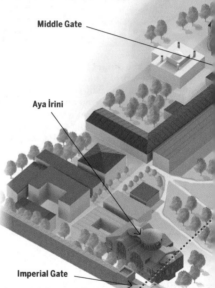

Harem Ticket Office

Middle Gate

Aya İrini

Imperial Gate

Imperial Council Chamber
This is where the Dîvân (Council) made laws, citizens presented petitions and foreign dignitaries were presented to the court. The sultan sometimes eavesdropped on proceedings through the window with the golden grill.

DON'T MISS

There are spectacular views from the terrace above the Konyalı Restaurant and also from the Marble Terrace in the Fourth Court.

Marble Terrace

This gorgeous terrace is home to the Baghdad and Revan Kiosks, the tiled imperial circumcision room and the İftariye Kameriyesi, a viewing platform with a gilded canopy. During Ramazan, the sultan would enjoy his *iftar* (breaking of the fast) here.

Circumcision Room

Baghdad Kiosk

Revan Kiosk

Kiosk of Mustafa Pasha

Library of Ahmet III

Head Physician's Pavilion

⑦

Dormitory of the Privy Chamber Arms & Armour

Sacred Safekeeping Rooms

...ence Chamber

...nded by a colonnade of 22 columns, this ...y restored pavilion was where the sultan ...a canopied throne to receive his grand ...and foreign dignitaries.

⑤

④

②

Mecidiye Kiosk

Outer Treasury

③

①

⑥

Terrace

Dormitory of the Expeditionary Force (Costume Collection)

Ticket Office

...te of Felicity

...s rococo-style gate was used ...state ceremonies, including ...sultan's accession and ...eral. A 1789 work by court ...nter Kostantin Kapidagli ...ords the enthronement ...emony of Sultan Selim III.

Palace Kitchens

Keeping the palace's 4000 residents fed was a huge task. Topkapı's kitchens occupied 10 domed buildings with 20 huge chimneys, and were workplace and home for 800 members of staff.

Imperial Treasury

One of the highlights here is the famous Topkapı Dagger, which was commissioned in 1747 by Sultan Mahmud I as a lavish gift for Nadir Shah of Persia. The shah was assassinated before it could be given to him.

ART DIRECTORS & TRIPI/ALAMY©

WOMEN OF THE HAREM

Islam forbade enslaving Muslims, so all of the concubines in Topkapı's Harem were foreigners or infidels. Girls were bought as slaves (often having been sold by their parents at a good price) or were received as gifts from nobles and potentates. Many of the girls were from Eastern Europe and all were noted for their beauty. The most famous of these was Haseki Hürrem (Joyous One), more commonly known as Roxelana, who was the consort of Süleyman the Magnificent. The daughter of a Ruthenian (Ukrainian) Orthodox priest, she was captured by Crimean Tatars who raided her home town and brought her to Constantinople to be sold in the slave market.

The chief black eunuch, the sultan's personal representative in administration of the Harem and other important affairs of state, was the third most powerful official in the empire, after the grand vizier and the supreme Islamic judge.

Second Court

The **Middle Gate** (Ortakapı or Bab-üs Selâm) led to the palace's Second Court, used for the business of running the empire. Only the sultan and the *valide sultan* (mother of the sultan) were allowed through the Middle Gate on horseback. Everyone else, including the grand vizier, had to dismount.

Like the First Court, the Second Court has an attractive parklike setting. Unlike typical European palaces, which feature one large building with outlying gardens, Topkapı is a series of pavilions, kitchens, barracks, audience chambers, kiosks and sleeping quarters built around a central enclosure.

The great **Palace Kitchens** on the right (east) as you enter have been closed to the public for a number of years while awaiting restoration. When they reopen they may hold a small portion of Topkapı's vast collection of Chinese celadon porcelain, valued by the sultans for its beauty but also because it was reputed to change colour if touched by poisoned food.

On the left (west) side of the Second Court is the ornate **Imperial Council Chamber** (Dîvân-ı Hümâyûn). The council met here to discuss matters of state, and the sultan sometimes eavesdropped through the gold grille high in the wall. The room to the right showcases clocks from the palace collection.

North of the Imperial Council Chamber can be found the **Outer Treasury**, where an impressive collection of Ottoman and European arms and armour is displayed.

Harem

The entrance to the Harem is beneath the Tower of Justice on the western side of the Second Court. If you decide to visit – and we highly recommend that you do – you'll need to buy a dedicated ticket.

As popular belief would have it, the Harem was a place where the sultan could engage in debauchery at will. In more prosaic reality, these were the imperial family quarters, and every detail of Harem life was governed by tradition, obligation and ceremony. The word 'harem' literally means 'forbidden' or 'private'.

The sultans supported as many as 300 concubines in the Harem, although numbers were usually lower than this. Upon entering the Harem, the girls would be schooled in Islam and in Turkish culture and language, as well as the arts of make-up, dress, comportment, music, reading, writing, embroidery and dancing. They then entered a meritocracy, first as ladies-in-waiting to the sultan's concubines and children, then to the sultan's mother and finally – if they were particularly attractive and talented – to the sultan himself.

TOPKAPI PALACE (TOPKAPI SARAYI)

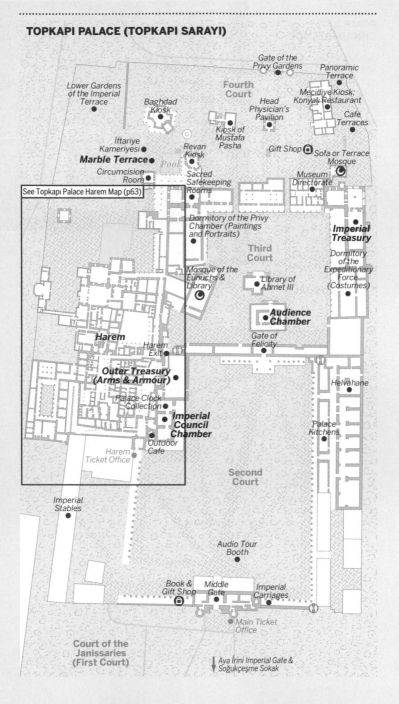

POMP & CIRCUMSTANCE

During the great days of the empire, foreign ambassadors were received at Topkapı on days when the janissaries (the sultan's personal bodyguard) were scheduled to receive their pay. Huge sacks of silver coins were brought to the Imperial Council Chamber in the Second Court and court officers would dispense the coins to long lines of the tough, impeccably costumed and faultlessly disciplined troops as the ambassadors looked on in admiration.

Circumcision Room (p66)

The so-called Spoonmaker's Diamond in the Topkapı collection is one of the largest diamonds in the world. According to legend, it was found in a rubbish dump in Eğrıkapı and purchased by a wily street peddler for three spoons before eventually being purchased by a grand vizier and becoming part of the Imperial Treasury.

The sultan was allowed by Islamic law to have four legitimate wives, who received the title of *kadın* (wife). If a wife bore him a son she was called *haseki sultan; haseki kadın* if it was a daughter.

Ruling the Harem was the *valide sultan* (mother of the reigning sultan), who often owned large landed estates in her own name and controlled them through black eunuch servants. Able to give orders directly to the grand vizier, her influence on the sultan, on the selection of his wives and concubines, and on matters of state was often profound.

The earliest of the 300-odd rooms in the Harem were constructed during the reign of Murat III (r 1574–95); the harems of previous sultans were at the now-demolished Eski Saray (Old Palace), near current-day Beyazıt Meydanı.

The Harem complex has six floors, but only one of these can be visited. This is approached via the **Carriage Gate**. Inside the gate is the Dome with Cupboards. Beyond it is a room where the Harem's eunuch guards were stationed. This is decorated with fine Kütahya tiles from the 17th century.

Beyond this room is the narrow **Courtyard of the Black Eunuchs**, also decorated with Kütahya tiles. Behind the marble colonnade on the left are the **Black Eunuchs' Dormitories**. In the early days white eunuchs were used, but black eunuchs sent as presents by the Ottoman governor of Egypt later took control. As many as 200 lived here, guarding the doors and waiting on the women of the Harem.

TOPKAPI PALACE HAREM

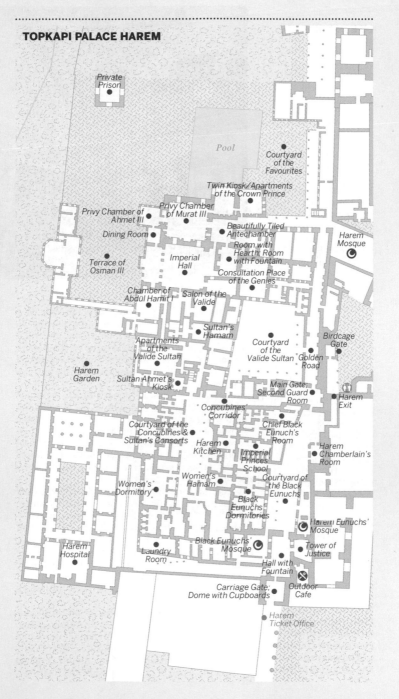

Private Prison

Pool

Courtyard of the Favourites

Twin Kiosk/Apartments of the Crown Prince

Privy Chamber of Murat III

Privy Chamber of Ahmet III

Beautifully Tiled Antechamber

Dining Room

Room with Hearth; Room with Fountain

Harem Mosque

Imperial Hall

Consultation Place of the Genies

Terrace of Osman III

Chamber of Abdül Hamit I

Salon of the Valide

Sultan's Hamam

Courtyard of the Valide Sultan

Birdcage Gate

Apartments of the Valide Sultan

Golden Road

Harem Garden

Sultan Ahmet's Kiosk

Main Gate; Second Guard Room

Harem Exit

Concubines' Corridor

Chief Black Eunuch's Room

Courtyard of the Concubines & Sultan's Consorts

Harem Chamberlain's Room

Harem Kitchen

Imperial Princes School

Women's Hamam

Courtyard of the Black Eunuchs

Women's Dormitory

Black Eunuchs Dormitories

Harem Eunuchs' Mosque

Harem Hospital

Black Eunuchs' Mosque

Tower of Justice

Laundry Room

Hall with Fountain

Carriage Gate; Dome with Cupboards

Outdoor Cafe

Harem Ticket Office

LIFE IN THE CAGE

In the early centuries of the empire, Ottoman princes were schooled as youths in combat and statecraft by direct experience. But as the Ottoman dynasty did not observe primogeniture (succession of the first-born), the death of the sultan regularly resulted in a bloodbath as his sons – often from different mothers – battled for the throne. This changed when Sultan Ahmet I (r 1603–20) couldn't bring himself to murder his brother Mustafa and decided instead to keep him imprisoned in Topkapı's Harem, so beginning the tradition of *kafes hayatı* (cage life). This house arrest, adopted in place of fratricide by succeeding sultans, meant that princes were kept ignorant of war and statecraft and usually rendered unfit to rule when the occasion arose, contributing to the decline of the empire's power and that of succeeding sultans even though in later years the dynasty observed primogeniture.

Sultan İbrahim I (r 1640–48), known as 'İbrahim the Crazy', spent his early life imprisoned in the *kafes* before succeeding his brother Murat IV in 1640. His reign was marked by extravagance and instability, and he was deposed and strangled in 1848.

Imperial Hall in the Harem

At the far end of the courtyard is the Main Gate into the Harem, as well as a guard room featuring two gigantic gilded mirrors. From this, a corridor on the left leads to the **Courtyard of the Concubines and Sultan's Consorts**. This is surrounded by baths, a laundry fountain, a laundry, dormitories and private apartments.

Further on is **Sultan Ahmet's Kiosk**, decorated with a tiled chimney, followed by the **Apartments of the Valide Sultan**, the centre of power in the Harem. From these ornate rooms the *valide sultan* oversaw and controlled her huge 'family'. Of particular note is the **Salon of the Valide** with its lovely 19th-century murals featuring bucolic views of İstanbul.

Past the adjoining **Courtyard of the Valide Sultan** is a splendid reception room with a large fireplace that leads to a vestibule covered in Kütahya and İznik tiles dating from the 17th century. This is where the princes, *valide sultan* and senior concubines waited before entering the handsome **Imperial Hall** for an audience with the sultan. Built during the reign of Murat III, the hall was redecorated in baroque style by order of Osman III (r 1754–57).

Nearby is the **Privy Chamber of Murat III**, one of the most sumptuous rooms in the palace. Dating from 1578, virtually all of its decoration is original and is thought to be the work of Sinan. The recently restored three-tiered marble fountain was designed to give the sound of cascading water and to make it difficult to eavesdrop on the sultan's conversations. The gilded canopied seating areas are later 18th-century additions.

Continue to the **Privy Chamber of Ahmed III** and peek into the adjoining dining room built in 1705. The latter is lined with wooden panels decorated with images of flowers and fruits painted in lacquer.

Northeast (through the door to the right) of the Privy Chamber of Murat III are two of the most beautiful rooms in the Harem – the **Twin Kiosk/Apartments of the Crown Prince**. These two rooms date from around 1600; note the painted canvas dome in the first room and the fine İznik tile panels above the fireplace in the second. The stained glass is also noteworthy.

To the east of the Twin Kiosk is the **Courtyard of the Favourites**. Over the edge of the courtyard (really a terrace) you'll see a large pool. Just past the courtyard (but on the floor above) are the many small dark rooms that comprised the *kafes* where brothers or sons of the sultan were imprisoned.

From here, a corridor leads east to a passage known as the Golden Road and then out into the palace's Third Court.

Note that the visitor route through the Harem changes when rooms are closed for restoration or stabilisation, so some of the areas mentioned here may not be open during your visit.

Third Court

The Third Court is entered through the **Gate of Felicity**. The sultan's private domain, it was staffed and guarded by white eunuchs. Inside is the **Audience Chamber**, constructed in the 16th century but refurbished in the 18th century. Important officials and foreign ambassadors were brought to this little kiosk to conduct the high business of state. The sultan, seated on a huge divan, inspected the ambassador's gifts and offerings as they were passed through the doorway on the left.

Right behind the Audience Chamber is the pretty **Library of Ahmet III**, built in 1719. Filled with light, it has comfortable reading areas and stunning inlaid woodwork.

On the eastern edge of the Third Court is the **Dormitory of the Expeditionary Force**, which now houses a rich collection of imperial robes, kaftans and uniforms worked in silver and gold thread. Also here is a fascinating collection of talismanic shirts, which were believed to protect the wearer from enemies and misfortunes of all kinds. Textile design reached its highest point during the reign of Süleyman the Magnificent, when the imperial workshops produced cloth of exquisite design and work. Don't miss Süleyman's gorgeous silk kaftan with its appliquéd tulip design.

On the other side of the Third Court are the **Sacred Safekeeping Rooms**. These rooms, sumptuously decorated with İznik tiles, house many relics of the Prophet. When the sultans lived here, the rooms were opened only once a year so that the imperial family could pay homage to the memory of the Prophet on the 15th day of the holy month of Ramazan. An imam sometimes sits in a glass box near the exit and recites from the Koran.

Next to the Sacred Safekeeping Rooms is the **Dormitory of the Privy Chamber**, which houses portraits of 36 sultans. The highlight is a wonderful painting of the **Enthronement Ceremony of Sultan Selim III** (1789) by Konstantin Kapidagli.

Imperial Treasury

Located on the eastern edge of the Third Court, Topkapı's Treasury features an incredible collection of objects made from or decorated with gold, silver, rubies, emeralds, jade, pearls and diamonds. The building itself was constructed during Mehmet the Conqueror's reign in 1460 and was used originally as reception rooms.

TULIP SULTAN

When he ascended to the throne aged 29, Sultan Ahmet III (r 1703–30) introduced many changes at Topkapı. He extended the palace Harem and he ordered that a number of new structures be built. These include the elegant street fountain outside the Imperial Gate that is named in his honour. Ahmet is best known, however, as the sultan who presided over the period known as the Lâle Devri (Tulip Period). He even introduced an annual festival to celebrate the blooming of this prized flower. Held over the three days surrounding the first full moon in April, this fête was staged in the gardens of the palace's Fourth Court, which was specially decorated with vases of tulips and tiny coloured glass lamps. Trilling nightingales in cages provided entertainment, as did palace musicians. Today the annual İstanbul Tulip Festival in April continues the tradition across the city.

Sultan Murat III (r 1574–95) had 112 children.

In the first room, look for the jewel-encrusted Sword of Süleyman the Magnificent and the Throne of Ahmed I (aka Arife Throne), which is inlaid with mother-of-pearl and was designed by Sedefkâr Mehmet Ağa, architect of the Blue Mosque. It's one of four imperial thrones on display here. In the second room, the tiny Indian figures, mainly made from seed pearls, are well worth seeking out. After passing through the third room and admiring the 16th-century gold-plated Ottoman helmet encrusted with turquoises, rubies and emeralds, you will come to the last and most impressive room, which is home to the Treasury's most famous exhibit: the **Topkapı Dagger**. The object of the criminal heist in Jules Dassin's 1963 film *Topkapı*, the dagger features three enormous emeralds on the hilt and a watch set into the pommel. Also here is the **Kaşıkçı (Spoonmaker's) Diamond**, a teardrop-shaped 86-carat rock surrounded by dozens of smaller stones. It was first worn by Mehmet IV at his accession to the throne in 1648.

Fourth Court

Pleasure pavilions occupy the palace's Fourth Court, also known as the Tulip Garden. These include the **Mecidiye Kiosk**, which was built by Abdül Mecit (r 1839–61) according to 19th-century European models. Beneath this is the Konyalı restaurant, which offers wonderful views from its terrace but is let down by the quality of its food. West of the Mecidiye Kiosk is the **Head Physician's Pavilion**. Interestingly, the head physician was always one of the sultan's Jewish subjects. Nearby, you can visit the late 17th-century **Kiosk of Kara Mustafa Pasha** (Sofa Köşkü), with its gilded ceiling, painted walls and delicate stained-glass windows. During the reign of Ahmet III, the Tulip Garden outside the kiosk was filled with the latest varieties of the flower.

Up the stairs at the end of the Tulip Garden is the **Marble Terrace**, a platform with a decorative pool, three pavilions and the whimsical **İftariye Kameriyesi**, a small structure commissioned by İbrahim I in 1640 as a picturesque place to break the fast of Ramazan.

Murat IV built the **Revan Kiosk** in 1636 after reclaiming the city of Yerevan (now in Armenia) from Persia. In 1639 he constructed the **Baghdad Kiosk**, one of the last examples of classical palace architecture, to commemorate his victory over that city. Notice its superb İznik tiles, painted ceiling and mother-of-pearl and tortoiseshell inlay. The small **Circumcision Room** (Sünnet Odası) was used for the ritual that admits Muslim boys to manhood. Built by İbrahim in 1640, the outer walls of the chamber are graced by particularly beautiful tile panels.

TOP SIGHT
BLUE MOSQUE

İstanbul's most photogenic building was the grand project of Sultan Ahmet I (r 1603–17), whose *türbe* (tomb) is located on the north side of the site facing Sultanahmet Park. The mosque's wonderfully curvaceous exterior features a cascade of domes and six slender minarets. Blue İznik tiles adorn the interior and give the building its unofficial but commonly used name.

Ahmet set out to build a monument that would rival and even surpass the nearby Aya Sofya in grandeur and beauty. Indeed the young sultan was so enthusiastic about the project that he is said to have worked with the labourers and craftsmen on site, pushing them along and rewarding extra effort. Ahmet did in fact come close to his goal of rivalling Aya Sofya, and in so doing achieved the added benefit of making future generations of hotel owners in Sultanahmet happy – a 'Blue Mosque view' from the roof terrace being the number-one selling point of the fleet of hotels in the area.

With the mosque's exterior, the architect, Sedefkâr Mehmet Ağa, managed to orchestrate the visual wham-bam effect that Aya Sofya achieved with its interior. Its curves are voluptuous, it has more minarets than any other İstanbul mosque (in fact, there was concern at the time of its construction that the sultan was being irreverent in specifying six minarets as the only equivalent was in Mecca) and the courtyard is the biggest of all the Ottoman mosques. The interior is conceived on a similarly grand scale: it features more than 21,000 İznik tiles, 260 windows and a huge central prayer space.

In order to fully appreciate the mosque's design you should approach it via the middle of the Hippodrome rather than entering from Sultanahmet Park. When inside the courtyard, which is the same size as the mosque's interior, you'll be able to appreciate the perfect proportions of the building. Walk towards the mosque through the gate in the peripheral

DON'T MISS

➡ The approach from the Hippodrome
➡ İznik tiles
➡ *Mimber*

PRACTICALITIES

➡ Sultanahmet Camii
➡ Map p240
➡ Hippodrome
➡ ⊘ closed to tourists during the 5 daily prayer times & Fri sermon
➡ 🚇 Sultanahmet

SULTAN AHMET I

Designed by Sedefkâr Mehmet Ağa and built between 1616 and 1619, Ahmet I's *türbe* is on the north side of the mosque facing Sultanahmet Park. Ahmet, who had ascended to the imperial throne aged 14, died one year after the mosque was constructed, aged only 27. Buried with him are his wife, Kösem, who was strangled to death in the Topkapı Harem, and his sons, Sultan Osman II (r 1618–22), Sultan Murat IV (r 1623–40) and Prince Beyazıt (murdered by order of Murat). Like the mosque, the *türbe* features fine İznik tiles.

Mosques built by the great and powerful usually included numerous public-service institutions, such as hospitals, soup kitchens and schools. Here, a large *medrese* (Islamic school of higher studies) on the northwestern side of the complex (closed to the public) and *arasta* (row of shops by a mosque; now the Arasta Bazaar) remain.

wall, noting on the way the small dome atop the gate: this is the motif Sedefkâr Mehmet Ağa uses to lift your eyes to heaven. As you walk through the gate, your eyes follow a flight of stairs up to another gate topped by another dome; through this gate is yet another dome, that of the ablutions fountain in the centre of the mosque courtyard. As you ascend the stairs, semidomes come into view: first the one over the mosque's main door, then the one above it, and another and another. Finally the main dome crowns the whole, and your attention is drawn to the sides, where forests of smaller domes reinforce the effect, completed by the minarets, which lift your eyes heavenward.

The mosque is such a popular tourist sight that admission is controlled so as to preserve its sacred atmosphere. Only worshippers are admitted through the main door; tourists must use the south door (follow the signs). Shoes must be taken off and women who haven't brought their own headscarf or are too scantily dressed will be loaned a headscarf and/or robe.

Inside, the **stained-glass windows** and **İznik tiles** immediately attract attention. Though the windows are replacements, they still create the luminous effects of the originals, which came from Venice. Tiles line the walls, particularly in the gallery (which is not open to the public); those downstairs are especially fine.

Once inside, it's easy to see that the mosque, which was constructed between 1606 and 1616, over 1000 years after Aya Sofya, is not as architecturally daring as its predecessor. Four massive pillars hold up the less ambitious dome, a sturdier solution lacking the innovation and grace of the 'floating' dome in Justinian's cathedral.

The semidomes and the dome are painted with graceful **arabesques**. Of note in the main space are the **müezzin mahfili** (*müezzin's* lodge), a raised platform where the *müezzin* repeats the call to prayer at the start of each service; the **mihrab**, which features a piece of the sacred Black Stone from the Kaaba in Mecca; and the high, elaborate **kursi** (chair) from which the imam gives the sermon on Friday. The beautifully carved white marble **mimber** with its curtained doorway at floor level features a flight of steps and a small kiosk topped by a spire.

JOHN SONES SINGING BOWL MEDIA / GETTY IMAGES ©

İSTANBUL ARCHAEOLOGY MUSEUMS

This superb museum (İstanbul Arkeoloji Müzeleri in Turkish) showcases archaeological and artistic treasures from the Topkapı collections. Housed in three buildings, its exhibits include ancient artefacts, classical statuary and an exhibition tracing İstanbul's history. There are many highlights, but the sarcophagi from the Royal Necropolis of Sidon are particularly striking.

The complex has three main parts: the Archaeology Museum (Arkeoloji Müzesi), the Museum of the Ancient Orient (Eski Şark Eserler Müzesi) and the Tiled Pavilion (Çinili Köşk). These museums house the palace collections formed during the late 19th century by museum director, artist and archaeologist Osman Hamdi Bey. The complex can be easily reached by walking down the slope from Topkapı's First Court, or by walking up the hill from the main gate of Gülhane Park.

Museum of the Ancient Orient

Immediately on the left after you enter the complex, this 1883 building has a collection of pre-Islamic items amassed from the expanse of the Ottoman Empire. Highlights include a series of large blue-and-yellow glazed-brick panels that once lined the processional street and the Ishtar Gate of ancient Babylon. The panels, which date from 604–562 BC, depict real and mythical animals such as lions, dragons and bulls.

Archaeology Museum

On the opposite side of the courtyard is this imposing neo-classical building housing an extensive collection of classical

DON'T MISS

- ➡ Glazed panels from ancient Babylon
- ➡ Alexander Sarcophagus
- ➡ Mourning Women Sarcophagus
- ➡ The Columned Sarcophagi of Anatolia
- ➡ Statuary Galleries
- ➡ *İstanbul Through the Ages* exhibition

PRACTICALITIES

- ➡ Map p238
- ➡ 212-520 7740
- ➡ www.istanbularkeoloji. gov.tr
- ➡ Osman Hamdi Bey Yokuşu, Gülhane
- ➡ adult/child under 12yr ₺15/free
- ➡ 9am-6pm Tue-Sun mid-Apr–Sep, to 4pm Oct–mid-Apr
- ➡ Gülhane

THE ALEXANDER SARCOPHAGUS

The Royal Necropolis of Sidon room in the Archaeology Museum showcases this famous piece of classical sculpture – so named not because it belonged to the Macedonian general, but because it depicts him among his army battling the Persians, who were led by King Abdalonymos (whose sarcophagus it is). Truly exquisite, the sarcophagus is carved out of Pentelic marble and dates from the last quarter of the 4th century BC. Alexander, on horseback, has a lion's head as a headdress. Remarkably, the sculpture retains remnants of its original red-and-yellow paintwork.

The Tiled Pavilion in the museum compound was originally an outer pavilion of Topkapı Palace. The sultan used it to watch sporting events being staged in the palace grounds below (now Gülhane Park).

statuary and sarcophagi plus a sprawling exhibit documenting İstanbul's history.

The main draws are two dimly lit rooms where the museum's major treasures – sarcophagi from the Royal Necropolis of Sidon and surrounding area – are displayed. These sarcophagi were unearthed in 1887 by Osman Hamdi Bey in Sidon (Side in modern-day Lebanon). The **Alexander Sarcophagus** and **Mourning Women Sarcophagus** are truly extraordinary works of art.

In the next room is an impressive collection of ancient grave-cult sarcophagi from Syria, Lebanon, Thessaloniki and Ephesus. Beyond that is a room called **The Columned Sarcophagi of Anatolia**, filled with amazingly detailed sarcophagi dating from between 140 and 270 AD. Many of these look like tiny temples or residential buildings; don't miss the **Sidamara Sarcophagus** from Konya.

Further rooms contain Lycian monuments and examples of Anatolian architecture from antiquity.

The museum's *Anatolia and Troy Through the Ages* and *Neighbouring Cultures of Anatolia, Cyprus, Syria and Palestine* exhibitions are upstairs, as is a fascinating albeit dusty exhibition called 'İstanbul Through the Ages' that traces the city's history through its neighbourhoods during different periods: Archaic, Hellenistic, Roman, Byzantine and Ottoman. It is likely that these exhibitions will be overhauled in the near future.

The museum's famed **Statuary Galleries** had been closed for renovation for a number of years at the time of writing and a completion date was not available. A downstairs gallery showcasing Byzantine artefacts was also closed.

Tiled Pavilion

The last of the complex's museum buildings is this handsome pavilion, constructed in 1472 by order of Mehmet the Conqueror. The portico, with its 14 marble columns, was constructed during the reign of Sultan Abdülhamid I (r 1774–89) after the original one burned down in 1737.

On display here are Seljuk, Anatolian and Ottoman tiles and ceramics dating from the end of the 12th century to the beginning of the 20th century. The collection includes İznik tiles from the period between the mid-14th and 17th centuries when that city produced the finest coloured tiles in the world. When you enter the central room you can't miss the stunning *mihrab* from the İbrahim Bey İmâret in Karaman, built in 1432.

TOP SIGHT
BASILICA CISTERN

This subterranean structure was commissioned by Emperor Justinian and built in 532. The largest surviving Byzantine cistern in İstanbul, it was constructed using 336 columns, many of which were salvaged from ruined temples and feature fine carved capitals. Its symmetry and sheer grandeur of conception are quite breathtaking, and its cavernous depths make a great retreat on summer days.

The cistern was originally known as the Basilica Cistern because it lay underneath the Stoa Basilica, one of the great squares on the first hill. Designed to service the Great Palace and surrounding buildings, it was able to store up to 80,000 cu metres of water delivered via 20km of aqueducts from a reservoir near the Black Sea, but was closed when the Byzantine emperors relocated from the Great Palace. Forgotten by the city authorities some time before the Conquest, it wasn't rediscovered until 1545, when scholar Petrus Gyllius was researching Byzantine antiquities in the city and was told by local residents that they were able to obtain water by lowering buckets into a dark space below their basement floors. Some were even catching fish this way. Intrigued, Gyllius explored before finally accessing the cistern through one of the basements. Even after his discovery, the Ottomans (who referred to the cistern as Yerebatan Saray) didn't treat the so-called 'Underground Palace' with the respect it deserved – it became a dumping ground for all sorts of junk, as well as corpses.

The cistern was cleaned and renovated in 1985 by the İstanbul Metropolitan Municipality and opened to the public in 1987. It's now one of the city's most popular tourist attractions. Walking along its raised wooden platforms, you'll feel the water dripping from the vaulted ceiling and see schools of ghostly carp patrolling the water – it certainly has bucketloads of atmosphere.

DON'T MISS

➡ Upside-down head of Medusa used as a column base

➡ Teardrop column

PRACTICALITIES

➡ Yerebatan Sarnıçı

➡ Map p240

➡ ☏212-512 1570

➡ www.yerebatan.com

➡ Yerebatan Caddesi 13

➡ admission officially ₺20 for foreigners but in reality ₺10

➡ ⏰9am-6.30pm mid-Apr–Sep, till 5.30pm Nov–mid-Apr

➡ 🚇Sultanahmet

◉ SIGHTS

◉ Sultanahmet

TOPKAPI PALACE PALACE
See p57.

AYA SOFYA MUSEUM
See p50.

BLUE MOSQUE MOSQUE
See p67.

**İSTANBUL ARCHAEOLOGY
MUSEUMS** MUSEUM
See p69.

BASILICA CISTERN CISTERN
See p71.

AYA SOFYA TOMBS TOMBS
Map p240 (Aya Sofya Müzesi Padişah Türbeleri; Kabasakal Caddesi; ⊘9am-5pm; ⊠Sultanahmet) **FREE** Part of the Aya Sofya complex but entered via Kabasakal Caddesi, these tombs are the final resting places of five sultans – Mehmet III, Selim II, Murad III, İbrahim I and Mustafa I – most of whom are buried with members of their families. The ornate interior decoration in the tombs features the very best Ottoman tilework, calligraphy and decorative paintwork.

Mehmet III's tomb dates from 1608 and Murad III's from 1599; both are adorned with particularly beautiful İznik tiles. Next to Murad's tomb is that of his five children; this was designed by Sinan and has simple but beautiful painted decoration.

Selim II's tomb, which was designed by Sinan and built in 1577, is particularly poignant, as it houses the graves of five of his sons, murdered on the same night in December 1574 to ensure the peaceful succession of the oldest, Murad III. It also houses the graves of 19 of Murad's sons, murdered in January 1595 to ensure Mehmet III's succession. They were the last of the royal princes to be murdered by their siblings – after this, the younger brothers of succeeding sultans were confined to the *kafes* (cage) in Topkapı Palace instead.

The fifth tomb is Aya Sofya's original Baptistry, converted to a mausoleum for sultans İbrahim I and Mustafa I during the 17th century.

GREAT PALACE MOSAIC MUSEUM MUSEUM
Map p240 (☑212-518 1205; Torun Sokak; admission ₺10; ⊘9am-5.30pm Tue-Sun mid-Apr–Sep, to 3.30pm Oct–mid-Apr; ⊠Sultanahmet) When archaeologists from the University of Ankara and the University of St Andrews (Scotland) excavated around the Arasta Bazaar at the rear of the Blue Mosque in the 1930s and 1950s, they uncovered a stunning mosaic pavement featuring hunting and mythological scenes. Dating from early Byzantine times, it was restored from 1983 to 1997 and is now preserved in this museum.

Thought to have been added by Justinian to the Great Palace of Byzantium, the pavement is estimated to have measured from 3500 to 4000 sq metres in its original form. The 250 sq metres that is preserved here is the largest discovered remnant – the rest has been destroyed or remains buried underneath the Blue Mosque and surrounding shops and hotels.

The pavement is filled with bucolic imagery and has a gorgeous ribbon border with heart-shaped leaves. In the westernmost room is the most colourful and dramatic picture, that of two men in leggings carrying spears and holding off a raging tiger.

The museum has informative panels documenting the floor's history, rescue and renovation.

HIPPODROME PARK
Map p240 (Atmeydanı; ⊠Sultanahmet) The Byzantine emperors loved nothing more than an afternoon at the chariot races, and this rectangular arena was their venue of choice. In its heyday, it was decorated by obelisks and statues, some of which remain in place today. Recently re-landscaped, it is one of the city's most popular meeting places and promenades.

Originally, the arena consisted of two levels of galleries, a central spine, starting boxes and the semicircular southern end known as the **Sphendone**, parts of which still stand. The level of galleries that once topped this stone structure was damaged during the Fourth Crusade and ended up being totally dismantled in the Ottoman period – many of the original columns were used in construction of the Süleymaniye Mosque.

The Hippodrome was the centre of Byzantium's life for 1000 years and of Ottoman life for another 400 years and has been the scene of countless political dramas. In Byzantine times, the rival chariot teams of 'Greens' and 'Blues' had separate sectarian connections. Support for a team was akin to membership of a political party and a team victory had important effects on policy. Occasionally, Greens and Blues joined forces against the emperor, as was the case in AD 532 when a chariot race was disturbed by protests against Justinian's high tax regime – this escalated into the Nika riots, so called after the protesters' cry of *Nika!* (Victory!), which led to tens of thousands of protesters being massacred in the Hippodrome by imperial forces. Not unsurprisingly, chariot races were banned for some time afterwards.

Ottoman sultans also kept an eye on activities in the Hippodrome. If things were going badly in the empire, a surly crowd gathering here could signal the start of a disturbance, then a riot, then a revolution. In 1826 the slaughter of the corrupt janissary corps (the sultan's personal bodyguards) was carried out here by the reformer Sultan Mahmut II. In 1909 there were riots here that caused the downfall of Abdülhamit II.

Despite the ever-present threat of the Hippodrome being the scene of their downfall, emperors and sultans sought to outdo one another in beautifying it, adorning the centre with statues from the far reaches of their empire. Unfortunately, many priceless statues carved by ancient masters have disappeared from their original homes here. Chief among the villains responsible for such thefts were the soldiers of the Fourth Crusade, who invaded Constantinople, a Christian ally city, in 1204. After sacking Aya Sofya, they tore all the plates from the **Rough-Stone Obelisk** (Map p240) at the Hippodrome's southern end in the mistaken belief that they were solid gold (in fact, they were gold-covered bronze). The Crusaders also stole the famous *quadriga* (team of four horses cast in bronze) a copy of which now sits atop the main door of the Basilica di San Marco in Venice (the original is inside the basilica).

Near the northern end of the Hippodrome, the little gazebo with beautiful stonework is known as **Kaiser Wilhelm's Fountain** (Map p240). The German emperor paid a state visit to Sultan Abdülhamit II in 1898 and presented this fountain to the sultan and his people as a token of friendship in 1901. The monograms on the dome's interior feature Abdülhamit's *tuğra* (imperial signature) and the first letter of Wilhelm's name, representing their political union.

The immaculately preserved pink granite **Obelisk of Theodosius** (Map p240) in the centre was carved in Egypt during the reign of Thutmose III (r 1549–1503 BC) and erected in the Amon-Re temple at Karnak.

ℹ MUSEUM PASS İSTANBUL

Most visitors spend at least three days in İstanbul and cram as many museum visits as possible into their stay, so the recent introduction of this discount pass (www.muze.gov.tr/museum_pass) is most welcome.

Valid for 72 hours from your first museum entrance, it costs ₺85 and allows entrance to Topkapı Palace and Harem, Aya Sofya, the İstanbul Archaeology Museums, the Museum of Turkish & Islamic Arts, the Great Palace Mosaics Museum and the İstanbul Museum of the History of Science & Technology in Islam. Purchased individually, admission fees to these sights will cost ₺125, so the pass represents a saving of ₺40. Its biggest benefit is that it allows you to bypass ticket queues and make your way straight into the museums – something that is particularly useful when visiting ever-crowded Aya Sofya.

As well as giving entry to these government-operated museums, the pass also gives discounts on entry to privately run museums including the Museum of Innocence (p125), the Pera Museum (p126) and the Rahmi M Koç Museum (p166); on ticket prices for the Bosphorus ferry tours operated by **İstanbul Şehir Hatları** (İstanbul City Routes; www.sehirhatlari.com.tr); and on guided walking tours operated by İstanbul Walks (p85).

The pass can be purchased from some hotels and also from the ticket offices at Aya Sofya, Topkapı Palace, the Great Palace Mosaics Museum and the İstanbul Archaeology Museums.

Theodosius the Great (r 379–95) had it brought from Egypt to Constantinople in AD 390. On the marble billboards below the obelisk, look for the carvings of Theodosius, his wife, sons, state officials and bodyguards watching the chariot-race action from the *kathisma* (imperial box).

South of the obelisk is a strange column coming up out of a hole in the ground. Known as the **Spiral Column** (Map p240), it was once much taller and was topped by three serpents' heads. Originally cast to commemorate a victory of the Hellenic confederation over the Persians in the battle of Plataea, it stood in front of the temple of Apollo at Delphi from 478 BC until Constantine the Great had it brought to his new capital city around AD 330. Though badly damaged in Byzantine times, the serpents' heads survived until the early 18th century. Now all that remains of them is one upper jaw, housed in the İstanbul Archaeology Museums (p69).

MARMARA UNIVERSITY REPUBLICAN MUSEUM MUSEUM

Map p240 (☉10am-6pm Tue-Sun; 🚇Sultanahmet) **FREE** Located at the southern end of the Hippodrome, this museum is housed in a handsome example of Ottoman Revivalism, a home-grown architectural style popular in the late 19th century. The university's collection of original prints and etchings by Turkish artists is displayed here.

★MUSEUM OF TURKISH & ISLAMIC ARTS MUSEUM

Map p240 (Türk ve İslam Eserleri Müzesi; www.tiem.gov.tr; Atmeydanı Caddesi 46; adult/child under 12yr ₺20/free; ☉refer to website; 🚇Sultanahmet) This Ottoman palace on the western edge of the Hippodrome was built in 1524 for İbrahim Paşa, childhood friend, brother-in-law and grand vizier of Süleyman the Magnificent. Undergoing a major renovation at the time of research, it has a magnificent collection of artefacts, including exquisite examples of calligraphy and one of the world's most impressive collections of antique carpets.

Born in Greece, İbrahim Paşa was captured in that country as a child and sold as a slave into the imperial household in İstanbul. He worked as a page in Topkapı, where he became friendly with Süleyman, who was the same age. When his friend became sultan, İbrahim was made in turn chief falconer, chief of the royal bedchamber and grand vizier. This palace was bestowed on him by Süleyman the year before he was given the hand of Süleyman's sister, Hadice, in marriage. Alas, the fairy tale was not to last for poor İbrahim. His wealth, power and influence on the monarch became so great that others wishing to influence the sultan became envious, chief among them Süleyman's powerful wife, Haseki Hürrem Sultan (Roxelana). After a rival accused İbrahim of disloy-

GREAT PALACE OF BYZANTIUM

Constantine the Great built the Great Palace soon after he declared Constantinople to be the capital of the Roman Empire in AD 330. Successive Byzantine leaders left their mark by adding to it, and the complex eventually consisted of hundreds of buildings over six levels. These included throne rooms, audience chambers, churches, chapels, stadiums and thermal baths, all enclosed by walls and set in terraced parklands stretching from the Hippodrome over to Hagia Sofia (Aya Sofya) and down the slope, ending at the sea walls on the Sea of Marmara. The palace was finally abandoned after the Fourth Crusade sacked the city in 1204, and its ruins were pillaged and filled in after the Conquest, becoming mere foundations of much of Sultanahmet and Cankurtaran.

Various pieces of the Great Palace have been uncovered – many by budding hotelier 'archaeologists'. The mosaics in the Great Palace Mosaic Museum (p72) once graced the floor of the complex, and excavations at the **Sultanahmet Archaeological Park** (Map p240) in Kabasakal Caddesi, near Aya Sofya, have uncovered other parts of the palace. Controversially, some of these excavations were subsumed into a new extension of the neighbouring luxury Four Seasons Hotel before public outcry stalled the project.

For more information, check out www.byzantium1200.com, which has computer-generated images that bring ancient Byzantium to life.

alty, Roxelana convinced her husband that İbrahim was a threat and Süleyman had him strangled in 1536.

Artefacts in the museum's collection date from the 8th and 9th centuries up to the 19th century. They include *müknames* (scrolls outlining an imperial decree) featuring the sultan's *tuğra* (monogram); Iranian book binding from the Safavid period (1501–1786); and Holbein, Lotto, Konya, Uşhak, Iran and Caucasia carpets.

AYA İRINI   CHURCH
Map p238 (Hagia Irene, Church of the Divine Peace; 1st Court, Topkapı Palace; adult/child under 12yr ₺20/free; ⊙9am-6pm Wed-Mon mid-Apr–Sep, to 4pm Oct–mid-Apr; 🚇Sultanahmet) Commissioned by Justinian in the 540s, this Byzantine church is almost exactly as old as its near neighbour, Aya Sofya. Used as an arsenal for centuries, it is now open to visitors but the entrance fee is exorbitant considering the fact that there are no exhibits inside.

The serenely beautiful interior and superb acoustics make this one of the most sought-after venues for the İstanbul Music Festival (p24). To attend a festival event here try your luck at the temporary box office located outside the church or online at Biletix (www.biletix.com).

CARPET MUSEUM   MUSEUM
Map p240 (Halı Müzesi; ☎212-512 6993; www.halimuzesi.com; Soğukçeşme Sokak; ⊙9am-4pm Tue-Sun; 🚇Sultanahmet or Gülhane) FREE Housed in an 18th-century *imaret* (soup kitchen) built behind the Aya Sofya complex, this recently opened museum is entered through a spectacular baroque gate and gives the visitor an excellent overview of the history of Anatolian carpet making. The carpets, which have been sourced from mosques throughout the country, date from the 14th to 20th centuries.

There are three galleries, each entered through Tardis-like humidity-controlled entrances. The first, in the *me'kel* (dining hall), features early Anatolian-era carpets with geometric and abstract designs; these are sometimes called Holbein carpets in honour of Dutch artist Hans Holbein the Younger, who often depicted them in his paintings. Also here are examples of the best-known type of Turkish carpets: Uşak (Ushak) carpets of the 16th and 17th centuries.

The second, in the *aşhane* (kitchen), displays rugs with Central and Eastern Ana-

tolian motifs including star-shaped medallions and keyholes; the latter is said to have been inspired by the mosque *mihrab*. Don't miss the particularly fine 19th-century Hereke rug that came from the Mustafa Mosque in Sirkeci.

The third, in the *fodlahane* (bakery), is the most impressive, with a huge 17th-century Uşak carpet from the Süleymaniye Mosque and another 19th-century example from the Blue Mosque.

The museum was free at the time of research, but an entry fee may apply in the future.

SOĞUKÇEŞME SOKAK   HISTORIC AREA
Map p238 (🚇Sultanahmet or Gülhane) Running between the Topkapı Palace walls and Aya Sofya, this cobbled street is named after the Soğuk Çeşme (Cold Fountain) at its southern end. It is home to the new Carpet Museum, to a row of faux-Ottoman houses functioning as a hotel and to an undoubtedly authentic restored Byzantine cistern that now operates as the hotel restaurant.

In the 1980s the Turkish Touring & Automobile Association (Turing) acquired a row of buildings on this street and decided to demolish most of them to build nine recreations of the prim Ottoman-style houses that had occupied the site in the previous two centuries. What ensued was a vitriolic battle played out on the pages of İstanbul's newspapers, with some experts arguing that the city would be left with a Disney-style architectural theme park rather than a legitimate exercise in conservation architecture. Turing eventually got the go-ahead (after the intervention of the Turkish president, no less) and in time opened all of the re-created buildings as Ayasofya Konakları, one of the first boutique heritage hotels in the city. Conservation theory aside, the street is particularly picturesque and worth a view.

CAFERAĞA MEDRESESI   HISTORIC BUILDING
Map p238 (www.tkhv.org; Soğukkuyu Çıkmazı 5, off Caferiye Sokak; ⊙8.30am-5pm; 🚇Sultanahmet) FREE This lovely little building tucked away in the shadows of Aya Sofya was designed by Sinan on the orders of Cafer Ağa, Süleyman the Magnificent's chief black eunuch. Built in 1560 as a school, it is now home to a cultural organisation teaching and promoting traditional Turkish handicrafts. The courtyard is home to the pleasant Caferağa Medresesi Çay Bahçesi (p83).

JOHN SONES SINGING BOWL MEDIA / GETTY IMAGES ©

1. İstanbul Archaeology Museums (p69)
Get up close with ancient sculptures

2. Spice Bazaar (p93)
Stalls here sell spices and *lokum* (turkish delight)

3. Topkapı Palace (p57)
Wandering through the main gate

4. Aya Sofya (p50)
The famous monument viewed from Sultanahmet Park

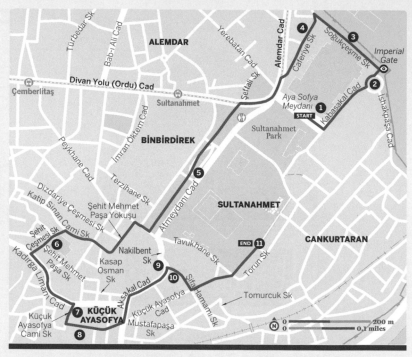

Neighbourhood Walk
Sultanahmet Saunter

START AYA SOFYA MEYDANI
FINISH ARASTA BAZAAR
LENGTH 2.3KM; TWO HOURS

Set off from Aya Sofya Meydanı and turn left into Kabaskal Caddesi to visit the ❶**Aya Sofya Tombs** (p72). After admiring their splendid interior decoration, head towards the ❷**Fountain of Sultan Ahmet III** (p57) outside Topkapı Palace. This kiosk once dispensed cold drinks of water or şerbet (sherbet) to thirsty Ottoman travellers.

Veer left into cobbled ❸**Soğukçeşme Sokak** (p75) and then turn left into Caferiye Sokak to visit the ❹**Caferağa Medresesi** (p75), where you can enjoy a glass of tea after admiring the elegant, Sinan-designed building. Back on Caferiye Sokak, continue until you reach the busy thoroughfare of Alemdar Caddesi and then walk alongside Sultanahamet Park to the ❺**Hippodrome** (p72), where horse-drawn chariots once stormed around.

Walk down Şehit Mehmet Paşa Yokuşu and continue down Katip Sinan Cami Sokak.

You will soon arrive at the ❻**Sokollu Şehit Mehmet Paşa Mosque** (p79) on the left-hand side of the street. After admiring its İznik tiles, veer left down Şehit Çeşmesi Sokak into the residential neighbourhood of Küçük Ayasofya. You will come to a busy but narrow road called Kadırga Limanı Caddesi. Veer left here and follow the road until you arrive at the sadly delapidated ❼**Çardaklı Hamam**, built in 1503. Turn right and you will see ❽**Little Aya Sofya** (p79), one of the most beautiful Byzantine buildings in the city.

Continue east along Küçük Ayasofya Caddesi and left up the hill at Aksakal Caddesi. At the crest is the ❾**Sphendone** (p72), originally part of the Hippodrome's southern stadium. Opposite is a huge carpet shop called ❿**Nakkaş**. Pop in here and ask a staff member to show you the restored Byzantine cistern in its basement.

From here, continue along Nakilbent Sokak and then veer right, down Şifa Hamamı Sokak, turning left into Küçük Ayasofya Caddesi and continuing straight ahead to visit the ⓫**Arasta Bazaar**, Sultanahmet's pre-eminent shopping precinct.

⊙ Küçük Ayasofya

LITTLE AYA SOFYA　　　　　　MOSQUE

Map p240 (Küçük Aya Sofya Camii, SS Sergius & Bacchus Church; Küçük Ayasofya Caddesi; 🚃Sultanahmet or Çemberlitaş) **FREE** Justinian and his wife Theodora built this little church sometime between 527 and 536, just before Justinian built Aya Sofya. You can still see their monogram worked into some of the frilly white capitals. The building is one of the most beautiful Byzantine structures in the city despite being thoroughly 'mosqueified' during a recent restoration.

Named after Sergius and Bacchus, the two patron saints of Christians in the Roman army, the building has been known as Little (Küçük in Turkish) Aya Sofya for much of its existence. Its dome is architecturally noteworthy and its plan – an irregular octagon – is quite unusual. Like Aya Sofya, its interior was originally decorated with gold mosaics and featured columns made from fine green and red marble. The mosaics are long gone, but the impressive columns remain. The church was converted into a mosque by the chief white eunuch Hüseyin Ağa around 1500; his tomb is to the north of the building. The minaret and *medrese* date from this time.

The *medrese* cells, arranged around the mosque's forecourt, are now used by secondhand booksellers and bookbinders. In the leafy forecourt there is a *çay bahçesi* (tea garden) where you can relax over a glass of tea.

SOKULLU ŞEHIT MEHMET PAŞA MOSQUE　　　　　　MOSQUE

Map p240 (Sokullu Mehmet Paşa Camii; cnr Şehit Çeşmesi & Katip Sinan Camii Sokaks, Kadırga; 🚃Sultanahmet or Çemberlitaş) Sinan designed this mosque in 1571, at the height of his architectural career. Besides its architectural harmony, the mosque is unusual because the *medrese* is not a separate building but actually part of the mosque structure, built around the forecourt. The interior walls and *mimber* are decorated with spectacular red-and-blue İznik tiles – some of the best ever made.

Though named after the grand vizier of the time, the mosque was actually sponsored by his wife Esmahan, daughter of Sultan Selim II. Inside are four fragments of the sacred Black Stone from the Kaaba in Mecca: one above the entrance framed in gold, two in the *mimber* and one in the *mihrab*.

⊙ Gülhane, Sirkeci & Eminönü

GÜLHANE PARK　　　　　　PARK

Map p238 (Gülhane Parkı; 🚃Gülhane) Gülhane Park was once the outer garden of Topkapı Palace, accessed only by the royal court. These days crowds of locals come here to picnic under the many trees, promenade past the formally planted flowerbeds, and enjoy wonderful views over the Golden Horn and Sea of Marmara from the Set Üstü Çay Bahçesi on the park's northeastern edge.

Recent beautification works have seen improvements to walkways and amenities, and have included the opening of a new museum, the İstanbul Museum of the History of Science & Technology in Islam.

Next to the southern entrance is the Alay Köşkü (Parade Kiosk), now open to the public as the Ahmet Hamdi Tanpınar Literature Museum Library.

Across the street and 100m northwest of the park's main gate is an outrageously curvaceous rococo gate leading into the precincts of what was once the grand vizierate, or Ottoman prime ministry, known in the West as the **Sublime Porte** (Map p238; 🚃Gülhane). Today the buildings beyond the gate hold various offices of the İstanbul provincial government (the Vilayeti).

AHMET HAMDI TANPINAR LITERATURE MUSEUM LIBRARY　　　　　　LIBRARY

Map p238 (Ahmet Hamdi Tanpınar Edebiyat Müze Kütüphanesi; 🕿212-520 2081; Gülhane Parkı; ☺10am-7pm Mon-Sat; 🚃Gülhane) **FREE** Built into the wall of Gülhane Park, the Alay Köşkü (Parade Kiosk) is where the sultan would sit and watch the periodic parades of troops and trade guilds that commemorated great holidays and military victories. It is now open to the public as a literature museum and library named in honour of novelist and essayist Ahmet Hamdi Tanpınar (1901–62).

Dating from the early 19th century, the kiosk is polygonal in shape and is beautifully decorated inside, with painted walls, stained-glass windows, chandeliers and highly polished wooden floors.

İSTANBUL MUSEUM OF THE HISTORY OF SCIENCE & TECHNOLOGY IN ISLAM　　　　　　MUSEUM

Map p238 (İstanbul İslam Bilim ve Teknoloji Tarihi Müzesi; 🕿212-528 8065; www.ibttm.org; Has Ahırlar Binaları, Gülhane Parkı; admission ₺10;

⏲9am-4.30pm Wed-Mon; 🚇Gülhane) Of interest to science buffs, the didactic exhibition in this museum argues that Islamic advances in science and technology preceded and greatly influenced those in Europe. Most of the exhibits are reconstructions of historical instruments and tools.

🍴 EATING

It's a shame the food served up in Sultanahmet eateries is largely mediocre. Too often lovely settings and great views are accompanied by disappointing meals. That said, we've eaten our way through the neighbourhood and fortunately, there are a few gems to be found. If you're in the Sirkeci neighbourhood at lunchtime, join the locals in Hocapaşa Sokak, a pedestrianised street lined with cheap eateries. Here, *lokantas* offer *hazır yemek* (ready-made dishes), *köftecis* dish out flavoursome meatballs, *kebapçıs* grill meat to order and the Hocapaşa Pidecisi serves pides straight from the oven. For more about eating ın Sirkeci, check out the website www.sirkecirestaurants.com.

🍴 Sultanahmet

EROL LOKANTASI   TURKISH €
Map p240 (📞212-511 0322; Çatal Çeşme Sokak 3, Cağaloğlu; portions ₺6-14; ⏲11am-9pm Mon-Sat; 📶; 🚇Sultanahmet) One of the last *esnaf lokantas* in Sultanahmet, Erol wouldn't win any awards for its interior design but might for its food – the dishes in the bain-marie are made fresh each day using seasonal ingredients and are really very good. Opt for a meat or vegetable stew served with buttery pilaf.

SEFA RESTAURANT   TURKISH €
Map p238 (📞212-520 0670; www.sefarestaurant.com.tr; Nuruosmaniye Caddesi 17, Cağaloğlu; portions ₺8-14, kebaps ₺13-20; ⏲7am-5pm; 📶; 🚇Sultanahmet) This popular place near the Grand Bazaar describes its cuisine as Ottoman, but what's really on offer are *hazır yemek* (ready-made dishes) and kebaps at extremely reasonable prices. You can order from an English menu or choose daily specials from the bain-marie. Try to arrive ear-

ly-ish for lunch because many of the dishes run out by 1.30pm. No alcohol.

KARADENIZ AILE PIDE
VE KEBAP SALONU   PIDE, KEBAP €
Map p240 (📞212-528 6290; www.karadenizpide.net; Hacı Tahsinbey Sokak 7, off Divan Yolu Caddesi; pides ₺12-17, kebaps ₺14-24; ⏲11am-11pm; 🚇Sultanahmet) The original Karadeniz (Black Sea)–style pide joint in this enclave off Divan Yolu, this popular place serves tasty pides and kebaps and is very popular with local shopkeepers. You can claim a table in the utilitarian interior (women usually sit upstairs) or on the cobbled lane. No alcohol.

Make sure that you don't get it confused with those nearby, which have very cheekily used versions of its name but are nowhere near as good. This one is on the corner of Biçki Yurdu Sokak.

SOFA CAFE RESTAURANT   RESTAURANT, BAR €
Map p240 (📞212-458 3630; Mimar Mehmet Ağa Caddesi 32, Cankurtaran; burgers ₺14, pastas ₺15-20, Turkish mains ₺17-35; ⏲11am-11pm; 🚇Sultanahmet) Ten candlelit tables beckon patrons into this friendly cafe-bar just off Akbıyık Caddesi. There's a happy hour (in fact three) between 3.30pm and 6.30pm each day and a decidedly laid-back feel. The food is cheap but tasty, the glasses of wine are generous and the Efes is cold, meaning that there's plenty to like.

TARIHI SULTANAHMET
KÖFTECISI SELIM USTA   KÖFTE €
Map p240 (📞212-520 0566; www.sultanahmetkoftesi.com; Divan Yolu Caddesi 12; köfte & beans ₺19; ⏲10.30am-10.30pm; 🚇Sultanahmet) This no-frills place near the Sultanahmet tram stop is the most famous eatery in the Old City for reasons that, frankly, elude us. It has been serving its slightly rubbery *ızgara köfte* (grilled meatballs) and bean salad to ultra-loyal locals since 1920, and shows no sign of losing their custom, as evidenced by the almost ubiquitous queue.

Accompany your *köfte* with the green pickled chillies that are served on the side, or ask the waiter for some spicy red chilli sauce. *Ayran* (yoghurt drink) is the drink of choice, so no alcohol.

ÇIĞDEM PASTANESI   CAFE €
Map p240 (Divan Yolu Caddesi 62a; cappuccino ₺7, glass of tea ₺2.50, pastries ₺1-4, cakes ₺2.50-7.50; ⏲8am-11pm; 🚇Sultanahmet) Strategically located on the main drag between Aya Sofya

HIPPIE HIPPIE SHAKE

Plenty of monuments in Sultanahmet evoke the city's Byzantine and Ottoman past, but there are few traces of an equally colourful but much more recent period in the city's history – the hippie era of the 1960s and 1970s. Back then the first wave of Intrepids (young travellers following the overland trail from Europe to Asia) descended upon İstanbul and can be said to have played a significant role in the Europeanisation of Turkey. The Intrepids didn't travel with itineraries, tour guides or North Face travel gear – their baggage embodied a rejection of materialism, a fervent belief in the power of love and a commitment to the journey rather than the destination. All that was leavened with liberal doses of drugs, sex and protest music, of course.

Sultanahmet had three central hippie hang-outs in those days: the Gülhane Hostel (now closed); a cafe run by Sitki Yener, the 'King of the Hippies' (now a leather shop on İnciliçavuş Sokak); and the still-operating **Lâle Pastanesi** (Map p240; ☑ info 212-522 2970; Divan Yolu Caddesi 6; ⏰ 7am-11pm; ⛔ Sultanahmet), known to hippies the world over as the Pudding Shop. Sadly, this retains few if any echoes of its counterculture past these days, substituting bland food in place of its former menu of psychedelic music and chillums of hash.

To evoke those days, we highly recommend Rory MacLean's *Magic Bus: On the Hippie Trail from Istanbul to India*, a thought-provoking and wonderfully written history/travelogue.

Meydanı and the Grand Bazaar, Çiğdem has been serving locals since 1961 and is still going strong. Pop in for a quick cup of tea or coffee accompanied by a cake, *börek* (filled pastry) or *acma* (Turkish-style bagel).

SEDEF BEYAZ   KEBAP €

Map p240 (Divan Yolu Caddesi 21b; döner from ₺6; ⏰ 11am-8.30pm; ⛔ Sultanahmet) Locals swear that this is the best döner kebap in Sultanahmet, and keep the chef busy shaving thin slices of meat or chicken with his enormous knife every lunchtime. A portion stuffed into fresh bread *(yarım ekmek)* costs ₺6 to ₺10 to take away, depending on the size and meat. Prices are higher in the next-door cafeteria.

AHIRKAPI BALIKÇISI   SEAFOOD €€

Map p240 (☑ 212-518 4988; Keresteci Hakkı Sokak 46, Cankurtaran; meze ₺5-30, fish ₺30-50; ⏰ 5.30-10pm; ⛔ Sultanahmet) For years we promised locals that we wouldn't review this neighbourhood fish restaurant. We sympathised with their desire to retain the place's low profile, particularly as it's tiny and authentically Turkish. However, other decent options are so scarce on the ground that we've finally decided to share the secret. Get here early to score a table.

COOKING ALATURKA   TURKISH €€

Map p240 (☑ 212-458 5919; www.cookingalaturka.com; Akbıyık Caddesi 72a, Cankurtaran; set lunch or dinner ₺55; ⏰ lunch Mon-Sat & dinner by reservation Mon-Sat; ☑; ⛔ Sultanahmet) Dutchborn owner/chef Eveline Zoutendijk and her Turkish colleague Fehzi Yıldırım serve a set four-course menu of simple Anatolian dishes at this hybrid cooking school and restaurant near the Blue Mosque. The menu makes the most of fresh seasonal produce, and can be tailored to suit vegetarians or those with food allergies (call ahead). No children under six years at dinner and no credit cards.

★ BALIKÇI SABAHATTIN   FISH €€€

Map p240 (☑ 212-458 1824; www.balikcisabahattin.com; Şeyit Hasan Koyu Sokak 1, Cankurtaran; mezes ₺10-30, fish ₺30-65; ⏰ noon-midnight; ⛔ Sultanahmet) The limos outside Balıkçı Sabahattın pay testament to its enduring popularity with the city's establishment, who join cashed-up tourists in enjoying its limited menu of meze and fish. The food here is the best in Sultanahmet, though the service is often harried. You'll dine under a leafy canopy in the garden (one section smoking, the other nonsmoking).

Be sure to choose your fish from the display near the restaurant entrance – cold mezes are chosen from trays brought to your table. If you're lucky, waiters will bring free desserts at the end of the meal (both the figs and the quince are delicious). This and water are included in a ₺5 cover charge.

★MATBAH   OTTOMAN €€€

Map p238 (☎212-514 6151; www.matbahrestau-rant.com; Ottoman Imperial Hotel, Caferiye Sokak 6/1; mezes ₺10-19, mains ₺28-60; ☺noon-11pm; 🖋; 🚇Sultanahmet) One of a growing number of İstanbul restaurants specialising in so-called 'Ottoman Palace Cuisine', Matbah offers dishes that were first devised in the palace kitchens between the 13th and 19th centuries. The menu changes with the sea-son and features unusual ingredients such as goose. Surrounds are attractive, the staff are attentive and there's live oud music on Friday and Saturday nights.

✗ Gülhane, Sirkeci & Eminönü

ŞEHZADE CAĞ KEBABI   KEBAP €

Map p238 (☎212-520 3361; Hocapaşa Sokak 3a, Sirkeci; kebap ₺15; ☺11.30am-7.30pm Mon-Sat; 🚇Sirkeci) Cooked on a horizontal rather than vertical spit, the Erzurum-style lamb kebap that this humble joint is known for is tender, very slightly charred and oh-so-delicious. Served on warm lavaş bread with a side-serve of tangy lemon, it's fast food of the highest order. Get here early at lunch-time to score one of the streetside tables.

GÜVENÇ KONYALI   TURKISH €

Map p238 (☎212-527 5220; Hocapaşa Hamam Sokak 4, Sirkeci; soups ₺8, mains & pides ₺12-25; ☺7am-9pm Mon-Sat; 🚇Sirkeci) Specialities from Konya in Central Anatolia are the draw at this bustling place just off the much-loved Hocapaşa Sokak food strip. Regulars come for the spicy bamya çorbası (sour soup with lamb and chickpeas), etli ekmek (flat bread with meat) and meltingly soft slow-cooked meats from the oven. No alcohol.

HOCAPAŞA PIDECISI   PIDE €

Map p238 (☎212-512 0990; www.hocapasa.com.tr; Hocapaşa Sokak 19, Sirkeci; pides ₺8-15; ☺11am-8pm; 🚇Sirkeci) This much-loved place has been serving piping-hot pides straight from its oven since 1964. Accompa-nied by pickles, they can be eaten at one of the outdoor tables or ordered paket (to go).

HAFIZ MUSTAFA   SWEETS €

Map p238 (www.hafizmustafa.com; Muradiye Caddesi 51, Sirkeci; börek ₺5, baklava ₺6-7.50, puddings ₺6; ☺7am-2am; 🚇Sirkeci) Making locals happy since 1864, this şekerlemeleri (sweets shop) sells lokum (Turkish delight), baklava, milk puddings, pastries and börek. Put your sweet tooth to good use in the upstairs cafe, or choose a selection of in-dulgences to take home (avoid the baklava, which isn't very good).

There's a second branch on **Divan Yolu Caddesi** (Map p240; ☎212-514 9068; Divan Yolu Caddesi 14, Sultanahmet; ☺9am-midnight; 🚇Sultanahmet) – look for the 'Edebiyat Kıraathanesi' sign – and a third on Hamidi-ye Caddesi (p104) close to the Spice Bazaar.

GÜLHANE KANDIL TESISLERI   TURKISH €

Map p238 (Gülhane Parkı; sandwiches ₺7.50-12.50, breakfast plate ₺19.50; ☺9am-5pm; 🚇Gülhane) In Spring, perfume from the pro-fusion of hyacinths blooming in Gülhane Park wafts over the outdoor tables of this garden cafe, which is built into the historic walls. It's a lovely spot for breakfast, a light lunch or a coffee break (Turkish coffee ₺5, tea ₺2) when the weather is kind.

🍷 DRINKING & 🍸 NIGHTLIFE

Sadly, there are few pleasant bars in Sultanahmet. Don't despair, though. Why not substitute tobacco or caffeine for alcohol and visit one of the atmospheric çay bahçesi dotted around the neighbourhood?

🍸 Sultanahmet

CAFE MEŞALE   NARGILE CAFE

Map p240 (Arasta Bazaar, Utangaç Sokak, Can-kurtaran; ☺24hr; 🚇Sultanahmet) Located in a sunken courtyard behind the Blue Mosque, Meşale is a tourist trap par excellence, but still has loads of charm. Generations of backpackers have joined locals in claiming one of its cushioned benches and enjoying a tea and nargile. It has sporadic live Turkish music and a bustling vibe in the evening.

DERVIŞ AILE ÇAY BAHÇESI   TEA GARDEN

Map p240 (Mimar Mehmet Ağa Caddesi; ☺7am-midnight Apr-Oct; 🚇Sultanahmet) Superbly located directly opposite the Blue Mosque, the Derviş beckons patrons with its com-fortable cane chairs and shady trees. Effi-cient service, reasonable prices and peer-less people-watching opportunities make it a great place for a leisurely tea, nargile and game of backgammon.

YEŞIL EV
BAR

Map p240 (Kabasakal Caddesi 5; ⊘noon-10.30pm; 🚇Sultanahmet) The elegant rear courtyard of this Ottoman-style hotel is a true oasis for those wanting to enjoy a quiet drink. In spring flowers and blossoms fill every corner; in summer the fountain and trees keep the temperature down. You can order a sandwich, salad or cheese platter if you're peckish.

CIHANNÜMA
BAR, RESTAURANT

Map p238 (☎212-520 7676; www.cihannumaistanbul.com; And Hotel, Yerebatan Caddesi 18; ⊘noon-midnight; 🚇Sultanahmet) We don't recommend eating at this restaurant on the top-floor of the And Hotel near Aya Sofya, but the view from its narrow balcony and glass-sheathed dining room is one of the best in the Old City (Aya Sofya, Blue Mosque, Topkapı Palace, Galata Tower and Bosphorus Bridge), so it's a great choice for a late-afternoon coffee or sunset drink.

CAFERAĞA MEDRESESI
ÇAY BAHÇESI
TEA GARDEN

Map p238 (Soğukkuyu Çıkmazı 5, off Caferiye Sokak; ⊘8.30am-4pm; 🚇Sultanahmet) On a fine day, sipping a çay in the gorgeous courtyard of this Sinan-designed *medrese* is a delight. Located close to both Aya Sofya and Topkapı Palace, it's a perfect pitstop between sights. There's simple food available at lunchtime.

HOTEL NOMADE TERRACE BAR
BAR

Map p240 (www.hotelnomade.com; Ticarethane Sokak 15, Alemdar; ⊘3-11pm; 🚇Sultanahmet) The intimate terrace of this boutique hotel overlooks Aya Sofya and the Blue Mosque. Settle down in a comfortable chair to enjoy a glass of wine, beer or freshly squeezed fruit juice. The only music that will disturb your evening reverie is the Old City's signature sound of the call to prayer.

KYBELE CAFE
BAR

Map p238 (www.kybelehotel.com; Yerebatan Caddesi 35; ⊘7.30am-11.30pm; 🚇Sultanahmet) The lounge bar-cafe at this hotel close to the Basilica Cistern is chock-full of antique furniture, richly coloured rugs and old etchings and prints, but its signature style comes courtesy of the hundreds of colourful glass lights hanging from the ceiling.

🍷 Gülhane, Sirkeci & Eminönü

SET ÜSTÜ ÇAY BAHÇESI
TEAHOUSE

Map p238 (Gülhane Parkı, Sultanahmet; ⊘9am-10.30pm; 🚇Gülhane) Come to this terraced tea garden to watch the ferries plying the route from Europe to Asia while at the same time enjoying an excellent pot of tea (1/2 person ₺8/14) accompanied by hot water (such a relief after the usual fiendishly strong Turkish brew). Add a cheap *tost* (toasted cheese sandwich; ₺3) to make a lunch of it.

☆ ENTERTAINMENT

HOCAPAŞA CULTURE
CENTRE
PERFORMING ARTS

Map p238 (Hodjapasha Culture Centre; ☎212-511 4626; www.hodjapasha.com; Hocapaşa Hamamı Sokak 3b, Sirkeci; performances adult ₺60-80, child under 12yr ₺40-50; 🚇Sirkeci) Occupying a beautifully converted 550-year-old *hamam* near Eminönü, this cultural centre stages a one-hour whirling dervish performance for tourists on Tuesday, Wednesday, Thursday, Saturday and Sunday evenings at 7pm, and a 1½-hour Turkish dance show on Tuesday, Thursday and Saturday at 9pm. Note that children under seven years are not admitted to the whirling dervish performance.

🛍 SHOPPING

The best shopping in Sultanahmet is found in and around the Arasta Bazaar, a historic arcade of shops that was once part of the *külliye* (mosque complex) of the Blue Mosque (Sultan Ahmet Camii). Some of Turkey's best-known rug and ceramic dealers have shops in the surrounding streets.

★COCOON
CARPETS, TEXTILES

Map p240 (☎212-638 6271; www.cocoontr.com; Küçük Ayasofya Caddesi 15 & 19; ⊘9am-6pm; 🚇Sultanahmet) There are so many rug and textile shops in İstanbul that choosing individual businesses to recommend is incredibly difficult. We had no problem whatsoever in singling this one out, though. Felt hats, felt-and-silk scarves and textiles from Central Asia are artfully displayed in one store, while rugs from Persia, Central Asia, the Caucasus and Anatolia adorn the other.

There's a third branch selling hamam items at Shop 93 in the **Arasta Bazaar** (Map p240; Arasta Bazaar 43, old door No 93; ⊘9am-7pm; ⌂Sultanahmet).

★ÖZLEM TUNA
JEWELLERY, HOMEWARES

Map p238 (⌧212-513 1361; www.ozlemtuna.com; 5th fl, Nemlizade Han, Ankara Caddesi 65, Eminönü; ⊘10am-5pm Mon-Fri, by arrangement Sat; ⌂Sirkeci) A leader in Turkey's contemporary design movement, Özlem Tuna produces super-stylish jewellery and homewares that she sells from her atelier overlooking Sirkeci train station. Her pieces use form and colours that reference the city (tulips, seagulls, gold, Bosphorus blue) and include hamam bowls, coffee and tea sets, serving bowls, trays, rings, earings, cufflinks and necklaces.

★JENNIFER'S HAMAM
BATHWARE

Map p240 (⌧212-518 0648; www.jennifershamam.com; Arasta Bazaar 135; ⊘9am-9pm Apr-Oct, 9am-7pm Nov-Mar; ⌂Sultanahmet) Owned by Canadian Jennifer Gaudet, this shop stocks top-quality hamam items including towels, robes and *peştemals* (bath wraps) produced using certified organic cotton on old-style shuttled looms. It also sells natural soaps and *keses* (coarse cloth mittens used for exfoliation). Prices are set, with no bargaining.

There's another branch within the **Arasta Bazaar** (Map p240; Arasta Bazaar 125; ⊘9am-9pm Apr-Oct, 9am-7pm Nov-Mar; ⌂Sultanahmet) and also nearby at **Öğül Sokak 20** (Map p240; Öğül Sokak 20; ⊘9am-6pm; ⌂Sultanahmet).

MEHMET ÇETINKAYA GALLERY
CARPETS, TEXTILES

Map p240 (⌧212-517 6808; www.cetinkayagallery.com; Tavukhane Sokak 7; ⊘9.30am-7.30pm; ⌂Sultanahmet) Mehmet Çetinkaya is known as one of the country's foremost experts on antique oriental carpets and kilims. His flagship store-cum-gallery stocks items that have artistic and ethnographic significance, and is full of treasures. There's a second shop selling rugs, textiles and objects in the **Arasta Bazaar** (Map p240; Arasta Bazaar 58; ⌂Sultanahmet).

KHAFTAN
ART, ANTIQUES

Map p240 (Nakilbent Sokak 33; ⊘9am-6.30pm; ⌂Sultanahmet) Gleaming Russian icons, delicate calligraphy (old and new), ceramics, Karagöz puppets and contemporary paintings are all on show in this attractive shop on the hill beneath the Hippodrome.

TULU
HOMEWARES

Map p240 (⌧212-518 8710; www.tulutextiles.com; Üçler Sokak 7; ⌂Sultanahmet) One of the new breed of contemporary homeware stores in İstanbul, Tulu is owned by American Elizabeth Hewitt, a textile collector and designer who produces a stylish range of cushions, bedding and accessories inspired by textiles from Central Asia. These are sold alongside an array of furniture, textiles and objects sourced in countries including Uzbekistan, India, Japan and Indonesia.

YILMAZ IPEKÇILIK
TEXTILES

Map p240 (⌧212-638 4579; www.yilmazipekcilik.com/en; İshakpaşa Caddesi 36; ⊘9am-9pm Mon-Sat, to 7pm winter; ⌂Sultanahmet) Well-priced hand-loomed silk textiles made in Antakya (Hatay) are on sale in this slightly out-of-the-way shop. Family-run, the business has been operating since 1950 and specialises in producing good-quality scarves, shawls and *peştemals*.

İZNIK CLASSICS
CERAMICS

Map p240 (⌧212-516 8874; www.iznikclassics.com; Utangaç Soka 13-17 k; ⊘9am-8pm; ⌂Sultanahmet) İznik Classics is one of the best places in town to seek out hand-painted collector-item ceramics made with real quartz and using metal oxides for pigments. Admire the range here or at the other branches at **Arasta Bazaar** (Map p240; Arasta Bazaar 119; ⌂Sultanahmet) and in the **Grand Bazaar** (Map p242; Serifaga Sokak 188, İç Bedesten; ⌂Beyazıt-Kapalı Çarşı).

GALERI KAYSERI
BOOKS

Map p240 (⌧212-516 3366; www.galerikayseri.com; Divan Yolu Caddesi 11 & 58; ⊘9am-9pm; ⌂Sultanahmet) These twin shops near the Sultanahmet tram stop offer a modest range of English-language fiction and a more impressive selection of books about İstanbul and Turkey. The second, smaller, shop is on the opposite side of the road half a block closer to Aya Sofya.

⚡ SPORTS & ACTIVITIES

★İSTANBUL WALKS
WALKING TOUR

Map p240 (☎212-516 6300; www.istanbulwalks. com; 2nd fl, Şifa Hamamı Sokak 1; walking tours €30-80, child under 6yr free; 🚇Sultanahmet) Specialising in cultural tourism, this company is run by history buffs and offers a large range of guided walking tours conducted by knowledgeable English-speaking guides. Tours concentrate on İstanbul's various neighbourhoods, but there are also tours of major monuments, a Turkish Coffee Trail, and a tour of the Bosphorus and Golden Horn by private boat. Student discounts are available.

AYASOFYA HÜRREM SULTAN HAMAMI
HAMAM

Map p240 (☎212-517 3535; www.ayasofya-hamami.com; Aya Sofya Meydanı 2; bath treatments €85-170, massages €40-75; ⊗8am-10pm; 🚇Sultanahmet) Reopened in 2011 after a meticulous restoration, this twin hamam is now offering the most luxurious traditional bath experience in the Old City. Designed by Sinan between 1556 and 1557, it was built just across the road from Aya Sofya by order of Süleyman the Magnificent and named in honour of his wife Hürrem Sultan, commonly known as Roxelana.

The building's three-year, US$13 million restoration was closely monitored by heritage authorities and the end result is wonderful, retaining Sinan's austere design but endowing it with an understated modern luxury. There are separate baths for males and females, both with a handsome *soğukluk* (entrance vestibule) surrounded by wooden change cubicles. Though relatively expensive, treatments are expert and the surrounds are exceptionally clean. The basic 35-minute treatment costs €85 and includes a scrub and soap massage, olive-oil soap and your personal *kese* (coarse cloth mitten used for exfoliation). In warm weather, a cafe and restaurant operate on the outdoor terrace.

COOKING ALATURKA
COOKING

Map p240 (☎0536 338 0896; www.cookingalaturka.com; Akbıyık Caddesi 72a, Cankurtaran; cooking class per person €65; 🚇Sultanahmet) Dutch-born Eveline Zoutendijk opened the first English-language Turkish cooking school in İstanbul in 2003 and since then

has built a solid reputation for her convivial classes, which offer a great introduction to Turkish cuisine and are suitable for both novices and experienced cooks. The delicious results are enjoyed over a five-course meal in the school's restaurant (p81).

AMBASSADOR SPA
HAMAM

Map p240 (☎212-512 0002; www.istanbulambassadorhotel.com; Ticarethane Sokak 19; Turkish bath treatments €40-60, remedial & aromatherapy massage €25-80; ⊗9am-10pm; 🚇Sultanahmet) There's no Ottoman ambience on offer at the shabby spa centre of this hotel just off Divan Yolu, but all treatments are private, meaning that you get the small hamam all to yourself. Best of all is the fact that the signature 60- or 75-minute 'Oriental Massage' package includes a facial massage, hamam treatment and expert 30-minute oil massage.

The spa's massage therapist Zeki Ulusoy is trained in sports, remedial and aromatherapy massage and he really knows his stuff – you'll float out of here at the end of a session. The 'Oriental Massage' treatment costs €50 to €60; a 50-minute 'Back to Traditions' package comprises a 20-minute body scrub and a 30-minute foam massage and costs €40.

CAĞALOĞLU HAMAMI
HAMAM

Map p238 (☎212-522 2424; www.cagalogluhamami.com.tr; Yerebatan Caddesi 34; bath, scrub & massage packages €50-110; ⊗8am-10pm; 🚇Sultanahmet) Built in 1741 by order of Sultan Mahmut I, this gorgeous hamam offers separate baths for men and women and a range of bath services that are – alas – radically overpriced considering how quick and rudimentary the wash, scrub and massage treatments are. Consider signing up for the self-service treatment (€30) only.

URBAN ADVENTURES
WALKING, CULTURAL TOURS

(☎0532 641 2822; www.urbanadventures.com; tours adult €25-39, child €20-30) The international tour company Intrepid offers a program of city tours including a popular four-hour guided walk around Sultanahmet and the Bazaar District. Also on offer is the 'Home Cooked İstanbul' tour, which includes a no-frills dinner with a local family in their home plus a visit to a neighbourhood teahouse for tea, a nargile and a game of backgammon.

Bazaar District

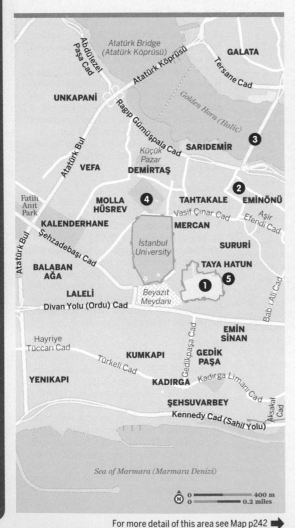

Neighbourhood Top Five

1 Enjoying getting lost in the labyrinthine laneways of the world's oldest shopping mall, the glorious **Grand Bazaar** (p88).

2 Shopping in and around the seductively scented **Spice Bazaar** (p93).

3 Viewing the Old City's skyline while walking across the **Galata Bridge** (p94) at sunset.

4 Visiting the remarkably intact *külliye* of the **Süleymaniye Mosque** (p91), the greatest of İstanbul's Ottoman monuments.

5 Lunching with the locals in and around the **Grand Bazaar** (p99).

For more detail of this area see Map p242 ➡

Explore: Bazaar District

There's loads to see in this district so you'll need to plan your time to make the most of it. Ideally, you should dedicate a full day to the bazaars, starting at the Grand Bazaar in the morning, having lunch and then walking down Mahmutpaşa Yokuşu to the Spice Bazaar and Eminönü.

Another day could be spent following our walking tour (p96). On this you'll visit two important Ottoman mosques and get a taste of local life while lunching at a regional eatery in the Kadınlar Pazarı (Women's Market) near the Roman-era Aqueduct of Valens.

Nothing much is open in this district on Sundays – visit Monday to Saturday only. And try to avoid the mosques at prayer times and from late morning to early afternoon on Friday, when weekly group prayers and sermons are held.

Local Life

➡ **Tahtakale** Locals shop in the streets between the Grand and Spice Bazaars rather than in the bazaars themselves. Head to Mahmutpaşa Yokuşu and Hasırcılar Caddesi to join them.

➡ **Kadınlar Pazarı** This atmospheric square in the Zeyrek neighbourhood is full of regional eateries and produce shops.

➡ **Fish sandwiches** The city's signature fast-food treat is best enjoyed with crowds of locals at the Eminönü ferry docks.

➡ **Nargile** Follow the evocative scent of apple tobacco to discover busy nargile (water pipe) cafes underneath the Galata Bridge or along Divan Yolu Caddesi.

Getting There & Away

➡ **Metro** To get here from Taksim Meydanı (Taksim Sq), take the Yenikapı service and alight at Vezneciler. From the exit, walk left (east) along Şehzadebaşı Caddesi until you reach Beyazıt Meydanı (Beyazıt Sq), next to the Grand Bazaar.

➡ **Tram** The neighbourhood is sliced into north and south by Ordu Caddesi, the western continuation of Divan Yolu Caddesi. The trams from Bağcılar and Cevizlibağ to Kabataş run along this major road, passing through Aksaray, past the Grand Bazaar, across Sultanahmet and then down the hill to Eminönü, where the Spice Bazaar is located.

Lonely Planet's Top Tip

If you are walking to the Grand Bazaar from Sultanahmet, you can avoid the traffic and touts along Divan Yolu Caddesi by instead heading up Yerebatan Caddesi, left into Nuruosmaniye Caddesi, across Cağaloğlu Meydanı, along pedestrianised Nuruosmaniye Caddesi and across Vezir Han Caddesi towards the Nuruosmaniye Mosque.

Best Places to Eat

➡ Develi Baklava (p98)
➡ Fatih Damak Pide (p98)
➡ Little Urfa (p95)
➡ Hamdi Restaurant (p100)
➡ Siirt Şeref Büryan Kebap (p98)

For reviews, see p98. ➡

Best Places to Shop

➡ Abdulla Natural Products (p102)
➡ Derviş (p103)
➡ Mekhann (p103)
➡ Ümit Berksoy (p102)
➡ Altan Şekerleme (p103)

For reviews, see p102. ➡

Best Mosque Architecture

➡ Süleymaniye Mosque (p91)
➡ Rüstem Paşa Mosque (p95)
➡ Şehzade Mehmet Mosque (p97)

For reviews, see p91. ➡

TOP SIGHT
GRAND BAZAAR

This colourful and chaotic bazaar is the heart of the Old City and has been so for centuries. Starting as a small vaulted *bedesten* (warehouse) built on the order of Mehmet the Conqueror in 1461, it grew to cover a vast area as laneways between the *bedesten*, neighbouring shops and *hans* (caravanserais) were roofed and the market assumed the sprawling, labyrinthine form that it retains today.

When here, be sure to peep through doorways to discover hidden *hans,* veer down narrow laneways to watch artisans at work and wander the main thoroughfares to differentiate treasures from tourist tat. It's obligatory to drink lots of tea, compare price after price and try your hand at the art of bargaining. Allow at least three hours for your visit; some travellers spend three days!

To learn more about day-to-day life in the bazaar, go to www.mygrandbazaar.com, which profiles some of the people who work here. For handy tips on how to bargain with the shopkeepers, see p17.

DON'T MISS

➡ İç (Inner) Bedesten

➡ Halıcılar Çarşışı Sokak

➡ Kuyumcular Caddesi

➡ Takkeçiler Sokak

➡ Sandal Bedesten

PRACTICALITIES

➡ Kapalı Çarşı, Covered Market

➡ Map p242

➡ ⏰ 8.30am-7pm Mon-Sat

➡ 🚻

➡ Ⓜ Vezneciler, 🚇 Beyazıt-Kapalı Çarşı

A Tour of the Bazaar

There are thousands of shops in the bazaar, and this can be overwhelming for the first-time visitor. By following this suggested itinerary, you should be able to develop an understanding of the bazaar's history, its layout and its important position as the hub of the surrounding retail precinct.

Start at the tram stop next to the tall column known as Çemberlitaş (p94). From here, walk down Vezir Han Caddesi and you will soon come to the entrance to the Vezir Han, a caravanserai built between 1659 and 1660 by the Köprülüs, one of the Ottoman Empire's most distinguished families. Five of its members served as Grand Vizier *(vezir)* to the sultan, hence its name. In Ottoman times, this *han* would have offered travelling merchants accommodation and a place to do business. Though gold manufacturers still work here, the *han* is in a sadly dilapidated state, as are the many (some experts say hundreds) of similar buildings dotted throughout the district. Look for the *tuğra* (monogram) of the sultan over the main gateway.

Continue walking down Vezir Han Caddesi until you come to a cobbled pedestrianised street on your left. Walk along this until you reach the Nuruosmaniye Mosque (p95). In front of you is one of the major entrances to the Grand Bazaar, the Nuruosmaniye Kapısı (Nuruosmaniye Gate, Gate 1), adorned by another *tuğra*. The narrow lanes behind the mosque are full of fast-food stands that are popular with the bazaar's shopkeepers.

Pass through the Nuruosmaniye Kapısı and into brightly lit **Kalpakçılar Caddesi**, the busiest street in the bazaar. Originally named after the makers of fur hats *(kalpakçılars)* who had their stores here, it's now full of jewellers, who pay up to US$100,000 per year in rent for this high-profile location. Start walking down the street and then turn right and take the marble stairs down to the **Sandal Bedesten**, a stone warehouse featuring 20 small domes. This warehouse has always been used for the storage and sale of fabric, although the current range of cheap textiles on sale couldn't be more different from the fine *sandal* (fabric woven with silk) that was sold here in the past.

Exit the Sandal Bedesten on its west (left) side, turning right into Sandal Bedesteni Sokak and then left into Ağa Sokak, which takes you into the oldest part of the bazaar, the **İç (Inner) Bedesten**, also known as the Eski (Old) Bedesten. This has always been an area where precious items are stored and sold, and these days it's where most of the bazaar's antique stores are located. Slave auctions were held here until the mid-19th century.

Exiting the *bedesten* from its south door, walk down to the first cross-street, Halıcılar Çarşışı Sokak, where popular shops including Abdulla Natural Products (p102) and Derviş (p103) are located. Also here is a good spot for a tea or coffee, Ethem Tezçakar Kahveci (p101).

Walking east (right) you will come to a major cross-street, **Kuyumcular Caddesi** (Street of the Jewellers). Turn left and walk past the little kiosk in the middle of the street. Built in the 19th century and known as the **Oriental Kiosk**, this now houses a jewellery store but was once home to the most famous *muhallebici* (milk-pudding shop) in the district. A little way further down, on the right-hand side of the street, is the entrance to the pretty **Zincirli (Chain) Han**, home to one of the bazaar's best-known carpet

MAHMUTPAŞA YOKUŞU

This busy thoroughfare links the Grand Bazaar with the Spice Bazaar at Eminönü. Locals come here to buy everything from wedding dresses to woollen socks, coffee cups to circumcision outfits. From the Grand Bazaar, leave the Mahmutpaşa Kapısı (Mahmutpaşa Gate, Gate 18) and walk downhill. Along the way you will pass one of the oldest hamams in the city: the **Mahmutpaşa Hamamı** (Map p242), now a shopping centre. If you veer left onto Tarakçılar Caddesi before coming to the hamam and walk all the way to Çakmakçılar Yokuşu you will see the historic **Büyük Valide Han** (Map p242), a huge and sadly dilapidated caravanserai built by order of Murad IV's mother in 1651. It once accommodated up to 3000 travelling merchants and their animals every night.

Over the bazaar's history, most silversmiths who have worked here have been of Armenian descent and most goldsmiths have been of Arabic or Aramaic descent – this is still true today.

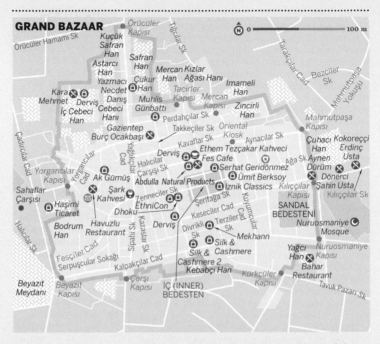

GRAND BAZAAR

merchants: Şişko Osman. Returning to Kuyumcular Caddesi, turn sharp left into Perdahçılar Sokak (Street of the Polishers). Walk until you reach Takkeçiler Sokak, where you should turn left. This charming street is known for its marble *sebils* (public drinking fountains) and shops selling kilims (pileless woven rugs). Turn right into Zenneciler Sokak (Street of the Clothing Sellers) and you will soon come to a junction with another of the bazaar's major thoroughfares: Sipahi Sokak (Avenue of the Cavalry Soldiers). Şark Kahvesi (p102), a traditional coffee house, is right on the corner. Sipahi Sokak becomes Yağlıkçılar Caddesi to the north (right) and Feraçeciler Sokak to the south (left).

Turn left into Sipahi Sokak and walk until you return to Kalpakçılar Caddesi. Turn right and exit the bazaar from the Beyazıt Kapısı (Beyazit Gate, Gate 7). Turn right again and walk past the market stalls to the first passage on the left to arrive at the **Sahaflar Çarşısı** (Old Book Bazaar; Map p242; Çadırcılar Caddesi, btwn Grand Bazaar & Beyazıt Mosque), which has operated as a book and paper market since Byzantine times. At the centre of its shady courtyard is a bust of İbrahim Müteferrika (1674–1745), who printed the first book in Turkey in 1732.

SALVATOR BARKI / GETTY IMAGES ©

TOP SIGHT
SÜLEYMANIYE MOSQUE

The Süleymaniye crowns one of İstanbul's seven hills and dominates the Golden Horn, providing a landmark for the entire city. Though it's not the largest of the Ottoman mosques, it is certainly one of the grandest and it is unusual in that many of its original *külliye* (mosque complex) buildings have been retained and sympathetically adapted for reuse.

Commissioned by Süleyman I, known as 'The Magnificent', the Süleymaniye was the fourth imperial mosque built in İstanbul and it certainly lives up to its patron's nickname. The mosque and its surrounding buildings were designed by Mimar Sinan, the most famous and talented of all imperial architects.

The Mosque

The mosque was built between 1550 and 1557. Though it's seen some hard times, having been damaged by fire in 1660 and then having its wonderful columns covered by cement and oil paint at some point after this, restorations in 1956 and 2010 mean that it's now in great shape. It's also one of the most popular mosques in the city, with worshippers rivalling the Blue and New Mosques in number.

The building's setting and plan are particularly pleasing, featuring gardens and a three-sided forecourt with a central domed ablutions fountain. The four **minarets** with their 10 beautiful *şerefes* (balconies) are said to represent the fact that Süleyman was the fourth of the Osmanlı sultans to rule the city and the 10th sultan after the establishment of the empire.

In the garden behind the mosque is a **terrace** offering lovely views of the Golden Horn. The street underneath once housed the *külliye's arasta* (row of shops), which was built into the retaining wall of the terrace. Close by was a five-level *mülazim* (preparatory school).

DON'T MISS
→ Mosque
→ *Türbes* (tombs)
→ *Külliye* (mosque complex)
→ View from terrace

PRACTICALITIES
→ Map p242
→ Professor Sıddık Sami Onar Caddesi
→ Ⓜ Vezneciler, 🚇 Laleli-Üniversite

SURROUNDING STREETS

The streets surrounding the mosque are home to what may well be the most extensive concentration of Ottoman timber houses on the Historic Peninsula, many of which are currently being restored as part of an urban regeneration project. To see some of these, head down Fetva Yokuşu, between the tabhane (inn for travelling dervishes) and Sinan's tomb, and then veer right into Namahrem Sokak and into Ayrancı Sokak. One of the many Ottoman-era houses here was once occupied by Mimar Sinan; it now houses a cafe. To see other timber houses in the area, take a walk down Kayserili Ahmetpaşa Sokak.

Although Sinan described the smaller Selimiye Mosque in Edirne as his best work, he chose to be buried here in the Süleymaniye complex, probably knowing that this would be the achievement that he would be best remembered for. His *türbe* (tomb) is just outside the mosque's walled garden, next to a disused *medrese* (seminary) building.

Inside, the building is breathtaking in its size and pleasing in its simplicity. Sinan incorporated the four buttresses into the walls of the building – the result is wonderfully 'transparent' (ie open and airy) and highly reminiscent of Aya Sofya, especially as the dome is nearly as large as the one that crowns the Byzantine basilica.

The *mihrab* (niche in a minaret indicating the direction of Mecca) is covered in fine İznik tiles, and other interior decoration includes window shutters inlaid with mother-of-pearl, gorgeous stained-glass windows, painted *muqarnas* (corbels with honeycomb detail), a new and quite spectacular persimmon-coloured floor carpet, painted pendentives and medallions featuring fine calligraphy.

The Külliye

Süleyman specified that his mosque should have the full complement of public services: *imaret* (soup kitchen), *medrese* (Islamic school of higher studies), hamam, caravanserai, *darüşşifa* (hospital) etc. Today the **imaret**, with its charming garden courtyard, houses the **Darüzziyafe restaurant** (Map p242) and is a lovely place to enjoy a çay. On its right-hand side (north) is a **tabhane** (inn for travelling dervishes) that was being restored at the time of research and on its left-hand side (south) is Lale Bahçesi, a popular tea garden set in a sunken courtyard.

The main entrance to the mosque is accessed via Professor Sıddık Sami Onar Caddesi, formerly known as **Tiryaki Çarşışı** (Market of the Addicts). The buildings here once housed three *medreses* and a primary school; they're now home to the Süleymaniye Library and a raft of popular streetside *fasülyecis* (restaurants specialising in beans) that were formerly teahouses selling opium (hence the street's former name). On the corner of Professor Sıddık Sami Onar Caddesi and Şifahane Sokak is the **darüşşifa**, also under restoration.

The still-functioning **Süleymaniye Hamamı** is on the eastern side of the mosque.

Türbes

To the right (southeast) of the main entrance is the cemetery, home to the **tombs** (Map p242) of Süleyman and his wife Haseki Hürrem Sultan (Roxelana). The tilework in both is superb. Peek through the windows of Süleyman's tomb to see jewel-like lights in the dome. In Roxelana's tomb, the many tile panels of flowers and the delicate stained glass produce a serene effect.

TOP SIGHT
SPICE BAZAAR

Vividly coloured spices are displayed alongside jewel-like *lokum* (Turkish delight) at this Ottoman-era marketplace, providing eye candy for the thousands of tourists and locals who make their way here every day. As well as spices and *lokum,* stalls sell dried herbs, caviar, nuts, honey in the comb, dried fruits and *pestil* (fruit pressed into sheets and dried). The number of stalls selling tourist trinkets increases annually, yet this remains a great place to stock up on edible souvenirs, share a few jokes with the vendors and marvel at the well-preserved building. It's also home to one of the city's oldest restaurants, Pandeli (p102).

The market was constructed in the 1660s as part of the New Mosque (p97); rent from the shops supported the upkeep of the mosque as well as its charitable activities, which included a school, hamam and hospital. The name Mısır Çarşısı (Egyptian Market) comes from the fact that the building was initially endowed with taxes levied on goods imported from Egypt. In its heyday, the bazaar was the last stop for the camel caravans that travelled the Silk Road from China, India and Persia.

On the west side of the market there are outdoor produce stalls selling fresh foodstuff from all over Anatolia, including a wonderful selectin on of cheeses. Also here is the most famous coffee supplier in İstanbul, Kurukahveci Mehmet Efendi (p104), established over 100 years ago. This is located on the corner of Hasırcılar Caddesi, which is full of shops selling foodstuffs and kitchenware.

At the time of research, the bazaar was opening on Sundays from 8am to 7pm, but this is subject to change.

DID YOU KNOW?

Leeches are still used for traditional medical treatments in Turkey. You'll see them being offered for sale in the outdoor market on the eastern side of the Spice Bazaar, alongside poultry and pot plants.

PRACTICALITIES

➜ Mısır Çarşısı, Egyptian Market

➜ Map p242

➜ ⊙8am-6pm Mon-Sat, 8am-7pm Sun

➜ 🚊Eminönü

◉ SIGHTS

GRAND BAZAAR MARKET
See p88.

SÜLEYMANIYE MOSQUE MOSQUE
See p91.

SPICE BAZAAR MARKET
See p93.

GALATA BRIDGE BRIDGE
Map p242 (Galata Köprüsü; 🚊Eminönü or Karaköy)
To experience İstanbul at its most magical, walk across the Galata Bridge at sunset. At this time, the historic Galata Tower is surrounded by shrieking seagulls, the mosques atop the seven hills of the city are silhouetted against a soft red-pink sky, and the evocative scent of apple tobacco wafts out of the nargile (water pipe) cafes under the bridge.

During the day, the bridge carries a constant flow of İstanbullus crossing to and from Beyoğlu and Eminönü, a handful or two of hopeful anglers trailing their lines into the waters below, and a constantly changing procession of street vendors hawking everything from fresh-baked *simits* (sesame-encrusted bread rings) to Rolex rip-offs. Underneath, restaurants and cafes serve drinks and food all day and night. Come here to enjoy a beer and nargile while watching the ferries making their way to and from the Eminönü and Karaköy ferry docks.

The present, quite ugly, bridge was built in 1992 to replace an iron structure dating from 1909 to 1912, which in turn had replaced two earlier structures. The iron bridge was famous for the ramshackle fish restaurants, teahouses and nargile joints that occupied the dark recesses beneath its roadway, but it had a major flaw: it floated on pontoons that blocked the natural flow of water and kept the Golden Horn from flushing itself free of pollution. In the late 1980s the municipality started to draw up plans to replace it with a new bridge that would allow the water to flow. A fire expedited these plans in the early 1990s and the new bridge was built a short time afterwards. The remains of the old, much-loved bridge were moved further up the Golden Horn near Hasköy.

ÇEMBERLİTAŞ MONUMENT
Map p242 (Hooped Column; Divan Yolu Caddesi; 🚊Çemberlitaş) Next to the Çemberlitaş tram stop, in a pigeon-packed plaza, you'll find one of the city's most ancient monuments: a column known as the Çemberlitaş that was erected by Constantine to celebrate the dedication of 'New Rome' (Constantinople) as capital of the Roman Empire in 330.

The column was placed in what was the grand Forum of Constantine and was topped by a statue of the great emperor himself in the guise of Apollo. It lost its crowning statue of Constantine in 1106 and was damaged in the 1779 fire that ravaged the nearby Grand Bazaar. Recently restored, it is a strange-looking remnant of the city's Roman past.

Also in this vicinity is the historic Çemberlitaş Hamamı (p105).

BEYAZIT MEYDANI SQUARE
Map p242 (Ⓜ Vezneciler, 🚊Beyazıt-Kapalı Çarşı)
Beyazıt Meydanı is officially called Hürriyet Meydanı (Freedom Sq), though everyone knows it simply as Beyazıt. In Byzantine times it was called the Forum of Theodosius. Today the square is home to street vendors, students from **İstanbul University** (Map p242) and plenty of pigeons, as well as a few policemen who like to keep an eye on student activities.

The square is backed by the impressive portal of İstanbul University. After the Conquest, Mehmet the Conqueror built his first palace here, a wooden structure called the Eski Sarayı (Old Seraglio). After Topkapı was built, the Eski Sarayı became home to women when they were pensioned out of the main palace – this was where *valide sultans* (mothers of the reigning sultans) came when their sultan sons died and they lost their powerful position as head of the Harem. The original building was demolished in the 19th century to make way for a grandiose Ministry of War complex designed by Auguste Bourgeois; this now houses the university. The 85m-tall **Beyazıt Tower** (Map p242) in its grounds sits on top of one of the seven hills on which Constantine the Great built the city, following the model of Rome. Commissioned by Mahmud II, the stone tower was designed by Senekerim Balyan and built in 1828 in the same location as a previous wooden tower. The tower was used by the İstanbul Fire Department to spot fires until 1993. The coloured lights on it indicate weather conditions – blue for clear and sunny, green for rain, yellow for fog and red for snow.

Both the university and tower are off-limits to travellers.

BEYAZIT MOSQUE
MOSQUE

Map p242 (Beyazıt Camii, Mosque of Sultan Beyazıt II; Beyazıt Meydanı, Beyazıt; MVezneciler, Beyazıt-Kapalı Çarşı) The second imperial mosque built in İstanbul (after the Fatih Camii), Beyazıt Camii was built between 1501 and 1506 by order of Beyazıt II, son of Mehmet the Conqueror. Architecturally, it links Aya Sofya, which obviously inspired its design, with great mosques such as the Süleymaniye, which are realisations of Aya Sofya's design fully adapted to Muslim worship.

The mosque's exceptional use of fine stone is noteworthy, with marble, porphyry, verd antique and rare granite featuring. The *mihrab* is simple, except for the rich stone columns framing it. The courtyard features 24 small domes and a central ablutions fountain.

Of the original *külliye* buildings, the *imaret* has been turned into a library. Unfortunately the once-splendid hamam has been closed for many years. Beyazıt's *türbe* is behind the mosque.

NURUOSMANIYE MOSQUE
MOSQUE

Map p242 (Nuruosmaniye Camii, Light of Osman Mosque; Vezir Han Caddesi, Beyazıt; Çemberlitaş) Facing Nuruosmaniye Kapısı, one of several gateways into the Grand Bazaar, this mosque was built in Ottomanbaroque style between 1748 and 1755. Construction was started by order of Mahmut I and finished by his successor Osman III.

Though it was meant to exhibit the sultans' 'modern' taste, the baroque building has very strong echoes of Aya Sofya, specifically the broad, lofty dome, colonnaded mezzanine galleries, windows topped with Roman arches and the broad band of calligraphy around the interior. Despite its prominent position on the busy pedestrian route from Cağaloğlu Meydanı and Nuruosmaniye Caddesi to the bazaar, it is surprisingly peaceful and contemplative inside.

RÜSTEM PAŞA MOSQUE
MOSQUE

Map p242 (Rüstem Paşa Camii; Hasırcılar Caddesi, Rüstem Paşa; MHaliç, Eminönü) Nestled in the middle of the busy Tahtakale shopping district, this diminutive mosque is a gem. Dating from 1560, it was designed by Sinan for Rüstem Paşa, son-in-law and grand vizier of Süleyman the Magnificent. A showpiece of the best Ottoman architecture and tilework, it is thought to have been

---

WORTH A DETOUR

LITTLE URFA

In recent decades, the Laleli and Aksaray neighbourhoods west of the Bazaar District have developed a reputation as being the centre of İstanbul's main red-light district, home to seedy nightclubs, petty crims and prostitutes from Eastern Europe. A sad fate for areas where *valide sultans* (mothers of the reigning sultans) once commissioned ornate imperial mosques and where Ottoman merchants built mansions so as to flaunt their wealth to the world.

These neighbourhoods possess another – much more interesting – claim to fame, though. For decades Aksaray has been home to a large concentration of immigrants from the southeast of Turkey. Many of these residents have opened food stands and restaurants serving dishes popular in their home region, and the streets immediately north of the Aksaray metro station have become known as 'Little Urfa' after the city on the Turkey–Syria border.

Every adventurous foodie should be sure to eat here at least once during their time in the city. Head to the streets around Sofular Caddesi and enjoy a sit-down Syrian-influenced feast at **Hatay Haskral Sofrası** (210-534 9707; www.hatayhaskralsofrasi.com; Ragıp Bey Sokak 25) or at **Akdeniz Hatay Sofrası** (212-444 7247; www.akdenizhataysofrasi.com.tr; Ahmediye Caddesi 44; mezes ₺7.50-9, mains ₺20-27;). Alternatively, pop into **Şanlı Urfa Zaman** (Simitçi Şakir Sokak 38) for a *ciğer* (liver) kebap; **Ehli Kebap** (212-631 3700; Simitçi Şakır Sokak 32) for a delicious and filling bowl of *bayran çorbası* (spicy lamb-based soup); or **Altın Pide ve Lahmacun** (Ragıp Bey Sokak 33; lahmacun ₺2.50-3.50, pide ₺5.50-7.50; 10am-10pm) for crispy *lahmacun* (thin pizza) straight from the traditional tiled oven.

If you decide to visit on a Sunday, the buffet brunch at Akdeniz Hatay Sofrası (open 8am to 1pm) offers an all-you-can-eat choice of 151 dishes for a mere ₺36, and draws customers from across the city.

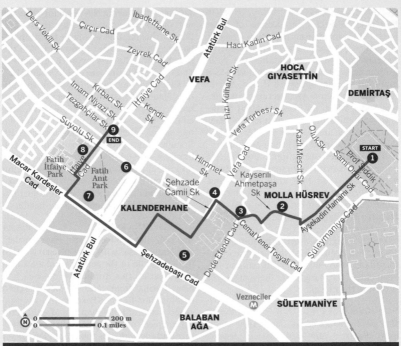

BAZAAR DISTRICT

🏃 Neighbourhood Walk
Ottoman Heartland

START SÜLEYMANIYE MOSQUE
FINISH KADINLAR PAZARI
LENGTH 2KM; TWO HOURS

Start at the **❶ Süleymaniye Mosque** (p91). From Professor Siddık Sami Onar Caddesi, enter narrow Ayşekadin Hamamı Sokak (look for the 'Süleymaniye Kütüphanesi' sign among the souvenir stands) and follow it and Kayserili Ahmetpaşa Sokak down through the Molla Hüsrev district, which is being restored. Kayserili Ahmetpaşa Sokak has some pretty timber houses built in the late 19th and early 20th centuries. These include the **❷ Kayserili Ahmet Paşa Konağı**, a three-storey mansion that was once home to a minister of the Ottoman navy and is now headquarters of the city's Directorate of Inspection of Conservation Implementation.

Follow the street and veer right, passing the soccer pitch, until you come to the **❸ Ekmekçizade Ahmetpaşa Medresesi**, built between 1603–17 by the son of a baker who rose up the ranks of Ottoman society to became a *defterdar* (first lord of the treasury).

From here, turn right and follow Cemal Yener Tosyalı Caddesi until you come to a junction with Vefa Caddesi. The famous **❹ Vefa Bozacısı** (p102) is close by – consider stopping to sample a glass of its *boza*. Back on Cemal Yener Tosyalı Caddesi, turn left into Şehzade Camii Sokak and through under the stone arch to reach the rear gate of the pretty **❺ Şehzade Mehmet Mosque** (p97). If the gate is closed, backtrack along Cemal Yener Tosyalı Caddesi and turn right into Dede Efedi Caddesi to access the main entrance on Şehzadebaşı Caddesi.

Next, head west; you'll see remnants of the majestic Byzantine **❻ Aqueduct of Valens** (p97) to your right. Cross Atatürk Bulvarı and then head towards the aqueduct through **❼ Fatih Anıt Park**. The huge monument in the middle of the park shows Mehmet the Conqueror (Fatih) astride his horse.

Passing a handsome Ottoman Revivalist building housing the **❽ Fatih İtfaiye (Fire Station)** on your left, head under the aqueduct and into the **❾ Kadınlar Pazarı (Women's Market)** on İtfaiye Caddesi, a vibrant local shopping precinct.

the prototype for Sinan's greatest work, the Selimiye in Edirne.

At the top of the two sets of entry steps there is a terrace and the mosque's colonnaded porch. You'll immediately notice the panels of İznik tiles set into the mosque's facade. The interior is covered in more tiles and features a lovely dome, supported by four tiled pillars.

The preponderance of tiles was Rüstem Paşa's way of signalling his wealth and influence – İznik tiles being particularly expensive and desirable. It may not have assisted his passage into the higher realm, though, because by all accounts he was a loathsome character. His contemporaries dubbed him Kehle-i-Ikbal (Louse of Fortune) because he was found to be infected with lice on the eve of his marriage to Mihrimah, Süleyman's favourite daughter. He is best remembered for plotting with Roxelana to turn Süleyman against his favourite son, Mustafa. They were successful and Mustafa was strangled in 1553 on his father's orders.

The mosque is easy to miss because it's not at street level. There's a set of access stairs on Hasırcılar Caddesi and another on the small street that runs right (north) off Hasırcılar Caddesi towards the Golden Horn.

NEW MOSQUE
MOSQUE

Map p242 (Yeni Camii; Yenicamii Meydanı Sokak, Eminönü; Eminönü) Only in İstanbul would a 400-year-old mosque be called 'New'. Dating from 1597, its design references both the Blue Mosque and the Süleymaniye Mosque, with a large forecourt and a square sanctuary surmounted by a series of semidomes crowned by a grand dome. The interior is richly decorated with gold leaf, coloured İznik tiles and carved marble.

Originally commissioned by Valide Sultan Safiye, mother of Sultan Mehmet III, the mosque was completed six sultans later in 1663 by order of Valide Sultan Turhan Hadice, mother of Sultan Mehmet IV.

The site had earlier been occupied by a community of Karaite Jews, radical dissenters from Orthodox Judaism. When the *valide sultan* decided to build her grand mosque here, the Karaites were moved to Hasköy, a district further up the Golden Horn that still bears traces of their presence.

The mosque was created after Ottoman architecture had reached its peak. Consequently, even its tiles are slightly inferior products, the late 17th century having seen a diminution in the quality of the products coming out of the İznik workshops. You will see this if you compare these tiles with the exquisite examples found in the nearby Rüstem Paşa Mosque, which are from the high period of İznik tilework. Nonetheless, it is a popular working mosque and a much-loved adornment to the city skyline. Note that it is closed to visitors on Fridays between 7am and 2pm.

Across the road from the mosque is the tomb of Valide Sultan Turhan Hadice, the woman who completed construction of the New Mosque. Buried with her are no fewer than six sultans, including her son Mehmet IV, plus dozens of imperial princes and princesses.

ŞEHZADE MEHMET MOSQUE
MOSQUE

Map p242 (Şehzade Mehmet Camii, Mosque of the Prince; Şehzadebaşı Caddesi, Kalenderhane; Vezneciler, Laleli-Üniversite) Süleyman the Magnificent built this mosque between 1543 and 1548 as a memorial to his son, Mehmet, who died of smallpox in 1543 at the age of 22. It was the first important mosque to be designed by Mimar Sinan. Although not one of his best works, it has a lovely setting, two beautiful minarets and attractive exterior decoration.

Among the many important people buried in tile-encrusted tombs on the mosque's eastern side are Prince Mehmet, his brothers and sisters, and two of Süleyman's grand viziers: Rüstem Paşa and İbrahim Paşa.

AQUEDUCT OF VALENS
LANDMARK

Map p242 (Atatürk Bulvarı, Zeyrek; Vezneciler) Rising majestically over the traffic on busy Atatürk Bulvarı, this limestone aqueduct is one of the city's most distinctive landmarks. Commissioned by the emperor Valens and completed in AD 378, it linked the third and fourth hills and carried water to a cistern at Beyazıt Meydanı before finally ending up at the Great Palace of Byzantium.

The aqueduct was part of an elaborate system sourcing water from the north of the city and linking more than 250km of water channels, some 30 bridges and over 100 cisterns within the city walls, making it one of the greatest hydraulic engineering achievements of ancient times. After the Conquest it supplied the Eski (Old) and Topkapı Palaces with water.

BAZAAR DISTRICT SIGHTS

CHURCH OF THE MONASTERY OF CHRIST PANTOKRATOR
MONASTERY

Map p242 (Zeyrek Camii; İbadethane Sokak, Zeyrek; Ⓜ Vezneciler) This church and a cistern are the only remaining structures of an important Byzantine monastery complex that also included a library, hospital and chapel. One of the finest examples of Byzantine architecture in İstanbul, it is the second-largest surviving Byzantine church in the city after Aya Sofya. Sorely neglected for centuries, it is currently undergoing a controversial restoration.

The monastery was commissioned by Empress Eirene in 1118 (she features in a mosaic at Aya Sofya with her husband Emperor John II Comnenus), who wanted to give succour to 'poor, sick, and suffering souls'. Building works were completed after her death. The north and south churches, dedicated to Christ Pantokrator and the Archangel Michael, were connected by an imperial chapel that was used as a mausoleum for the Komnenos and Palaiologos dynasties.

After the Conquest, the church was converted into a mosque named in honour of Molla Zeyrek, a well-known scholar who lived during the reign of Sultan Mehmed II.

Until recently, the building was listed by the World Monument Fund (WMF) as one of the world's 100 most endangered cultural heritage sites. It is now undergoing an excruciatingly slow restoration that was instigated and initially funded by the WMF but has since been tended out to private contractors, who are applying liberal amounts of ugly pink concrete to the stone walls. The interior of the northern section of the church has been unsympathetically (we would say incompetently) stabilised with ugly metal braces and decorated with dreadful faux-marble painted walls. It is now functioning as a mosque.

When visiting, be sure to admire the view of the Golden Horn from the garden terrace of the adjacent cafe-restaurant, Zeyrekhane (p101).

EATING

Generations of shoppers have worked up an appetite around the Grand Bazaar. Fortunately there have always been eateries to meet this need, including a range of good *lokantas* and fast-food stands. Down near the water there aren't too many choices – a fish sandwich on the quay at Eminönü, a döner kebap at Bereket Döner in the Küçük Pazar or a more formal meal at Hamdi Restaurant are your best bets.

★ DEVELI BAKLAVA
SWEETS €

Map p242 (☑ 212-512 1261; Hasırcılar Caddesi 89, Eminönü; portions ₺8-9; ☺ 6.30am-7pm Mon-Sat; Ⓜ Haliç, ☒ Eminönü) As with many things Turkish, there's a ritual associated with eating baklava. Aficionados don't use a knife and fork. Instead, they turn their baklava upside down with the help of an index finger and thumb, and pop it into the mouth. To emulate them, head to this famous shop close to the Spice Bazaar, one of the city's best *backlavacıs*.

The baklava here is made with butter and real sugar (inferior products use glucose) and it's absolutely delicious. Try the classic with your choice of nut filling, or try the indulgent *bülbül yuvası* (nightingale's nest), a pastry filled with *kaymak* (clotted cream) and pistachio. Those in the know (and with a big appetite) tend to order Develi's Gaziantep-style *katmer* (flaky pastry stuffed with pistachio and *kaymak*), which takes around 15 minutes to cook and comes to your table piping hot. Bliss!

★ FATIH DAMAK PIDE
PIDE €

(☑ 212-521 5057; www.fatihdamakpide.com; Büyük Karaman Caddesi 48, Zeyrek; pide ₺12-16; ☺ 11am-11pm; Ⓜ Vezneciler) It's worth making the trek to this *pidecisi* overlooking the Fatih İtfaiye Park near the Aqueduct of Valens, as its reputation for making the best Karadeniz (Black Sea)–style pide on the Historic Peninsula is well deserved and the free pots of tea served with meals are a nice touch.

Toppings are pretty well standard – the *sucuklu-peynirli* (sausage and cheese) option is particularly tasty, but there's also an unusual *bafra pidesi* (rolled-up pide; ₺12) on offer. No alcohol.

SIIRT ŞEREF BÜRYAN KEBAP
ANATOLIAN €

(☑ 212-635 8085; www.serefburyan.com; Itfaye Caddesi 4, Kadın Pazarı; büryan ₺12, perde pilavi ₺12; ☺ 9.30am-10pm Sep-May, till midnight Jun-Aug; Ⓜ Vezneciler) Those who enjoy investigating regional cuisines should head to this four-storey eatery in the Kadın Pazarı (Women's Market) near the Aqueduct of Valens. It specialises in two dishes that are a speciality of the southeastern city of Siirt: *büryan* (lamb slow-cooked in a pit) and

CHEAP EATS: THE GRAND BAZAAR

Lunch is an important part of the day for the shopkeepers, artisans and porters who work in and around the Grand Bazaar. As well as providing an excuse for a welcome break, it's also a chance to chat with fellow workers and catch up with the local gossip. Of the hundreds of food stands in the streets and laneways in and around the bazaar, the following are our favourites. Most have a few stools for customers, a few are take-away only.

Note that when ordering döner kebap or kokoreç (seasoned grilled intestines) in ekmek (bread), you will usually have to choose from three sizes: çeyrek (a quarter of a loaf), yarım (half a loaf) or bütün (a whole loaf). The term dürüm ('wrapped') applies when meat is served in thin lavaş bread.

Gazientep Burç Ocakbaşı (Map p242; Parçacılar Sokak 12, off Yağlıkçılar Caddesi, Grand Bazaar; kebaps ₺13-22; ☺noon-4pm Mon-Sat; ⓂVezneciler, 🚇Beyazıt-Kapalı Çarşı) The usta (master chef) at this simple place presides over a charcoal grill where choice cuts of meats are cooked to perfection. We particularly recommend the spicy Adana kebap and the delectable dolması (eggplant and red peppers stuffed with rice and herbs).

Dönerci Şahin Usta (Map p242; ☎212-526 5297; www.donercisahinusta.com; Kılıççlar Sokak 7-9, Nuruosmaniye; döner kebap from ₺7; ☺11am-3pm Mon-Sat; 🚇Çemberlitaş) Ask any shopkeeper in the Grand Bazaar about who makes the best döner in the immediate area, and he is likely to give the same answer: 'Şahin Usta, of course!'

Pak Pide & Pizza Salonu (Map p242; ☎212-513 7664; Paşa Camii Sokak 16, Mercan; pides ₺7-10; ☺11am-3pm Mon-Sat; 🚇Eminönü or Beyazıt-Kapalı Çarşı) Finding this worker's pideçisi is an adventure in itself (it's hidden in the steep narrow lanes behind the Büyük Valide Han) but your quest will pay off when you try the fabulous pides, which are served straight from the oven.

Aynen Dürüm (Map p242; Muhafazacılar Sokak 29; dürüm kebap ₺8; ☺7am-6pm Mon-Sat; 🚇Çemberlitaş) You'll find this perennially busy place just inside the Grand Bazaar's Kılıççlar Kapısı (Kılıççılar Gate), near where the currency dealers ply their noisy trade. Patrons are free to doctor their choice of grilled meat (we like the chicken) with pickled cucumber, grilled and pickled green chillies, parsley, sumac and other accompaniments that are laid out on the communal bench.

Dürümcü Raif Usta (Map p242; ☎212-528 5997; Küçük Yıldız Han Sokak 6, Mahmutpaşa; dürüm kebap ₺9; ☺11.30am-6pm Mon-Sat; 🚇Çemberlitaş) The assembly line of staff assisting the usta at this place attests to the excellence and popularity of its speciality, Adana or Urfa kebap served with raw onion and parsley and wrapped in lavaş bread. Note that the Adana is spicy, Urfa isn't.

Kokoreççi Erdinç Usta (Map p242; ☎212-514 6029; Kılıçlar Sokak 33, Nuruosmaniye; kokoreç from ₺4; ☺9am-6pm Mon-Sat; 🚇Çemberlitaş) Devotees of offal flock here for the kokoreç: seasoned lamb intestines stuffed with sweetbreads or other offal, seasoned with red pepper and oregano, wrapped around a skewer and grilled over charcoal.

Meşhur Dönerci Hacı Osman'ın Yeri (Map p242; Fuat Paşa Caddesi 16, Mercan; döner kebap from ₺3.50; ☺11am-5pm Mon-Sat; ⓂVezneciler, 🚇Beyazıt-Kapalı Çarşı) This döner stand occupying an elegant Ottoman sebil (fountain) outside the Ali Paşa Camii is hugely popular with students from nearby İstanbul University.

Bena Dondurmaları (Map p242; ☎212-520 5440; Gazi Atik Ali Paşa Camii 12b; ice cream per scoop ₺0.75, desserts ₺2.50-5; ☺10am-6pm Mon-Sat; 🚇Çemberlitaş) There's inevitably an afternoon queue in front of this tiny dondurma (Turkish ice cream) shop In the courtyard of the Atik Ali Paşa Camii near the Çemberlitaş tram stop. Though the dondurma is an undeniable draw, we tend to opt for the fırın sütlaç (rice pudding) or decadent trileçe (cream-soaked sponge cake with a caramel topping).

FISH SANDWICHES

The city's favourite fast-food treat is undoubtedly the *balık ekmek* (fish sandwich), and the most atmospheric place to try one is at the Eminönü end of the Galata Bridge. Here, in front of fishing boats tied to the quay, are a number of stands where mackerel fillets are grilled, crammed into fresh bread and served with salad; a generous squeeze of bottled lemon is optional but recommended. A sandwich will set you back a mere ₺6 or so, and is delicious accompanied by a glass of the *şalgam suyu* (sour turnip juice) sold by nearby pickle vendors.

There are plenty of other places around town to try a *balık ekmek* – head to any *iskele* (ferry dock) and there's bound to be a stand nearby. Alternatively, **Fürreyya Galata Balıkçısı** (www.furreyyagalata.com), a tiny place opposite the Galata Tower, serves an excellent version for ₺8.

perde pilavi (chicken and rice cooked in pastry). Both are totally delicious.

The *büryan* here is cooked in pits at the rear of the restaurant and is meltingly tender. It's served on flat bread with crispy bits of lamb fat and a dusting of salt. *Perde pilavi* is made with rice, chicken, almonds and currants that are encased in a thin pastry shell and then baked until the exterior turns golden and flaky. Order either with a glass of frothy homemade *ayran* (yoghurt drink) and you'll be happy indeed. Note that on weekends, the food tends to run out by 9pm. No alcohol.

★ BEREKET DÖNER   KEBAP ₵

Map p242 (Hacı Kadın Caddesi, cnr Tavanlı Çeşme Sokak, Küçük Pazar; döner ekmek ₺3; ⊙11am-8pm Mon-Sat; Ⓜ Halıc or Vezneciler) The best döner in the district (maybe even the city) can be found at this local eatery in the rundown Küçük Pazar shopping strip between Eminönü and Atatürk Bulvarı. Definitely worth the trek.

BAHAR RESTAURANT   TURKISH ₵

Map p242 (Yağcı Han 13, off Nuruosmaniye Sokak, Nuruosmaniye; soups ₺5, dishes ₺10-17; ⊙11am-4pm Mon-Sat; Ⓠ Çemberlitaş) Tiny Bahar

('Spring') is popular with local shopkeepers and is always full, so arrive early to score a table. Dishes change daily and with the season – try the flavourful lentil soup, tasty *hünkar beğendi* (literally 'Sultan's Delight'; lamb or beef stew served on a mound of rich eggplant purée) or creamy macaroni. The latter is made only once per week. No alcohol.

KURU FASULYECI
ERZINCANLI ALI BABA   TURKISH ₵

Map p242 (www.kurufasulyeci.com; Professor Sıddık Sami Onar Caddesi 11, Süleymaniye; beans with pilaf & pickles ₺12; ⊙7am-7pm; ⊅; Ⓜ Vezneciler, Ⓠ Laleli-Üniversite) Join the crowds of hungry locals at this long-time favourite opposite the Süleymaniye Mosque. It's been dishing up its signature *kuru fasulye* (white beans cooked in a spicy tomato sauce) accompanied by pilaf (rice) and pickles since 1924. The next-door *fasulyeci* (restaurant specialising in beans) is nearly as old and serves up more of the same. No alcohol.

MAVI HALIÇ PIDECISI   PIDE ₵

Map p242 (Kutucular Caddesi 28, Eminönü; pides ₺7-12; ⊙11am-6pm; Ⓜ Haliç, Ⓠ Eminönü) Fight your way through the crowds of shoppers that jam Hasırcılar Caddesi and you'll eventually come to this tiny *pideçisi*, which is known for its *kıymalı* (ground beef and tomato) pide.

HAMDI RESTAURANT   KEBAP ₵₵

Map p242 (☎212-528 8011; www.hamdi-restorant.com.tr; Kalçın Sokak 17, Eminönü; mezes ₺9-14, kebaps ₺25-32; Ⓜ Haliç, Ⓠ Eminönü) Hamdi Arpacı arrived in İstanbul in the 1960s and almost immediately established a street stand near the Spice Bazaar where he grilled and sold tasty kebaps made according to recipes from his hometown Urfa, in Turkey's southeast. His kebaps became so popular with locals that he soon acquired this nearby building, which has phenomenal views from its top-floor terrace.

A meal here offers views of the Old City, Golden Horn and Galata, as well as tasty food and a bustling atmosphere. Try the *yoğurtlu şakşuka* (yoghurt meze with fried eggplant, peppers and potato), the *içli köfte* (meatballs rolled in bulgur) and the *lahmacun* (thin, meat-topped pizza) followed by any of the kebaps and you'll leave replete and happy – extremely replete if you finish with the house-made baklava, *katmer* or *künefe*. Any place this good is always going to be busy, so make sure you book, and don't forget to request a rooftop table with a view (outside if the weather is hot).

One slight caveat: staff work hard and are clearly encouraged to turn tables over as fast as possible. Don't expect much in terms of personal service, and be prepared for little time between courses.

SUR OCAKBAŞI   KEBAP €€

(☏212-533 8088; www.surocakbasi.com; İtfaiye Caddesi 27; kebaps ₺13-25; Ⓜ️Vezneciler) Indulge in some peerless people-watching while enjoying the grilled meats at this popular place in the Kadınlar Pazarı. The square is always full of locals shopping or enjoying a gossip, and tourists were a rare sight before Anthony Bourdain filmed a segment of *No Reservations* here and blew Sur's cover.

There are plenty of options on offer: consider the mixed kebap plate, the *içli köfte* (deep-fried lamb and onion meatballs with a bulgur coating) and the *çiğ köfte* (meat pounded with spices and eaten raw). No alcohol, but there's homemade *ayran*.

HAVUZLU RESTAURANT   TURKISH €€

Map p242 (☏212-527 3346; www.havuzlurestaurant.com; Gani Çelebi Sokak 3, Grand Bazaar; portions ₺13-20, kebaps ₺23; ⏲11am-5pm Mon-Sat; 🍴; Ⓜ️Vezneciler, 🚇Beyazıt-Kapalı Çarşı) After a morning spent in the Grand Bazaar, many visitors choose to park their shopping bags at this well-known *lokanta*. A lovely space with a vaulted ceiling, Havuzlu (named after the small fountain at its entrance) serves up simple but tasty fare to hungry hordes of tourists and shopkeepers – go early when the food is freshest. No alcohol.

FES CAFE   CAFE €€

Map p242 (Ali Baba Türbe Sokak 25, Nuruosmaniye; sandwiches ₺14-22, salads ₺16-20, pasta ₺18-20; ⏲closed Sun; 🍴; 🚇Çemberlitaş) After a morning spent trading repartee with the touts in the Grand Bazaar, you'll be in need of a respite. Those who want a cafe with a Western-style ambience and menu are sure to be happy with this stylish cafe just outside the Nuruosmaniye Gate. Sandwiches, salads and pastas feature on the menu. There's a second **branch** (Map p242; ☏212-527 3684; Halıcılar Caddesi 62, Grand Bazaar; ⏲9.30am-6.30pm Mon-Sat; 🚇Beyazıt-Kapalı Çarşı) inside the Grand Bazaar.

🍷 DRINKING & NIGHTLIFE

Like most parts of the Old City, the area around the Grand Bazaar is conservative and there are few places serving alcohol. There are loads of *çay bahçesis* (tea gardens), nargile cafes and *kahvehanıs* (coffeehouses) to visit, though.

⭐MIMAR SINAN TERAS CAFE   NARGILE CAFE

Map p242 (☏212-514 4414; www.mimarsinanterascafe.com; Mimar Sinan Han, Fetva Yokuşu 34-35, Süleymaniye; ⏲8am-1am; Ⓜ️Vezneciler or Haliç, 🚇Laleli-Üniversite) A magnificent panorama of the city can be enjoyed from the spacious outdoor terrace of this popular student cafe in a ramshackle building located in the shadow of the Süleymaniye Mosque. Head here during the day or in the evening to admire the view over a coffee, unwind with a nargile or enjoy a glass of çay and game of backgammon.

⭐ERENLER NARGILE VE ÇAY BAHÇESI   TEA GARDEN

Map p242 (Yeniçeriler Caddesi 35, Beyazıt; ⏲7am-midnight; 🚇Beyazıt-Kapalı Çarşı) Set in the vine-covered courtyard of the Çorlulu Ali Paşa Medrese, this nargile cafe near the Grand Bazaar is the most atmospheric in the Old City.

ZEYREKHANE   CAFE

Map p242 (www.zeyrekhane.com; İbadethane Arkası Sokak 10, Zeyrek; ⏲9.30am-10pm Tue-Sun; Ⓜ️Vezneciler) This lovely cafe opposite the Byzantine Church of the Monastery of Christ Pantokrator has a garden terrace offering magnificent views of the Golden Horn and Süleymaniye Mosque. It's a great choice for a coffee or sunset aperitif in the warm weather.

LALE BAHÇESI   TEA GARDEN

Map p242 (Şifahane Caddesi, Süleymaniye; ⏲9am-11pm; Ⓜ️Vezneciler, 🚇Laleli-Üniversite) Make your way down the stairs into the sunken courtyard opposite the Süleymaniye Mosque to discover this charming outdoor teahouse, which is popular with students from the nearby theological college and İstanbul University.

ETHEM TEZÇAKAR KAHVECI   CAFE

Map p242 (Halıcılar Çarşışı Sokak, Grand Bazaar; ⏲8.30am-7pm Mon-Sat; Ⓜ️Vezneciler, 🚇Beyazıt-Kapalı Çarşı) Bekir Tezçakar's family has

---

NARGILES

While in town, be sure to visit a *çay bahçesi* (tea garden). These atmosphere-rich venues are frequented by locals who don't drink alcohol and are often redolent with apple-scented smoke from nargiles (water pipes), their substitute indulgence.

When ordering a nargile, you'll need to specify what type of tobacco you would like. Most people opt for *elma* (when the tobacco has been soaked in apple juice, giving it a sweet flavour and scent), but it's possible to order it unadulterated *(tömbeki)*. A nargile usually costs ₺15 to ₺25 and can be shared (you'll be given individual plastic mouthpieces).

---

been at the helm of this tiny coffee shop for four generations. Smack bang in the middle of the bazaar's most glamorous retail strip, its traditional brass-tray tables and wooden stools are a good spot to enjoy a break and watch the passing parade of shoppers.

ŞARK KAHVESI · CAFE

Map p242 (Oriental Coffeeshop; Yağlıkçılar Caddesi 134, Grand Bazaar; ⊗8.30am-7pm Mon-Sat; Ⓜ︎Vezneciler, ⊞Beyazıt-Kapalı Çarşı) The Şark's arched ceiling betrays its former existence as part of a bazaar street; years ago some enterprising *kahveci* (coffeehouse owner) walled up several sides and turned it into a cafe. Located on one of the bazaar's major thoroughfares, it's popular with both stall-holders and tourists.

PANDELI · CAFE

Map p242 (www.pandeli.com.tr; Spice Bazaar, Eminönü; ⊗noon-4pm Mon-Sat; ⊞Eminönü) Pandeli's three salons are encrusted with stunning turqoise-coloured İznik tiles and furnished with chandeliers and richly upholstered banquettes. Though its location above the main entrance to the Spice Bazaar makes it a popular lunch spot for tourists (locals wouldn't dream of eating here), we suggest visiting for a tea or coffee after the main lunch service instead.

KAHVE DÜNYASI · CAFE

Map p242 (Nuruosmaniye Caddesi 79; ⊗7.30am-9.30pm; ⊞Çemberlitaş) The name means 'Coffee World', and this coffee chain has the local world at its feet. The secret of its success lies in the huge coffee menu, reasonable prices, delicious chocolate spoons (yes, you read that correctly), comfortable seating and free wi-fi. The filter coffee is better than its espresso-based alternatives.

There's another **branch** (Map p242; Kızıhan Sokak 18, Eminönü; ⊞Eminönü) near the Spice Bazaar in Eminönü.

VEFA BOZACISI · BOZA BAR

Map p242 (www.vefa.com.tr; cnr Vefa & Katip Çelebi Caddesis, Molla Hüsrev; boza ₺3; ⊗8am-midnight; Ⓜ︎Vezneciler, ⊞Laleli-Üniversite) This famous *boza* bar was established in 1876 and locals still flock here to drink the viscous tonic, which is made from water, sugar and fermented barley and has a slight lemony tang. Topped with dried chickpeas and a sprinkle of cinnamon, it has a reputation for building up strength and virility, and tends to be an acquired taste.

In summer, the bar also serves *şıra,* a fermented grape juice.

🔒 SHOPPING

The city's two most famous shopping destinations – the Grand and Spice Bazaars – are in this district. In between the two is the vibrant local shopping neighbourhood of Tahtakale.

★ABDULLA NATURAL PRODUCTS · TEXTILES, BATHWARE

Map p242 (www.abdulla.com; Halıcılar Çarşışı Sokak 62, Grand Bazaar; ⊗8.30am-7pm Mon-Sat; Ⓜ︎Vezneciler, ⊞Beyazıt-Kapalı Çarşı) The first of the Western-style designer stores to appear in this ancient marketplace, Abdulla sells top-quality cotton bed linen and towels, handspun woollen throws from Eastern Turkey, cotton *peştemals* (bath wraps) and pure olive-oil soap. There's another branch located in the **Fes Cafe** (Map p242; Ali Baba Türbe Sokak 25, Nuruosmaniye; ⊞Çemberlitaş) in Nuruosmaniye.

★ÜMIT BERKSOY · JEWELLERY

Map p242 (📞212-522 3391; İnciler Sokak 2-6, Grand Bazaar; ⊗8.30am-7pm Mon-Sat; Ⓜ︎Vezneciler, ⊞Beyazıt-Kapalı Çarşı) Jeweller Ümit Berksoy handcrafts gorgeous Byzantine-style rings, earings and necklaces using gold and old coins as well as more contemporary pieces at his tiny atelier just outside the İç Bedesten.

★**DERVIŞ** TEXTILES, BATHWARE
Map p242 (www.dervis.com; Keseciler Caddesi 33-35, Grand Bazaar; ⏱8.30am-7pm Mon-Sat; ⓂVezneciler, ⒷBeyazıt-Kapalı Çarşı) 🍃 Gorgeous raw cotton and silk *peştemals* share shelf space here with traditional Turkish dowry vests and engagement dresses. If these don't take your fancy, the pure olive-oil soaps and old hamam bowls are sure to step into the breach. There are other branches in **Halıcılar Çarşısı Sokak** (Map p242; Halıcılar Çarşışı Sokak 51, Grand Bazaar) and in the **Cebeci Han** (Map p242; ⓙ0532 256 0107; Cebeci Han 10, Grand Bazaar), also in the bazaar.

MEKHANN TEXTILES
Map p242 (ⓙ212-519 9444; Divrikli Sokak 49, Grand Bazaar; ⏱8.30am-7pm Mon-Sat; ⓂVezneciler, ⒷBeyazıt-Kapalı Çarşı) Bolts of richly coloured hand-woven silk from Uzbekistan and a range of finely woven shawls join finely embroidered bedspreads and pillow slips on the crowded shelves of this Grand Bazaar store, which sets the bar high when it comes to quality.

ALTAN ŞEKERLEME FOOD & DRINK
Map p242 (ⓙ212-522 5909; www.altansekerleme.com; Kıble Çeşme Caddesi 68, Eminönü; ⏱8am-7pm Mon-Sat, 9am-6pm Sun; ⓂHaliç, ⒷEminönü) It's not just kids who like candy stores. İstanbullus of every age have been coming to this shop in the Küçük Pazar (Little Bazaar) precinct below the Süleymaniye Mosque since 1865, lured by its cheap and delectable *lokum* (Turkish delight), *helva* (a sweet made from sesame seeds) and *akide* (hard candy).

MUHLIS GÜNBATTI TEXTILES
Map p242 (www.muhlisgunbatti.net; Perdahçılar Sokak 48, Grand Bazaar; ⏱8.30am-7pm Mon-Sat; ⓂVezneciler, ⒷBeyazıt-Kapalı Çarşı) One of the most famous stores in the Grand Bazaar, Muhlis Günbattı specialises in *suzani* fabrics from Uzbekistan. These beautiful bedspreads, tablecloths and wall hangings are made from fine cotton embroidered with silk. As well as the textiles, it stocks top-quality carpets, brightly coloured kilims and a small range of antique Ottoman fabrics richly embroidered with gold.

YAZMACI NECDET DANIŞ TEXTILES
Map p242 (Yağlıkçılar Caddesi 57, Grand Bazaar; ⏱8.30am-7pm Mon-Sat; ⓂVezneciler, ⒷBeyazıt-Kapalı Çarşı) Fashion designers and buyers from every corner of the globe know that

when in İstanbul, this is where to come to source top-quality textiles. It's crammed with bolts of fabric of every description – shiny, simple, sheer and sophisticated – as well as *peştemals*, scarves and clothes. Murat Danış next door is part of the same operation.

HAŞIMI TICARET ANTIQUES
Map p242 (Ali Paşa Han, Grand Bazaar; ⏱8.30am-7pm Mon-Sat; ⓂVezneciler, ⒷBeyazıt-Kapalı Çarşı) Head towards the Sahaflar Çarşışı from the Yorganciler Kapısı (Gate 11) to find this veritable Aladdin's Cave of a shop, which is crammed with old wooden boxes and other artefacts sourced from Turkey, Afghanistan and Pakistan. Bargain hard.

SERHAT GERIDÖNMEZ JEWELLERY
Map p242 (Şerifağa Sokak 69, Old Bazaar, Grand Bazaar; ⏱9am-7pm Mon-Sat; ⓂVezneciler, ⒷBeyazıt-Kapalı Çarşı) There are plenty of jewellers in the Grand Bazaar, but few sell objects as gorgeous as the expertly crafted copies of Hellenistic, Roman and Byzantine pieces on offer at this tiny store.

AK GÜMÜŞ HANDICRAFTS
Map p242 (Gani Çelebi Sokak 8, Grand Bazaar; ⏱9am-7pm Mon-Sat; ⒷBeyazıt-Kapalı Çarşı, ⒷVezneciler) Specialising in Central Asian tribal arts, this delightful store stocks an array of felt toys and hats, as well as jewellery and other objects made using coins and beads.

KOÇ DERI LEATHER CLOTHING
Map p242 (www.kocderi.com/en/; Kürkçüler Çarşısı 22-46, Grand Bazaar; ⏱8.30am-7pm; ⓂVezneciler, ⒷBeyazıt-Kapalı Çarşı) If you fancy a leather jacket or coat, Koç is bound to have something that suits. It's one of the bazaar's busiest stores and certainly the most stylish of the leather outlets here.

DHOKU CARPETS
Map p242 (www.dhoku.com; Takkeçiler Sokak 58-60, Grand Bazaar; ⏱8.30am-7pm Mon-Sat; ⓂVezneciler, ⒷBeyazıt-Kapalı Çarşı) One of the new generation of rug stores opening in the bazaar, Dhoku (meaning 'texture') sells artfully designed wool kilims in resolutely modernist designs. Its sister store, **Ethni-Con** (Map p242; www.ethnicon.com; Takkeçiler Sokak, Grand Bazaar), opposite this store, sells similarly stylish rugs in vivid colours and can be said to have started the current craze in contemporary kilims.

WORTH A DETOUR

ANTIQUES, ANYONE?

Those seeking out authentic Ottoman souvenirs should visit the **Horhor Antikacılar Çarşışı** (Horhor Antique Market; Horhor Bit Pazarı; Kırık Talumba Sk, Aksaray; ⊙varies according to shop; 🚇Aksaray), a decrepit building in Aksaray that is home to five floors of shops selling antiques, curios and bric-a-brac of every possible description, quality and condition.

To get there, catch the tram to Aksaray, cross Atatürk Bulvarı, pass the Valide Sultan Mosque and veer right when the main road divides. Horhor Caddesi is to your right, going up the hill. The market is on Kırık Talumba Sokak, on the right-hand side near the top of the hill.

Note that the market is closed on Sundays, and also be aware that it is illegal to take antiquities out of the country. This certainly applies to anything Byzantine, and can also apply to Ottoman items that are more than 200 years old.

SEVAN BIÇAKÇI   JEWELLERY

Map p242 (www.sevanbicakci.com; Gazi Sinan Paşa Sokak 16, Nuruosmaniye; ⊙10am-6pm Mon-Sat; 🚇Çemberlitaş) Inspired by the monuments and history of his much-loved İstanbul, flamboyant jeweller Sevan Bıçakçı creates wearable art that aims to impress. His flagship store is in the Kutlu Han near the Grand Bazaar's Nuruosmaniye Gate.

SOFA   ART, JEWELLERY

Map p242 (☎212-520 2850; www.kashifsofa. com; Nuruosmaniye Caddesi 53, Nuruosmaniye; ⊙9.30am-6.30pm Mon-Sat; 🚇Çemberlitaş) Investigation of Sofa's three floors of artfully arranged clutter reveals an eclectic range of pricey jewellery, prints, textiles, calligraphy, Ottoman miniatures and contemporary Turkish art.

SILK & CASHMERE   CLOTHING

Map p242 (www.silkcashmere.com; Nuruosmaniye Caddesi 69, Nuruosmaniye; ⊙9.30am-7pm Mon-Sat; 🚇Çemberlitaş) The Nuruosmaniye branch of this popular chain sells cashmere and silk-cashmere-blend cardigans, jumpers, tops and shawls. All are remarkably well priced considering their quality. There's another, smaller, store inside the

Grand Bazaar (Map p242; Kalpakçılar Caddesi 74; 🚇Vezneciler, 🚇Beyazıt-Kapalı Çarşı).

ALI MUHIDDIN HACI BEKIR   FOOD

Map p242 (www.hacibekir.com.tr; Hamidiye Caddesi 31 & 33, Eminönü; ⊙8am-8pm Mon-Sat; 🚇Eminönü) Many people think that this historic shop, which has been operated by members of the same family for over 200 years, is the best place in the city to buy *lokum*. Choose from *sade* (plain), *cevizli* (walnut), *fıstıklı* (pistachio), *badem* (almond) or *roze* (rose water). There are other branches in Beyoğlu (p139) and Kadıköy (p153).

HAFIZ MUSTAFA   SWEETS

Map p242 (☎212-513 3610; www.hafizmustafa. com; Hamidiye Caddesi 84; ⊙8am-8pm Mon-Sat, 9am-8pm Sun; 🚇Eminönü) Located opposite Ali Muhıddin Hacı Bekir, Hafız Mustafa sells excellent *lokum*. You can buy a small bag of freshly made treats to sample, plus gift boxes to take home. Best of all, staff are happy to let you taste before buying (within reason, of course). There are other branches in Sirkeci (p82) and Sultanahmet (p82).

VAKKO İNDIRIM   CLOTHING, ACCESSORIES

Map p242 (Vakko Sale Store; Sultan Hamamı Caddesi 8a, Eminönü; ⊙9.30am-6pm Mon-Sat; 🚇Eminönü) This remainder outlet of İstanbul's famous fashion store should be on the itinerary of all bargain hunters. Top-quality men's and women's clothing – often stuff that's been designed and made in Italy – is sold here for a fraction of its original price.

ARMINE   CLOTHING

Map p242 (www.armine.com; Mahmutpaşa Yokuşu 181, Eminönü; ⊙10am-6pm Mon-Sat; 🚇Eminönü) İstanbul is a fashionable city with a highly idiosyncratic style. In Bebek and Beyoğlu the fashion might be for tight jeans, revealing jackets and chunky jewellery, but in the city's conservative neighbourhoods, there's little make-up and even less flesh on show. Wildly popular Armine is where Zara style meets the headscarf, and it's an exemplar of affordable Islamic chic.

KURUKAHVECI MEHMET EFENDI   COFFEE

Map p242 (www.mehmetefendi.com; cnr Tahmis Sokak & Hasırcılar Caddesi, Eminönü; ⊙9am-6pm Mon-Sat; 🚇Eminönü) Caffeine addicts are regularly spotted queuing outside this, the flagship store of İstanbul's most famous coffee purveyor. Join them to buy a packet of the freshest beans in town.

UCUZCULAR BAHARAT
SPICES

Map p242 (www.ucuzcular.com.tr; Spice Bazaar 51, Eminönü; ⊙8am-6.30pm, high season 9am-6pm Sun; ⓜEminönü) Showcasing the colour and fragrance of hundreds of spices, Ucuzcular concocts its own spice blends and will vacuum pack them for travellers who are keen to add them to their luggage.

MEHMET KALMAZ BAHARAT
BEAUTY

Map p242 (Spice Bazaar 41, Eminönü; ⊙8am-6.30pm Mon-Sat, high season 9am-6pm Sun; ⓜEminönü) One of the few shops in the Spice Bazaar that specialises in potions and lotions, this old-fashioned place sells remedies to make women younger, others to make men stronger, and a royal love potion that, we guess, is supposed to combine the two. It also stocks spices, bath accessories, teas and medicinal herbs.

MALATYA PAZARI
FOOD

Map p242 (www.malatya-pazari.com; Spice Bazaar 20-44, Eminönü; ⊙8am-6.30pm Mon-Sat, high season 9am-6pm Sun; ⓜEminönü) The city of Malatya in central-eastern Turkey is famous for its apricots, and this shop with three branches near the Spice Bazaar's Tahmis Caddesi doorway stocks the cream of the crop, dried both naturally and chemically. Its other quality dried fruit and nuts eclipse all others in this bazaar.

PAŞABAHÇE
GLASSWARE

Map p242 (☎212-522 1622; www.pasabahce.com; Nuruosmaniye Caddesi 66, Nuruosmaniye; ⓜÇemberlitaş) A retail branch of the popular Turkish glassware brand.

🏃 SPORTS & ACTIVITIES

İSTANBULODOS
PHOTOGRAPHY TOUR

(☎0535 675 6491; www.istanbulodosviaggio.com; tours per group €110) Having lived in İstanbul for many years, New York–born photographer Monica Fritz recently made the decision to share some of the secrets she has learned about the city with fellow shutterbugs. Her five-hour tours of the Grand Bazaar introduce participants to hidden *hans* and passageways as well as taking to the roof à la James Bond in *Skyfall*.

Monica also offers tours of Galata, Balat and the Asian suburbs. The cost covers groups of up to 10 participants and includes lunch in a local eatery.

ÇEMBERLITAŞ HAMAMI
HAMAM

Map p242 (☎212-522 7974; www.cemberlitashamami.com; Vezir Han Caddesi 8; self-service ₺60, bath, scrub & soap massage ₺90; ⊙6am-midnight; ⓜÇemberlitaş) There won't be too many times in your life when you'll get the opportunity to have a Turkish bath in a building dating back to 1584, so now might well be the time to do it – particularly as this twin hamam was designed by the great architect Sinan and is among the most beautiful in the city.

The building was commissioned by Nurbanu Sultan, wife of Selim II and mother of Murat III. Both of its bath chambers have a huge marble *sıcaklık* (circular marble heat platform) and a gorgeous dome with glass apertures. The *camekan* (entrance hall) for men is original, but the women's version is new.

It costs around ₺60 to add an oil massage to the standard bath package, but all massages and treatments here are perfunctory so we'd suggest giving this a miss and opting for the cheaper self-serve option. Tips are meant to be covered in the treatment price and there's a 20% discount for ISIC student-card holders.

GEDİKPAŞA HAMAMI
HAMAM

Map p242 (☎212-517 8956; www.gedikpasahamami.com; Emin Sinan Hamamı Sokak 65-67, Gedikpaşa; bath, scrub & soap massage ₺70; ⊙men 6am-midnight, women 9am-11pm; ⓜÇemberlitaş) This Ottoman-era hamam has been operating since 1475. Its shabby interior isn't as beautiful as those at Çemberlitaş and Cağaloğlu, but services are cheaper and there are separate hamams, small dipping pools and saunas for both sexes. Best of all is the fact that the masseuses in the women's section occasionally break into song while working.

The operators will sometimes transport guests to and from Sultanahmet hotels at no charge – ask your hotel to investigate this option.

Western Districts

Neighbourhood Top Five

1 Admiring the exquisite mosaics and frescoes adorning the interior of one of İstanbul's Byzantine treasures, the **Kariye Museum** (Chora Church; p108).

2 Taking a ferry up the Golden Horn to visit **Eyüp** (p113), home to İstanbul's most important Islamic shrine.

3 Visiting the Greek Orthodox **Patriarchal Church of St George** (p112), one of Turkey's major pilgrimage destinations.

4 Sampling dishes enjoyed by Süleyman the Magnificent and other sultans at **Asitane** (p115) restaurant.

5 Exploring the streets around the **Yavuz Sultan Selim Mosque** (p111) in the fascinating Çarşamba district.

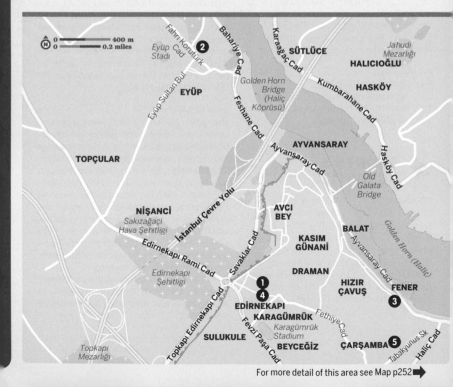

For more detail of this area see Map p252 ➡

Explore: Western Districts

It's a great shame that so few visitors head to this fascinating part of town. Try to dedicate at least one day of your stay to exploring the area; two would be better.

Spend the first of these taking the Golden Horn ferry trip from Eminönü, first alighting at Ayvansaray to visit the Kariye Museum (Chora Church) and then continuing to Eyüp (p113).

If you are able to spend a second day here, we highly recommend that you start your day in the Bazaar District and then continue uphill towards the Fatih and Yavuz Sultan Selim Mosques.

Note that these districts are deathly quiet at night and on Sundays, so you're best off exploring during the day on weekdays or Saturday.

Local Life

➡**Produce shopping** Locals shop along Fevzi Paşa Caddesi in Fatih, on Murat Molla Caddesi in Çarşamba, along Vodina Caddesi in Balat and at the Çarşamba Pazarı (Wednesday Market) in Fatih.

➡**Gathering spots** Popular local gathering spots include the terrace of the Yavuz Sultan Selim Mosque (p111) and the forecourts of the Eyüp Sultan Mosque (p114)and Fatih Mosque (p111).

➡**Ferry hopping** Regular commuters enjoy catching up with friends and neighbours over a glass of tea on the Haliç (Golden Horn) ferry.

Getting There & Away

➡**Ferry** The most enjoyable way to access these suburbs is to take the Haliç (Golden Horn) ferry from Eminönü, which stops at Ayvansaray near Edirnekapı and at Eyüp.

➡**Bus** Regular services travel from Eminönü along Mürsel Paşa Caddesi (at various points also called Abdülezel Paşa Caddesi and Sadrazam Ali Paşa Caddesi), which follows the shore of the Golden Horn through Balat, Fener and Ayvansaray and on to Eyüp. From Eminönü there are also regular services to Fatih and Edirnekapı along Fevzi Paşa Caddesi (the continuation of Macar Kardeşler and Şehzadebaşı Caddesis). We have provided information about relevant bus routes in our reviews.

Lonely Planet's Top Tip

If you plan to visit Fatih, try to do so on Wednesdays, when the Çarşamba Pazarı (Wednesday Market) is held in the streets around the Fatih Mosque.

Best Places to Eat & Drink

➡ Asitane (p115)
➡ Pierre Loti Café (p115)

For reviews, see p115.➡

Best Churches

➡ Patriarchal Church of St George (p112)
➡ Church of St Stephen of the Bulgars (p114)
➡ Church of St Mary of the Mongols (p112)

For reviews, see p111.➡

Best Byzantine Sites

➡ Kariye Museum (p108)
➡ Fethiye Museum (p111)

For reviews, see p108.➡

WESTERN DISTRICTS

TOP SIGHT
KARIYE MUSEUM (CHORA CHURCH)

İstanbul has more than its fair share of Byzantine monuments, but few are as drop-dead gorgeous as this mosaic-laden church. Nestled in the shadow of Theodosius II's monumental land walls and now a museum overseen by the Aya Sofya curators, it receives a fraction of the visitor numbers that its big sister attracts but offers an equally fascinating insight into Byzantine art.

The building was originally known as the Church of the Holy Saviour Outside the Walls (Chora literally means 'country' and Kariye is the Turkish version of the ancient Greek word Khora, which means the same thing), reflecting the fact that when it was first built it was located outside the original city walls built by Constantine the Great. Within a century the church and the monastery complex in which it was located were engulfed by Byzantine urban sprawl and enclosed within a new set of walls built by Emperor Theodosius II. Around AD 500, the Emperor Anastasius and his court moved from the Great Palace of Byzantium in Sultanahmet to the Palace of Blachernae, a new complex built close to the point where Theodosius' land walls met the old sea walls on the Golden Horn. Its proximity to the Chora Monastery led to the monastery expanding and being rebuilt in 536 during the rule of Justinian.

What you see today isn't Justinian's church, though. That building was destroyed during the Iconoclastic period (711–843) and reconstructed at least five times, most significantly in the 11th, 12th and 14th centuries. Today the Chora consists of five main architectural units: the nave, the two-storied structure (annex) added to the north,

GEORGE TSAFOS / GETTY IMAGES ©

DON'T MISS

➡ Khalke Jesus
➡ Genealogy of Christ
➡ Mary and the Baby Jesus
➡ Frescoes in parecclesion

PRACTICALITIES

➡ Kariye Müzesi
➡ Map p164
➡ Floorplan p254
➡ 212-631 9241
➡ www.ayasofyamuzesi.gov.tr
➡ Kariye Camii Sokak, Edirnekapı
➡ admission ₺15
➡ ⊙9am-6pm Thu-Tue mid-Apr–Sep, to 5pm Oct–mid-Apr
➡ 31E, 32, 36K & 38E from Eminönü, 87 from Taksim, Ayvansaray

the inner and the outer narthexes, and the chapel for tombs (parecclesion) to the south.

Virtually all of the interior decoration – the famous mosaics and the less renowned but equally striking frescoes – dates from 1312 and was funded by Theodore Metochites. One of the museum's most wonderful mosaics (item 48), found above the door to the nave in the inner narthex, depicts Theodore offering the church to Christ.

Metochites also established a very large and rich library inside the monastery; unfortunately, no traces of this or the other monastery buildings have survived.

The structure and environs of the church weren't the only thing to change over the years – after centuries of use as a church, the building became a mosque during the reign of Beyazıt II (1481–1512), and the 14th-century belfry was replaced by a minaret. The church was converted into a museum in 1945.

The best way to get to this part of town is to catch the Haliç (Golden Horn) ferry from Eminönü to Ayvansaray and walk up the hill along Dervişzade Sokak, turn right into Eğrikapı Caddesi and then almost immediately left into Şişhane Caddesi. From here you can follow the remnants of Theodosius II's land walls, passing the Palace of Constantine Porphyrogenitus on your way. From Şişhane Caddesi, veer left into Vaiz Sokak just before you reach the steep stairs leading up to the ramparts of the wall, then turn sharp left into Kariye Sokak and you'll come to the museum.

Mosaics

Most of the interior is covered with mosaics depicting the lives of Christ and the Virgin Mary. Look out for the **Khalke Jesus** (item 33), which shows Christ and Mary with two donors – Prince Isaac Comnenos and Melane, daughter of Mikhael Palaiologos VIII (only scant remains exist, alas). This is under the right dome in the inner narthex. On the dome itself is a stunning depiction of **Jesus and his ancestors** (the Genealogy of Christ; item 27). On the narthex's left dome is a serenely beautiful mosaic of **Mary and the Baby Jesus surrounded by her ancestors** (item 34).

In the nave *(naos)* are three mosaics: of **Christ** (item 50c), of **Mary and the Baby Jesus** (item 50b) and of the **Assumption of the Virgin** (item 50a) – turn around to see this, as it's over the main door you just entered. The 'infant' being held by Jesus is actually Mary's soul.

THE CHORA'S PATRON

Theodore Metochites was born in Constantinople in 1270, the son of a senior official in the court of Michael VIII Palaiologos. In 1290 he was accepted into the court of Andronikos II and was appointed logothetes, the official responsible for the treasury. This made him the highest Byzantine official after the emperor. In 1316 Metochites was appointed by the emperor as *ktetor* (donor) for the restoration of the Chora Monastery. When the restoration of the monastery was completed in 1321, he was granted the title of grand logothetes. Metochites lost his position as grand logothetes in 1328 when Emperor Andronikos II was dethroned, and was banished from Constantinople. He was allowed to return in 1330 and chose to become a priest in the monastery that he had so generously endowed. He died in 1332 and is buried in a grave niche in the parecclesion.

After visiting the museum, consider sampling the Ottoman dishes on offer at the Asitane restaurant (p115), which is in the basement of the Kariye Oteli next door.

Frescoes

To the right of the nave is the parecclesion, a side chapel built to hold the tombs of the church's founder and his relatives, close friends and associates. This is decorated with frescoes that deal with the themes of death and resurrection, depicting scenes taken from the Old Testament. The striking painting in the apse known as the **Anastasis** (item 51) shows a powerful Christ raising Adam and Eve out of their sarcophagi, with saints and kings in attendance. The gates of Hell are shown under Christ's feet. Less majestic but no less beautiful are the **frescoes adorning the dome** (item 65), which show Mary and 12 attendant angels.

Though no one knows for certain, it is thought that the frescoes were painted by the same masters who created the mosaics. Theirs is an extraordinary accomplishment, as the paintings, with their sophisticated use of perspective and exquisitely portrayed facial expressions, are reminiscent of those painted by the Italian master Giotto (c 1266–1337), the painter who more than any other ushered in the Italian Renaissance and who was painting at around the same time.

Marble

The nave and the narthexes feature very fine, multicoloured marblework. The marble door in the north axis of the nave is an imitation of the bronze-and-wood doors of the 6th century, and is one of the few surviving examples of its kind.

Restoration

Between 1948 and 1958 the church's interior decoration was carefully restored under the auspices of the Byzantine Society of America. Plaster and whitewash covering the mosaics and frescoes were removed and everything was cleaned. In 2013 a second major restoration commenced. This will be undertaken in stages, involves closure of parts of the museum and is likely to take a number of years (the estimated date of completion is August 2015). At the time of research the nave and the two-storey annexes on the northern side of the building were closed for stage one of the restoration. Stage two will see the inner narthex closed and stage three the outer narthex and parecclesion. It may not be worth visiting during stage three.

Despite signs clearly prohibiting the use of camera flashes in the museum, many visitors wilfully ignore this rule, endangering these wonderful mosaics and frescoes. Please don't be one of them.

⊙ SIGHTS

KARIYE MUSEUM (CHORA CHURCH) MUSEUM
See p108.

MIHRIMAH SULTAN MOSQUE MOSQUE
Map p164 (Mihrimah Sultan Camii; Ali Kuşçu Sokak, Edirnekapı; ⬚31E, 32, 36K & 38E from Eminönü, 87 from Taksim) The great Sinan put his stamp on the entire city, and this mosque, constructed in the 1560s next to the Edirnekapı section of the historic land walls, is one of his best works. Commissioned by Süleyman the Magnificent's favourite daughter, Mihrimah, it features a wonderfully light and airy interior with delicate stained-glass windows and an unusual 'bird cage' chandelier.

Occupying the highest point in the city, the mosque's dome and one slender minaret are major adornments to the city skyline; they are particularly prominent on the road from Edirne. Remnants of the *külliye* (mosque complex) include a still-functioning **hamam** (Map p252; Ali Kuşçu Sokak, Edirnekapı) on the corner of Ali Kuşçu and Eroğlu Sokaks.

FATIH MOSQUE MOSQUE
(Fatih Camii, Mosque of the Conqueror; Fevzi Paşa Caddesi, Fatih; ⬚31E, 32, 336E, 36KE & 38E from Eminönü, 87 from Taksim) The Fatih was the first great imperial mosque built in İstanbul following the Conquest. Mehmet the Conqueror chose to locate it on the hilltop site of the ruined Church of the Apostles, burial place of Constantine and other Byzantine emperors. Mehmet decided to be buried here as well – his tomb is behind the mosque and is inevitably filled with worshippers.

The original *külliye*, finished in 1470, was enormous. Set in extensive grounds, it included 15 charitable establishments such as *medreses* (Islamic schools of higher studies), a hospice for travellers and a caravanserai. Many of these still stand – the most interesting is the multidomed *tabhane* (inn for travelling dervishes) to the southeast of the mosque. Its columns are said to have been originally used in the Church of the Apostles.

Unfortunately, the mosque you see today is not the one Mehmet built. The original stood for nearly 300 years before toppling in an earthquake in 1766. The current baroque-style mosque was constructed between 1767 and 1771.

The front courtyard of the mosque is a favourite place for locals to congregate. On Wednesday the streets behind and to the north of the mosque host the **Çarşamba Pazarı** (Fatih Pazarı, Wednesday Market), a busy weekly market selling food, clothing and household goods.

FETHIYE MUSEUM MUSEUM
Map p252 (Fethiye Müzesi, Church of Pammakaristos; www.ayasofyamuzesi.gov.tr; Fethiye Caddesi, Çarşamba; admission ₺5; ⊙9am-6pm Thu-Tue mid-Apr–Sep, to 5pm Oct–mid-Apr; ⬚33ES, 44B, 36C, 90, 399B&C from Eminönü, 55T from Taksim) Not long after the Conquest, Mehmet the Conqueror visited this 13th-century church to discuss theological questions with the Patriarch of the Orthodox Church. They talked in the southern side chapel known as the **parecclesion**, which is decorated with gold mosaics and is now open as a small museum.

The church was endowed by a nephew of Emperor Michael VIII Palaiologos and built between 1292 and 1294; the chapel was endowed by the benefactor's wife (the inscription around Christ's head at the base of the half dome reads 'The nun Maria gave the promise of salvation in the name of her husband, the victorious and deserving protostrator Michael Glabas Ducas') and dates from 1315. It was the seat of the Christian Orthodox Patriarchate from 1455 to 1587, after which time it was converted into a mosque and named Fethiye (Conquest) to commemorate Sultan Murat III's victories in Georgia and Azerbaijan.

In the paracclesion, the most impressive of the mosaics are the **Pantokrator and 12 Prophets** adorning the dome, and the **Deesis** (Christ with the Virgin and St John the Baptist) in the apse.

YAVUZ SULTAN SELIM MOSQUE MOSQUE
Map p164 (Sultan Selim Camii, Mosque of Yavuz Selim; Yavuz Selim Caddesi, Çarşamba; ⊙tomb 9am-5pm; ⬚90 from Eminönü) The sultan to whom this mosque was dedicated (Süleyman the Magnificent's father, Selim I, known as 'the Grim') was by all accounts a nasty piece of work. He is famous for having killed his father, two of his brothers, six of his nephews and three of his own sons. Odd, then, that İstanbullus love his mosque so much.

The reason becomes clear when a visit reveals the mosque's position atop the Old City's fifth hill. Its terrace has panoramic views over the Golden Horn and is a popular picnic and relaxation spot. Selim's *türbe* (tomb) is in the garden behind the mosque.

The mosque is located in the fascinating Çarşamba district, one of the city's most conservative enclaves. Women in black chadors and men with long beards and traditional clothing are seen everywhere, often hurrying to prayers at the İsmail Ağa Mosque, headquarters of the Nakşibendi Tarikatı, a Sufi sect. The huge sunken park next door was originally a 5th-century open Roman cistern; it's now home to playing fields, basketball courts and an excellent children's playground.

The building itself, constructed between 1522 and 1529, has a simple but elegant design. Inside, its mother-of-pearl inlay and painted woodwork provide the most distinctive features.

PATRIARCHAL CHURCH OF ST GEORGE
CHURCH

Map p252 (St George in the Phanar; www.ec-patr.org; Sadrazam Ali Paşa Caddesi, Fener; ⊘8.30am-4.30pm; ▣33ES, 44B, 36C, 90, 399B&C from Eminönü, 55T from Taksim) Dating from 1836, this church is part of the Greek Patriarchate, a compound of buildings nestled behind the historic sea walls fronting the Golden Horn. Inside are artefacts including Byzantine mosaics, religious relics and a wood-and-inlay patriarchal throne. The most eye-catching feature is an ornately carved wooden iconostasis (screen of icons) that was restored and lavishly gilded in 1994.

The patriarchal throne is in the middle of the nave. Made of walnut inlaid with ivory, mother-of-pearl and coloured wood, it is thought to date from the last years of Byzantium.

Other treasures include the 11th-century mosaic icon that is on the south wall to the right of the iconostasis. This shows the Virgin Mary holding and pointing to the Christ Child, and was originally created for the Byzantine church of Pammakaristos (now the Fethiye Museum).

Look for the Column of Christ's Flagellation in the southern corner of the nave. The church claims that this is a portion of the column to which Jesus Christ was bound

and whipped by Roman soldiers before the Crucifixion. It was supposedly brought to Constantinople by St Helen, mother of the first Christian emperor, Constantine.

Note that the church is closed between 9.15am and 12.20pm for Sunday service when the Patriarch is in residence (usually once per month).

CHURCH OF ST MARY OF THE MONGOLS
CHURCH

Map p252 (Church of Theotokos Panaghiotissa, Kanlı Kilise; Tevkii Cafer Mektebi Sokak, Fener; ⊘9am-5pm Sat & Sun; ▣33ES, 44B, 36C, 90, 399B&C from Eminönü, 55T from Taksim) Consecrated in the 13th century and saved from conversion into a mosque by the personal decree of Mehmet the Conqueror, this is the only church in İstanbul to remain in Greek hands ever since Byzantine times. It was named after Princess Maria Palaiologina, an illegitimate daughter of Emperor Michael VIII Palaiologos.

Maria was sent from Byzantium to marry Hulagu, the Great Khan of the Mongols, in 1265. By the time she arrived in his kingdom he had died (we guess it was a very long trip), so she was forced to marry his son Abagu instead. On Abagu's death she returned to Byzantium and retired to a convent attached to this church.

The church is usually open on weekends. If the doors aren't open, ring the bell on the outside gate to attract the attention of the caretaker.

GÜL MOSQUE
MOSQUE

Map p252 (Gül Camii; cnr Gül Camii & Şerefiye Sokaks, Fener; ▣33ES, 44B, 36C, 90, 399B&C from Eminönü, 55T from Taksim) This mosque started life as the 11th-century Church of St Theodosia. Legend has it that one day before the Conquest, worshippers filled the church with rose petals in St Theodosia's honour and prayed for her intervention against the Ottomans. Their prayers went unanswered, but the invaders renamed the building Gül (Rose) Mosque after the petals they found on entering.

But legends, however evocative, are rarely true. In reality, the building was used as a shipyard warehouse after the Conquest and wasn't converted into a mosque until the reign of Beyazıt II (r 1481–1512). The central, extremely high, dome is an Ottoman addition and the pretty minaret dates from the rule of Selim II (r 1512–20).

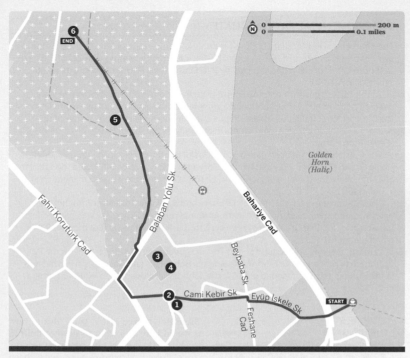

🏃 Neighbourhood Walk
Exploring Eyüp

START EYÜP İSKELESI
FINISH PIERRE LOTI CAFÉ
LENGTH 1KM; ONE HOUR

Take the Haliç (Golden Horn) ferry from Karaköy or Eminönü and disembark at Eyüp. Cross busy Bahariye Caddesi, walk through the park and veer slightly right into Eyüp İskele Sokak, following it to pedestrian-only Cami Kebir Sokak, which is lined with stalls selling religious souvenirs and tourist tat. At the top of the street is the ❶ **Tomb of Sokullu Mehmet Paşa** (p115), an Ottoman grand vizier. The tomb is next to ❷ **Eyüp Meydanı**, where pilgrims and family groups congregate around the fountain and street vendors sell fairy floss, *macun* (luridly coloured twisted candy on a stick), *kağıt helvas* (wafers filled with sweet sesame paste) and snacks. Family groups often include young boys dressed up in white satin suits with spangled caps and coloured sashes emblazoned with the word '*Maşallah*' ('May God Protect Him'). These lads are on the way to their *sünnet* (circum-

cision) and have made a stop beforehand at this holy place.

On the northern edge of the square is the ❸ **Eyüp Sultan Mosque** (p114) and the ❹ **Tomb of Ebu Eyüp el-Ensari**, the most important religious site in İstanbul. Enter the mosque's courtyard, which is shaded by a huge plane tree; the mosque is to your right and the tomb, rich with silver, gold and crystal chandeliers and coloured İznik tiles, is to your left.

After visiting both, walk out of the main gate and turn right into Balaban Yolu Sokak. Walk around the mosque complex (keeping it to your right) until you see a set of stairs and a cobbled path going uphill into the ❺ **Eyüp Sultan Mezarlığı** (Cemetery of the Great Eyüp), where many important Ottomans are buried. It's worth wandering off the path and through the cemetery, as many of the headstones and tombs feature fine calligraphy and statuary. Walk uphill for approximately 15 minutes to reach your final destination, the ❻ **Pierre Loti Café** (p115), where you can admire a panoramic view of the Golden Horn.

THE ECUMENICAL PATRIARCHATE

The Ecumenical Patriarchate of Constantinople (Rum Ortodoks Patrikhanesi) is the symbolic headquarters of the Greek Orthodox church, the 'Mother Church' of Eastern Orthodox Christianity. It has been led by 270 Ecumenical Patriarchs since its establishment in AD 330.

To the Turkish government, the Ecumenical Patriarch is a Turkish citizen of Greek descent nominated by the church and appointed by the government as an official in the Directorate of Religious Affairs. In this capacity he is the religious leader of the country's Orthodox citizens and is known officially as the Greek Patriarch of Fener (Fener Rum Patriği).

The Patriarchate has been based in a series of churches over its history, including Hagia Eirene (Aya İrini; 272–398), Hagia Sofya (Aya Sofya; 398–1453) and the Church of Pammakaristos (Fethiye Museum; 1456–1587). It moved to its current location in Fener in 1601.

The relationship between the Patriarchate and the wider Turkish community has been strained in the past, no more so than when Patriarch Gregory V was hanged for treason after inciting Greeks to overthrow Ottoman rule at the start of the Greek War of Independence (1821–32).

Current tensions are focused on the Turkish government's refusal to allow the Patriarchate to reopen the Orthodox Theological School of Halki, located on Heybeliada in the Princes' Islands. Opened in 1844, the school was closed by government order in 1971.

CHURCH OF ST STEPHEN
OF THE BULGARS   CHURCH

Map p164 (Sveti Stefan Church; Mürsel Paşa Caddesi 85, Fener; ☒33ES, 44B, 36C, 90, 399B&C from Eminönü, 55T from Taksim) These days we're accustomed to kit homes and assemble-yourself furniture from Ikea, but back in 1871, when this Gothic Revival-style church was constructed from cast-iron pieces shipped down the Danube and across the Black Sea from Vienna on 100 barges, the idea was extremely novel.

The building's interior features screens, a balcony and columns all cast from iron; it is extremely beautiful, with the gilded iron glinting in the hazy light that filters in through stained-glass windows.

The congregation are members of the Bulgarian Orthodox Exarchate (Bulgarian Orthodox Church), which broke away from the Greek Ecumenical Orthodox Patriarchate in 1872. This is the church's İstanbul base.

The building was closed for restoration at the time of research.

PALACE OF CONSTANTINE
PORPHYROGENITUS   HISTORIC BUILDING

Map p252 (Palace of the Sovereign, Tekfur Sarayı; Hoca Çakır Caddesi, Edirnekapı; ☒31E, 32, 36K & 38E from Eminönü, 87 from Taksim) Though only a shell these days, the remnants of this Byzantine palace give a good idea of how it would have looked in its heyday. Built in the late 13th or early 14th century, the large three-storied structure may have been an annex of the nearby imperial Palace of Blachernae, of which few traces exist today.

The building's later uses were not so regal: after the Conquest it functioned in turn as a menagerie for exotic wild animals, a brothel, a poorhouse for destitute Jews and a pottery.

The structure was undergoing restoration works at the time of research. When these are completed an entry fee may be levied.

EYÜP SULTAN MOSQUE   MOSQUE

Map p164 (Eyüp Sultan Camii, Mosque of the Great Eyüp; Camii Kebir Sokak, Eyüp; ⊙tomb 9.30am-4.30pm; ☒36CE, 44B or 99 from Eminönü, ⊛Eyüp) This important complex marks the supposed burial place of Ebu Eyüp el-Ensari, a friend of the Prophet's who fell in battle outside the walls of Constantinople while carrying the banner of Islam during the Arab assault and siege of the city from 674 to 678. His tomb is İstanbul's most important Islamic shrine.

Eyüp's grave was identified in a location outside the city walls immediately after the Conquest, and Sultan Mehmet II decided to build a grand tomb to mark its location.

The mosque complex that he commissioned became the place where the Ottoman princes came for the Turkish equivalent of a coronation ceremony: girding the Sword of Osman to signify their power and their title as *padişah* (king of kings), or sultan. In 1766 Mehmet's building was levelled by an earthquake; a new mosque was built on the site by Sultan Selim III in 1800.

Be careful to observe the Islamic proprieties when visiting, as this is an extremely sacred place for Muslims, ranking fourth after the big three: Mecca, Medina and Jerusalem. It's always busy on weekends and religious holidays.

TOMB OF SOKULLU MEHMET PAŞA TOMB

(Sokullu Mehmed Paşa Türbe; Cami Kebir Sokak, Eyüp; 🚍36CE, 99, 448 from Eminönü, 🚢Eyüp) Designed by Mimar Sinan and constructed around 1572, this *türbe* was part of a *külliye* commissioned by Ottoman statesman Sokullu Mehmet Paşa (c 1506–79). Assassinated in 1579, he was buried here next to his wife Ismihan, the daughter of Sultan Selim II. Inside, the stained glass is particularly noteworthy. The *külliye*'s *medrese*, which is nearby, is currently under restoration.

Sokullu Mehmet Paşa's life story is fascinating. Born in Bosnia, he was captured by Ottoman troops and recruited into the *devşirme,* the annual intake of Christian youths into the janisseries (this also happened to Sinan). After converting to Islam he rose through the ranks, holding important positions such as high admiral of the fleet, before becoming grand vizier for 14 years under two sultans: Süleyman the Magnificent and Selim II. During his time in office he amassed a great fortune and commissioned religious buildings including the Sokullu Şehit Mehmet Paşa Mosque (p79) in Sultanahmet.

🍴 EATING & DRINKING

KÖMÜR TURK MUTFAĞI TURKISH €

(☎212-521 9999; www.komurturkmutfagi.com; Fevzi Paşa Caddesi 18, Fatih; veg portions ₺7-8, meat portions ₺10-15, grills ₺13-32; ⊗5am-11pm; 🗗; 🚍31E, 32, 336E, 36KE & 38E from Eminönü, 87 from Taksim) Located amid the wedding-dress shops on Fatih's main drag is this five-floor *Türk mutfağı* (Turkish kitchen) where brides-to-be join businessmen and worshippers from the nearby Fatih Mosque

for lunch. The gleaming ground-floor space has a huge counter where ready-made dishes are displayed and where fresh meat and fish can be cooked to order.

KÖFTECI ARNAVUT KÖFTE €

Map p252 (☎212-531 6652; Mürsel Paşa Caddesi 139, Balat; köfte ₺9, piyaz ₺4; ⊗11am-7pm Mon-Sat; 🚍33ES, 44B, 36C, 90, 399B&C from Eminönü, 55T from Taksim) Unsigned and unassuming, this famous *köftecisi* first opened in 1947 and is overseen by the son of the original 'Armenian meatball seller'. It is known for it *köfte* (meatballs) served with *piyaz* (white-bean salad). Look for the run-down red-brick building with white wooden windows on the ground floor; there are usually a couple of tables and some stools outside.

TARIHI HALIÇ İŞKEMBECISI TURKISH €

Map p252 (☎212-534 9414; www.haliciskembecisi.com; Abdülezel Paşa Caddesi 315, Fener; soup ₺11; ⊗24hr; 🚍33ES, 36C, 44B, 90, 399B&C from Eminönü, 55T from Taksim) Locals swear by the hangover-fighting properties of *işkembe* (tripe soup) and often make late-night pilgrimages to this, the most famous *işkembecisi* in the city. The most popular tables are on the upstairs terrace.

⭐ASITANE OTTOMAN €€€

Map p252 (☎212-635 7997; www.asitanerestaurant.com; Kariye Oteli, Kariye Camii Sokak 6, Edirnekapı; starters ₺16-26, mains ₺32-50; ⊗11am-midnight; 🗗; 🚍31E, 32, 36K & 38E from Eminönü, 87 from Taksim, 🚢Ayvansaray) This elegant restaurant next to the Kariye Museum serves Ottoman dishes devised for the palace kitchens at Topkapı, Edirne and Dolmabahçe. Its chefs have been tracking down historic recipes for years, and the menu is full of versions that will tempt most modern palates, including vegetarians. Dine inside or in the pretty outdoor courtyard during summer.

⭐PIERRE LOTI CAFÉ CAFE

Map p164 (Gümüşsuyu Balmumcu Sokak 1, Eyüp; ⊗8am-midnight; 🚢Eyüp) Many visitors head to this hilltop cafe after visiting the Eyüp Sultan Mosque (p114). Named for the famous French novelist who is said to have come here for inspiration, it offers lovely views across the Golden Horn and is a popular weekend destination for locals, who relax over tea, coffee, ice cream and nargiles (water pipes).

Beyoğlu

GALATA | TOPHANE | KARAKÖY | İSTIKLAL | ÇUKURCUMA | CİHANGİR

Neighbourhood Top Five

❶ Visiting cultural centres such as **İstanbul Modern** (p119), **SALT Beyoğlu** (p126), **ARTER** (p125) and **SALT Galata** (p120) to see why international artists, collectors and critics think that İstanbul has one of the world's most-exciting visual-art scenes.

❷ Seeing dervishes whirl in a 15th-century *semahane* (whirling-dervish hall) at the **Galata Mevlevi Museum** (p124).

❸ Admiring Orhan Pamuk's ambitious and thought-provoking conceptual art project, the **Museum of Innocence** (p125).

❹ Investigating the cafe and bar scenes in **Karaköy**, **Cihangir** and **Asmalımescit** (p134).

❺ Sampling the sights, smells and flavours in the historic **Balık Pazarı** (p129).

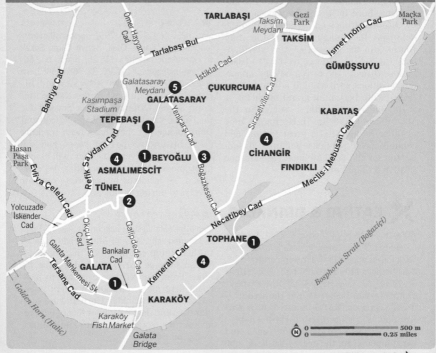

For more detail of this area see Map p244 and p248 ➡

Explore: Beyoğlu

If you have the time, it makes sense to spread your exploration of this neighbourhood over two days. The first day could be spent in Tophane, Karaköy, Galata and Tünel, visiting sights such as the İstanbul Modern and wandering around the fascinating streets. The second day could be spent walking from Taksim Meydanı (Taksim Square) along İstiklal Caddesi, veering off into the districts of Cihangir, Çukurcuma, Asmalımescit and Tepebaşı.

If you only have one day, start in Taksim Meydanı and work your way down İstiklal Caddesi, exploring the Balık Pazarı, heading into Tepebaşı to visit the Pera Museum, then making your way through Galata down to Karaköy.

Even if you are staying in another neighbourhood, it makes sense to follow the lead of locals and head here every night for dinner, bar-hopping and clubbing.

Local Life

→**Streetside Cafes** Take a break and enjoy tea at old-fashioned outdoor cafes such as Hazzo Pulo Çay Bahçesi (p135) off İstiklal Caddesi, Kardeşler Cafe in Cihangir and Cafe Gündoğdu in the square below Galata Tower.

→**Football & Nargile** If you're in town when a Süper Lig or UEFA match is being played, head to one of the Tophane nargile cafes (p134) to drink tea, smoke a nargile (water pipe) and join the fans in making your team allegiances clear.

→**Tea by the Bosphorus** To enjoy a million-dollar view with a cheap glass of tea, try the ramshackle *çay bahçesi* (tea gardens) at the edge of the Bosphorus opposite the Fındıklı tram stop. There's even a kids' playground nearby to make toddlers happy.

Getting There & Away

→**Tram** A tram runs from Cevizlibağ and Bağcılar in the city's west to Kabataş near Taksim Meydanı in Beyoğlu, stopping at Sultanahmet, Eminönü and Karaköy en route.

→**Funicular** It's a steep uphill walk from all tram stops to İstiklal, so most commuters use the funiculars that link Karaköy with Tünel Meydanı and Kabataş with Taksim Meydanı.

→**Metro** Trains travel between Yenikapı on the Sea of Marmara and Taksim Meydanı, stopping at Vezneciler in the Old City, on a bridge over the Golden Horn and in Şişhane (near Tünel Meydanı) en route. From Taksim, another train heads to Nişantaşı and the ritzy residential and commercial suburbs to its north.

→**Bus** Buses to every part of the city leave from the bus interchanges underneath Taksim Meydanı and near the tram stop at Kabataş.

Lonely Planet's Top Tip

The neighbourhoods within Beyoğlu all have distinct and fascinating characters. Be sure to veer off İstiklal Caddesi and explore districts such as Cihangir, Çukurcuma, Asmalımescit and Galata.

✖ Best Places to Eat

→ Antiochia (p130)
→ Karaköy Güllüoğlu (p128)
→ Klemuri (p130)
→ Meze by Lemon Tree (p132)
→ Zübeyir Ocakbaşı (p131)

For reviews, see p128.➡

◉ Best Places to Drink

→ Dem (p134)
→ Karabatak (p134)
→ Mikla (p135)
→ Tophane Nargile Cafes (p134)
→ 360 (p135)
→ Unter (p134)

For reviews, see p134.➡

☆ Best Places to Party

→ Babylon (p137)
→ MiniMüzikHol (p136)
→ Indigo (p135)

For reviews, see p134.➡

BEYOĞLU

TOP SIGHT
İSTIKLAL CADDESI

Once called the Grand Rue de Pera but renamed İstiklal (Independence) in the early years of the Republic, Beyoğlu's premier boulevard is a perfect metaphor for 21st-century Turkey. A long pedestrianised strip cluttered with shops, cafes, cinemas and cultural centres, it showcases İstanbul's Janus-like personality, embracing modernity one minute and happily bowing to tradition the next.

At its northern end is frantically busy Taksim Meydanı, the symbolic heart of the modern city and the site of loud and sometimes violent anti-government protests in recent years. At its southern end is the relatively tranquil district of Galata, home to crooked cobblestone lanes and traces of a fortified settlement built by Genoese merchants in the 13th century.

In the 19th century, new ideas brought from Europe by traders and diplomats walked into Ottoman daily life down the streets of Pera (as Beyoğlu was originally called). The Europeans who lived here imported new fashions, machines, arts and manners to the city. This part of town had telephones, the world's second-oldest underground train (the Tünel), tramways (one still functioning), electric light and modern municipal government. There were even European-style patisseries and shopping arcades, a number of which have been retained. In contrast, the Historic Peninsula (Old City or Old Stamboul) on the opposite side of the Golden Horn kept its oriental bazaars, great mosques, draughty palaces, narrow streets and traditional values.

Today promenading along the length of İstiklal is the most popular activity in town, and huge crowds of İstanbullus head here in the early evening and on weekends to shop in the multinational chain stores, see exhibitions at galleries including SALT Beyoğlu and ARTER, listen to the street buskers, drink coffee and party in *meyhanes* (taverns). We highly recommend that you join them.

DON'T MISS

➜ Çiçek Pasajı (p127)
➜ Balık Pazarı (p129)
➜ SALT Beyoğlu (p126)
➜ ARTER (p125)

PRACTICALITIES

➜ Independence Ave
➜ Map p244

TOP SIGHT
İSTANBUL MODERN

In the past decade İstanbul's contemporary-art scene has boomed. Facilitated by the active cultural philanthropy of the country's industrial dynasties – many of which have built extraordinary arts collections – museum buildings are opening nearly as often as art exhibitions. İstanbul Modern, funded by the Eczcıbaşı family, is the big daddy of them all.

Opened with great fanfare in 2005, this huge converted shipping terminal has a stunning location right on the shores of the Bosphorus at Tophane and is easily accessed by tram from Sultanahmet.

The museum's curatorial program is twofold: the 1st floor highlights the Eczcıbaşı family's collection of Turkish 20th-century and contemporary art using a thematic approach; and the downstairs spaces host temporary exhibitions from local and international artists. While the 1st floor exhibits are interesting – look for works by Şekere Ahmet Ali Paşa (1841–1907), Orhan Peker (1926–78), İsmet Doğan (1957–), Ömer Kaleşi (1932–), Cihat Burak (1915–94), Tayfun Erdoğmuş (1958–), İhsan Cemal Karaburçak (1897–1970), Avni Arbaş (1919–2003), Selma Gürbüz (1960–), Alaaddin Aksoy (1942–), Fahreinissa Zeid (1901–91), Nurullah Berk (1906–82) and Adnan Çoker (1927–) – it's the temporary exhibitions and permanent installations in the downstairs spaces that stand out.

Make sure you check out what is showing in the main temporary gallery (it's always good), the photography gallery and the pop-up exhibition spaces. Of the permanent works on display, don't miss *False Ceiling* (installation; Richard Wentworth; 1995–2005) downstairs and *The Road to Tate Modern* (video; Erkan Özgen and Şener Özmen; 2003), an ironic reworking of Cervantes' *Don Quixote,* in one of the upstairs projection rooms. Also of note are the museum's cafe and gift shop.

DON'T MISS

➡ Shows in the main temporary gallery
➡ *False Ceiling*
➡ *The Road to Tate Modern*

PRACTICALITIES

➡ İstanbul Modern Sanat Müzesi
➡ Map p248
➡ www.istanbulmodern. org
➡ Meclis-i Mebusan Caddesi, Tophane
➡ adult/student/under 12yr ₺17/9/free
➡ ⊙10am-6pm Tue, Wed & Fri-Sun, to 8pm Thu
➡ 🚊Tophane

SIGHTS

◉ Galata, Tophane & Karaköy

İSTANBUL MODERN ART GALLERY
See p119.

GALERI MANÂ GALLERY
Map p248 (☑212-243 6666; www.galerimana. com; Ali Paşa Değirmeni Sokak 16-18, Karaköy; ⊕11am-6pm Tue-Sat; ⓐTophane) Occupying a converted 19th-century wheat mill in the midst of the city's most happening enclave, Galeri Manâ is perhaps the most interesting of the many commercial galleries to open over the past few years. Its stable of artists includes up-and-coming local and international names such as Abbas Akhavan and Deniz Gül, as well as established practitioners such as Sarkis.

ELIPSIS GALLERY GALLERY
Map p248 (☑212-244 0900; www.elipsisgallery. com; cnr Hoca Tahsin & Akçe Sokaks, Karaköy; ⊕11am-7pm Tue-Fri, noon-6pm Sat; ⓐTophane) Showing the work of contemporary photographers from Turkey and overseas, Elipsis has built a solid reputation over the past few years and is always worth a visit.

JEWISH MUSEUM OF TURKEY MUSEUM
Map p248 (500 Yil Vakfi Türk Musevileri, The Quincentennial Foundation Jewish Museum of Turkey; ☑212-244 4474; www.muze500.com; Perçemli Sokak, Karaköy; admission ₺10; ⊕10am-4pm Mon-Thu, 10am-2pm Fri & Sun; ⓐKaraköy) Housed in the ornate 19th-century Zullfaris synagogue near the Galata Bridge, this museum was established in 2001 to commemorate the 500th anniversary of the arrival of the Sephardic Jews in the Ottoman Empire. Its modest but extremely well-intentioned collection comprises photographs, papers and objects that document the mostly harmonious coexistence between Jews and the Muslim majority in this country.

The history of the Jews in Turkey is as long as it is fascinating. When Mehmet II conquered the city in 1453, he recognised the last Byzantine chief rabbi, Moshe Kapsali, as the chief rabbi of İstanbul and said 'The God has presented me with many lands and ordered me to take care of the dynasty of his servants Abraham and Jacob...Who, among you, with the consent of God, would like to settle in İstanbul, live in peace in the shade of the figs and vineyards, trade freely and own property?' Alas, this enlightened state didn't last through the centuries, and Jewish Turks were made to feel considerably less welcome when racially motivated 'wealth taxes' were introduced in 1942 and violence against Jews and other minorities was unleashed in 1955, prompting many families to flee the country. More recently, Islamist terrorists have bombed synagogues on a number of occasions. Despite these recent events, the museum chooses to focus on the positive rather than the negative.

Approximately 23,000 Jews currently live in Turkey, with most residing in İstanbul. Sephardic Jews make up around 96% of this number, while the rest are primarily Ashkenazic. Today there are a total of 16 synagogues in İstanbul, all of which are Sephardic except for one. For a list of these see www.jewish-europe.net/turkey/ en/synagogue.

SALT GALATA CULTURAL CENTRE
Map p248 (☑212-334 2200; www.saltonline.org/ en; Bankalar Caddesi 11, Karaköy; ⊕noon-8pm Tue-Sat, to 6pm Sun; ⓐKaraköy) **FREE** The descriptor 'cultural centre' is used a lot in İstanbul, but is often a misnomer. Here at SALT Galata it really does apply. Housed in a magnificent 1892 bank building designed by Alexandre Vallaury and cleverly adapted by local architectural firm Mimarlar Tasarım, this cutting-edge institution offers an exhibition space, auditorium, arts research library, cafe and glamorous rooftop restaurant.

Funded by the Garanti Bank, SALT aims to be a centre of learning and debate in the city and hosts regular conferences, lectures and workshops. The building also houses a small Ottoman Bank Museum.

ARAB MOSQUE MOSQUE
Map p248 (Arap Camıı; Galata Mahkemesi Sokak, Galata; ⓐKaraköy) Built by the Genoese in 1337, this fortress-like mosque was the largest of İstanbul's Latin churches. Converted to a mosque after the Conquest, it was given to the recently arrived community of Spanish Muslims after their expulsion from Spain and arrival in İstanbul in the late 15th century. Notable features include the stone exterior and a magnificent wooden ceiling.

Neighbourhood Walk
Galatasaray to Galata

START GALATASARAY MEYDANI
FINISH SALT GALATA
LENGTH 1.4KM; TWO HOURS

Start this walk in front of the ❶ **Galatasaray Lycée**, a prestigious public school located on the busy corner of İstiklal and Yeniçarşı Caddesis. Established in 1868 by Sultan Abdül Aziz, it educates the sons of İstanbul's elite.

Walking south down İstiklal, you'll pass the neo-Gothic ❷ **St Anthony's Cathedral** on your left. Built between 1906 and 1911, it is one of two churches fronting the street in this stretch.

Further south are two of the city's newest and most exciting gallery spaces – ❸ **SALT Beyoğlu** (p126) and ❺ **ARTER** (p125). Both are housed in historic buildings that have been imaginatively adapted.

Just before ARTER is the ❹ **Netherlands Consulate General**, a handsome 1855 building by the Swiss-born Fossati Brothers, who designed many buildings for Sultan Abdülmecit I.

After passing the ❻ **Russian Consulate**, another grand embassy designed by the Fossati brothers, veer left down Kumbaracı Caddesi and then into the first street on your right.

Walk up the hill past ❼ **Christ Church** and then turn right into one of Beyoğlu's most interesting shopping streets, Serdar-ı Ekram Caddesi. Check out its edgy boutiques and consider having a break at bohemian ❽ **Mavra** (p128) or laid-back ❾ **Aheste** (p129).

Continue straight ahead to ❿ **Galata Tower** (p124) and then head down winding Camekan and Bereketzade Medresesi Sokaks. You'll eventually come to the sculptural ⓫ **Camondo Stairs**, commissioned and paid for by the famous Jewish banking family of the same name. At the bottom is Bankalar Caddesi, centre of the city's prosperous banking industry in the 19th century. It's now home to ⓬ **SALT Galata** (p120), where you can end your walk enjoying a coffee in the cafe or, if late in the day, a drink or meal in the rooftop restaurant.

SALVATOR BARKI / GETTY IMAGES ©

GARY YEOWELL / GETTY IMAGES ©

KASA GALERI
GALLERY

Map p248 (☏212-292 4939; http://kasagaleri.
sabanciuniv.edu; Bankalar Caddesi 2, Karaköy;
⊙10am-5pm Mon-Sat; ⓐKaraköy) FREE Kasa
Galeri is located in the basement vault of the
Minerva Han, a splendid Islamic Revival-
style building that was built as the Greek-
owned Bank of Athens in the early 20th
century. Funded by Sabaci University, it
supports and exhibits collaborative international art projects that are experimen-
tal in nature. It also offers residencies and
shows to emerging Turkish artists.

SCHNEIDERTEMPEL ART CENTER
GALLERY

Map p248 (Schneidertempel Sanat Merkezi;
www.schneidertempel.com; Felek Sokak 1, Galata; ⊙10.30am-5pm Mon-Fri, noon-4pm Sun;
ⓐKaraköy) Housed in a synagogue dating
from 1894, the Schneidertempel (Tailors'
temple) exhibits work by local Jewish artists, as well as frequent exhibitions from
abroad. Quality varies, but we've seen
some excellent photographic exhibitions
here.

GALATA TOWER
TOWER

Map p248 (Galata Kulesi; Galata Meydanı, Galata;
admission ₺19; ⊙9am-8pm; ⓐKaraköy) The cy-
lindrical Galata Tower stands sentry over
the approach to 'new' İstanbul. Constructed in 1348, it was the tallest structure in the
city for centuries, and it still dominates the
skyline north of the Golden Horn. Its ver-
tiginous upper balcony offers 360-degree
views of the city, but we're not convinced
that the view (though spectacular) justifies
the steep admission cost.

Be warned that queues can be long and
the viewing balcony can get horribly over-
crowded. An elevator goes most of the way
to the top, but there is one flight of stairs
to climb.

CHRIST CHURCH
CHURCH

Map p248 (Crimean Memorial Church; ☏0555
810 1010; Serdar-i Ekrem Sokak 52, Galata; ⊙ser-
vices 10am Sun; ⓂŞişhane, ⓐKaraköy, then
funicular to Tünel) The cornerstone of this
Gothic-style Anglican church was laid in
1858 by Lord Stratford de Redcliffe, known
as 'The Great Elchi' (*elçi*, meaning ambassador) because of his paramount influence
in mid-19th-century Ottoman affairs. The
largest of the city's Protestant churches, it
was dedicated in 1868 as the Crimean Memorial Church and restored and renamed
in the mid-1990s.

Inside, there is a painted rood screen by
Scottish artist Mungo McCosh that depicts
notable İstanbul residents (mainly expats).
Services are so wonderfully High that they
would almost be at home at St Peter's.

To visit, attend the Sunday service or
SMS chaplain Ian Sherwood to organise a
convenient time.

DEPO
CULTURAL CENTRE

Map p248 (☏212-292 3956; www.depoistanbul.
net; Lüleci Hendek Caddesi 12, Tophane; ⊙11am-
7pm Tue-Sun; ⓂŞişhane, ⓐTophane) Occupying
a former tobacco warehouse, this alternative space is operated by **Anadolu Kültür**
(www.anadolukultur.org), a not-for-profit organisation that facilitates artistic collabo-
ration, promotes cultural exchange, and
stimulates debates on social and political issues relevant to Turkey, the South Caucasus,
the Middle East and the Balkans. It hosts
talks, art exhibitions and film screenings.

GALATA MEVLEVI MUSEUM
MUSEUM

Map p248 (Galata Mevlevihanesi Müzesi; www.me
kder.org; Galipdede Caddesi 15, Tünel; admission
₺5; ⊙9am-4pm Tue-Sun; ⓂŞişhane, ⓐKaraköy,
then funicular to Tünel) The *semahane* (whirling-
dervish hall) at the centre of this *tekke*
(dervish lodge) was erected in 1491 and
renovated in 1608 and 2009. It's part of a
complex including a *meydan-ı şerif* (courtyard), *çeşme* (drinking fountain), *türbesi*
(tomb) and *hamuşan* (cemetery). The oldest of six historic Mevlevihaneleri (Mevlevi
tekkes) remaining in İstanbul, the complex
was converted into a museum in 1946.

The Mevlevi *tarika* (order), founded in
the central Anatolian city of Konya during
the 13th century, flourished throughout the
Ottoman Empire. Like several other orders,
the Mevlevis stressed the unity of human-
kind before God regardless of creed.

Taking their name from the great Sufi
mystic and poet, Celaleddin Rumi (1207–
73), called Mevlana (Our Leader) by his
disciples, Mevlevis seek to achieve mysti-
cal communion with God through a *sema*
(ceremony) involving chants, prayers, music and a whirling dance. This *tekke's* first
şeyh (sheikh) was Şemaî Mehmed Çelebi, a
grandson of the great Mevlana.

Dervish orders were banned in the early
days of the Turkish republic because of their
ultraconservative religious politics. Although
the ban has been lifted, only a handful of
functioning *tekkes* remain in İstanbul, including this one and the İstanbul Bilim Sanat

Kültür ve Eğitim Derneği in Fatih. Konya remains the heart of the Mevlevi order.

Beneath the *semahane* is an interesting exhibit that includes displays of Mevlevi clothing, turbans and accessories. The *mahfiller* (upstairs floor) houses the *tekke's* collection of traditional musical instruments, calligraphy and *ebru* (paper marbling).

The *hamuşan* is full of stones with graceful Ottoman inscriptions, including the tomb of Galip Dede, the 17th-century Sufi poet whom the street is named after. The shapes atop the stones reflect the headgear of the deceased, each hat denoting a different religious rank.

⊙ İstiklal & Around

İSTIKLAL CADDESI   STREET
See p118.

ARTER   GALLERY
Map p248 (☎212-243 3767; www.arter.org.tr; İstiklal Caddesi 211; ⊙11am-7pm Tue-Thu, noon-8pm Fri-Sun; MŞişhane, ⬚Karaköy, then funicular to Tünel) FREE A stunning marble spiral staircase, prominent location on İstiklal Caddesi and international exhibition program featuring the likes of Mona Hatoum, Sarkis, Marc Quinn, Patricia Piccinini and Sophia

Pompéry make this four-floor art space one of the most prestigious art venues in town.

★MUSEUM OF INNOCENCE   MUSEUM
Map p248 (Masumiyet Müzesi; ☎212-252 9748; www.masumiyetmuzesi.org; Dalgıç Sokak 2, off Çukurcuma Caddesi, Çukurcuma; adult/student ₺25/10; ⊙10am-6pm Tue-Sun, till 9pm Thu; MTaksim, ⬚Tophane) The painstaking attention to detail in this fascinating museum/piece of conceptual art will certainly provide every amateur psychologist with a theory or two about its creator, Nobel Prize–winning novelist Orhan Pamuk. Vitrines display a quirky collection of objects that evoke the minutiae of İstanbullu life in the mid-to-late 20th century, when Pamuk's novel of the same name is set.

Occupying a modest 19th-century timber house, the museum relies on its vitrines, which are reminiscent of the work of American artist Joseph Cornell, to retell the story of the love affair of Kemal and Füsun, the novel's protagonists. These displays are both beautiful and moving; some, such as the installation using 4213 cigarette butts, are as strange as they are powerful.

Pamuk's 'Modest Manifesto for Museums' is reproduced on a panel on the ground floor. In it, he asserts 'The resources that are channeled into monumental, symbolic

BEYOĞLU SIGHTS

SEEING THE DERVISHES WHIRL

If you thought the Hare Krishnas or the Harlem congregations were the only religious orders to celebrate their faith through music and movement, think again. Those sultans of spiritual spin known as the 'whirling dervishes' have been twirling their way to a higher plane ever since the 13th century and show no sign of slowing down.

There are a number of opportunities to see dervishes whirling in İstanbul. The best known of these is the weekly ceremony in the *semahane* (whirling dervish hall) in the **Galata Mevlevi Museum** in Tünel. This one-hour ceremony is held on Saturdays and Sundays at 5pm and costs ₺40 per person. Come early (preferably days ahead) to buy your ticket.

Another, much longer and more authentic, ceremony is held at the **EMAV Silivrikapı Mevlana Cultural Center** (EMAV Silivrikapı Mevlana Kültür Merkezi; www. emav.org; Yeni Tavanlı Çeşme Sokum 8, Silivrikapı; ⬚Çapa-Şehremini) on Thursday evenings between 7.30pm and 11pm. This includes a Q&A session (in Turkish), prayers and a *sema* (ceremony). You'll need to sit on the ground for a long period. Admission is by donation.

For a more touristy experience, the **Hocapaşa Culture Centre** (p83), housed in a beautifully converted 15th-century hamam near Eminönü, presents whirling dervish performances five evenings per week throughout the year.

Remember that the ceremony is a religious one – by whirling, the adherents believe that they are attaining a higher union with God – so don't talk, leave your seat or take flash photographs while the dervishes are spinning or chanting.

museums should be diverted to smaller museums that tell the stories of individuals'. The individuals in this case are fictional, of course, and their story is evoked in a highly nostalgic fashion, but in creating this museum Pamuk has put his money where his mouth is and come out triumphant.

SALT BEYOĞLU
CULTURAL CENTRE

Map p244 (✆212-377 4200; www.saltonline.org/en; İstiklal Caddesi 136; ✆noon-8pm Tue-Sat, to 6pm Sun; MŞişhane, Karaköy, then funicular to Tünel) Its three floors of exhibition space, bookshop, walk-in cinema and cafe make SALT Beyoğlu nearly as impressive as its Galata-based sibling. Occupying a former apartment building dating from the 1850s, it shows the work of both high-profile and emerging international and local artists.

GALERIST
GALLERY

Map p248 (www.galerist.com.tr; 1st fl, Meşrutiyet Caddesi 67, Tepebaşı; ✆11am-7pm Tue-Sat; MŞişhane, Karaköy, then funicular to Tünel) Owned by architect Melkan Gürsel Tabanlıoğlu and serious (ie mega-moneyed) art collector Taha Tatlıcı, Galerist occupies the 1st floor of a beautiful 18th-century building in one of the city's most fashionable enclaves. It shows Turkish and international artists working in a variety of media. The gallery's second space is located in the rapidly gentrifying Golden Horn suburb of Hasköy.

GALERI NEV
GALLERY

Map p244 (✆212-252 1525; www.galerinevistanbul.com; 4th fl, Mısır Apt, İstiklal Caddesi 163; ✆11am-6.30pm Tue-Sat; MŞişhane, Karaköy, then funicular to Tünel) One of the city's oldest and most impressive commercial galleries, Nev numbers many of the country's best-known modernists among its stable of artists.

GALERI APEL
GALLERY

Map p244 (✆212-292 7236; www.galleryapel.com; Hayriye Caddesi 5a, Galatasaray; ✆11.30am-6.30pm Tue-Sat, closed Aug; MTaksim, Kabataş, then funicular to Taksim) This long-established commercial gallery behind the Galatasaray Lycée has a large stable of Turkish artists working in a number of media. Its shows are always worth a visit.

PERA MUSEUM
MUSEUM

Map p244 (Pera Müzesi; ✆212-334 9900; www.peramuzesi.org.tr; Meşrutiyet Caddesi 65, Tepebaşı; adult/student/child under 12yr ₺15/8/free; ✆10am-7pm Tue-Sat, noon-6pm Sun; MŞişhane, Karaköy, then funicular to Tünel) Head here to admire works from Suna and İnan Kıraç's splendid collection of paintings featuring Turkish Orientalist themes, which are displayed on the museum's 2nd floor. A changing program of thematic exhibitions drawing on the collection provides fascinating glimpses into the Ottoman world from the 17th to the early 20th

---

WORTH A DETOUR

NIŞANTAŞI

If you're a dab hand at air-kissing and striking a pose over a caffe latte, you'll feel totally at home in Nişantaşı. Serious shoppers, visiting celebs, PR professionals and the city's gilded youth gravitate towards this upmarket enclave, which is located about 2km north of Taksim Meydanı and is accessed via the metro (Osmanbey stop). Bars, restaurants, boutique hotels and international fashion and design shops are found in the streets surrounding the main artery, Teşvikiye Caddesi, prompting some locals to refer to that area as Teşvikiye.

If you decide to spend a day or half-day shopping here, consider taking a break and eating at **Hünkar** (✆212-225 4665; www.hunkarlokantasi.com; Mim Kemal Öke Caddesi 21; veg portions ₺9-10, meat portions ₺18-35; ✆noon-10.30pm; MOsmanbey), one of the best *lokantas* (eatery serving ready-made food) in the city, or at Slow Food–favourite **Kantın** (✆212-219 3114; www.kantin.biz; Akkavak Sokak 30; mains ₺18-32; ✆11.30am-9pm Mon-Sat; MOsmanbey).

Nişantaşı is the fashion hub of the city, and the queen of the local industry is undoubtedly **Gönül Paksoy** (✆212-261 9081; Atiye Sokak 6a; ✆10am-7pm Mon-Sat; MOsmanbey), who creates and sells pieces that transcend fashion and step into art. The major fashion strip is Abdi İpekçi Caddesi, home to Turkish and international designers and the city's most glamorous department store, **Beymen** (✆212-373 4800; www.beymen.com.tr; Abdi İpekçi Caddesi 23; 10am-8pm Mon-Sat, noon-8pm Sun; MOsmanbey).

century. Some works are realistic, others highly romanticised – all are historically fascinating.

The most beloved painting in the Turkish canon – Osman Hamdı Bey's *The Tortoise Trainer* (1906) – is the stand-out work in the Kıraç collection and is always part of the 2nd-floor display, but there's plenty more to see in the museum, including a permanent exhibit of Kütahya tiles and ceramics, and a somewhat esoteric collection of Anatolian weights and measures on the 1st floor. The 5th floor hosts a constantly changing program of international travelling exhibitions.

PERA PALACE HOTEL   HISTORIC BUILDING

Map p248 (Pera Palas Oteli; www.perapalace. com; Meşrutiyet Caddesi 52, Tepebaşı; **M**Şişhane, **@**Karaköy, then funicular to Tünel) The Pera Palas was a project of Georges Nagelmackers, the Belgian entrepreneur who linked Paris and Constantinople with his famous *Orient Express* train service. The 1892 building has undergone a €23-million restoration in recent years and claims to have regained its position as İstanbul's most glamorous hotel. Its ground floor is open to the public.

Nagelmackers founded the Compagnie Internationale des Wagons-Lits et Grands Express Européens in 1868. The *Orient Express* service first operated in 1883 and Nagelmackers soon realised that İstanbul had no suitably luxurious hotels where his esteemed passengers could stay. His solution was to build one himself, and he commissioned the fashionable İstanbul-born but French-trained architect Alexandre Vallaury to design it.

On opening, the hotel advertised itself as having 'a thoroughly healthy situation, being high up and isolated on all four sides', and 'overlooking the Golden Horn and the whole panorama of Stamboul'. Its guests included Agatha Christie, who supposedly wrote *Murder on the Orient Express* in Room 411; Mata Hari, who no doubt frequented the elegant bar with its lovely stained-glass windows and excellent eavesdropping opportunities; and Greta Garbo, who probably enjoyed her own company in one of the spacious suites.

The bar in the ground-floor lounge is a pleasant spot for a drink, but neither the restaurant nor the tearoom off the foyer are worthy of a visit.

PATISSERIE LEBON   HISTORIC BUILDING

Map p248 (İstiklal Caddesi 172; **M**Şişhane, **@**Karaköy, then funicular to Tünel) In Pera's heyday, there was no more glamorous spot to see and be seen than Patisserie Lebon. Its gorgeous art nouveau interior featured chandeliers, a decorative tiled floor and large tiled wall panels designed by Alexandre Vallaury, the architect of the Pera Palace Hotel. Though now sadly functioning as a fast-food joint, much of its interior has been retained.

The patisserie is one of the best-loved buildings in Beyoğlu, as much for its history as for its interior design. After decades as the Lebon, the business was taken over by Avedis Çakır in 1940 and renamed Patisserie Markiz. It continued to trade until the 1960s, when Pera's decline and a lack of customers led to its closure. Fortunately, closure didn't mean destruction – the building was boarded up and left just as it had been, fittings and all. In the 1970s local artists and writers lobbied the authorities to have the patisserie and adjoining shopping arcade added to the country's register of historical buildings; this occurred in 1977, ensuring the entire building's preservation.

In late 2003 the magnificently restored patisserie reopened to great acclaim. It had a short-lived and much-lamented second life as an upmarket patisserie, but has recently been reinvented as Yemek Kulübü, a cafe serving cheap coffee and food. Still, the interior means that a stop here remains well worthwhile.

ÇIÇEK PASAJI   HISTORIC BUILDING

Map p244 (Flower Passage; İstiklal Caddesi; **M**Taksim, **@**Kabataş, then funicular to Taksim) Back when promenading down the Rue de Pera (now İstiklal Caddesi) was the height of fashion, the Cité de Pera building was İstanbul's most glamorous address. Built in 1876 and decorated in Second Empire style, it housed a shopping arcade and apartments. The arcade is now known as the Çiçek Pasajı and is full of boisterous *meyhanes* (taverns).

As Pera declined in the mid-20th century, so too did this building. Its once-stylish shops gave way to rough *meyhanes* where beer barrels were rolled out onto the pavement, marble slabs were balanced on top, wooden stools were arranged and enthusiastic revellers caroused the night away. It continued in this vein until the late 1970s, when parts of the building collapsed. When

BEYOĞLU SIGHTS

it was reconstructed, the arcade acquired a glass canopy to protect pedestrians from bad weather, its makeshift barrels and stools were replaced with solid wooden tables and benches, and its broken pavement was covered with smooth tiles. These days its raffish charm is nearly gone and most locals bypass the touts and the mediocre food on offer here and instead make their way behind the passage to the bars and *meyhanes* on or around Nevizade Sokak.

AKBANK ART CENTRE CULTURAL CENTRE

Map p244 (Akbank Sanat; ☑212-252 3500; www.akbanksanat.com; İstiklal Caddesi 8; ☺10.30am-7.30pm Tue-Sat; ⓠKabataş, then funicular to Taksim Meydanı) Turkey's big banks and philanthropic trusts vie with each other to be seen as the greatest sponsor of the arts. İstiklal is a showcase for their generosity, and with this venue Akbank joins SALT Beyoğlu and ARTER in offering a showcase for the city's thriving arts scene. It has an art gallery, performance hall, dance studio, music-listening studio and arts library.

The centre is the venue for the Akbank-sponsored İstanbul Jazz and Short Film Festivals as well as for performances by the Akbank Chamber Orchestra.

TAKSIM MEYDANI SQUARE

Map p244 (Ⓜ Taksim, ⓠKabataş, then funicular to Taksim) Named after the 18th-century stone *taksim* (water storage unit) on its western side, this square is the symbolic heart of modern İstanbul. Hardly a triumph of urban design, it has recently been closed to traffic and covered in unsightly concrete. The location of the 2013 Gezi protests, it is closely patrolled by police and is best avoided during demonstrations.

The **Atatürk Cultural Centre** (AKM, Atatürk Kültür Merkezi; Map p244; ⓠKabataş, then funicular to Taksim) on the square's eastern edge was designed by Hayati Tabanlioğlu in 1956–57 and appears to best advantage at night, when its elegant steel mesh is illuminated. It is currently closed for restoration.

The **Republic Monument** (Cumhuriyet Anıtı; Map p244000) in the centre of the square was created by Canonica, an Italian sculptor, in 1928. This features Atatürk, his assistant and successor, İsmet İnönü, and other revolutionary leaders.

Plans to redevelop Gezi Park on the northeast side of the square as a shopping mall were stalled after protests in May and

June 2013, and it is unclear whether the development will go ahead or not. Local activists stand firm in their opposition, citing it as one of many current instances of public space being sold off to private developers without proper public consultation or approval. The site, which has been a park since the early 1940s, was previously occupied by an Ottoman military barracks and is one of the few remaining public green spaces in Beyoğlu.

✖ EATING

As is the case in all big international cities, the dining scene in İstanbul can change at a fast and furious pace, meaning that what's hot one month can be closed due to lack of patrons the next. At the time of research there was lots of hype around high-end Beyoğlu restaurants such as Yenı Lokanta, Gaspar and Sekiz İstanbul that we can't in good conscience recommend – they are perfect examples of style triumphing over substance. What we do recommend are the many eateries in this part of town that take pride in serving traditional Turkish regional food or the growing number of casual places delivering clever modern rifts on old-fashioned favourites using locally sourced, seasonal produce.

✖ Galata, Tophane & Karaköy

★ KARAKÖY GÜLLÜOĞLU SWEETS, BÖREK €

Map p248 (www.karakoygulluoglu.com; Kemankeş Caddesi, Karaköy; portion baklava ₺5-10, portion börek ₺6-7; ☺8am-11pm; ⓠKaraköy) This Karaköy institution has been making customers deliriously happy and dentists obscenely rich since 1947. Head to the register and order a *porsiyon* (portion) of whatever baklava takes your fancy (*fıstıklı* is pistachio, *cevizli* walnut and *sade* plain), preferably with a glass of tea. Then hand your ticket over to the servers. The *börek* (filled pastry) here is good, too.

MAVRA CAFE, BAR €

Map p248 (☑212-252 7488; Serdar-ı Ekrem Caddesi 31a, Galata; breakfast ₺9-27, sandwiches & burgers ₺9-22, pastas ₺15-20; ☺9.30am-2am

Mon-Sat, till midnight Sun; Ⓜ Şişhane, 🚋 Karaköy, then funicular to Tünel) Serdar-ı Ekrem Caddesi is one of the most interesting streets in Galata, full of ornate 19th-century apartment blocks, avant-garde boutiques and mellow cafes. Mavra was the first of the cafes to open on the strip, and remains one of the best, offering simple food and drinks (caffè latte ₺6, beer ₺9) amid decor that is thrift-shop chic.

NAMLI
DELICATESSEN €

Map p248 (www.namligida.com.tr; Rıhtım Caddesi 1, Karaköy; ⊙7am-10pm; 🚶; 🚋 Karaköy) As well as being one of the best delicatessens in the city, Namlı offers a sit-down or takeaway selection of salad and mezes. There's another branch on **Harıcılar Caddesi** (Map p242; www.namlipastirma.com.tr; Hasırcılar Caddesi 14-16; ⊙6.30am-7pm Mon-Sat; 🚶; 🚋 Eminönü) next to the Spice Market in Eminönü.

AHESTE
CAFE €€

Map p248 (☎212-245 4345; www.ahestegalata. com; Serdar-ı Ekrem Caddesi 30, Galata; breakfast ₺9-21, soups ₺12-15, sandwiches ₺18-22; ⊙9am-midnight; Ⓜ Şişhane, 🚋 Karaköy) A perfect example of the casual, design-driven cafe model that has been trending in İstanbul over the past few years, Aheste is a small place that's equally alluring for breakfast, morn-

ing tea, lunch or dinner. The home-baked cakes and pastries are European-style and delicious, the perfect accompaniment to good Italian-style coffee. Meals are light and packed with flavour.

KARAKÖY LOKANTASI
TURKISH €€

Map p248 (☎212-292 4455; www.karakoylokan tasi.com; Kemankeş Caddesi 37a, Karaköy; mezes ₺8-18, portions ₺8-14, mains ₺19-25; ⊙noon-4pm & 6pm-midnight Mon-Sat, 6pm-midnight Sun; 🚶; 🚋 Karaköy) Known for its gorgeous tiled interior, genial owner and bustling vibe, Karaköy Lokantası serves tasty and well-priced food to its loyal local clientele. It functions as a *lokanta* (eatery serving ready-made food) during the day, but at night it morphs into a *meyhane* (tavern), with slightly higher prices. Bookings are essential for dinner.

CAFE PRIVATO
CAFE €€

Map p248 (☎212-293 2055; http://privatocafe. com; Tımarcı Sokak 3b; breakfast ₺30; ⊙9am-midnight; Ⓜ Şişhane, 🚋 Karaköy, then funicular to Tünel) This enclave off Galipdede Caddesi in Galata has been reinvented over the past couple of years, trading in its rough-and-ready heritage for up-to-the-minute casual-chic credentials. Privato is the best-loved of the new cafe arrivals and is well worth

BEYOĞLU EATING

BEYOĞLU'S HISTORIC FISH MARKET

Opposite the grandiose entrance to the 1868 Galatasaray Lycée, one of the city's most prestigious educational institutions, is the much-loved **Balık Pazarı** (Fish Market; Map p244; Şahne Sokak, off İstiklal Caddesi, Galatasaray; 🚋). At its entrance are stands selling *midye tava* (skewered mussels fried in hot oil), *kokoreç* (seasoned lamb or mutton intestines wrapped around a skewer and grilled over charcoal) and other snacks. Further inside are shops selling fish, caviar, fruit, vegetables and other produce; most of these are in Duduodaları Sokak on the left (southern) side of the market.

Many of the shops have been here for close on a century and have extremely loyal clienteles – check out **Sütte Şarküteri** (Map p244; ☎212-293 9292; Duduodaları Sokak 13; ⊙8am-10pm) for its delicious charcuterie, *kaymak* (clotted cream) and takeaway sandwiches; **Tarihi Beyoğlu Ekmek Fırını** (Map p244; Duduodaları Sokak 5) for fresh bread; **Üç Yıldız Şekerleme** (Map p244; ☎212-293 8170; www.ucyildizsekerleme.com; Duduodaları Sokak 7; ⊙7am-8.30pm Mon-Sat, 9am-6pm Sun) for jams, *lokum* (Turkish delight) and sweets; **Petek Turşuları** (Map p244; Duduodaları Sokak 6) for pickles; and **Reşat Balık Market** (Map p244; ☎212-293 6091; Sahne Sokak 30) for caviar and the city's best *lakerda* (strongly flavored salted bonito).

At 24a, look for the gigantic black doors to the courtyard of the **Üç Horan Ermeni Kilisesi** (Armenian Church of Three Altars; Map p244; Sahne Sokak 24a), which dates from 1838. Visitors can enter the church providing the doors are open. On the opposite side of the street is the neoclassical **Avrupa Pasajı** (European Passage; Map p244000), an attractive arcade full of shops that once sold antiques but now seem to stock little except tourist tat.

visiting for its *köy kahvaltası* (village breakfast) or for a drink (espresso and Turkish coffee, herbal tea, house-made *limonata*).

TARIHI KARAKÖY
BALIK LOKANTASI
FISH €€

Map p248 (📞212-243 4080; Kardeşim Sokak 30, Karaköy; fish soup ₺8, mains ₺20-38; ⊘noon-4pm Mon-Sat; 🚇Karaköy) Seafood is expensive in most of İstanbul's restaurants, so it's always a pleasure to sample the fresh and perfectly prepared fish dishes at this old-style fish restaurant in the run-down quarter behind the Karaköy Balıkcılar Çarşısı (Karaköy Fish Market). No frills, no alcohol, no dinner service. Don't get it mixed up with its far-more-expensive sibling, Tarihi Karaköy Balıkçısı Grifin.

KIVA HAN
ANATOLIAN €€

Map p248 (📞212-292 9898; www.galatakivahan. com; Galata Kulesi Meydanı 4, Galata; veg portions ₺12-18, meat portions ₺14-25; ⊘11am-11pm; 🖋; 🚇Karaköy) Located in the shadow of Galata Tower, this *lokanta* specialises in seasonal dishes from the different regions of Turkey. Make your choice of the daily dishes after inspecting the bain-marie. Seating is inside or on the *meydanı* (square).

LOKANTA MAYA
MODERN TURKISH €€€

Map p248 (📞212-252 6884; www.lokantamaya. com; Kemankeş Caddesi 35a, Karaköy; starters ₺16-28, mains ₺34-52; ⊘noon-5pm & 7-11pm Mon-Sat; 🖋; 🚇Karaköy) Critics and chowhounds alike adore the dishes created by chef Didem Şenol at her stylish restaurant near the Karaköy docks. The author of a successful cookbook focusing on Aegean cuisine, Didem's food is light, flavoursome, occasionally quirky and always assured. You'll need to book for dinner; lunch is cheaper and more casual.

İSTANBUL MODERN
CAFE/RESTAURANT
INTERNATIONAL €€€

Map p248 (📞212-292 2612; Meclis-i Mebusan Caddesi, Tophane; pizzas ₺25-37, pasta ₺25-43, mains ₺34-76; ⊘10am-midnight; 🖋; 🚇Tophane) The cafe/restaurant at İstanbul's pre-eminent contemporary art museum offers an 'industrial arty' vibe and great views over the Bosphorus when there are no cruise ships moored in front. The pasta is home-made, pizzas are Italian-style and there's a small (but less-impressive) range of modern Turkish dishes on offer, too. For a table on the terrace you'll need to book ahead.

✖ İstiklal & Around

ASMALI CANIM CIĞERIM
ANATOLIAN €

Map p248 (Minare Sokak 1, Asmalımescit; portion ₺22, half portion ₺14; 🚇Karaköy, then funicular to Tünel) The name means 'my soul, my liver', and this small place behind the Ali Hoca Türbesi specialises in grilled liver served with herbs, *ezme* (spicy tomato sauce) and grilled vegetables. If you can't bring yourself to eat offal, fear not – you can substitute the liver with lamb if you so choose. No alcohol, but *ayran* (yoghurt drink) is the perfect accompaniment.

İNCI PASTANESI
DESSERTS €

Map p244 (Mis Sokak 18; tea & dessert ₺10; ⊘7am-midnight; 🚇Karaköy, then funicular to Tünel) A Beyoğlu institution, İnci was forced out of its historic İstiklal Caddesi premises in 2012 but has reopened here and continues to delight devotees with its profiteroles covered in chocolate sauce. We're also particularly partial to the moist chocolate cake filled with candied fruit, but usually ask the staff to hold the chocolate topping.

HELVETIA LOKANTA
TURKISH €

Map p248 (General Yazgan Sokak 8-12, Asmalımescit; soup ₺6, portions ₺5-13; ⊘8am-10pm Mon-Sat; 🖋; Ⓜ Şişhane, 🚇Kabataş, then funicular to Tünel) This tiny *lokanta* is popular with locals (particularly of the vegetarian and vegan variety) who pop in here for inexpensive soups, salads and stews cooked fresh each day. No alcohol, and cash only.

★KLEMURI
ANATOLIAN €€

Map p244 (📞212-292 3272; www.klemuri.com; Büyük Parmakkapi Sokak 2; starters ₺8-12, mains ₺12-23; ⊘noon-11pm Mon-Sat; 🖋; ⓂTaksim, 🚇Kabataş, then funicular to Taksim) The Laz people hail from the Black Sea region, and their cuisine relies heavily on fish, kale and dairy products. One of only a few Laz restaurants in the city, Klemuri serves delicious home-style cooking in bohemian surrounds. There's a well-priced wine list, a dessert *(Laz böreği)* that has attained a cult following and interesting choices for vegetarians and vegans.

★ANTIOCHIA
ANATOLIAN €€

Map p248 (📞212-292 1100; www.antiochiacon cept.com; General Yazgan Sokak 3c, Asmalımescit; mezes ₺10-12, mains ₺18-28; ⊘lunch Mon-Fri, dinner Mon-Sat; 🚇Karaköy, then funicular to

CAFE CHAINS

In recent years the city's fashionable streets and shopping malls have been colonised by an ever-proliferating colony of concept cafes. With designer interiors, strong visual branding, international menus and reasonable prices, these chains have been embraced by young İstanbullus with alacrity, and are great places to spend an hour or so people-watching over a coffee, drink or meal. Look out for branches of the following:

House Cafe The most glamorous of them all, with interiors by the uber-fashionable Autoban architectural group, menus by Australian/UK-trained chef Coşkun Uysal and prominent locations, including İstiklal Caddesi, Teşvikiye Caddesi in **Nişantası** (Teşvikiye Caddesi 146; M Osmanbey), Sofyalı Sokak in **Asmalımescit** (Map p248; www. thehousecafe.com.tr; Sofyalı Sokak; ☑; ☒ Karaköy, then funicular Taksim), İskele Meydanı on the Bosphorus, and in the Kanyon and İstinye Park shopping malls. Best branch: **İskele Meydanı** (Map p250; İskele Meydanı 42; breakfast platters ₺24, sandwiches ₺15-26, pizzas ₺17.50-27.50, mains ₺16.50-29.50; ☺9am-1am Mon-Thu, to 2am Fri & Sat, to 10.30pm Sun; ☒ Kabataş Lisesi) – go for the Sunday brunch.

Kitchenette House-baked bread and pastries are the hallmarks of these popular outfits, which are found in locations such as **Taksim** (Map p244; www.kitchenette.com. tr; Tak-ı Zafer Caddesi 3; ☒ Kabataş, then funicular to Taksim), **Ortaköy** (Map p250; cnr Eski Vapur İslelesi & Sağlık Sokaks, Ortaköy; ☒ Kabataş Lisesi) and the Kanyon shopping mall. Best branch: Bebek, which occupies all three floors of a stunning art deco building opposite the Bebek ferry dock.

Midpoint A laid-back West Coast American feel is evident at these mall-style diners, which feature sleek but anonymous interiors and huge menus, featuring wraps, salads, crepes, burgers and quesadillas. Best branch: **İstiklal Caddesi** (Map p248; www.midpoint.com.tr; İstiklal Caddesi 187; ☒ Karaköy, then funicular Tünel), which has a terrace complete with Bosphorus view.

Tünel) Dishes from the southeastern city of Antakya (Hatay) are the speciality at this foodie destination. Mezes are dominated by wild thyme, pomegranate syrup, olives, walnuts and tangy home-made yoghurt, and the kebaps are equally flavoursome – try the succulent *şiş et* (grilled lamb) or *dürüm* (wrap filled with minced meat, onions and tomatoes). There's a discount at lunch.

★ZÜBEYIR OCAKBAŞI
KEBAPS ₺₺

Map p244 (☑212-293 3951; Bekar Sokak 28; meze ₺7-9, kebaps ₺22-45; ☺noon-1am; ☒ Kabataş, then funicular to Taksim) Every morning the chefs at this popular *ocakbaşı* (grill house) prepare fresh, top-quality meats to be grilled over their handsome copper-hooded barbecues that night: spicy chicken wings and Adana kebaps, flavoursome ribs, pungent liver kebaps and well-marinated lamb *şiş kebaps*. Their offerings are famous throughout the city, so booking a table is essential.

ÇUKUR MEYHANE
TURKISH ₺₺

Map p244 (☑212-244 5575; Kartal Sokak 1; mezes ₺7-16, mains ₺12-17; ☺noon-1am Mon-Sat; ☑; M Taksim, ☒ Kabataş, then funicular to Taksim)

Despite their long and much-vaunted tradition in the city, it is becoming increasingly difficult to find *meyhanes* serving good food. Standards have dropped in many of our old favourites (sob!), and we are constantly on the search for replacements. Fortunately, Çukur fits the bill. On offer are a convivial atmosphere, great food and relatively cheap prices. Book ahead on weekends.

ENSTİTÜ
CAFE, RESTAURANT ₺₺

Map p244 (www.istanbulculinary.com; Meşrutiyet Caddesi 59, Tepebaşı; starters ₺10-20, mains ₺15-30; ☺7.30am-10pm Mon-Fri, 10am-10pm Sat; ☑; M Şişhane, ☒ Karaköy, then funicular to Tünel) This chic but casual venue would be equally at home in Soho, Seattle or Sydney. A training venue for the **İstanbul Culinary Institute** (Enstitü; Map p244; ☑212-251 2214; www. istanbulculinary.com; Meşrutiyet Caddesi 59, Tepebaşı), it offers freshly baked cakes and pastries, a limited lunch menu that changes daily and a more-sophisticated dinner menu that makes full use of seasonal products. Prices are a steal considering the quality of the food.

GRAM
MODERN TURKISH €€

Map p248 (☎212-243 1048; www.grampera.com; Meşrutiyet Caddesi 107, Asmalımescit; soup ₺11, small/large salad plate ₺16/25, mains ₺22-33; ⊙10.30am-6.30pm Mon-Fri, 10.30am-6.30pm Sat; ⓂŞişhane, 🚇Karaköy, then funicular to Tünel) London has Ottolenghi, İstanbul has Gram. This pocket-sized place in fashionable Asmalımescit embraces the open kitchen concept and serves its daily changing menu of fresh and healthy dishes to a coterie of ultra-loyal regulars. Arrive early at lunchtime to claim a place at the shared tables in the rear kitchen/dining room. We love the self-service salad spread.

ASMALI CAVIT
TURKISH €€

Map p248 (Asmalı Meyhane; ☎212-292 4950; Asmalımescit Sokak 16, Asmalımescit; mezes ₺6-20, mains ₺18-24; 🍷; ⓂŞişhane, 🚇Karaköy, then funicular to Tünel) Cavit Saatcı's place is an old-style *meyhane* that, like other old-timers on this street, has stood the test of time and retained a local following. The menu offers all the usual dishes (mezes, fried calamari, *börek* stuffed with meat, fried liver, kebaps). Bookings essential.

KAFE ARA
CAFE €€

Map p244 (Tosbağ Sokak 8a, Galatasaray; sandwiches ₺16-22, salads ₺16-25; ⊙7.30am-midnight Mon-Thu, to 1am Fri & Sat, to 10pm Sun; 🍷; ⓂŞişhane, 🚇Kabataş, then funicular to Taksim) This casual cafe is named after its owner, legendary local photographer Ara Güler. It occupies a converted garage with tables and chairs spilling out into a wide laneway opposite the Galatasaray Lycée and serves an array of well-priced salads, sandwiches and Turkish staples such as *köfte* (meatballs) and *sigara böreği* (pastries filled with cheese and potato). No alcohol.

SOFYALI 9
TURKISH €€

Map p248 (☎212-252 3810; www.sofyali.com.tr; Sofyalı Sokak 9, Asmalımescit; mezes ₺4-18, mains ₺15-30; ⊙noon-1am; 🍷; ⓂŞişhane, 🚇Karaköy, then funicular to Tünel) Tables at this *meyhane* are hot property on a Friday or Saturday night, and no wonder. The food is tasty, and the atmosphere convivial. Stick to mezes rather than ordering mains – choose cold dishes from the waiter's tray and order hot ones from the menu – the *kalamar* (calamari) and *Anavut ciğeri* (Albanian fried liver) are delicious.

ÇOKÇOK
THAI €€

Map p244 (☎212-292 6496; www.cokcok.com.tr; Meşrutiyet Caddesi 51, Tepebaşı; starters ₺16-33, salads ₺17-32, mains, ₺17-40; ⊙6-11.30pm Mon, noon-11.30pm Tue-Sun; 🍷; ⓂŞişhane, 🚇Kabataş, then funicular to Tünel) The fragrances of lemongrass, coriander (cilantro) and kaffir-lime lure diners into this sleek restaurant on Tepebaşı's main drag. Huge servings of dishes from the classic Thai repertoire go down well with a Tiger or Efes beer. It's one of the best Asian restaurants in the city, so book ahead to be sure of a table.

★MEZE BY LEMON TREE
MODERN TURKISH €€€

Map p248 (☎212-252 8302; www.mezze.com.tr; Meşrutiyet Caddesi 83b, Tepebaşı; mezes ₺10-30, 4-course degustation menu for 2 people ₺160; ⊙7-11pm; 🍷; ⓂŞişhane, 🚇Karaköy, then funicular to Tünel) Chef Gençay Üçok creates some of the most interesting – and delicious – modern Turkish food seen in the city and serves it in an intimate restaurant opposite the Pera Palace Hotel. We suggest opting for the degustation menu or sticking to the wonderful mezes here rather than ordering mains. Bookings essential.

DUBLE MEZE BAR
MODERN TURKISH €€€

Map p248 (☎212-244 0188; www.dublemezebar.com; 7th fl, Meşrutiyet Caddesi 85; cold mezes ₺10-18, hot mezes ₺16-40; ⊙6pm-2am; 🍷; ⓂŞişhane, 🚇Karaköy, then funicular to Taksim) Commanding expansive Golden Horn views from its location atop the Palazzo Donizetti Hotel, Duble is an exciting modern take on the traditional *meyhane* experience. On sultry nights, local glamour pusses love nothing better than claiming a designer chair in the glass-sheathed dining space, ordering a cocktail and grazing the menu of 35 different mezes.

MIKLA
MODERN TURKISH €€€

Map p248 (☎212-293 5656; www.miklarestaurant.com; Marmara Pera Hotel, Meşrutiyet Caddesi 15, Tepebaşı; prix fixe à la carte dinner menu ₺160; ⊙6-11.30pm Mon-Sat; ⓂŞişhane, 🚇Karaköy, then funicular to Tünel) Local celebrity chef Mehmet Gürs is a master of Mod Med, and the Turkish accents on the menu here make his food memorable. Extraordinary views, luxe surrounds and professional service complete the experience. In summer be sure to have a drink at the rooftop bar beforehand.

DELICATESSAN   RESTAURANT, BAR €€€
Map p248 (☑212-244 8454; www.delicatessen
istanbul.com; Oteller Sokak 10, Asmalımescit;
starters ₺13-30, sandwiches ₺28-33, mains ₺25-
50; ☑; M Şişhane, ☒ Karaköy, then funicular
to Tünel) Owner Elif Yalın runs this new
bar-cafe-restaurant in Asmalımescit with
charm and competence. The front bar is
definitely a place to party (great cocktails
and a hugely popular 'bar bite Thursday')
but the rear restaurant is more restrained.
The menu is modern Mediterranean with
Turkish accents; servings are generous and
there's an impressive wine list.

HACI ABDULLAH   LOKANTA €€€
Map p244 (www.haciabdullah.com.tr; Sakız
Ağacı Caddesi 9a; veg portions ₺14-25, meat
portions ₺26-47; ☺noon-10.30pm; ☑; M Taksim, ☒ Kabataş, then funicular to Taksim) This
upmarket İstanbul institution (it was established in 1888) serves a good range of
hazır yemek (ready-made food). There's no
alcohol, but the range of delicious desserts
(try the quince dessert with clotted cream)
well and truly compensates. Come for lunch
rather than dinner and be prepared for
the double-whammy of cover and service
charges.

✖ Çukurcuma & Cihangir

DATLI MAYA   BAKERY €
Map p248 (www.datlimaya.com; Türkgücü Caddesi 59, Cihangir; cakes & pastries ₺2-5; ☺8am-
10pm; M Taksim, ☒ Kabataş, then funicular to
Taksim) A tiny cafe-bakery located behind
the Firuz Ağa Mosque in Cihangir, Datlı
Maya is as popular as it is fashionable.
The old wood-fired oven produces cakes,
lahmacuns (Arabic pizzas), pides (Turkish-
style pizza), *böreks* and breads, all of which
can be taken away or enjoyed in the tiny upstairs dining area.

JOURNEY   INTERNATIONAL, CAFE €€
Map p248 (☑212-244 8989; www.journeycihang
ir.com; Akarsu Yokuşu 21, Cihangir; breakfast ₺14-
25, sandwiches ₺16-19, mains ₺16-39; ☺9am-
2am; ☑; M Taksim, ☒ Kabataş, then funicular
to Taksim) This classy lounge cafe located
in the expat enclave of Cihangir serves
a great range of Mediterranean comfort
foods, including sandwiches, soups, pizzas
and pastas. Most of the dishes use organic
produce, there's a thoughtful wine list, and

vegetarian and vegan options are on offer.
The crowd is 30-something and the ambience is laid-back.

SOCIAL   RESTAURANT, BAR €€
Map p244 (☑212-293 3040; Sıraselviler Caddesi
72, Cihangir; salads ₺18-25, pasta ₺17-32, burgers ₺21-24; ☺8am-3.30am; ☎☑; M Taksim,
☒ Kabataş, then tram to Taksim) The spacious
courtyard at the rear of this hipster hang-
out is the main draw, but the food provides
strong backup. A huge menu features fresh
and delicious salads, authentic burgers, and
an array of sandwiches, pastas and pizzas.
Patrons drink everything from coffee to
cocktails, and particularly enjoy the party
vibe on Friday and Saturday nights.

JASH   ANATOLIAN €€
Map p248 (☑212-244 3042; www.jashistan bul.
com; Cihangir Caddesi 9, Cihangir; mezes ₺9-
22, mains ₺22-45; ☺noon-11pm; M Taksim,
☒ Kabataş, then funicular to Taksim) Armenian
specialities such as *topik* (a cold meze made
with chickpeas, pistachios, onion, flour,
currants, cumin and salt) make an appearance on the menu of this bijou *meyhane*
in trendy Cihangir. Come on the weekend,
when an accordian player entertains diners and unusual dishes including *harisa*
(chicken with a hand-forged wheat and butter sauce) are on offer.

DEMETI   TURKISH €€
Map p248 (☑212-244 0628; www.demeti.com.tr;
Şimşirci Sokak 6; mezes ₺8-20, mains
₺16-25; ☺4pm-2am Mon-Sat; ☑; M Taksim,
☒ Kabataş, then funicular to Taksim) This modern *meyhane* has a friendly feel and simple
but stylish decor. Reservations are a must if
you want one of the four tables on the terrace, which have an unimpeded Bosphorus
view. There's occasional live music.

KAHVE 6   CAFE €€
Map p248 (☑212-293 0849; Anahtar Sokak 13,
Cihangir; breakfast ₺11-19, sandwiches ₺10-19,
pastas ₺15-19; ☺9am-10pm; ☎☑; M Taksim,
☒ Kabataş, then funicular to Taksim) An expat
haven in Cihangir, Kahve Altı (Coffee 6)
has a pretty interior salon where patrons
take advantage of free wi-fi and a popular
rear courtyard where groups of friends ren-
dezvous. The menu is simple but deserves
kudos for its emphasis on local, natural
and seasonal produce (often organic). No
alcohol.

🍷 DRINKING & NIGHTLIFE

There are hundreds of bars in Beyoğlu, with the major bar strips being Balo, Nevizade and Sofyalı Sokaks. As a rule, drinks are much cheaper at street-level venues than at rooftop bars. Note that many of the Beyoğlu clubs close over the warmer months (June to September), when the party crowd moves down to Turkey's southern coasts. We've listed some popular gay bars and clubs; for other options, check the dedicated pages in the monthly *Time Out İstanbul* (www. timeoutistanbul.com/en/) magazine.

🍸 Galata, Tophane & Karaköy

★TOPHANE NARGILE CAFES   CAFE
Map p248 (off Necatibey Caddesi, Tophane; ⊙24hr; ☐Tophane) This atmospheric row of nargile cafes behind the Nusretiye Mosque is always packed with locals enjoying tea, nargile and snacks. Follow your nose to find it – the smell of apple tobacco is incredibly enticing. It costs around ₺50 for a 'VIP package' (tea, one nargile and some snacks to share) or around ₺25 for tea and nargile only.

★KARABATAK   CAFE
Map p248 (⌀212-243 6993; www.karabatak.com; Kara Ali Kaptan Sokak 7, Karaköy; ⊙8.30am-10pm Mon-Fri, 9.30am-10pm Sat & Sun; ☐Tophane) Hipster central for caffeine fans, Karabatak imports Julius Meinl coffee from Vienna and uses it to conjure up some of the city's best coffee. The outside seating is hotly contested, but the quiet tables inside can be just as alluring. Take your choice from filter, espresso or Turkish brews and order a panino (filled bread roll) or sandwich if you're hungry.

★DEM   TEAHOUSE
Map p248 (⌀212-293 9792; www.demkarakoy. com; Hoca Tahsin Sokak 17, Karaköy; ⊙10am-10pm; ☐Tophane) We have witnessed long-term expat residents of İstanbul fight back tears as they read the menu at Dem. Their reaction had nothing to do with the price list (which is very reasonable) and everything to do with the joy of choosing from 60 types of freshly brewed tea, all served in fine china cups and with milk on request.

A selection of panini, wraps, cakes and scones is also on offer, and everything is served on streetside tables or under the ultrachic Zettel'z 5 lightfitting in the main space.

★UNTER   BAR
Map p248 (⌀212 244-5151; http://unter.com.tr; Kara Ali Kaptan Sokak 4, Karaköy; ⊙9am-midnight Tue-Thu & Sun, till 2am Fri & Sat; ☐Tophane) This scenester-free zone epitomises the new Karaköy style: it's glam without trying too hard, and has a vaguely arty vibe. The ground-floor windows open to the street in fine weather, allowing the action to spill outside during busy periods. Good cocktails and a wine list strong in boutique Thracian drops are major draws, as is the varied food menu.

FERAHFEZA   BAR, RESTAURANT
Map p248 (⌀212-243 5154; 5th fl, Kemankeş Caddesi 31, Karaköy; ⊙5pm-2am Mon-Sat; ☐Tophane) Perched on the top floor of İstanbul's Architectural Institute and boasting an appropriately stylish decor, FerahFeza is best known as a restaurant, but we've found the food overpriced and underwhelming on our visits. Instead, we recommend heading here on Thursday nights after 9pm when multigenerational ensembles perform jazz sets that delight the decidedly design-driven crowd.

X BAR   BAR
Map p248 (7th fl, İstanbul Foundation for Culture & Arts, Sadı Konuralp Caddesi 5, Şişhane; ⊙noon-midnight Mon-Sat; ⓜŞişhane, ☐Karaköy, then funicular to Tünel) High culture meets serious glamour on the top floor of the İstanbul Foundation for Culture and Arts (İKSV) building. Our meals here haven't been worth their hefty price tags, so we suggest limiting yourself to a sunset aperitif or two – the Golden Horn view is simply extraordinary and there's a good list of wines by the glass.

ATÖLYE KULEDIBI   BAR
Map p248 (Galata Kulesi Sokak 4, Galata; ⊙noon-midnight Mon-Thu, to 2am Fri & Sat; ⓜŞişhane, ☐Karaköy, then funicular to Tünel) Good music (sometimes live jazz) and a welcoming atmosphere characterise this bohemian place near Galata Tower.

SENSUS WINE BAR   WINE BAR
Map p248 (www.sensuswine.com; Büyük Hendek Sokak 5, Galata; ⊙10am-11pm; ⓜŞişhane,

Karaköy, then funicular to Tünel) Set in a stone basement lined with wine bottles, this bar underneath the Anemon Galata Hotel has a great concept, but needs to work on its customer service. There are close to 300 bottles of local wine to choose from.

♥ İstiklal & Around

★MIKLA
BAR

Map p248 (www.miklarestaurant.com; Marmara Pera Hotel, Meşrutiyet Caddesi 15, Tepebaşı; ⊗from 6pm Mon-Sat summer only; ⓂŞişhane, Karaköy, then funicular to Tünel) It's worth overlooking the occasional uppity service at this stylish rooftop bar to enjoy what could well be the best view in İstanbul. After a few drinks, consider moving downstairs to eat in the classy restaurant.

★360
BAR

Map p244 (www.360istanbul.com; 8th fl, İstiklal Caddesi 163; ⊗noon-2am Sun-Thu, to 4am Fri & Sat; ⓂŞişhane, Karaköy, then funicular to Tünel) İstanbul's most famous bar, and deservedly so. If you can score one of the bar stools on the terrace you'll be happy indeed – the view is truly extraordinary. It morphs into a club after midnight on Friday and Saturday, when a cover charge of around ₺40 applies.

INDIGO
CLUB

Map p244 (http://indigo-istanbul.com; 1st-5th fl, Mısır Apt, 309 Akarsu Sokak, Galatasaray; ⊗10pm-5am Fri & Sat, closed summer; ⓂTaksim, Kabataş, then funicular to Taksim) This is Beyoğlu's electronic music temple and dance-music enthusiasts congregate here on weekends for their energetic kicks. The program spotlights top-notch local and visiting DJs or live acts.

BAYLO
BAR, RESTAURANT

Map p248 (www.baylo.com.tr; Meşrutiyet Caddesi 107a, Tepebaşı; ⊗6.30pm-1am Tue-Thu, to 2.30am Fri & Sat; ⓂŞişhane, Karaköy, then funicular to Tünel) In recent years the lower section of Asmalımescit has undergone a huge transformation. Glamour rules rather than grunge, and this bar is a perfect example. The elegant interior provides a perfect backdrop for the 30-something bankers, architects and other professionals who head here after a busy day at the office.

MANDA BATMAZ
COFFEEHOUSE

Map p244 (Olivia Geçidi 1a, off İstiklal Caddesi; ⊗9.30am-midnight; ⓂŞişhane, Karaköy, then funicular to Tünel) He's been working at this tiny coffeehouse for two decades, so Cemil Pilik really knows his stuff when it comes to making Turkish coffee. The name translates as 'so thick that even a water buffalo won't sink in it', and Cemil's brew is indeed as viscous as it is smooth.

HAZZO PULO ÇAY BAHÇESI
TEA GARDEN

Map p244 (Tarihi Hazzo Pulo Pasaji, off İstiklal Caddesi; ⊗9am-midnight; ⓂŞişhane, Karaköy, then funicular to Tünel) There aren't as many traditional teahouses in Beyoğlu as there are on the Historic Peninsula, so this picturesque cobbled courtyard full of makeshift stools and tables is beloved of local 20-somethings. Order from the waiter and then pay at the small cafe near the narrow arcade entrance.

OFF PERA
CLUB

Map p248 (Gönül Sokak 14a, Asmalımescit; ⊗10pm-4am Tue-Sat; ⓂŞişhane, Karaköy, then funicular to Tünel) You'll need to squeeze your way into this tiny club, but once inside your persistence is sure to pay off. The DJs perch on a balcony over the bar and the multi-aged crowd spills out onto the street to smoke and catch its breath. Go on a Tuesday night, when Turkish pop dominates the sound system after midnight.

LEB-I DERYA
BAR, RESTAURANT

Map p248 (www.lebiderya.com; 6th fl, Kumbaracı Yokuşu 57, Galata; ⊗4pm-2am Mon-Thu, to 3am Fri, 10am-3am Sat, to 2am Sun; ⓂŞişhane, Karaköy, then funicular to Tünel) On the top floor of a dishevelled building off İstiklal, Leb-i Derya has wonderful views across to the Old City and down the Bosphorus, meaning that seats on the small outdoor terrace or at the bar are highly prized. Note that the venue can close early on quiet winter nights.

LEB-I DERYA RICHMOND
BAR, RESTAURANT

Map p248 (☎212-243 4375; www.lebiderya.com; 6th fl, Richmond Hotel, İstiklal Caddesi 227; ⊗11am-2am Mon-Thu, to 3am Fri, 10am-3am Sat, 10am-2am Sun; ⓂŞişhane, Karaköy, then funicular to Tünel) Perched on an upper floor of the Richmond Hotel, the sleek younger sister of perennial favourite Leb-i Derya is a good spot for a late-night drink. The crowd here is dominated by visitors to the city, who love the Bosphorus and Old City vistas framed by the huge windows.

MÜNFERIT
BAR, RESTAURANT

Map p248 (☎212-252 5067; Yeniçarşı Caddesi 19, Galatasaray; ☺7am-1am Mon-Sat; ⓂTaksim, ⓀKabataş, then funicular to Taksim) This upmarket bar-restaurant designed by the Autoban Design Partnership is among the most glamorous watering holes in town. Though the restaurant's pricey take on nouvelle *meyhane* food lacks assurance, the bar is fabulous, serving expertly made cocktails and good wine by the glass to a formidably fashionable crowd who often ends up dancing the night away.

NUTERAS
BAR, RESTAURANT

Map p248 (www.nupera.com.tr/nuteras; 6th fl, NuPera Bldg, Meşrutiyet Caddesi 67, Tepebaşı; ☺noon-1am Mon-Thu, noon-4am Fri & Sat summer only; ⓂŞişhane, ⓀKaraköy, then funicular to Tünel) This bar-restaurant attracts a fashionable crowd to the rooftop terrace of the NuPera Building. Its Golden Horn view is spectacular and the after-dinner club scene is trés chic.

LITERA
BAR, RESTAURANT

Map p244 (www.literarestaurant.com; 5th fl, Yenicarşı Caddesi 32, Galatasaray; ☺11am-4am; ⓂŞişhane, ⓀKaraköy, then funicular to Tünel) Occupying the 5th floor of a handsome building downhill from Galatasaray Meydanı, Litera revels in its extraordinary views of the Old City, Asian side and Bosphorus, and has an outdoor terrace. It hosts plenty of cultural events, as befits its location in the Goethe Institut building.

URBAN
BAR

Map p244 (www.urbanbeyoglu.com; Kartal Sokak 6a, Galatasaray; ☺11am-1am; ⓂTaksim, ⓀKabataş, then funicular to Taksim) A tranquil bolthole in the midst of İstiklal's mayhem, Urban is where the preclub crowd congregates at night and where many of them can be found kicking back over a coffee during the day. The vaguely Parisienne interior is a clever balance of grunge and glamour.

LOVE DANCE POINT
GAY

(☎212-232 5683; www.lovedp.net; Cumhuriyet Caddesi 349, Harbiye; ☺11.30pm-5am Fri & Sat; ⓂTaksim or Osmanbey) Well into its second decade, LDP is easily the most Europhile of the local gay venues, hosting gay musical icons and international circuit parties. Hardcutting techno is thrown in with gay anthems and Turkish pop. This place attracts the well travelled and the unimpressionable, as well as straight hipsters from nearby Nişantaşı.

CLUB 17
GAY

Map p244 (Zambak Sokak 17; ☺11pm-5am; ⓂTaksim, ⓀKabataş, then funicular to Taksim) Rent boys outnumber regulars at this narrow bar. At closing time the crowd spills out onto the street to make final hook-up attempts possible. It's quiet during the week but jampacked late on Friday and Saturday.

BIGUDI
GAY

Map p244 (terrace fl, Mis Sokak 5; ☺10.30pm-5am Sat; ⓂTaksim, ⓀKabataş, then funicular to Taksim) The city's only lesbian club is open for one night only and is resolutely off-limits to non-females. To find it, look for the Dizzel Bar on the ground floor and then head upstairs. The **Şarlo Cafe Pub** (Map p244; 5th fl, Mis Sokak 5; ☺4pm-1am; ⓂTaksim, ⓀKabataş, then funicular to Taksim) on the 5th floor is open to women, men and the transgendered, and offers special events including a queer tango night every second Wednesday.

ARAF
CLUB

Map p244 (www.araf.com.tr; 5th fl, Balo Sokak 32; ☺5pm-4am Tue-Sun; ⓂTaksim, ⓀKabataş, then funicular to Taksim) Grungy English teachers, Erasmus exchange students and Turkish-language students have long claimed this as their favoured destination, listening to world music and swilling some of the cheapest club beer in the city. Wednesday night is comedy night.

🍷 Çukurcuma & Cihangir

⭐MINIMÜZIKHOL
CLUB

Map p244 (MMH; ☎212-245 1718; www.minimuzikhol.com; Soğancı Sokak 7, Cihangir; ☺10pm-late Wed-Sat; ⓂTaksim, ⓀKabataş, then funicular to Taksim) The mothership for inner-city hipsters, MMH is a small, slightly grungy venue near Taksim that hosts the best dance party in town on weekends and live sets by local and international musicians midweek. It's best after 1am.

KIKI
BAR, CLUB

Map p244 (☎212-243 5306; www.kiki.com.tr; Sıraselviler Caddesi 42, Cihangir; ☺6pm-2am Mon-Wed, to 4am Thu-Sat; ⓂTaksim, ⓀKabataş, then funicular to Taksim) Kiki has a loyal clientele who enjoys its burgers and drinks, but mainly comes for the music (DJs and live sets). Regulars tend to head to the rear courtyard. There's a second branch in Ortaköy (p146).

CIHANGIR 21 · BAR

Map p248 (☏212-251 1626; Coşkun Sokak 21, Cihangir; ⊙9am-2.30am; Ⓜ Taksim, 🚡 Kabataş, then funicular to Taksim) The great thing about this neighbourhood place is its inclusiveness – the regulars include black-clad boho types, besuited professionals, expat loafers and quite a few characters who defy categorisation. There's beer on tap (Efes and Miller), a smokers' section and a bustling feel after work hours; it's quite laid-back during the day.

5 KAT · BAR, RESTAURANT

Map p244 (www.5kat.com; 5th fl, Soğancı Sokak 7, Cihangir; ⊙5pm-1am Mon-Fri, 11am-1am Sat & Sun; Ⓜ Taksim, 🚡 Kabataş) This İstanbul institution has been around for over two decades and is a great alternative for those who can't stomach the style overload at many of the high-profile Beyoğlu bars. In winter drinks are served in the boudoir-style bar on the 5th floor; in summer action moves to the outdoor roof terrace. Both have great Bosphorus views.

SMYRNA · BAR

Map p248 (Akarsu Yokuşu 29, Cihangir; ⊙9am-2am; Ⓜ Taksim, 🚡 Kabataş, then funicular to Taksim) The original boho bar on Cihangir's main entertainment strip, Smyrna has a relaxed atmosphere, retro decor and a self-consciously liter-arty clientele. If you decide to make a night of it here (and many do), there's simple food available.

WHITE MILL · BAR

Map p248 (☏212-292 2895; www.whitemill cafe.com; Susam Sokak 13, Cihangir; ⊙9.30am-1.30am; Ⓜ Taksim, 🚡 Kabataş, then funicular to Taksim) Forget the hard-edged interior – the draw here is the leafy rear garden, which is a perfect place to while away a lazy summer afternoon or evening and is super-popular for weekend brunch. The chefs here were early converts to the locovore/organic movement and work hard to keep the faith.

TEK YÖN · GAY

Map p244 (1st fl, Siraselviler Caddesi 63, Taksim; ⊙10pm-4am; Ⓜ Taksim, 🚡 Kabataş, then funicular to Taksim) This sleek premises features the city's largest gay dance floor as well as a garden popular with smokers and cruisers. The core clientele is hirsute and fashion-challenged (and that includes the drag queens). Cuddly bears abound.

☆ ENTERTAINMENT

☆ Galata, Tophane & Karaköy

SALON · LIVE MUSIC

Map p248 (☏212-334 0752; www.saloniksv.com; ground fl, İstanbul Foundation for Culture & Arts, Sadi Konuralp Caddesi 5, Şişhane; ⊙Oct-May; Ⓜ Şişhane, 🚡 Karaköy, then funicular to Tünel) This intimate performance space in the İstanbul Foundation for Culture & Arts (İKSV) building hosts live contemporary music (classical, jazz, rock, alternative and world music) as well as theatrical and dance performances; check the website for program and booking details. Before or after the show, consider having a drink at X Bar (p134), in the same building.

NARDIS JAZZ CLUB · JAZZ

Map p248 (☏212-244 6327; www.nardisjazz.com; Kuledibi Sokak 14, Galata; ⊙9.30pm-12.30am Mon-Thu, 10.30pm-1.30am Fri & Sat, closed Aug; Ⓜ Şişhane, 🚡 Karaköy) Named after a Miles Davis track, this intimate venue near the Galata Tower is run by jazz guitarist Önder Focan and his wife Zuhal. Performers include gifted amateurs, local jazz luminaries and visiting international artists. It's small, so you'll need to book if you want a decent table.

NUBLU İSTANBUL · JAZZ

Map p248 (☏212-249 7712; www.nubluistanbul. net; Gradiva Hotel, Voyvoda Sokak 2/1, Karaköy; ⊙10pm-3am Wed-Sun Oct-May; 🚡 Karaköy) This ultra-cool basement venue in the Gradiva Hotel is run by – or at least in association with – New York–based jazz saxophonist and composer, İlhan Ersahin. It closes during summer, but has a busy and never predictable program for the rest of the year. Check the club's website or Facebook page for what's on.

☆ İstiklal & Around

★BABYLON · LIVE MUSIC, CLUB

Map p248 (www.babylon.com.tr; Şehbender Sokak 3, Asmalımescit; ⊙lounge from 5pm, club from 8.30pm from 10.30pm Fri & Sat, closed summer; Ⓜ Şişhane, 🚡 Karaköy, then funicular to Tünel) İstanbul's pre-eminent live-music venue has been packing the crowds in since 1999 and shows no sign of losing its mojo.

The eclectic program often features big-name international music acts, particularly during the festival season. Most of the action occurs in the club, but there's also a lounge with DJ; access this from Jurnal Sokak.

MUNZUR CAFE & BAR
LIVE MUSIC

Map p244 (☑212-245 4669; www.munzurcafebar. com; Hasnun Galip Sokak 17, Galatasaray; ☺1pm-4am, music from 9pm; Ⓜ Taksim, ⓐKabataş, then funicular to Taksim) Hasnun Galip Sokak in Galatasaray is home to a number of *Türkü evleri*, Kurdish-owned bars where musicians perform live, emotion-charged *halk meziği* (folk music). This simple place, which is two decades old, has stood the test of time and is well worth a visit. It has a great line-up of singers and expert *bağlama* (lute) players.

GARAJISTANBUL
CULTURAL CENTRE

Map p244 (☑212-244 4499; www.garajistanbul. org; Kaymakem Reşet Bey Sokak 11a, Galatasaray; Ⓜ Şişhane, ⓐKabataş, then funicular to Tünel) This performance space occupies a former parking garage in a narrow street behind İstiklal Caddesi and is about as edgy as the city's performance scene gets. It hosts contemporary dance performances, poetry readings, theatrical performances and live jazz.

JOLLY JOKER
LIVE MUSIC

Map p244 (www.jjistanbul.com; Balo Sokak 22; ☺from 10pm Wed-Sat, closed summer; Ⓜ Taksim, ⓐKabataş, then funicular to Taksim) The gig-goers among the lively multinational crowd here gravitate towards the upstairs bilevel performance hall, which hosts Turkish rock, alternative and pop outfits. Check the website for schedules and cover charges.

🛍 SHOPPING

🛍 Galata & Tophane

★ HIÇ
HOMEWARES, HANDICRAFTS

Map p248 (☑212-251 9973; www.hiccrafts.com; Lüleci Hendek Caddesi 35, Tophane; ☺10.30am-7pm Mon-Sat; Ⓜ Şişhane, ⓐTophane) Interior designer Emel Güntaş is one of İstanbul's style icons, and this recently opened contemporary crafts shop in Tophane is a favourite destination for the city's design mavens. The stock includes cushions, carpets, kilims (pileless woven rugs), silk scarves, lamps, furniture, glassware, porcelain and felt crafts. Everything here is artisan-made and absolutely gorgeous.

İKSV TASARIM MAĞAZASI
JEWELLERY, HOMEWARES

Map p248 (İKSV Gift Shop; ☑212-334 0830; www.iksvtasarim.com; İstanbul Foundation for Culture & Arts, Sadi Konuralp Caddesi 5, Şişhane; ☺10am-7pm Mon-Sat; Ⓜ Şişhane, ⓐKaraköy, then funicular to Tünel) A secret to sourcing a great souvenir of your trip to İstanbul? Ignore the mass-produced junk sold in many shops around the city and instead head to a museum or gallery store like this one. Run by the İstanbul Foundation for Culture & Arts (İKSV), it sells jewellery, ceramics and glassware designed and made by local artisans.

İSTANBUL MODERN GIFT SHOP
GIFTS

Map p248 (www.istanbulmodern.org; Meclis-i Mebusan Caddesi, Tophane; ☺10am-6pm Tue, Wed & Fri-Sun, 10am-8pm Thu; ⓐTophane) It's often difficult to source well-priced souvenirs and gifts to take home, but this stylish shop in the İstanbul Modern gallery boasts plenty of options. It stocks T-shirts, CDs, stationery, coffee mugs, homewares, jewellery and cute gifts for kids.

OLD SANDAL
SHOES

Map p248 (☑212-292 8647; www.oldsandal.com. tr; Serdar-ı Ekrem Sokak 10a, Galata; ☺11am-7.30pm; Ⓜ Şişhane, ⓐKaraköy, then funicular to Tünel) Owning a pair of Hülya Samancı's handmade shoes, boots or sandals is high on many local wishlists. Pop into this tiny store in the shadow of the Galata Tower to admire these 100% leather creations for men and women.

ARZU KAPROL
CLOTHING

Map p248 (☑212-252 7571; www.arzukaprol. net; Serdar-ı Ekrem Sokak 22, Galata; Ⓜ Şişhane, ⓐKaraköy, then funicular to Tünel) Parisian-trained and lauded throughout Turkey for her exciting designs, Arzu Kaprol's collections of women's clothing and accessories feature in Paris Fashion Week and are stocked by international retailers including Harrods in London. This store showcases her sleek prêt á porter range.

İRONI
HOMEWARES

Map p248 (☎212-245 7803; www.ironi.com.tr; Camekan Sokak 4e, Galata; ⊙10.30am-8pm; 🚇Karaköy) Güney İnan's range of silver-plated Turkish-style homewares includes plenty of options for those wanting to take home a souvenir of their trip. The tea sets (tray, glasses with holders, sugar bowls) are extremely attractive, as are the light fittings.

SELDA OKUTAN
JEWELLERY

Map p248 (☎212-514 1164; www.seldaokutan. com; Ali Paşa Değirmeni Sokak 10a, Tophane; ⊙Mon-Sat; 🚇Tophane) Selda Okutan's sculptural pieces featuring tiny naked figures have the local fashion industry all aflutter. Come to her design studio in Tophane to see what all the fuss is about.

🔒 İstiklal & Around

★NAHIL
HANDICRAFTS, BATHWARE

Map p244 (☎212-251 9085; www.nahil.com.tr; Bekar Sokak 17; ⊙10am-7pm Mon-Sat; 🚇Taksim, 🚇Kabataş, then funicular to Taksim) The felting, lacework, embroidery, all-natural soaps and soft toys in this lovely shop are made by economically disadvantaged women in Turkey's rural areas and all profits are returned to them, ensuring that they and their families have better lives.

LALE PLAK
MUSIC

Map p248 (☎212-293 7739; Galipdede Caddesi 1, Tünel; ⊙noon-7pm; 🚇Şişhane, 🚇Karaköy, then funicular to Tünel) This small shop is crammed with CDs, including a fine selection of Turkish classical, jazz and folk music. It's a popular hang-out for local musicians.

ALI MUHIDDIN HACI BEKIR
FOOD & DRINK

Map p244 (☎212-244 2804; www.hacibekir.com. tr; İstiklal Caddesi 83; 🚇Taksim, 🚇Kabataş, then funicular to Taksim Meydanı) The Beyoğlu branch of the famous *lokum* (Turkish delight) shop.

ARTRIUM
ART, JEWELLERY

Map p248 (☎212-251 4302; www.artrium.com.tr; Müellif Sokak 12, Tünel; ⊙Mon-Sat; 🚇Şişhane, 🚇Karaköy, then funicular to Tünel) Crammed with antique ceramics, calligraphy, maps, prints and jewellery, this Aladdin's cave of a shop is most notable for the exquisite miniatures by Iranian artist Haydar Hatemi.

BEYOĞLU OLGUNLAŞMA ENSTİTÜSÜ
HANDICRAFTS

Map p244 (www.beyogluolgunlasma.k12.tr; İstiklal Caddesi 28; ⊙9am-5pm Mon-Fri; 🚇Taksim, 🚇Kabataş, then funicular to Taksim) This is the ground-floor retail outlet-gallery of the Beyoğlu Olgunlaşma Enstitüsü, a textile school where students in their final year of secondary school learn crafts such as felting, embroidery, knitting and lacemaking. It sells well-priced examples of their work, giving them a taste of its commercial possibilities.

TEZGAH ALLEY
CLOTHING

Map p248 (Terkoz Cikmazı, off İstiklal Caddesi; ⊙Mon-Sat; 🚇; 🚇Şishane, 🚇Karaköy, then funicular to Tünel) Put your elbows to work fighting your way to the front of the *tezgah* (stalls) in this alleyway off İstiklal Caddesi, which are heaped with clothing for under ₺20 per piece. Turkey is a major centre of European clothing manufacture, and the items here are sometimes factory run-ons from designer or major chain-store orders. The 'Terkos Pasajı' sign marks the spot.

DENIZLER KITABEVI
MAPS, PRINTS

Map p248 (☎212-249 8893; www.denizlerkitabevi.com; İstiklal Caddesi 199a; ⊙9.30am-7.30pm Mon-Sat; 🚇Taksim, 🚇Karaköy, then funicular to Tünel) One of the few interesting shops remaining on İstiklal, Denizler Kitabevi sells antique maps, books, prints and postcards.

PAŞABAHÇE
GLASS

Map p248 (☎212-244 0544; www.pasabahce.com; İstiklal Caddesi 314; ⊙10am-8pm; 🚇Taksim, 🚇Karaköy, then funicular to Tünel) Established in 1934, this local firm manufactures excellent glassware from its factory on the Bosphorus. Three floors of glassware, vases and decanters feature and prices are very reasonable. Styles are both traditional and contemporary. There are other stores at the Zorlu, İstinye Park and Kanyon shopping malls, as well as near the Grand Bazaar (p105).

MEPHISTO
MUSIC

Map p244 (☎212-249 0696; www.mephisto.com.tr; İstiklal Caddesi 125; ⊙9am-midnight; 🚇Kabataş, then funicular to Taksim) If you manage to develop a taste for local music while you're in town, this popular store is the place to indulge it. As well as a huge CD collection of Turkish popular music, there's a select range of Turkish folk, jazz and classical music. It also stocks DVDs and has an upstairs cafe. There's another branch in Kadıköy (p153).

İSTANBUL KITAPÇISI
BOOKS

Map p248 (☑212-292 7692; www.istanbulkitapci si.com; İstiklal Caddesi 146; ☉10am-6.45pm Mon-Sat, noon-6.45pm Sun; Ⓜ Şişhane, Ⓕ Karaköy, then funicular to Tünel) This bookshop is run by the municipality and as a consequence its prices are very reasonable. It stocks some English-language books about İstanbul, and a good range of maps, CDs, postcards and prints.

🏠 Çukurçuma & Cihangir

A LA TURCA
CARPETS, ANTIQUES

Map p244 (☑212-245 2933; www.alaturcahouse. com; Faikpaşa Sokak 4, Çukurcuma; ☉10.30am-7.30pm Mon-Sat; Ⓜ Taksim, Ⓕ Kabataş, then funicular to Taksim) Antique Anatolian kilims and textiles are stacked alongside top-drawer Ottoman antiques in this fabulous shop in Çukurcuma. This is the best area in the city to browse for antiques and curios, and A La Turca is probably the most interesting of its retail outlets. Ring the doorbell to gain entrance.

BERRIN AKYÜZ
CLOTHING

Map p248 (☑212-251 4125; www.berrinakyuz. com; Akarsu Yokuşu 22, Cihangir; ☉10am-9pm Mon-Sat; Ⓜ Taksim, Ⓕ Kabataş, then funicular to Taksim) Local lasses love the reworked vintage clothing on offer at this Cihangir boutique, and no wonder. It's well priced and extremely stylish. There's another branch in Üsküdar.

LEYLA ESKI EŞYA PAZARLAMA
CLOTHING

Map p244 (Altıpatlar Sokak 6, Çukurcuma; ☉11am-5.30pm; Ⓜ Taksim, Ⓕ Kabataş, then funicular to Taksim) If you love old clothes, you'll adore Leyla Seyhanlı's boutique. Filled to the brim with piles of vintage embroidery and outfits, it's a rummager's delight. It stocks everything from 1950s taffeta party frocks to silk-embroidery cushion covers that would have been at home in the Dolmabahçe Palace linen cupboard.

MARIPOSA
CLOTHING

Map p248 (☑212-249 0483; www.atolyemari posa.com; Şimşirci Sokak 11a, Cihangir; ☉10am-8pm Mon-Fri, 11am-8.30pm Sat & Sun; Ⓜ Taksim, Ⓕ Kabataş, then funicular to Taksim) Designer Banu One turns out a particularly fetching line in floral frocks at her Cihangir atelier. Fashionistas will adore the fact that she not only makes to order, but also designs and tailors unique ensembles. As well as the dresses, coats and jackets on the racks, the shop sells pretty bedspreads and pillowslips.

LA CAVE WINE SHOP
FOOD & DRINK

Map p248 (La Cave Şarap Evi; ☑212-243 2405; www.lacavesarap.com; Sıraselviler Caddesi 109, Cihangir; ☉9.30am-8pm; Ⓜ Taksim, Ⓕ Kabataş, then funicular to Taksim) Its enormous selection of local and imported wine makes La Cave a good stop for tipplers. The staff can differentiate a Chablis from a Chardonnay, and though they don't speak much English, they are always happy to give advice on the best Turkish bottles to add to your cellar.

🏃 SPORTS & ACTIVITIES

KILIÇ ALI PAŞA HAMAMI
HAMAM

Map p248 (☑212-393 8010; http://kilicalipasa hamami.com; Hamam Sokak 1, off Kemeraltı Caddesi, Tophane; self-service ₺100, bath service ₺130; ☉women 8am-4pm, men 4.30pm-midnight; Ⓕ Tophane) It took seven years to develop a conservation plan for this 1580 Sinan-designed building and complete the meticulous restoration and boy oh boy, it was worth the wait. The hamam's interior is simply stunning and the place is run with total professionalism, ensuring a clean and enjoyable Turkish bath experience.

Commissioned by Admiral Kılıç Ali Paşa, who also endowed the nearby mosque and *medrese* (seminary), the hamam was originally used by the *levends* (marine forces in the Ottoman navy) but fell into disrepair last century. It reopened in late 2012.

Beşiktaş, Ortaköy & Kuruçeşme

Neighbourhood Top Five

❶ Getting a glimpse into the public and private lives of the last Ottoman sultans at **Dolmabahçe Palace** (p143).

❷ Viewing 19th-century Ottoman painting in a Crown Prince's residence at the **National Palaces Painting Museum** (p144).

❸ Admiring the ornately decorated 19th-century imperial caïques (ornately decorated wooden rowboats) at the recently renovated **İstanbul Naval Museum** (p144).

❹ Tiptoeing through the tulips and visiting a royal hideaway in **Yıldız Park** (p144).

❺ Wandering the streets surrounding the waterside *meydanı* (main square) in the former fishing village of **Ortaköy** (p145).

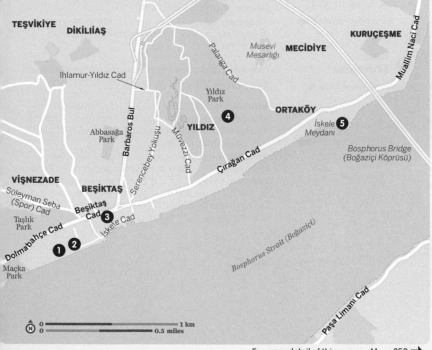

For more detail of this area see Map p250 ➡

Lonely Planet's Top Tip

It can be difficult to get past the door staff at the superclubs on the Golden Mile if you're not a celebrity or socialite. If you're keen to party with the glitterati, consider making a booking at one of the club restaurants, which should ensure that you get automatic entrance.

✕ Best Places to Eat

➡ Vogue (p145)

➡ Zuma (p145)

For reviews, see p145.

◉ Best Ottoman Palaces

➡ Dolmabahçe Palace (p143)

➡ Yıldız Şale (p144)

➡ Çırağan Palace (p144)

For reviews, see p143. ➡

◉ Best Museums

➡ İstanbul Naval Museum (p144)

➡ National Palaces Painting Museum (p144)

For reviews, see p144. ➡

Explore: Beşiktaş to Kuruçeşme

This part of town has the largest concentration of Ottoman palaces and pavilions in İstanbul, so history and architecture buffs will find it satisfying to spend a day or two exploring. Start by walking to Dolmabahçe Palace from the tram stop at Kabataş, and then walk or bus your way down to Yıldız Park and Çırağan Palace. Be warned, though, that getting back to Kabataş or Taksim by bus or taxi is usually a slow process due to constant traffic jams along Çırağan, Muallim Naci and Kuruçeşme Caddesis.

The waterside suburb of Ortaköy has considerable charm, particularly on warm summer nights when its main square is crowded with locals dining at its waterside restaurants or enjoying an after-dinner coffee and ice cream by the water. It's a good place to kick off an evening of clubbing at the venues along the Golden Mile.

Local Life

➡**Picnic in the Park** You don't need to organise a portable BBQ and folding furniture to enjoy an al fresco lunch in popular Yıldız Park (p144; although many locals do).

➡**İskele Idling** Watch the ferries head in and out of dock while lingering in the **cafes and bars** (Map p250) behind Bahçeşehir University next to the Beşiktaş İskelesi (Beşiktaş Ferry Dock).

➡**Kümpir** Join the crowds tucking into stuffed potatoes and savoury pancakes from the **stands** (Map p250) behind the Ortaköy Mosque.

Getting There & Away

➡**Buses** Lines 22, 22RE and 25E travel from Kabataş along Çırağan, Muallim Naci and Kuruçeşme Caddesis and on to the Bosphorus suburbs. Lines 40, 40T and 42T travel from Taksim.

➡**Ferries** Regular services run between Beşiktaş and the Asian shore. There are also commuter services from Eminönü to Beşiktaş every 10 minutes on weekdays between 5.20pm and 6.55pm, and from Eminönü to Ortaköy at 5.50pm, 6.10pm, 6.30pm and 6.40pm. Unfortunately, there are no return services to Eminönü.

SALVATOR BARKI / GETTY IMAGES ©

TOP SIGHT
DOLMABAHÇE PALACE

It's fashionable for architects and critics influenced by the less-is-more aesthetic of the Bauhaus masters to sneer at buildings such as Dolmabahçe. Enthusiasts of Ottoman architecture also decry this final flourish of the imperial dynasty, finding that it has more in common with the Paris Opera than with traditional pavilion-style buildings such as Topkapı. But whatever the critics might say, this 19th-century imperial residence with its formal garden and waterside location is a clear crowd favourite.

The palace, which is entered via an ornate imperial gate, is divided into three sections: the over-the-top **Selâmlık** (Ceremonial Quarters), the slightly more restrained **Harem** and the **Veliaht Dairesi** (Apartments of the Crown Prince), now home to the National Palaces Painting Museum (p144). The Selâmlık and Harem are visited on a compulsory – and dreadfully rushed – combined guided tour; the Veliaht Dairesi can be visited on your own.

The tourist entrance to the palace is near the ornate **Clock Tower**, built between 1890 and 1894. There's an outdoor cafe nearby with premium Bosphorus views and cheap prices (yes, really).

Note that visitor numbers in the palace are limited to 3000 per day and this ceiling is often reached on weekends and holidays – come midweek if possible, and even then be prepared to queue (often for a long period and in full sun). If you arrive before 3pm, you must buy a joint ticket for the Selâmlık and Harem; after 3pm you can visit only one. The Selâmlık, with its huge chandeliers and crystal staircase made by Baccarat, is the more impressive of the two.

Note that admission to the palace is not covered by the Museum Pass İstanbul.

DON'T MISS

➡ Selâmlık
➡ Harem
➡ National Palaces Painting Museum

PRACTICALITIES

➡ Dolmabahçe Sarayı
➡ Map p156
➡ ☎212-327 2626
➡ www.millisaraylar.gov.tr
➡ Dolmabahçe Caddesi, Beşiktaş
➡ adult Selâmlık ₺30, Harem ₺20, joint ticket ₺40, student/child under 7yr ₺5/free
➡ ⏰9am-3.30pm Tue-Wed & Fri-Sun Apr-Oct, to 2.30pm Nov-Mar
➡ 🚇Kabataş then walk

◉ SIGHTS

DOLMABAHÇE PALACE

PALACE

See p143.

NATIONAL PALACES
PAINTING MUSEUM

GALLERY

Map p250 (Milli Saraylar Resim Müzesi; ☎212-236 9000; Dolmabahçe Caddesi, Beşiktaş; ⊙9am-4pm Tue, Wed & Fri-Sun; ☐Akaretler, ☐Kabataş then walk) Reopened in 2014 after a long restoration, the Veliaht Dairesi (Apartments of the Crown Prince) in Dolmabahçe Palace now showcase the palace's collection of paintings. Highlights include the downstairs 'Turkish Painters 1870–1890' room, which includes two Osman Hamdi Bey works, and the upstairs 'İstanbul views' room, which is home to 19th-century street scenes by Germain Fabius Brest. Tickets are included in the ticket price and the gallery can be accessed from the palace grounds.

İSTANBUL NAVAL MUSEUM

MUSEUM

Map p250 (İstanbul Deniz Müzesi; ☎212-327 4345; www.denizmuzeleri.tsk.tr; Beşiktaş Caddesi 6, Beşiktaş; adult ₺6, student & child free; ⊙9am-5pm Tue-Sun Oct–mid-Apr, 9am-5pm Tue-Fri, 10am-6pm Sat & Sun mid-Apr–Sep; ☐Bahçeşehir Unv) Established over a century ago to celebrate and commemorate Turkish naval history, this museum has recently been undergoing a prolonged and major renovation. Its architecturally noteworthy copper-clad exhibition hall opened in 2013 and showcases a spectacular collection of 19th-century imperial caïques, ornately decorated wooden rowboats used by the royal household. Exhibits about naval battles are located in a downstairs gallery, as is part of the chain that stretched across the Golden Horn during Mehmet the Conqueror's assault on Constantinople.

The next stage of the renovation will see the museum's original building reopened with exhibits including 'The Navy in the Turkish Republic' and 'Cartography and Navigational Instruments'; the latter is likely to focus on the achievements of the 16th-century cartographer Piri Reis.

In the square opposite the museum is the Sinan-designed tomb of the admiral of Süleyman the Magnificent's fleet, Barbaros Heyrettin Paşa (1483–1546), better known as Barbarossa.

The museum is located on the Bosphorus shore close to the Beşiktaş bus station and ferry dock. Outside, dolmuşes (minibuses) run up to Taksim Meydanı (Taksim Sq) and to Harbiye, where Turkey's major military museum, the **Askeri Müze** (Military Museum; ☎212-233 2720; Vali Konağı Caddesi; adult/student & child ₺10/free; ⊙9am-5pm Wed-Sun), is located. The Ottoman military band known as the Mehter performs there most days between 3pm and 4pm.

ÇIRAĞAN PALACE

PALACE

Map p250 (Çırağan Sarayı; Çırağan Caddesi 84, Ortaköy; ☐Çırağan) Not satisfied with the architectural exertions of his predecessor at Dolmabahçe, Sultan Abdül Aziz (r 1861–76) built his own grand residence at Çırağan, only 1.5km away. Here, architect Nikoğos Balyan, who had also worked on Dolmabahçe, created an interesting building melding European neoclassical with Ottoman and Moorish styles. The palace is now part of the Çırağan Palace Kempinski Hotel.

YILDIZ PARK

PARK

Map p250 (Yıldız Parkı; Çırağan Caddesi, Yıldız; chalet museum adult/child ₺10/5; ⊙chalet museum 9am-4.30pm Tue, Wed & Fri-Sun; ☐Yahya Efendi) **FREE** This large and leafy retreat is alive with birds, picnicking families and young couples enjoying a bit of hanky-panky in the bushes. At its highest point is a **şale** (Yıldız Chalet Museum; Map p250; ☎212-259 4570; www.millisaraylar.gov.tr; adult/child ₺10/5; ⊙9am-4.30pm Tue-Wed & Fri-Sun Apr-Oct, until 3.30pm Nov-Mar), or chalet, commissioned by Sultan Abdül Hamit II as a hunting lodge. Built in 1880, this was converted into a guesthouse for visiting foreign dignitaries in 1889 and is now a museum. The best time to visit the park is in April, when its spring flowers (including thousands of tulips) bloom.

The **şale** is at the top of the hill, enclosed by a wall. After being expanded and renovated for the use of Kaiser Wilhelm II of Germany in 1889, it underwent a second extension in 1898 to accommodate a huge ceremonial hall. After his imperial guest departed, the sultan became quite attached to his 'rustic' creation and decided to live here himself, forsaking the palaces of Dolmabahçe and Çırağan on the Bosphorus shore.

Turkish-speaking guides conduct compulsory half-hour tours through the building every 15 minutes on weekends (less frequently on weekdays). The chalet isn't as plush as Dolmabahçe, but it's far less crowded. In fact, on weekdays it's often empty.

The tour visits a reception hall with French furniture and an ornate painted ceiling; the ceremonial hall with its magnificent Hereke carpet; and a series of bedrooms, bathrooms and salons.

Around 500m past the turn-off to Yıldız şale, you'll come to the **Malta Köşkü** (Map p250; Yıldız Parkı), now a restaurant and function centre. Built in 1870, this was where Abdül Hamit imprisoned his brother Murat V, whom he had deposed in 1876. The terrace here has a view of the Bosphorus and is a pleasant spot for a light lunch, tea or coffee.

If you continue walking past the Malta Köşkü for 10 minutes, you'll arrive at **Yıldız Porselen Fabrikası** (Yıldız Porcelain Factory; Map p250; ☎212-260 2370; admission ₺5; ☯9am-6pm Mon-Fri). This factory is housed in a wonderful building designed by Italian architect Raimondo D'Aronco, who introduced the art nouveau style to İstanbul.

The steep walk uphill from Çırağan Caddesi to the şale takes 15 to 20 minutes. If you come to the park by taxi, have it take you up the steep slope to the şale. A taxi from Taksim Meydanı to the top of the hill should cost around ₺12.

ORTAKÖY MOSQUE   MOSQUE
Map p250 (Ortaköy Camii; Büyük Mecidiye Camii; İskele Meydanı, Ortaköy; ☒Ortaköy) This elegant baroque structure was designed by Nikoğos Balyan, one of the architects of Dolmabahçe Palace, and was built for Sultan Abdül Mecit I between 1853 and 1855. Today, the modern Bosphorus Bridge looms behind it, providing a fabulous photo opportunity for those wanting to illustrate İstanbul's 'old meets new' character. This mosque was being restored at the time of research.

Within the mosque hang several masterful examples of Arabic calligraphy executed by Abdül Mecit, who was an accomplished calligrapher.

The mosque fronts onto İskele Meydanı, the hub of this former fishing village and home to a pretty fountain and waterfront cafes. On weekends the square and surrounding streets host an unremarkable but popular street market.

✗ EATING

There are plenty of eateries in Beşiktaş and Ortaköy, though few deserve to be singled out for recommendation. On weekends in Ortaköy, locals flock to the _kümpir_ (stuffed potato) and waffle stands behind the Ortaköy Mosque or to the branches of the Kitchenette (p131) and House Cafe (p131) chains.

AŞŞK KAHVE   CAFE ₺₺
(☎212-231 9172; www.asskkahve.com; Muallim Naci Caddesi 64b, Kuruçeşme; brunch ₺12-30; ☯9am-midnight, closed Mon winter; ☒; ☒Kuruçeşme) Aşk means 'love' in Turkish, and here it's given an extra ş. We've no idea why, but posit that it may be a reference to how much locals love a leisurely breakfast, which is the place's raison d'être. Go early to snaffle a table by the water, preferably on a weekend. It's accessed via the stairs behind the Macrocenter.

VOGUE   INTERNATIONAL ₺₺₺
Map p250 (☎212-227 4404; www.vogueuerestaurant.com; 13th fl, A Blok, BJK Plaza, Spor Caddesi 92, Akaretler, Beşiktaş; starters ₺26-50, mains ₺30-75; ☯noon-2am Mon-Sat, 10.30am-2am Sun; ☒; ☒Akaretler) It seems as if Vogue has been around for almost as long as the Republic. In fact, this sophisticated bar-restaurant in an office block in Beşiktas opened over a decade ago. It's a favourite haunt of the Nişantaşı powerbroker set, who like to have a drink at the terrace bar before moving into the restaurant for dinner.

ZUMA   JAPANESE ₺₺₺
Map p250 (☎212-236 2296; www.zumarestaurant.com; Salhane Sokak 7, Ortaköy; mains ₺50-100; ☯lunch from noon Mon-Fri, 1pm Sat & Sun, dinner from 7pm daily; ☒; ☒Kabataş Lisesi) Izakaya-style dishes from the robata grill and raw treats from the sushi bar draw a loyal crew of locals to this branch of the popular London restaurant, but the main draw is the amazing waterside location. There's also a sake bar and lounge on the top floor.

BANYAN   ASIAN ₺₺₺
Map p250 (☎212-259 9060; www.banyanrestaurant.com; 3rd fl, Salhane Sokak 3, Ortaköy; starters ₺14-39, sushi rolls ₺18-29, mains ₺30-85; ☯noon-midnight; ☒; ☒Kabataş Lisesi) The menu here travels around Asia, featuring Thai, Japanese, Indian, Vietnamese and

Chinese dishes including soups, sushi, satays and salads. The food claims to be good for the soul, and you can enjoy it while revelling in the exceptional views of the Ortaköy Mosque and Bosphorus Bridge from the terrace. There's a 10% discount at lunch.

♀ DRINKING & NIGHTLIFE

The stretch of Muallim Naci Caddesi running between Ortaköy and Kuruçeşme is often referred to as the Golden Mile, a reference to the string of high-profile nightclubs located on this part of the Bosphorus shoreline. The best time to visit these clubs is during summer, when they are open nightly and their waterside terraces provide a truly magical setting in which to party. A night here won't suit everyone, though: drinks are super-expensive, the food in the club restaurants is poor quality (and also expensive), the entrance policies are inconsistent, and the door staff are notoriously rude and tip-hungry. There's usually a cover charge on Friday and Saturday nights, although if you have a restaurant reservation you will often escape this.

REINA   CLUB
Map p250 (📞212-259 5919; www.reina.com.tr; Muallim Naci Caddesi 44, Ortaköy; 🚇Ortaköy) According to its website, Reina is where

'foreign heads of state discuss world affairs, business people sign agreements of hundred billions of dollars and world stars visit'. In reality it's where Turkey's C-list celebrities congregate, the city's nouveaux riches flock and an occasional tourist gets past the doorman to ogle the spectacle. The Bosphorus location is truly extraordinary.

SORTIE   CLUB
Map p250 (📞212-327 8585; www.sortie.com.tr; Muallim Naci Caddesi 54, Kuruçeşme; 🚇Şifa Yurdu) Sortie has long vied with Reina for the title of reigning queen of the Golden Mile, nipping at the heels of its rival dowager. It pulls in the city's glamourpusses and poseurs, all of whom are on the lookout for the odd celebrity guest.

ÇIRAĞAN PALACE
KEMPINSKI HOTEL   BAR
Map p250 (📞212-326 4646; www.ciragan-palace.com; Çırağan Caddesi 32, Ortaköy; 🚇Çırağan) Nursing a mega-pricey drink or coffee at one of the Çırağan's terrace tables and watching the scene around the city's best swimming pool, which is right on the Bosphorus, lets you sample the lifestyle of the city's rich and famous.

KIKI   BAR, CLUB
Map p250 (📞212-258 5524; http://kiki.com.tr; Osmanzade Sok 8, Ortaköy; ⊙5pm-1am Tue-Fri, to 5am Fri & Sat, to midnight Sun) An Ortaköy offshoot of the popular Cihangir venue.

LOCAL KNOWLEDGE

THE BIG THREE

The Big Three (Üç Büyükler) teams in the national Super League (SüperLig) are Galatasaray (nickname: the Lions), Fenerbahçe (the Golden Canaries) and Beşiktaş (the Black Eagles). All are based in İstanbul, and locals are extravagantly proud of them. Indeed, when Galatasaray became the first Turkish team to win a UEFA Cup back in 2000, locals went wild with excitement – in many eyes it was probably the most significant event since the Conquest.

There is one other team based in the city: Kasımpaşa SK (the Apaches).

Eighteen teams from all over Turkey compete from August to May. Each season, three move up from the second league into the first and three get demoted. The top team of the first league plays in the UEFA Cup. Matches are usually held on the weekend, often on a Saturday night. Tickets are sold at the *stadyum* (stadium) on the day of the match, but most fans purchase them ahead of time through Biletix (www.biletix). Open seating is affordable; covered seating – which has the best views – can be very pricey.

Although violence at home games is not unknown, most matches are fine. If you're worried, avoid the Galatasaray and Fenerbahçe clashes, as the supporters of these arch-rivals occasionally become overly excited and throw a few punches.

🛍 SHOPPING

LOKUM FOOD

(☎212-287 1528; www.lokumistanbul.com; Arnavutköy-Bebek Caddesi 15, Arnavutköy; ⊙9am-7pm Mon-Sat; 🚌Arnavutköy) *Lokum* (Turkish delight) is elevated to the status of artwork at this boutique on the border of Kuruçeşme and Arnavutköy. Owner/creator Zeynep Keyman aims to bring back the delights, flavours, knowledge and beauty of Ottoman-Turkish products such as *lokum*, *akide* candies (traditional boiled lollies), cologne water and scented candles. The gorgeous packaging makes these treats perfect gifts.

🏃 SPORTS & ACTIVITIES

FOUR SEASONS ISTANBUL AT THE BOSPHORUS SPA

Map p250 (☎212-381 4000; www.fourseasons.com/bosphorus; Çırağan Caddesi 28, Beşiktaş; 30/45min hamam experience €100/150; ⊙9am-9pm; 🚌Bahçeşehir Unv or Çırağan) The spa at this luxury hotel has wow factor in spades. Features include a stunning indoor pool area, steam room, spa, sauna and meditation areas. The gorgeous marble hamam is the perfect choice if you're looking for an indulgent – rather than utilitarian – Turkish bath experience, You'll get full-day access to the spa facilities with any treatment.

BEŞİKTAŞ, ORTAKÖY & KURUÇEŞME SHOPPING

Kadıköy

Neighbourhood Top Five

1 Taking a **ferry ride** (p153) between Europe and Asia.

2 Wandering around the **Kadıköy Produce Market** (p150).

3 Signing up for an expertly guided **foodie walk** (p153).

4 Following the aroma of freshly roasted coffee beans to **Fazıl Bey** (p152).

5 Shopping for **homewares and speciality foodstuffs** (p153) in the streets around the Kadıköy Produce Market.

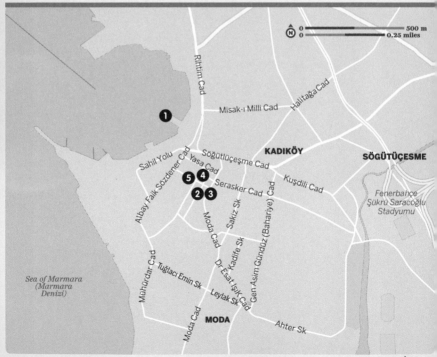

For more detail of this area see Map p253 ➡

Explore: Kadıköy

Located on the Anatolian (Asian) side of the city, Kadıköy is a short but atmospheric ferry ride from the European shore and offers a very different – and authentically local – experience to those travellers who are keen to cross continents.

İstanbullus come here from every corner of the city to stock up on speciality food items, fresh-from-the-farm produce and kitchenware items. To join them and see the suburb at its bustling best, you should head here on a morning any day except Sunday.

We suggest catching the ferry here, exploring the market and then enjoying lunch before heading back to the *iskele* (ferry dock) for your return trip or heading to nearby Üsküdar to visit its imperial mosques.

Local Life

→**Coffee Culture** Locals love to catch up over cups of sugar-sweetened *Türk kahve* (Turkish coffee) in the Seraskanter Caddesi *kahvehanıs* (coffeehouses).

→**Beer and Backgammon** Enjoying a late-afternoon beer and game of *tavla* (backgammon) is a popular pastime at the Kadife Sokak bars.

→**Football** Ultra-loyal Canary fans flock to Fenerbahçe's Şükrü Saracoğlu Stadium for home matches and can be found in the suburb's restaurants and bars before and after games.

Getting There & Away

→**Ferry** Boats travel to/from Eminönü and Karaköy, occasionally stopping at Haydarpaşa en route.

KADIKÖY

✖ Best Places to Eat

→ Çiya Sofrası (p151)
→ Kadı Nımet Balıkçılık (p151)

For reviews, see p151.➡

◉ Best Detour

→ Üsküdar (p151)

🍷 Best Places to Drink

→ Fazıl Bey (p152)
→ Kadife Sokak (p151)

For reviews, see p151.➡

KADIKÖY PRODUCE MARKET

An aromatic, colourful and alluring showcase of the best fresh produce in the city, the Kadıköy Pazarı (Market) is foodie central for locals and is becoming an increasingly popular destination for tourists. Equally rewarding to explore independently or on a guided culinary walk, it's small enough to retain a local feel yet large enough to support a variety of specialist traders.

Getting here involves crossing from Europe to Asia and is best achieved on a ferry – from the deck you'll be able to admire the domes and minarets studding the skylines of both shores and watch seagulls swooping overhead. Once you've arrived, cross Rihtim Caddesi in front of the *iskele* (ferry dock) and walk up Muvakkithane or Yasa Caddesis to reach the centre of the action. The best produce shops are in Güneşlibahçe Sokak – you'll see fish glistening on beds of crushed ice, displays of seasonal fruits and vegetables, combs of amber-hued honey, tubs of tangy pickles, bins of freshly roasted nuts and much, much more.

Eating and drinking opportunities are plentiful: creamy yoghurt and honey at Etabal, regional Anatolian specialities at Çiya Sofrası, the catch of the day at Kadı Nımet Balıkçılık and the city's best Turkish coffee at Fazıl Bey. For gifts to take home, consider *lokum* (Turkish delight) from Ali Muhıddın Hacı Bekir, coffee from Fazıl Bey or olive-oil soap from one of the herbalists in Güneşlibahçe Sokak.

For a serious immersion into the local food culture, sign up for a walk with İstanbul Eats (p153) or Turkish Flavours (p153) – both companies use guides who know loads about food and also know the best local places to eat it.

DON'T MISS

➡ Etabal
➡ The Serasker Caddesi *khavehani*
➡ Çiya Sofrası

PRACTICALITIES

➡ Kadıköy Pazarı
➡ Map p253
➡ The streets around Güneşlibahçe Sokak
➡ ⊘Mon-Sat
➡ ⊠Kadıköy

EATING

ETABAL
HONEY €

Map p253 (☑216-414 9977; www.etabal.com.
tr; Güneşli Bahçe Sokak 28; yoghurt & honey tub
₺4; ⓔKadıköy) To sample one of the market's
greatest treats, stop at this honey shop and
ask for a serve of yoghurt with a generous
swirl of honey from the comb on top. Simply sensational.

BAYLAN PASTANESI
SWEETS €

Map p253 (☑216-336 2881; www.baylanpastane
si.com.tr; Muvakkithane Caddesi 9; ☺7am-10pm;
ⓔKadıköy) Its front window and interior have
stood the test of time (the cafe opened in
1961 and its appearance has hardly changed
since this time), and so too has the popularity of this Kadıköy institution. Regulars tend
to order a decadent ice cream sundae or an
espresso coffee and house-made macaroon.

ÇIYA SOFRASI
ANATOLIAN €€

Map p253 (www.ciya.com.tr; Güneşlibahçe Sokak
43; mezes ₺7-8, portions ₺16-22; ☺11am-11pm;
ⓔKadıköy) Known throughout the culinary
world, Musa Dağdeviren's *lokanta* (eatery serving ready-made food) showcases
dishes from the region surrounding the
chef/owner's home city of Gaziantep and is
a wonderful place to try Turkish regional
specialities. Its next-door *kebapçı* (kebaps
₺18 to ₺40) sells a huge variety of tasty meat
dishes. Neither sells alcohol.

KADI NIMET BALIKÇILIK
FISH €€

Map p253 (☑216-348 7389; Seraser Caddesi
10a; mezes ₺7-16, fish mains ₺15-35; ☺noon-
midnight; ⓔKadıköy) Tucked in behind the
market's best fish stall, which has the same
owners, is this much-loved restaurant.
Make your choice from the cold mezes on
display, choose your fish and let the waiters
do the rest. Cold beer or rakı are the usual
accompaniments.

🍷 DRINKING & NIGHTLIFE

**The two major bar strips are Kadife
Sokak (aka Barlar or Bar Sokak) and the
southern end of Güneşlibahçe Sokak,
although Moda Caddesi is starting to
give them a run for their money.**

WORTH A DETOUR

ÜSKÜDAR

A working-class suburb with a conservative population, Üsküdar isn't blessed with the
restaurants, bars and cafes that give Kadıköy such a vibrant and inclusive edge, but it
does have one very big asset – an array of magnificent imperial mosques. Foremost
among these is the **Atik Valide Mosque** (Atik Valide Camii; Valide Imaret Sokak; ⓔÜsküdar),
designed by Sinan for the Valide Sultan Nurbanu, wife of Selim II (The Sot) and mother
of Murat III. Dating from 1583, it has retained most of the buildings in its original *külliye*
(mosque complex) and has a commanding location on Üsküdar's highest hill. The nearby
Çinili Mosque (Çinili Camii, Tiled Mosque; Çinili Hamam Sokak; ⓔÜsküdar) is dwarfed in
comparison, but is notable for the multicoloured İznik tiles that adorn its interior. Slightly
further up the hill is one of the few architecturally notable modern mosques in the city,
the **Şakirin Mosque** (cnr Huhkuyusu Caddesi & Dr Burhanettin Üstünel Sokak; ◻6, 9A, 11P,
11V, 12A, 12C). Designed by Hüsrev Tayla and featuring an interior by Zeynap Fadıllıoğlu, it
is located opposite the Zeynep Kamil Hospital on the road to Kadıköy.

Down by the *iskele* (ferry dock) are the **Mihrimah Sultan Mosque** (Mihrimah Sultan
Camii; Paşa Limanı Caddesi; ⓔÜsküdar), a Sinan design from 1547–48 that was commissioned by the daughter of Süleyman the Magnificent; and the **Yeni Valide Mosque**
(Yeni Valide Camii, New Queen Mother's Mosque; Demokrasi Meydanı; ⓔÜsküdar), commissioned by Ahmet III for his mother. South of the *iskele* is yet another Sinan design: the
diminutive 1580 **Şemsi Ahmed Paşa Mosque** (Şemsi Paşa Camii, Kuskonmaz Camii;
Paşa Limanı Caddesi; ⓔÜsküdar). Next to this is a popular waterside *çay bahçesi* (tea garden) where you can enjoy a tea, coffee or soft drink while admiring the view and watching the ever-present group of anglers trying their luck in the choppy waters below.

To get here from Kadıköy, take bus 12 or 12A from the bus station in front of the Turyol *iskele* or one of the many dolmuşes picking up passengers nearby. From Üsküdar,
ferries travel back to Eminönü, Karaköy, Kabataş and Beşiktaş.

LOCAL KNOWLEDGE

İSTANBUL'S FOOD CULTURE

Ansel Mullins and Yigal Schleifer produce **Istanbul Eats** (http://istanbuleats.com), an excellent blog that investigates the traditional food culture of the city, and are the authors of *Istanbul Eats: Exploring the Culinary Backstreets*, a pocket-sized publication available in bookshops throughout the city. Here, they recommend some of their favourite eating destinations:

Favourite Old City Food Destinations

Şehzade Cağ Kebabı (p82) This place continues to astound us. We've been polling everyone we meet from Erzurum and they all agree on the quality and authenticity of this place.

Develi Baklava (p98) For *katmer* (flaky pastry stuffed with pistachio and clotted cream). We can't understand how *katmer* can be so delicious and so hard to find in İstanbul.

Erol Lokantası (p80) Everyone should have 'their' local *lokantası* (eatery serving ready-made food), even when on a short trip. Everyone is treated like an old regular here and the food is excellent if predictable.

Favourite Beyoğlu Food Destinations

Çukur Meyhane (p131) A classic, cheap *meyhane* (tavern) with exceptional food.

Tarihi Karaköy Balık Lokantası (p130) Simple, fresh fish at its best.

Antiochia (p130) Always our top pick for the Syrian–inspired cuisine of Hatay.

Favourite Produce Market in İstanbul

It's not the biggest market, but we love the element of surprise present at the weekly Inebolu Pazari in Dolapdere. Along with the predictable staples of the Kastamonu area where all of these vendors live, one week you might find some strange mushrooms and the following week a wonderful sour homemade yoghurt. This is as close as İstanbul gets to the countryside 'farmers' markets we've enjoyed throughout Turkey.

Best Foodie Strip

The Kadiköy Produce Market, with Çiya Sofrası (p151) as the jewel in the crown.

Most Exciting Food Trend

We are encouraged to see established chefs focusing their attention on the regional specialities of Anatolia (rather than those of Italy, France and East Asia, as was the previous trend!). While İstanbul is extremely rich in traditional restaurants on the humble end of the scale, it is lacking in exciting Turkish fine-dining restaurants.

Worst Food Trend

Food courts! Shopping malls are popping up like mushrooms in İstanbul and bringing with them the local-restaurant-slaying forces of Jamie Oliver, Pinkberry and, of course, Colonel Sanders.

Most Lamented (ie Disappearing) Food Tradition

İstanbullus of a certain generation fondly remember the haunting call in winter nights of the *bozacı* (street vendor selling *boza* drink), but this is something that is becoming increasingly rare. The itinerant liver sandwich man is also almost extinct. We do hope the global streetfood craze will reach Turkey and revive some of these old local traditions.

★**FAZIL BEY**   COFFEEHOUSE
Map p253 (www.fazilbey.com; Serasker Caddesi 3; ⊙daily; 🚇Kadıköy) Making the call as to who makes the best Turkish coffee in İstanbul is no easy task, but our vote goes to Fazil Bey, the best-loved *khavehan* (coffeeshop) on Serasker Caddesi. Enjoying a cup while watching the passing parade of shoppers has been a popular local pastime since 1923.

KARGA BAR BAR

Map p253 (📞216-449 1725; www.kargabar.
org; Kadife Sokak 16; ⊗11am-2am; 🚇Kadıköy)
Karga is one of the most famous bars in
the city, offering cheap drinks, loud music
and avant-garde art on its walls. There's a
small courtyard downstairs to enjoy a late-
afternoon beer.

☆ ENTERTAINMENT

SÜREYYA OPERA HOUSE CLASSICAL MUSIC

Map p253 (📞216-346 1533, 216-346 1532, 216-
346 1531; www.sureyyaoperasi.org; Gen Asim
Gumduz (Bahariye) Caddesi 29) Built in 1927
and used for many years as a cinema, this
bijou building was restored and opened as
an opera house in 2007. It is the base of the
İstanbul State Opera and Ballet.

🛍 SHOPPING

SOY HOMEWARES

Map p253 (📞216-330 0030; www.soy.com.
tr; Leylek Sokak 20b; ⊗call for appointment;
🚇Kadıköy) A few years ago, entrepreneur
and committed foodie Emir Ali Enç identified a market opportunity for quality copper cookware made in Turkey. The resulting
range of handmade serving bowls, coffee
pots and saucepans has quickly developed
a loyal fan base both here and overseas, and
can be seen at his showroom on the edge of
Kadıköy and Moda. If you are keen to purchase a pot or two, you'll need to give Emir
a lead time of seven to 10 days. Alternatively,
orders can be shipped overseas.

MESUT GÜNEŞ TEXTILES

Map p253 (📞216-337 6215; www.mesutgunes.
com.tr; Yasa Caddesi 46; ⊗8.30am-6pm Mon-
Sat; 🚇Kadıköy) It may not look like much
from the front, but this shop often sells top-
quality towels and sheets manufactured in
Turkey for major international brands (eg
Frette) for a fraction of their usual price.

ALI MUHIDDIN HACI BEKIR FOOD & DRINK

Map p253 (📞216-336 1519; Muvakkithane Caddesi 61; 🚇Kadıköy) The Kadıköy branch
of İstanbul's most famous purveyors of
lokum.

MEPHISTO MUSIC

Map p253 (📞216-414 3519; www.mephisto.com.
tr; Muvakkithane Caddesi 5; 🚇Kadıköy) The
Kadıköy branch of the city's best-known
music store.

🏃 SPORTS & ACTIVITIES

FERRY TRIP BETWEEN
EUROPE & ASIA BOAT TRIP

(www.sehirhatlari.com.tr/en; one way ₺4) Every day ferries from the fleet operated by
İstanbul Şehir Hatları ply a short stretch
of the Sea of Marmara between the city's
European and Asian shores. The 30-minute
ride to Kadıköy from Eminönü or Karaköy
offers wonderful views, a ubiquitous escort
of seagulls and an occasional dolphin spot-
ting. You can even enjoy a cheap glass of tea
on board.

★ İSTANBUL EATS WALKING TOUR

(http://istanbuleats.com/; tour per person
US$125) The seriously committed foodies
at this award-winning outfit offer a daily
5½ hour 'Two Markets, Two Continents'
tour that visits the Karaköy Produce Market and then makes its way via ferry to
Kadıköy and neighbouring Moda to sample plenty of local specialities.

TURKISH FLAVOURS WALKING TOUR

(📞0532 218 0653; www.turkishflavours.com;
tour per person US$145) A well-regarded out-
fit offering foodie walks, Turkish Flavours
runs a five-hour 'Market Tour' that starts at
Eminönü's Spice Market and then takes a
ferry to Kadıköy, where it tours the Karaköy
Produce Market and finishes with a lavish
lunch at Çiya Sofrası.

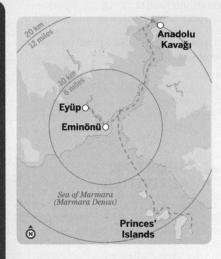

Day Trips

The Bosphorus p155
Running from the Galata Bridge all the way to the Black Sea (Karadeniz), 32km north, the mighty Bosphorus Strait has been İstanbul's major thoroughfare ever since classical times.

The Golden Horn p164
This stretch of water to the north of the Galata Bridge offers visitors a glimpse into the suburbs and lifestyles of working-class İstanbul. Get here before it gentrifies.

Princes' Islands p167
A favourite day-trip destination for İstanbullus, the Adalar (Islands) lie in the Sea of Marmara, about 20km southeast of the city. Come here to escape the sensory overload of the big smoke.

The Bosphorus

Explore

The Bosphorus deserves at least one day of your time; two days (one for each shore) is even better.

To spend a day exploring the European shore, purchase a one-way ticket for the Long Bosphorus Tour ferry trip leaving from Eminönü, alight at Sarıyer and work your way back to Kabataş or Taksim by bus, stopping at the Sadberk Hanım Museum, the Sakıp Sabancı Museum, the fortress at Rumeli Hisarı, and the waterside suburbs of Bebek and/or Ortaköy on the way.

To spend a day exploring the Asian shore, purchase a one-way ticket for the Long Bosphorus Tour ferry trip leaving from Eminönü, alight at Anadolu Kavağı and work your way back along that shore by bus, stopping to visit Hıdiv Kasrı, Küçüksu Kasrı and Beylerbeyi Palace before getting off the bus at Üsküdar and catching a ferry back to Eminönü, Karaköy or Kabataş.

The Best...

➡ **Sight** Beylerbeyi Palace (p160)
➡ **Place to Eat** Tapasuma (p163)
➡ **Place to Drink** On the ferry

Top Tip

If you buy a return ticket on the Long Bosphorus Tour, you'll be forced to spend three hours in the tourist-trap village of Anadolu Kavağı. It's much better to buy a one-way ticket and alight there, at Sarıyer or at Kanlıca and make your way back to town by bus. Alternatively, take the Dentur Avraysa hop-on/hop-off tour from Kabataş.

Getting There & Away

➡ **Ferry** Most day-trippers take the Long Bosphorus Tour (Uzun Boğaz Turu) operated by Istanbul Şehir Hatları (İstanbul City Routes; www.sehirhatlari.com.tr). The ferry travels the entire length of the strait in a 90-minute *tek yön* (one-way) trip and departs from the *iskele* (ferry dock) at Eminönü daily at 10.35am. From April to October there is an extra service at 1.35pm. A ticket costs ₺25 return *çift* (return), ₺15 one way. The ferry stops at Beşiktaş, Kanlıca, Sarıyer, Rumeli Kavağı and Anadolu Kavağı (the turnaround point). It's not possible to get on and off the ferry at stops along the way using the same ticket. The ferry returns from Anadolu Kavağı at 3pm (plus 4.15pm from April to October).

From March to October, İstanbul Şehir Hatları also operates a two-hour Short Bosphorus Tour (Kısa Boğaz Turu) that leaves Eminönü daily at 2.30pm, picking up passengers in Ortaköy 20 minutes later. It travels as far as the Fatih Bridge before returning to Eminönü. Tickets cost ₺12 one way. From November to February, the service is limited to Saturdays, Sundays and holidays.

On Saturday evenings between early June and mid-September there is a special Moonlit Night Cruise (Mehtaplı Geceler Turu) leaving from Bostancı and picking up passengers in Eminönü at 6.25pm. After further pick-ups in Üsküdar and Beşiktaş, the ferry makes its way up the strait to Anadolu Kavağı, stops there for two hours and then returns at 10.30pm, arriving at Eminönü just past midnight. On board, Turkish musicians entertain passengers. Tickets cost ₺20 one way.

Note that if you have a Museum Pass İstanbul you will receive a 25% discount on the ticket prices of these tours.

Check www.sehirhatlari.com.tr for timetable and fare updates for all ferry services, as these often change.

A newly introduced and attractive alternative to the Long Bosphorus Tour is to take the hop-on/hop-off tour from Kabataş operated by Dentur Avraysa (✆444 6336; www.denturavrasya.com) from the *iskele* behind the petrol station at Kabataş. This costs ₺15 one way, leaves six times daily at 12.45pm, 1.45pm, 2.45pm, 3.45pm, 4.45pm and 5.45pm, and allows passengers to alight at Emirgan, Küçüksu Kasrı and Beylerbeyi Sarayı and then reboard the ferry on the same ticket. It would be very rushed to try and make three stops within one afternoon (you would need to take the first service), but two stops is achievable. Just be aware that Küçüksu Kasrı and Beylerbeyi Sarayı close at 3.30pm (winter) and 4.30pm (summer).

Another option is to buy a ticket for a cruise on a private excursion boat. Although these only take you as far as Anadolu Hisarı and back (without stopping), the fact that the boats are smaller means that you travel closer to the shoreline and are able to see a lot more. The entire trip

Bosphorus Cruise

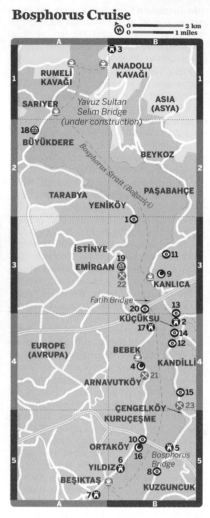

0 — 2 km
0 — 1 miles

takes about 90 minutes and tickets cost
₺12 one way. A number of companies offer
these tours from Eminönü; of these Turyol
is probably the most reputable. Its boats
leave from the dock on the western side of
the Galata Bridge hourly from 11am to 6pm
on weekdays and every 45 minutes or so
from 11am to 7.15pm on weekends. Boats
operated by other companies leave from
near the Boğaz İskelesi, from near the Haliç
İskelesi and from the Ahirkapı İskelesi near
Sultanahmet. There's also a full 5½-hour
tour operated by Dentur/Avraysa leaving
daily at 11.15am from behind the petrol station at Kabataş (one way ₺20). It stops for
three hours in Anadolu Kavağı.

➡Bus From Sarıyer, buses 25E and 40 head
south to Emirgan. From Emirgan, buses 22,
22RE and 25E head to Kabataş, and 40, 40T
and 42T go to Taksim. All travel via Rumeli
Hisarı, Bebek, Ortaköy, Yıldız and Beşiktaş.

If you decide to catch the ferry to Anadolu Kavağı and make your way back to town
by bus, catch bus 15A, which leaves from a
square straight ahead from the ferry terminal en route to Kavacık. Get off at Kanlıca to
visit Hıdıv Kasrı or to transfer at Beykoz to
bus 15, which will take you south to Üsküdar
via Çengelköy, the Küçüksu stop (for Küçüksu Kasrı) and the Beylerbeyi Sarayı stop (for

Beylerbeyi). Bus 15F or 15BK take the same route but continue to Kadıköy.

All bus tickets and commuter ferry trips cost ₺4 (₺2.15 with an İstanbulkart).

....

Need to Know

➡**Area Code** ☑212 (European shore), ☑216 (Asian shore)
➡**Duration** Long/short tour six/two hours
➡**Cost** Long/short tour ₺25/15

◎ SIGHTS

◎ Departure Point: Eminönü

Our write-up follows the route of the Long Bosphorus Tour. Hop onto the boat at the Boğaz İskelesi (Bosphorus Ferry Dock) on the Eminönü quay near the Galata Bridge. It's always a good idea to arrive 30 minutes or so before the scheduled departure time and manoeuvre your way to the front of the queue that builds near the doors leading to the dock. When these open and the boat can be boarded, you'll need to move fast to score a good seat. The best spots are on the sides of the upper deck at the bow.

The Asian shore is to the right side of the ferry as it cruises up the strait, Europe is to the left. When you start your trip, watch out for the small island of **Kız Kulesi** (☸Üsküdar), just off the Asian shore near Üsküdar. One of the city's most distinctive landmarks, this 18th-century structure has functioned as a lighthouse, quarantine station and restaurant. It also featured in the 1999 James Bond film, *The World Is Not Enough.*

Just before the first stop at Beşiktaş, you'll pass the grandiose Dolmabahçe Palace (p143), built on the European shore of the Bosphorus by Sultan Abdül Mecit between 1843 and 1854.

◎ Beşiktaş to Kanlica

After a brief stop at Beşiktaş, Çırağan Palace (p144), once home to Sultan Abdül Aziz and now a luxury hotel, looms up on the left. Next to it is the long yellow building occupied by the prestigious Galatasaray University. On the Asian shore is the **Fethi Ahmed Paşa Yalı**, a wide white building with a red-tiled roof that was built in the pretty suburb of Kuzguncuk in the late 18th century. The word *yalı* comes from the Greek word for 'coast', and describes the timber summer residences along the Bosphorus built by Ottoman aristocracy and foreign ambassadors in the 17th, 18th and 19th centuries, now all protected by the country's heritage laws.

A little further along on your left is the pretty Ortaköy Mosque (p145), which was being restored at the time of research. The mosque's dome and two minarets are dwarfed by the adjacent **Bosphorus Bridge**, opened in 1973 on the 50th anniversary of the founding of the Turkish Republic.

Under the bridge on the European shore are two huge *yalıs:* the red-roofed **Hatice Sultan Yalı**, once the home of Sultan Murad V's daughter, Hatice; and the **Fehime Sultan Yalı**, home to Hatice's sister Fehime. Both are undergoing massive restorations and will be reimagined as a luxury hotel. On the Asian side is the ornate Beylerbeyi Palace (p160) – look for its whimsical marble bathing pavilions on the shore; one was for men, the other for the women of the harem.

Past the small village of Çengelköy on the Asian side is the imposing **Kuleli Military School** (Çengelköy; ☸Eminönü-Kavaklar tourist ferry), built in 1860 and immortalised in İrfan Orga's wonderful memoir, *Portrait of a Turkish Family.* Look out for its two 'witch-hat' towers.

Almost opposite Kuleli on the European shore is **Arnavutköy** (Albanian Village), which boasts a number of gabled Ottoman-era wooden houses and Greek Orthodox churches. On the hill above it are buildings formerly occupied by the American College for Girls. Its most famous alumni was Halide Edib Adıvar, who wrote about the years she spent here in her 1926 work, *The Memoir of Halide Edib.*

Arnavutköy runs straight into the glamorous suburb of **Bebek**, known for its upmarket shopping and chic cafe-bars such as Mangerie and Lucca. It also has the most glamorous Starbucks in the city (right on the water, and with a lovely terrace). Bebek's shops surround a small park and the Ottoman Revivalist–style **Bebek Mosque**; to the east of these is the ferry dock, to the

DAY TRIPS THE BOSPHORUS

Eyüp Sultan Mosque (p114)
Important Muslim sacred place

Princes' Islands (p167)
fayton (horse-drawn carriage) ride
on the car-less Princes' Islands

The Bosphorus (p155)
Aerial view of İstanbul and Ortaköy
Mosque

south is the **Egyptian consulate building** (Bebek; ⚓Eminönü-Kavaklar tourist ferry), thought by some critics to be the work of Italian architect Raimondo D'Aronco. This gorgeous art nouveau mini-palace was built for Emine Hanım, mother of the last khedive of Egypt, Abbas Hilmi II. It's the white building with two mansard towers and an ornate wrought-iron fence.

Opposite Bebek on the Asian shore is **Kandilli**, the 'Place of Lamps', named after the lamps that were lit here to warn ships of the particularly treacherous currents at the headland. Among the many *yalıs* here is the huge red **Kont Ostrorog Yalı**, built in the 19th century by Count Leon Ostorog, a Polish adviser to the Ottoman court; Pierre Loti visited here when he visited İstanbul in the 1890s. A bit further on, past Kandilli, is the long, white **Kıbrıslı (Cypriot) Mustafa Emin Paşa Yalı**, which dates from 1760.

Next to the Kıbrıslı are the **Büyük Göksu Deresi** (Great Heavenly Stream) and **Küçük Göksu Deresi** (Small Heavenly Stream), two brooks that descend from the Asian hills into the Bosphorus. Between them is a fertile delta, grassy and shady, which

the Ottoman elite thought perfect for picnics. Foreign residents referred to it as 'The Sweet Waters of Asia'.

If the weather was good, the sultan joined the picnic, and did so in style. Sultan Abdül Mecit's answer to a simple picnic blanket was **Küçüksu Kasrı** (☎216-332 3303; Küçüksu Caddesi, Beykoz; adult/student/child under 7yr ₺5/1/free; ⏰9am-4.30pm Tue, Wed & Fri-Sun Apr-Oct, till 3.30pm Nov-Mar; ⚓Küçüksu), an ornate hunting lodge built in 1856–7. Earlier sultans had wooden kiosks here, but architect Nikoğos Balyan designed a rococo gem in marble for his monarch. You'll see its ornate cast-iron fence, boat dock and wedding-cake exterior from the ferry.

Close to the Fatih Bridge are the majestic structures of **Rumeli Hisarı** (Fortress of Europe; ☎212-263 5305; Yahya Kemal Caddesi 42; admission ₺10; ⏰9am-noon & 12.30-4.30pm Thu-Tue; ⚓Rumeli Hisarı) and **Anadolu Hisarı** (Fortress of Anatolia). Mehmet the Conqueror had Rumeli Hisarı built in a mere four months in 1452, in preparation for his siege of Byzantine Constantinople. For its location, he chose the narrowest point of the Bosphorus, opposite Anadolu Hisarı, which Sultan Beyazıt I had

---

⊙ TOP SIGHT
BEYLERBEYI PALACE

Every sultan needed a place to escape to, and this 26-room palace built in 1865 was the place for Abdül Aziz I (r 1861–76). The baroque-style building was designed by Sarkis Balyan, brother of Nikoğos (architect of Dolmabahçe), and it delighted both Abdül Aziz and the foreign dignitaries who visited. The palace's last imperial 'guest' was the former sultan Abdül Hamit II, who spent the last years of his life (1913–18) under house arrest here.

The compulsory guided tour whips you past rooms decorated with frescoes of naval scenes, Bohemian crystal chandeliers, Ming vases and sumptuous Hereke carpets. The interior features a grand *selamlik* (ceremonial quarters) and a small but opulent harem. Highlights include the downstairs hall with the huge marble pool used for cooling during summer, the elaborately painted and gilded sultan's apartment, and the dining room with chairs covered in gazelle skin. After the tour, you can enjoy a glass of tea in the garden cafe.

The easiest way to visit Beylerbeyi is to take the Dentur Avraysa hop-on/hop-off tour from Kabataş.

DON'T MISS

➡ Hall with Pool
➡ Blue Hall
➡ Valide Sultan's Reception Rooms

PRACTICALITIES

➡ Beylerbeyi Sarayı
➡ www.millisaraylar.gov.tr
➡ Abdullah Ağa Caddesi, Beylerbeyi
➡ adult/student/child under 7yr ₺20/₺5/free
➡ ⏰9am-4.30pm Tue, Wed & Fri-Sun Apr-Oct, till 3.30pm Nov-Mar
➡ ⚓Beylerbeyi Sarayı

built in 1394. By doing so, Mehmet was able to control all traffic on the strait, cutting the city off from resupply by sea.

To speed Rumeli Hisarı's completion, Mehmet ordered each of his three viziers to take responsibility for one of the three main towers. If the tower's construction was not completed on schedule, the vizier would pay with his life. Not surprisingly, the work was completed on time. The useful military life of the mighty fortress lasted less than one year. After the conquest of Constantinople, it was used as a glorified Bosphorus tollbooth for a while, then as a barracks, a prison and finally as an open-air theatre.

Within Rumeli Hisarı's walls are park-like grounds, an open-air theatre and the minaret of a ruined mosque. Steep stairs (with no barriers, so beware!) lead up to the ramparts and towers; the views of the Bosphorus are magnificent. Just next to the fortress is a clutch of cafes and restaurants, the most popular of which is **Kale Cafe & Pastane** (✆212-265 0097; Yahya Kemal Caddesi 16, Rumeli Hisarı).

The ferry doesn't stop at Rumeli Hisarı; you can either leave the ferry at Kanlıca and catch a taxi across the Fatih Bridge (this will cost around ₺20 including the bridge toll) or you can visit on your way back to town from Sarıyer. Though it's not open as a museum, visitors are free to wander about Anadolu Hisarı's ruined walls.

There are many architecturally and historically important *yalıs* in and around Anadolu Hisarı. These include the **Köprülü Amcazade Hüseyin Paşa Yalı**, a cantilevered boxlike structure built for one of Mustafa II's grand viziers in 1698. The oldest *yalı* on the Bosphorus, it is currently undergoing a major renovation. Next door, the **Zarif Mustafa Paşa Yalı** was built in the early 19th century by the official coffee maker to Sultan Mahmud II. Look for its upstairs salon, which juts out over the water and is supported by unusual curved timber struts.

Almost directly under the **Fatih Bridge** on the European shore is the huge stone four-storey **Tophane Müşiri Zeki Paşa Yalı**, a mansion built in the early 20th century for a field marshall in the Ottoman army. Later, it was sold to Sabiha Sultan, daughter of Mehmet VI, the last of the Ottoman sultans, and her husband İmer Faruk Efendi, grandson of Sultan Abdül Aziz. When the sultanate was abolished in 1922, Mehmet walked from this palace onto a British warship, never to return to Turkey.

Past the bridge on the Asian side is **Kanlıca**, the ferry's next stop. This charming village is famous for the rich and delicious yoghurt produced here, which is sold on the ferry and in two cafes on the shady waterfront square. The small **Gâzi İskender Paşa Mosque** in the square dates from 1560 and was designed by Mimar Sinan.

High on a promontory above Kanlıca is Hıdiv Kasrı (p162), a gorgeous art nouveau villa built by the last khedive of Egypt as a summer residence for use during his family's annual visits to İstanbul. You can see its square white tower (often flying a Turkish flag) from the ferry.

◉ Kanlıca to Sarıyer

On the opposite shore is the wealthy suburb of Emirgan, home to the impressive **Sakıp Sabancı Museum** (Sakıp Sabancı Müsezi; ✆212-277 2200; http://muze.sabanciuniv.edu; Sakıp Sabancı Caddesi 42, Emirgan; adult/student/child under 8yr ₺15/8/free; ◷10am-5.30pm Tue, Thu & Fri-Sun, to 7.30pm Wed; ⛴Emirgan), which hosts international travelling art exhibitions. Inside the museum grounds is one of İstanbul's most stylish eateries, MüzedeChanga, with an extensive terrace and magnificent Bosphorus views.

On the hill above Emirgan is **Emirgan Woods**, a huge public reserve that is particularly beautiful in April, when it is carpeted with thousands of tulips.

North of Emirgan, there's a ferry dock near the small yacht-lined cove of **İstinye**. Nearby, on a point jutting out from the European shore, is the suburb of **Yeniköy**. This was a favourite summer resort for the Ottomans, as indicated by the cluster of lavish 18th- and 19th-century *yalıs* around the ferry dock. The most notable of these is the frilly white **Ahmed Afif Paşa Yalı**, designed by Alexandre Vallaury, architect of the Pera Palas Hotel in Beyoğlu, and built in the late 19th century.

On the opposite shore is the village of **Paşabahçe**, famous for its glassware

TOP SIGHT
HIDIV KASRI

The Ottomans conquered Egypt in 1517. After surviving a challenge to their rule by the French from 1798 to 1801, they again lost control in 1805, this time to an Albanian-born military commander of the Ottoman army in Egypt called Muhammed Ali, who was given quasi-independence and the title of *hıdiv* (khedive or viceroy) by the sultan.

The Egyptian khedives maintained close ties with the Ottoman Empire and often spent summers in İstanbul. In 1906 Khedive Abbas Hilmi II built himself this palatial art nouveau villa on the most dramatic promontory on the Bosphorus. It became the property of the municipality in the 1930s.

Restored after decades of neglect, the villa now functions as a restaurant and cafe. The building is an architectural gem and the garden is superb, especially during the İstanbul International Tulip Festival in April.

The villa is a 20-minute walk from the *iskele* (ferry dock). Head left (north) up Halide Edip Adivar Caddesi and turn right into the second street (Kafadar Sokak). Turn left into Hacı Muhittin Sokağı and walk up the hill until you come to a fork in the road. Take the left fork and follow the 'Hadiv Kasrı' signs to the villa's car park and garden.

DON'T MISS

➡ The garden
➡ The entrance lobby
➡ Main dining room

PRACTICALITIES

➡ Khedive's Villa
➡ www.beltur.com.tr
➡ Çubuklu Yolu 32, Çubuklu
➡ admission free
➡ ⊙9am-10pm
➡ 🚢Kanlıca

---

factory. A bit further on is the fishing village of Beykoz, which has a graceful ablutions fountain, the **İshak Ağa Çeşmesi**, dating from 1746, near the village square. Much of the land along the Bosphorus shore north of **Beykoz** is a military zone.

Originally called Therapia for its healthy climate, the little cove of **Tarabya** on the European shore has been a favourite summer watering place for İstanbul's well-to-do for centuries, though modern developments such as the horrendous multistorey Grand Hotel Tarabya right on the promontory have poisoned much of its charm. For an account of Therapia in its heyday, read Harold Nicolson's 1921 novel *Sweet Waters*. Nicolson, who is best known as Vita Sackville-West's husband, served as the third Secretary in the British embassy in Constantinople between 1912 and 1914, the years of the Balkan wars, and clearly knew Therapia well. In the novel, the main character, Eirene, who was based on Vita, spent her summers here.

North of the village are some of the old summer embassies of foreign powers. When the heat and fear of disease increased in the warm months, foreign ambassadors would retire to palatial residences, complete with lush gardens, on this shore. The region for such embassy residences extended north to the village of Büyükdere, notable for its churches, summer embassies and the **Sadberk Hanım Museum** (☎212-242 3813; www.sadberkhanimmuzesi.org.tr; Piyasa Caddesi 27-29; adult/student ₺7/2; ⊙10am-4.30pm Thu-Tue; 🚢Sarıyer). Named after the wife of the late Vehbi Koç, founder of Turkey's foremost commercial empire, the museum is housed in a graceful old *yalı* and is a showcase for her extraordinary private collection of antiquities and Ottoman heirlooms. This includes İznik and Kütahya ceramics, Ottoman silk textiles and needlework, and an exquisite collection of diadems from the Mycenaean, Archaic and Classical periods. To get here, alight from the ferry at Sarıyer and walk left (south) from the ferry dock for approximately 10 minutes.

The residents of **Sarıyer**, the next village up from Büyükdere on the European shore, have traditionally made a living by fishing, and the area around the ferry terminal (the next stop) is full of fish restaurants.

☉ Sarıyer to Anadolu Kavaği

From Sarıyer, it's only a short trip to **Rumeli Kavağı**, a sleepy place where the only excitement comes courtesy of the arrival and departure of the ferry. To the south of the town is the shrine of the Muslim saint **Telli Baba**, reputed to be able to find suitable husbands for young women who pray there.

Anadolu Kavağı, on the opposite shore, is where the Long Bosphorus Tour finishes its journey. Once a fishing village, its local economy now relies on the tourism trade and its main square is full of mediocre fish restaurants and their touts.

Perched above the village are the ruins of **Anadolu Kavağı Kalesi** (Yoros Kalesi; Anadolu Kavağı; 🚢Eminönü-Kavaklar tourist ferry), a medieval castle that originally had eight massive towers in its walls. Built by the Byzantines, it was restored and reinforced by the Genoese in 1350, and later by the Ottomans. Unfortunately, the castle is in such a serious state of disrepair that it has been fenced so that no-one can enter and enjoy its spectacular Black Sea views. As a result, we suggest giving the steep 25-minute walk up here a miss.

🍴 EATING & DRINKING

SÜTIŞ
CAFE €

(🖉212-323 5030; www.sutis.com.tr; Sakıp Sabancı Caddesi 1, Emirgan; ☉6am-1am; 🚌22, 22RE & 25E from Kabataş, 40, 40T & 42T from Taksim) The Bosphorus branch of this popular chain has an expansive and extremely comfortable terrace overlooking the water. It's known for serving all-day breakfasts and milk-based puddings – we recommend the *simit* (sesame-encrusted bread ring) with honey and *kaymak* (clotted cream). Watching the valet parking ritual on weekends is hilarious.

TAPASUMA
MODERN TURKISH €€€

(🖉216-401 1333; www.tapasuma.com; Kuleli Caddesi 43, Çengelköy; ☉11.30am-midnight; 🚌15) Set in a restored 19th-century *rakı* distillery (*suma* is a Turkish word meaning unadulterated spirit), this recently opened, super-stylish restaurant associated with the luxury Sumahan on the Water hotel has a waterside location and a jetsetter vibe. The menu focusses on Turkish mezes with a modern twist, which are artfully displayed on an 8m-long marble bar.

For a unique experience, call the restaurant to book and ask to be picked up from Kabataş on the hotel's private launch – crossing the Bosphorus in a private boat is a truly wonderful experience.

MÜZEDECHANGA
MODERN TURKISH €€€

(🖉212-323 0901; www.changa-istanbul.com; Sakıp Sabancı Müzesi, Sakıp Sabancı Caddesi 42, Emirgan; starters ₺20-34, mains ₺40-55; ☉10.30am-1am Tue-Sun; 🚌22, 22RE & 25E from Kabataş, 40, 40T & 42T from Taksim) A glamorous terrace with Bosphorus views is the main draw of this design-driven restaurant at the Sakıp Sabancı Museum. The food is good, if overpriced, and is best enjoyed at a weekend brunch. If you don't feel like visiting the museum, door staff will waive the entry fee and point you towards the restaurant.

ANTICA LOCANDA
ITALIAN €€€

(🖉212-287 9745; www.anticalocanda.com.tr; Satış Meydanı 12, Arnavutköy; starters ₺20-38, mains ₺35-65, pizzas (lunch only) €20-30; ☉6.30-11pm Tue, noon-2.30 & 6.30-11pm Wed-Sat, noon-4pm Sun; 🚌22, 22RE & 25E from Kabataş, 40, 40T & 42T from Taksim) Milanese-born chef Gian Carlo Talerico and his Turkish wife Beldan Erkkul converted this former residence of the Aya Strati Taksiarhi Greek Orthodox Church complex into an elegant trattoria in 2011 and keep a loyal coterie of locals happy with their takes on classic Italian dishes including grills, pastas and pizzas.

LUCCA
BAR

(🖉212-257 1255; www.luccastyle.com; Cevdetpaşa Caddesi 51b, Bebek; 🚌22, 22RE & 25E from Kabataş, 40, 40T & 42T from Taksım) Ecstatically embraced by the in-crowd when it first opened in 2005, Lucca's star shows no sign of waning. Glam young things flock here on Friday and Saturday nights to see and be seen, but the mood is more relaxed during the week. Food choices are global, the caffe latte reigns supreme during the day and cocktails claim the spotlight at night.

The Golden Horn

Explore

You can explore the Haliç (Golden Horn) in half a day by boarding the ferry in Karaköy or Eminönü, alighting once at either Hasköy (for the Rahmi M Koç Museum) or Eyüp (for the Eyüp Sultan Mosque) and then reboarding a ferry for the return trip.

If you have a full day, you could visit both of these sights and also visit Aynalıkavak Kasrı before or after visiting the Rahmi M Koç Museum. Another good option is to alight at Ayvansaray on your return trip, follow the historic land walls up the hill and visit the Kariye Museum (Chora Church).

The Best...

➡ **Sight** Rahmi M Koç Museum (p166)
➡ **Local Life** Eyüp Meydanı
➡ **Place to Drink** Pierre Loti Café (p115)

Top Tip

If visiting the Eyüp Sultan Mosque, dress appropriately (no shorts or skimpy skirts and tops). Females should bring a scarf or shawl to use as a head covering

Getting There & Away

➡ **Ferry** Haliç ferries leave Üsküdar hourly from 7.30am to 8.45pm and travel up the Golden Horn to Eyüp, picking up most of their passengers at Eminönü; the last ferry returns from Eyüp at 8.45pm. Note that services are reduced on Sundays and holidays. The ferry trip takes 55 minutes

Golden Horn Cruise

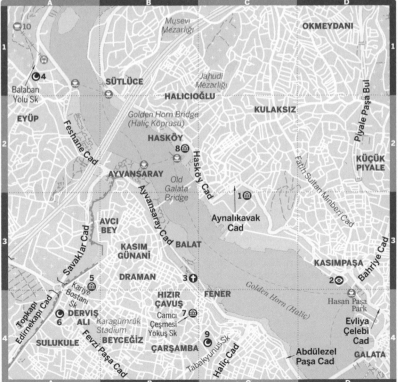

(35 minutes from Eminönü) and costs ₺4 per leg (₺2.15 if you use an İstanbulkart). Check www.sehirhatlari.com.tr for timetable and fare updates.

⮞**Bus** If you wish to return from Eyüp by bus rather than ferry, buses 36CE, 44B and 99 travel from outside the ferry stop at Eyüp via Balat, Fener and Karaköy to Eminönü. Bus 39 travels to Aksaray via Edirnekapı, allowing you to stop and visit the Kariye Museum. To return to Taksim from Hasköy or Sütluce by bus, take bus 36T, 54HT or 54HŞ. For Eminönü, take bus 47, 47E, 47Ç or 47N. All bus tickets cost ₺4 (₺2.15 if you use an İstanbulkart).

Need to Know
⮞**Area Code** ☏212
⮞**Duration** Ferry one way 55 minutes
⮞**Cost** ₺4

⊙ SIGHTS

⊙ Departure Point: Eminönü

These ferries start in Üsküdar on the Asian side and stop in Karaköy before taking on most of their passengers at the Haliç İskelesi (Golden Horn Ferry Dock) on the western side of the Galata Bridge at Eminönü. The dock is behind a car park next

to the Zindanhan Jewellery building. The ferry then passes underneath the Atatürk Bridge and stops at Kasımpaşa on the opposite side of the Golden Horn. This area is where the Ottoman imperial naval yards were located between the 16th and early 20th centuries, and some of the original building stock remains. The palace-like building to the left of the *iskele* is the 19th-century **Bahriye Nezareti**, where the Ministry for the Navy was once based. It is currently undergoing a major restoration. On the hill above is an 18th-century building that was originally the Naval Academy but was converted to a hospital in the 1850s; French soldiers were treated here during the Crimean War.

There are plans to redevelop the shipyards here into a huge complex including shops, hotels and restaurants, although locals seem sceptical that this will go ahead in the near future.

⊙ Kasımpaşa to Hasköy

As the ferry makes its way to the next stop, Hasköy, you can see the fascinating Western District suburbs of Fener and Balat on the western (left) shore.

Fener is the traditional home of the city's Greek population, and although few Greeks are resident these days, a number of important Greek Orthodox sites remain. The prominent red-brick building on the hill is the Phanar Greek Orthodox College, the oldest house of learning in İstanbul. The school has been housed in Fener since before the Conquest – the present building dates from 1881–83. Sadly, it currently has a total enrolment of less than 100 students.

The Gothic Revival church building you can see in the waterside park is the Church of St Stephen of the Bulgars (p114).

The next suburb, Balat, was once home to a large proportion of İstanbul's Jewish population but is now crowded with migrants from the east of the country.

Passing the derelict remains of the original Galata Bridge on its way, the ferry then docks at Hasköy. In the Ottoman period, this part of the city was home to a naval shipyard and a sultan's hunting ground. Today it has two sights of interest to visitors, the Rahmi M Koç Museum, which

TOP SIGHT
RAHMI M KOÇ MUSEUM

This splendid museum (Rahmi M Koç Müzesi in Turkish) is dedicated to the history of transport, industry and communications in Turkey. Its collection of artefacts from İstanbul's industrial past is highly eclectic, giving the impression of being a grab-bag of cool stuff collected over the decades or donated to the museum by individuals, organisations or companies who didn't know what else to do with it. This might sound like we're damning the museum with faint praise, but this is far from the case – in fact, we highly recommend a visit, particularly if you are travelling with children.

The museum is in two parts: a new building on the Golden Horn side of the road and a restored and converted Byzantine stone building opposite. The exhibits concerned with forms of transport are particularly fascinating: you can sit in a classic car; take a cruise on a restored 1936 steam tug (summer weekends only); enter the cabin of a Douglas DC-3 Dakota; board a 1944 US naval submarine; or take a short trip on a working narrow-gauge railway (summer weekends only).

Excellent interpretive panels in Turkish and English are provided. There's also a restaurant right on the waterfront.

DON'T MISS

➡ Sultan Abdul Aziz's railway carriage
➡ Historical car collection

PRACTICALITIES

➡ www.rmk-museum.org.tr
➡ Hasköy Caddesi 5, Hasköy
➡ museum adult/student & child ₺12.50/6, submarine ₺7/5
➡ ☺10am-5pm Tue-Fri, to 6pm/8pm Sat & Sun winter/summer
➡ ▣47, 47E, 47Ç, 47N from Eminönü & 36T, 54HT, 54HŞ from Taksim, ⛴Hasköy

is located directly to the left of the ferry stop (Hasköy İskelesi); and **Aynalıkavak Pavilion** (Aynalıkavak Kasrı; ☎212-256 9750; www.millisaraylar.gov.tr; Aynalıkavak Caddesi, Hasköy; adult/student & child ₺5/1; ☺9am-4.30pm Tue, Wed & Fri-Sun Apr-Oct, to 3.30pm Nov-Mar), a short walk away. This ornate 18th-century imperial hunting pavilion is set in a pretty garden and now houses a collection of historic musical instruments. To get there, walk southeast (right) along Hasköy Caddesi, veer left into Okmeydanı Caddesi and then right into Sempt Konağı Sokak, which runs into Kasimpaşa-Hasköy Caddesi.

⊙ Hasköy to Sütlüce

The ferry's next stop is at **Ayvansaray** on the opposite shore. On the way, look out for three imperial mosques on the western skyline: the Süleymaniye (p91), Yavuz Sultan Selim (p111) and Mihrimah Sultan (p111).

From Ayvansaray, you can visit the Kariye Museum (Chora Church; p108) or walk up to Edirnekapı to see a well-preserved section of the historic city walls.

From Ayvansaray, the ferry crosses to **Sütlüce** and then returns to the western shore to terminate at **Eyüp**. This conservative suburb is built around the Eyüp Sultan Mosque (p114), one of the most important religious sites in Turkey. This ends at the Pierre Loti Café, where you can stop for a tea or coffee and enjoy panoramic views.

 EATING & DRINKING

This isn't a part of town known for its eating and drinking options. Your best options for lunch are the cafes and restaurants in the Rahmi M Koç Museum complex (there are three). For a tea or coffee break, head to the Pierre Loti Café (p115) in Eyüp.

Princes' Islands

....

Explore

This is a great day trip, particularly as the ferry ride is so enjoyable. If you manage to catch an early ferry, you will be able to spend the morning on Heybeliada and the afternoon on Büyükada (or vice versa).

The islands are busiest on holidays and in summer, and ferries can be unpleasantly crowded on weekends at this time; consider visiting midweek instead. In winter many hotels, restaurants and shops close for the season.

....

The Best...

➡**Sight** Haghia Triada Monastery (p168), Heybeliada

➡**Place to Eat** Heyamola Ada Lokantası (p169), Heybeliada

➡**Place to Drink** Yücetepe Kır Gazinosu Restaurant (p169), Büyükada

....

Top Tip

One of the wonderful things about the Princes' Islands is that they are largely car-free zones. Be sure to enjoy a *fayton* (horse-drawn carriage) ride while you're here.

....

Getting There & Away

➡**Ferry** At least eight municipal ferries run to the islands daily from 6.50am to 7.40pm (to 9pm June to mid-September), departing from the Adalar İskelesi (Adalar Ferry Dock) at Kabataş. The most useful departure times for day-trippers are 8.40am, 10.40am and noon (8.30am, 9.30am, 10.30am and 11.30am June to mid-September). On summer weekends, board the vessel and grab a seat at least half an hour before departure time unless you want to stand the whole way. The trip costs ₺6 (3.85₺ with an İstanbulkart) to the islands and the same for each leg between the islands and for the return trip. To be safe, check the timetable at www.sehirhatlari.com.tr, as the schedule often changes.

Ferries return to İstanbul every two hours or so. The last ferry of the day leaves Büyükada at 8.15pm and Heybeliada at 8.30pm (10.40pm and 10.55pm June to mid-September).

There are also regular Mavi Marmara ferries operated by Dentur Avraysa. These are on smaller boats and leave from the *iskele* behind the petrol station at Kabataş. As there are only two stops (Heybeliada and Büyükada) the trip is faster. Ferries depart Kabataş every 30 minutes from 9.30am to 11.30am, at 1pm and then hourly from 2.30pm to 7.30pm. The last return service is at 7.30pm. Tickets cost ₺6; İstanbulkarts are not valid.

....

Need to Know

➡**Area Code** ☑216

➡**Location** 20km southeast of İstanbul

➡**Duration** 80 minutes Heybeliada, 95 minutes Büyükada

◉ SIGHTS

◉ Departure Point: Kabataş

After boarding, try to find a seat on the right side of the ferry so that you can view the various islands as the ferry approaches them.

Heading towards the Sea of Marmara, passengers are treated to fine views of Topkapı Palace, Aya Sofya and the Blue Mosque on the right and Kız Kulesi, Haydarpaşa train station and the distinctive minaret-style clock towers of Marmara University on the left. After a fire in 2011 and its decommissioning as a rail hub, Haydarpaşa train station was placed on the World Monument Fund's international watch list of endangered buildings. Its future was unknown at the time of research and many locals were concerned that it would undergo unsympathetic conversion into a hotel and shopping mall.

After a quick stop at Kadıköy, the ferry makes its way to the first island in the group, Kınalıada. This leg takes 30 minutes. After that, it's another 15 minutes to

SLEEPING ON THE PRINCES' ISLANDS

You'll need to book ahead if you want to stay overnight in summer. Both of the recommendations below are open year-round.

Merit Halki Palace (☑216-351 0025; www.halkipalacehotel.com; Refah Şehitleri Caddesi 94; s/d €110/160; @🛜🏊) This old-fashioned place commands wonderful water views and has comfortable though chintzy rooms equipped with ceiling fans. There's a large pool and two terraces where meals can be enjoyed.

More Cafe & Pansiyon (☑216-382 8833; http://morecafepansiyon.com; Malul Gazi Caddesi 2, Büyükada; s/d €55/65, without bathroom €50/60; ❄🛜; 🚢Büyükada) Homey midrange choice in a handsome wooden villa with a tranquil garden. Guests inevitably comment on the friendly service.

the island of Burgazada and another 15 minutes again to Heybeliada, the second-largest and perhaps the most charming of the islands.

◉ Heybeliada

Heybeliada (Heybeli for short and Halki in Greek) is popular with day-trippers, who come here on weekends to walk in the pine groves and swim from the tiny (but crowded) beaches. The island's major landmark is the hilltop **Haghia Triada Monastery** (☑216-351 8563; ⊙open daily, appointments essential; 🚢Heybeliada), which is perched above a picturesque line of poplar trees in a spot that has been occupied by a Greek monastery since Byzantine times. The current monastery buildings date from 1844 and housed a Greek Orthodox theological school until 1971, when it was closed on the government's orders; the Ecumenical Orthodox Patriarchate is waging an ongoing campaign to have it reopened. There's a small church with an ornate altar and an internationally renowned library that is home to many old and rare manuscripts. To visit the library, you'll need to gain special permission from the abbot, Metropolitan Elpidophoros. A *fayton* will charge ₺30 to bring you here from the centre of town.

The delightful walk from the *iskele* up to the Merit Halki Palace hotel at the top of Refah Şehitleri Caddesi passes a host of large wooden villas set in lovingly tended gardens. Many laneways and streets lead to a picnic spot and lookout points. To find the hotel, turn right as you leave the ferry and head past the waterfront restaurants and cafes to the plaza with the Atatürk statue. From here walk up İşgüzar Sokak,

veering right until you hit Refah Şehitleri Caddesi. If you don't feel like walking up to the hotel (it's uphill but not too steep), you can hire a bicycle (per hour/day ₺10/25) from one of the shops in the main street, or a *fayton* to take you around the island. A 25-minute tour *(küçük turu)* costs ₺45 and a one-hour tour *(büyük turu)* costs ₺58; the *fayton* stand is behind the Atatürk statue. Some visitors spend the day by the **pool** (weekdays/weekends ₺40/60) at the Merit Halki Palace, which is a good idea as the waters around the island aren't very clean and many of the beaches are privatised. Towels and chaise longues are supplied, and there's a pleasant terrace restaurant for meals or drinks.

◉ Büyükada

The largest island in the group, Büyükada (Great Island), is impressive as viewed from the ferry, with gingerbread villas climbing up the slopes of the hill and the bulbous twin cupolas of the Splendid Otel providing an unmistakable landmark.

The **ferry terminal** is an attractive building in the Ottoman Revival style; it dates from 1899.

The island's main drawcard is the **Greek Orthodox Monastery of St George**, located in the 'saddle' between Büyükada's two highest hills. To walk here, head from the ferry to the clock tower in İskele Meydanı (Dock Sq). The shopping district (with cheap eateries) is left along Recep Koç Sokak. Bear right onto 23 Nisan Caddesi, then head along Çankaya Caddesi up the hill to the monastery; when you come to a fork in the road, veer right. The walk, which takes at least one hour, takes you past a long progression of impressive wooden villas set in gardens. About a quarter of the way up on the left is the Büyükada Kültür Evi, a charming spot where you can enjoy a tea or coffee in a garden setting. After 40 minutes or so you will reach a reserve called 'Luna Park' by the locals. The monastery is a 25-minute walk up an extremely steep hill from here. As you ascend, you'll sometimes see pieces of cloth tied to the branches of trees along the path – each represents a prayer, most made by female supplicants visiting the monastery to pray for a child.

There's not a lot to see at the monastery. A small and gaudy church is the only building of note, but there are panoramic views from the terrace, as well as the pleasant Yücetepe Kır Gazinosu restaurant. From its tables you will be able to see all the way to İstanbul and the nearby islands of Yassıada and Sivriada.

The new **Museum of the Princes' Islands** (Adalar Müzesi Hangar Müze Alanı; ☑216-382 6430; www.adalarmuzesi.org; Aya Nikola Mevkii; adult/child under 12yr ₺5/free, free Wed; ◎9am-7pm Tue-Sun Mar-Nov, to 6pm Dec-Feb) is also worth a visit, with exhibits covering local lifestyle, famous residents, food etc. Housed in an old helicopter hangar, it's very hard to locate (there is no street signage). To get here, it's best to take a *fayton* (₺26).

Bicycles are available for rent in several of the town's shops (per hour/day ₺10 /40), and shops on the market street can provide picnic supplies. The *fayton* stand is to the left of the clock tower. Hire one for a long tour of the town, hills and shore (₺80, 70 to 75 minutes) or a shorter tour (₺70). It costs ₺30 to be taken to Luna Park.

✖ EATING & DRINKING

YÜCETEPE KIR GAZINOSU RESTAURANT   TURKISH ₺

(☑216-382 1333; www.yucetepe.com; Monastery of St George, Büyükada; mezes ₺6-8, mains ₺12-16; ◎daily Apr-Oct, Sat & Sun only Nov-Mar) At the very top of the hill where the Monastery of St George is located, this simple place has benches and chairs on a terrace overlooking the sea and İstanbul. Dishes are simple but good – the *köfte* (meatballs) are particularly tasty. You can also enjoy a beer or glass of tea here.

HEYAMOLA ADA LOKANTASI   TURKISH ₺₺

(☑216-351 1111; www.heyamolaadalokantasi. com; Mavi Marmara Yalı Caddesi 30b, Heybeliada; mezes ₺9-12, fish ₺18-20, set brunch ₺25; ◎9am-midnight, closed Mon Nov-Apr; ▣Heybeliada) Opposite the İDO dock, this busy place wows customers with a huge array of mezes (try the baked saganaki cheese), delicious fish mains (order *mezgit* if it's on offer), and an interesting and affordable wine list featuring plenty of boutique labels.

PELIKAN BALIKÇISI   FISH ₺₺

(☑216-382 1282; www.pelikanbalik.com; Şehit Recep Koç Caddesi 20, Büyükada; fish soup ₺7, fish mains ₺15-30 or by kg; ◎11am-9.30pm, to midnight Jun-Aug; ▣Büyükada) The cheery slogan (Hello Fish!) on the sign outside this simple place one street back from the waterfront promenade says it all. Fresh fish is available daily, with yesterday's leftovers used in the tasty fish soup. The friendly waiters probably won't care if you opt for a fish sandwich or a plate of fried *hamsi* (anchovy) instead of the more-expensive grills on offer.

Sleeping

Every accommodation style is available in İstanbul. You can live like a sultan in a world-class luxury hotel, bunk down in a dorm bed or settle into a stylish boutique establishment. The secret is to choose the neighbourhood that best suits your interests, and then look for accommodation that will suit your style and budget – there are loads of options to choose from.

Accommodation Trends

Despite what certain members of the EU may think, İstanbul is a European city and accommodation styles and prices here are similar to those in most major European capitals. Recent trends have seen customers moving away from the small midrange and budget hotels that dominate Sultanahmet towards the apartments and boutique hotels that have been opening in Beyoğlu. Some of these boutique hotels offer chic bars, spas, gyms and other trappings of the international designer lifestyle. The up-and-coming accommodation enclave is the hitherto under-represented Karaköy neighbourhood.

Accommodation Styles

The boutique hotels in Beyoğlu and along the Bosphorus are hip rather than historic, even though many of them occupy handsome 19th-century apartment blocks or mansions. Most have been fitted out by architects versed in international modernism, and have interiors that would suit Stockholm, Sydney or a host of other cities as much as they do İstanbul. In most of Sultanhmet's hotels, the decor is different. These places are often owned and run by locals who are originally from the east of the country and have a resolutely Anatolian aesthetic – you'll see lots of carpets and kilims, silk bedspreads and *nazar boncuks* (the blue glass beads that Turks believe protect against the evil eye). That said, there are a number of Sultanahmet hotels that seem to have melded the best of both worlds, delivering quietly elegant interiors with Anatolian or Ottoman flourishes.

Rates & Reservations

Hotels here are busy, so you should book your room as far in advance as possible, particularly if you are visiting during the high season (Easter to May, Septembe to October and Christmas/New Year). Recent years have seen significant fluctuations in tourist numbers in İstanbul, so most hotels now use yield management systems when setting their rates. This means that in quiet times prices can drop dramatically (sometimes by as much as 50%) and in busy times they can skyrocket. As a result, you should treat our prices as a guide only – it is possible that the price you are quoted will be quite different. Note that most hotels in İstanbul set their prices in euros, and we have listed them as such here.

Lonely Planet's Top Choices

Hotel Empress Zoe (p174) Atmospheric boutique choice near Aya Sofya perfectly balancing charm and comfort.

Hotel Ibrahim Pasha (p174) Chic contemporary style with Ottoman overtones; overlooks the Blue Mosque.

Marmara Guesthouse (p173) Family-run budget pension in the heart of Sultanahmet.

Marmara Pera (p177) Excellent value for money in a vibrant entertainment precinct.

Sirkeci Mansion (p175) Wonderful family choice with impressive service, entertainment program and facilities.

Witt Istanbul Hotel (p177) Sleek suite rooms in bohemian Cihangir.

Best by Budget

€

Cheers Hostel (p173) Airy dorm rooms, streetside terrace and a lovely winter lounge.

Hotel Alp Guesthouse (p173) Attractive, well-priced rooms and a great roof terrace.

Hotel Peninsula (p173) Simple rooms and a friendly atmosphere.

Marmara Guesthouse (p173) Three-star rooms for one-star prices.

€€

Hotel Empress Zoe (p174) Keenly priced rooms and slightly more expensive suites overlooking a courtyard garden.

Hotel Uyan (p175) The lower end of the midrange, with some super-cheap singles.

Marmara Pera (p177) Five-star location and facilities for three-star prices.

€€€

Four Seasons Istanbul at the Bosphorus (p176) Restaurants, impressive spa, luxe rooms and spectacular pool.

Sumahan on the Water (p176) A classy Bosphorus retreat accessed via the hotel's private launch.

Witt Istanbul Hotel (p177) Huge, super-stylish suite rooms and a great breakfast.

Best for Families

Four Seasons Istanbul at the Bosphorus (p176) Baby-sitting service, a pool and a garden.

Sarı Konak Hotel (p175) Kitchenettes in all suites; some suites with bathtubs.

Sirkeci Mansion (p175) Indoor pool, family rooms with bathtub and in-house dining.

Ahmet Efendi Evi (p174) Homey atmosphere and DVD player in family rooms.

Best Rooftop Views

Hotel Ibrahim Pasha (p174) Intimate rooftop bar overlooking the Blue Mosque and Palace of İbrahim Paşa.

Tomtom Suites (p177) Bar-restaurant overlooking the Bosphorus and Old City.

Arcadia Blue Hotel (p176) In-house bar-restaurant overlooking Aya Sofya, the Blue Mosque, the Bosphorus and the Sea of Marmara.

Best Newcomers

Armaggan Bosporus Suites (p176) Luxury and privacy on the Bosphorus shore.

Burckin Suites Hotel (p175) Well-priced rooms in a convenient location between Sultanahmet and the Grand Bazaar.

Vault Karaköy (p177) The latest and most impressive hotel opened by the trend-setting House Hotel group.

Best In-House Restaurants

Ottoman Hotel Imperial (p175) Delicious Ottoman palace cuisine in attractive surrounds.

Sumahan on the Water (p176) Cafe tables next to the water or chic dining in the meze bar.

NEED TO KNOW

Price Ranges
We use the following coding to indicate the high-season price per night of an en suite double room with breakfast:

€ less than €90

€€ €90–€200

€€€ more than €200

Tax
Value-added tax of 8% is added to all hotel bills. This is usually included in the price quoted when you book.

Airport Transfers
Most hotels will provide a free airport transfer from Atatürk International Airport if you stay three nights or more. This sometimes only applies to bookings made through hotel websites.

Discounts
Many hotels offer a discount of between 5% and 10% for cash payments if you book through the hotel website rather than a booking site. Room rates in the low season (November to Easter excluding Christmas and New Year) are usually discounted; the prices we have provided in each review range from the low-season rate to the high-season rate.

Breakfast
Breakfast is almost always included in the room rate. A standard Turkish breakfast buffet includes fresh bread, jams, yoghurt, sheep's milk cheese, boiled eggs, olives, tomatoes, cucumber and tea or coffee. Often cakes and *böreks* (filled pastries) are added to the mix.

SLEEPING

Where to Stay

Neighbourhood	For	Against
Sultanahmet & Around	Most of the major monuments and museums are located here, so it's very convenient for sightseeing; a handy tram service travels to Beyoğlu.	Carpet touts can be annoying, but the biggest drawback is the lack of decent places to eat and drink.
Bazaar District	Quiet, and way off the tourist trail.	Very quiet at night; few eating choices at night and solo travellers may not feel comfortable walking through some streets after dark.
Beyoğlu	The best bars, restaurants and clubs are found here, as is the greatest concentration of boutique hotels and apartment rentals. Tram and metro services connect it with the historic peninsula, and a metro links it with ritzy shopping, commercial and residential suburbs to its northeast.	Violent demonstrations can erupt around Taksim Sq; lots of bars and nightclubs mean that the streets around İstiklal Caddesi and in Cihangir and Karaköy can be noisy.
Kadıköy	The city's best produce market is located here, making it great for self-caterers; loads of bars and restaurants; lovely ferry ride to the Old City or a quick metro trip.	Streets around the market can be noisy in the morning (market trade) and at night (bars); you'll be dependent on public transport and taxis to explore the rest of the city.
The Bosphorus	Rooms and restaurants overlooking the water are romantic, and there's something truly magical about hopping aboard hotel launches to criss-cross the Bosphorus between Asia and Europe.	The distance from the historic peninsula is considerable, so the trip back to your hotel can be tiring after a full day of sightseeing; eating and drinking choices around the hotels here can be limited.

🛏 Sultanahmet & Around

⭐MARMARA GUESTHOUSE · PENSION €
Map p240 (📞212-638 3638; www.marmaraguesthouse.com; Terbıyık Sokak 15, Cankurtaran; s €30-70, d €40-85, f €60-100; ❄@🛜; 🚇Sultanahmet) There are plenty of family-run pensions in Sultanahmet, but few can claim the Marmara's levels of cleanliness and comfort. Manager Elif Aytekin and her family go out of their way to make guests feel welcome, offering plenty of advice and serving a delicious breakfast on the vine-covered, sea-facing roof terrace. Rooms have comfortable beds, good bathrooms and double-glazed windows.

Members of the same family operate the similarly impressive **Saruhan Hotel** (Map p242; 📞212-458 7608; www.saruhanhotel.com; Cinci Meydanı Sokak 34, Kadırga; s €30-65, d €35-75, f €52-105; ❄@🛜; 🚇Çemberlitaş) in the predominantly residential pocket of Kadirga.

HOTEL ALP GUESTHOUSE · HOTEL €
Map p240 (📞212-517 7067; www.alpguesthouse.com; Adliye Sokak 4, Cankurtaran; s €35-60, d €55-80, f €80-110; ❄@🛜; 🚇Sultanahmet) The Alp lives up to its location in Sultanahmet's premier small-hotel enclave, offering a range of attractive, well-priced rooms. Bathrooms are small but very clean, and there are plenty of amenities. The roof terrace is one of the best in this area, with great sea views, comfortable indoor and outdoor seating, and free tea and coffee.

HOTEL PENINSULA · HOTEL €
Map p240 (📞212-458 6850; www.hotelpeninsula.com; Adliye Sokak 6, Cankurtaran; s €30-55, d €35-70, f €80-130; ❄@🛜; 🚇Sultanahmet) Hallmarks here are friendly staff, comfortable rooms and bargain prices. There's a terrace with sea views and hammocks, and a breakfast room with outdoor tables. Basement rooms are dark, but have reduced prices (d €30 to €55, f €65 to €90). The same owners operate the slightly more expensive and comfortable **Grand Peninsula** (Map p240; 📞212-458 7710; www.grandpeninsulahotel.com; Cetinkaya Sokak 3, Cankurtaran; s €35-50, d €45-80, f €85-100; ❄@🛜), a few streets away.

ZEYNEP SULTAN HOTEL · HOTEL €
Map p238 (📞212-514 5001; www.zeynepsultanhotel.com; Zeynep Sultan Camii Sokak 25, Alamdar; s €39-69, d €49-79; ❄@🛜; 🚇Sultanahmet or Gülhane) There aren't many hotels in the world that can boast a Byzantine chapel in the basement, but this one can. Room decor doesn't date back in time quite as far, but it's certainly faded. Front rooms are nice and light, with clean but basic bathrooms and satellite TV. Breakfast is served on the rear terrace with an Aya Sofya view.

HANEDAN HOTEL · HOTEL €
Map p240 (📞212-516 4869; www.hanedanhotel.com; Adliye Sokak 3, Cankurtaran; s €30-55, d €45-70, f €70-110; ❄@🛜; 🚇Sultanahmet) The 11 rooms at this cheap, clean and comfortable choice feature double-glazed windows, satellite TV and small white marble bathrooms. One large and two interconnected rooms are perfect for families, and the pleasant roof terrace overlooks the sea and Aya Sofya.

CHEERS HOSTEL · HOSTEL €
Map p238 (📞212-526 0200; www.cheershostel.com; Zeynep Sultan Camii Sokak 21, Cankurtaran; dm €16-22, d €60-80, tr €90-120; ❄@🛜; 🚇Gülhane) The dorms here are worlds away from the impersonal barracks-like spaces in bigger hostels. Bright and airy, they feature wooden floorboards, rugs, lockers and comfortable beds; most have air-con. Bathrooms are clean and plentiful. It's a great choice in winter because the cosy rooftop bar has an open fire and a great view. Private rooms aren't as nice.

BAHAUS HOSTEL · HOSTEL €
Map p240 (📞212-638 6534; www.bahausistanbul.com; Bayram Fırını Sokak 11, Cankurtaran; dm €11-24, d €60-70, without bathroom €50-60; @🛜; 🚇Sultanahmet) A small, clean and secure operation, Bahaus stands in stark and welcome contrast to the huge institutional-style hostels found on nearby Akbıyık Caddesi. Dorms (some female-only with bathroom) have curtained bunks with good mattresses, reading lights and lockers; they can be hot in summer. Top marks go to the plentiful bathrooms, entertainment program and rooftop terrace bar.

METROPOLIS HOSTEL · HOSTEL €
Map p240 (📞212-518 1822; www.metropolishostel.com; Terbıyık Sokak 24, Cankurtaran; dm €11-18, d €88-140, without bathroom €64-88; ❄@🛜; 🚇Sultanahmet) Located in a quiet street where a good night's sleep is assured, this friendly place offers a mix of dorms – at least one female-only and all

with comfortable beds, reading lamps and private lockers. Showers and toilets are clean but in limited supply. Guests love the rooftop terrace with its sea views and enjoy the busy entertainment program.

AHMET EFENDI EVI   PENSION €
Map p240 (☑212-518 8465; www.ahmetefendi-evi.com; Keresteci Hakkı Sokak 23, Cankurtaran; s €35-65, d €45-80, f €65-140; ✳@☎; ◙Sultan-ahmet) Mr Ahmet's House has a true home-away-from-home feel and is a particularly good choice for families. In a predominant-ly residential area (a rarity in Sultanahmet), it offers nine rooms that vary in size; the family rooms have kettles and DVD players.

BIG APPLE HOSTEL   HOSTEL €
Map p240 (☑212-517 7931; www.hostelbigapple.com; Bayram Fırını Sokak 12, Cankurtaran; dm €15-21, s €50-75, d €55-85; ✳@☎; ◙Sultanahmet) It may be lacking a traveller vibe, but the compensations at this recently renovated hostel include six- and 14-bed air-conditioned dorms with comfortable beds, as well as hotel-style private rooms with private bathroom and satellite TV. Added to this is a rooftop bar-breakfast room with sea views.

★ HOTEL IBRAHIM PASHA   BOUTIQUE HOTEL €€
Map p240 (☑212-518 0394; www.ibrahimpasha.com; Terzihane Sokak 7; r standard €100-195, deluxe €145-285; ✳@☎; ◙Sultanahmet) This exemplary designer hotel has a great loca-tion just off the Hippodrome, a comfortable lounge with open fire, and a terrace bar with knockout views of the Blue Mosque. All of the rooms are gorgeous but some are small – opt for a deluxe one if possible. Urbane owner Mehmet Umur is a mine of information about the city.

★ HOTEL EMPRESS ZOE   BOUTIQUE HOTEL €€
Map p240 (☑212-518 2504; www.emzoe.com; Akbıyık Caddesi 10, Cankurtaran; s €65-90, d €110-140, ste €160-275; ✳☎; ◙Sultanahmet) Named after the feisty Byzantine Empress, this is one of the most impressive boutique hotels in the city. There's a range of room types but the garden suites are particularly enticing as they overlook a gorgeous flower-filled courtyard where breakfast is served in warm weather. You can enjoy an early evening drink there, or while admiring the sea view from the terrace bar.

APARTMENT LIVING

We all daydream about packing our bags and escaping to live in another country at some stage in our lives. In İstanbul, it's easy to hire an apartment and do just that for a week or two.

There's a rapidly proliferating number of short-term apartment rentals on offer here, all of which are furnished and most of which come with amenities such as wi-fi, washing machines and weekly maid service. Many are located in historic apartment blocks and offer spectacular views – just remember that the usual trade-off for this is a steep flight of stairs.

The following companies are worth investigating; most have three- or four-day minimum rental periods:

1001 Nites (www.1001nites.com; apt €100-135) Run by a long-term American resident. Locations in Sultanahmet, Çukurcuma and Cihangir.

Galateia Residence (Map p248; ☑212-245 3032; www.galateiaresidence.com; Şahkulu Bostan Sokak 9, Galata; apt from €140; ✳☎; Ⓜ Şişhane, ◙Karaköy, then funicular to Tünel) Serviced apartments in a wonderful location close to Galata Tower. Perfect for busi-ness travellers, but a 30-day minimum stay applies.

Istanbul Apartments (☑0212-249 5065; www.istanbulapt.com; apt from €50; ✳@) Run by an urbane Turkish couple, with properties in Cihangir, Tarlabası and off İstiklal.

istanbul!place Apartments (http://istanbulplace.com/; apt 1-bed €80-121, 2-bed €109-230, 3-bed €115-270) Stylish and well-set-up apartments in the Galata district managed by an English-Turkish couple.

Manzara Istanbul (☑212-252 4660; www.manzara-istanbul.com; apt per night from €70; ✳☎) Long-standing operation run by a Turkish-German architect. Locations are mainly in Galata, Cihangir and Kabataş.

★ SIRKECI MANSION HOTEL €€

Map p238 (📞212-528 4344; www.sirkecimansion.com; Taya Hatun Sokak 5, Sirkeci; standard r €120-215, superior & deluxe r €220-325, f €220-295; ✳@🏵🏊; 🚇Gülhane) The owners of this terrific hotel overlooking Gülhane Park know what keeps guests happy – rooms are impeccably clean, well sized and loaded with amenities. It has a restaurant where a lavish breakfast is served, an indoor pool and a hamam. Top marks go to the incredibly helpful staff and the complimentary entertainment program, which includes walking tours and afternoon teas.

SARI KONAK HOTEL BOUTIQUE HOTEL €€

Map p240 (📞212-638 6258; www.istanbulhotelsarikonak.com; Mimar Mehmet Ağa Caddesi 26, Cankurtaran; s & d €59-179, tr €79-199, ste €119-299; ✳@🏵; 🚇Sultanahmet) Guests here enjoy relaxing on the roof terrace with its Sea of Marmara and Blue Mosque views, but also take advantage of the comfortable lounge and courtyard downstairs. Rooms are similarly impressive – the deluxe rooms are spacious and elegantly decorated, the superior rooms are nearly as nice, and standard rooms, though small, are very attractive. Suites have kitchenettes.

BURCKIN SUITES HOTEL HOTEL €€

Map p242 (📞212-638 5521; www.burckinhotel.com; Klodfarer Caddesi 18, Binbirdirek; s €50-109, d €60-119; ✳@🏵; 🚇Sultanahmet) An offer of four-star amenities at three-star prices is always enticing, and such is the case here. Rooms are small but the decor is attractive and there are plenty of amenities. The main draw is the rooftop terrace restaurant-bar, which has a wonderful view of Aya Sofya and the Sea of Marmara.

OTTOMAN HOTEL IMPERIAL HOTEL €€

Map p238 (📞212-513 6150; www.ottomanhotelimperial.com; Caferiye Sokak 6; s from €110, d from €130, ste from €215; ✳@🏵; 🚇Sultanahmet) This four-star hotel is in a wonderfully quiet location just outside the Topkapı Palace walls. Its large and comfortable rooms have plenty of amenities and are decorated with Ottoman-style objets d'art – opt for one with an Aya Sofya view or one in the rear annexe. No roof terrace, but the excellent Matbah (p82) restaurant is based here.

HOTEL UYAN HOTEL €€

Map p240 (📞212-518 9255; www.uyanhotel.com; Utangaç Sokak 25, Cankurtaran; s €50-60, d standard €75-99, deluxe €95-200; ✳@🏵; 🚇Sultanahmet) The Uyan's quietly elegant decor nods towards the Ottoman style, but never goes over the top – everyone will feel at home here. Rooms are comfortable and most are of a decent size; the exceptions are the budget singles, which are tiny but serviceable. Breakfast is enjoyed in the top-floor space or on the terrace.

HOTEL NOMADE BOUTIQUE HOTEL €€

Map p240 (📞212-513 8172; www.hotelnomade.com; Ticarethane Sokak 15, Alemdar; s €60-100, d €70-110; ✳🏵; 🚇Sultanahmet) Designer style and budget pricing don't often go together, but the Nomade bucks the trend. Just a few steps off busy Divan Yolu, it offers simple rooms that some guests find too small – request the largest possible. Everyone loves the roof-terrace bar (smack-bang in front of Aya Sofya).

DERSAADET HOTEL HOTEL €€

Map p240 (📞212-458 0760; www.hoteldersaadet.com; Kapıağası Sokak 5, Küçük Aya Sofya; s €70-105, d standard €70-130, d & tr deluxe €110-160; ✳@🏵; 🚇Sultanahmet) 'Dersaadet' means 'Place of Happiness' in Turkish – and guests are inevitably happy at this well-run place. A restored Ottoman house, it offers extremely comfortable rooms; three have charming hamam-style bathrooms and half have sea views. The terrace restaurant has Sea of Marmara and Blue Mosque views.

OSMAN HAN HOTEL HOTEL €€

Map p240 (📞212-458 7702; www.osmanhanhotel.com; Çetinkaya Sokak 1, Cankurtaran; d & tw €80-140, t €130-169; ✳@🏵; 🚇Sultanahmet) Amenity levels at this small hotel are high – rooms have comfortable beds, free minibars, tea/coffee facilities and satellite TV; opt for a slightly larger deluxe room if possible, as the bathrooms in the standard rooms are cramped (request 41 or 42). The breakfast room and terrace have sea views, and guests are free to use the kitchen.

ERTEN KONAK BOUTIQUE HOTEL €€

Map p240 (📞212-458 5000; www.ertenkonak.com; Akbıyık Değirmeni Sokak, Cankurtaran; standard r €80-140, executive r €100-160; ✳@🏵; 🚇Sultanahmet) Lovers of antiques and collectables will enjoy staying in this historic wooden *konak* (mansion), which has been completely rebuilt in recent years. Public areas are full of objects d'art and all 16 rooms are attractively decorated.

SLEEPING SULTANAHMET & AROUND

Standard rooms are cramped – opt for a deluxe room if possible. No roof terrace, but the glassed winter garden compensates.

HOTEL ŞEBNEM
HOTEL €€

Map p240 (☑212-517 6623; www.sebnemhotel.net; Adliye Sokak 1, Cankurtaran; s €50-80, d €60-120, f €80-140; ❄@🛜; ⛴Sultanahmet) Simplicity is the rule at the Şebnem, and it works a treat. Rooms have wooden floors, recently renovated bathrooms and comfortable beds; two have a private courtyard garden. The large terrace upstairs functions as a bar and nargile cafe and has views over the Sea of Marmara.

EMINE SULTAN HOTEL
HOTEL €€

Map p240 (☑212-458 4666; www.eminesultanhotel.com; Kapıağası Sokak 6, Cankurtaran; s €75-85, d €105-120; ❄@🛜; ⛴Sultanahmet) Solo female travellers and families will feel particularly at home here because manager Özen Dalgın is as friendly as she is efficient, and the rest of the staff follow her lead. Rooms have a pretty cream-and-pink decor and some have sea views. A delicious breakfast is served in the upstairs breakfast room, which overlooks the Sea of Marmara.

ARCADIA BLUE HOTEL
HOTEL €€€

Map p240 (☑212-516 9696; www.hotelarcadiablue.com; İmran Öktem Caddesi 1, Bindirbirek; s €125-255, d €135-255, sea view r €165-355; ❄@🛜; ⛴Sultanahmet) Views of Aya Sofya, the Blue Mosque, the Bosphorus and the Sea of Marmara certainly make breakfast

or the complimentary afternoon aperitivo memorable at the terrace restaurant-bar of this recently renovated hotel. Rooms are extremely comfortable; all are a good size but the sea-view versions are worth their higher price tag. There's a hamam (charged) and a gym (free).

🛏 Bazaar District

HAYRIYE HANIM KONAĞI
BOUTIQUE HOTEL €€

Map p242 (HHK Hotel; ☑212-513 0026; www.hhkhotel.com; Hayriye Hanım Sokak 19, Süleymaniye; s €60-148, d €65-158; ❄🛜❄; Ⓜ Haliç, ⛴Beyazıt-Kapalı Çarşı) We're in two minds about HHK's claim to boutique status, as levels of comfort and service don't quite justify this. However, views are impressive and there's a small outdoor pool, which is almost unprecedented in the Old City. Occupying a restored Ottoman timber house, its location in the shabby area below the Süleymaniye Mosque may not be to all tastes.

🛏 Beyoğlu

WORLD HOUSE HOSTEL
HOSTEL €

Map p248 (☑212-293 5520; www.worldhouseistanbul.com; Galipdede Caddesi 85, Galata; dm €14-18, d €68, tr €78; @🛜; Ⓜ Şişhane, ⛴Karaköy, then funicular to Tünel) Hostels in İstanbul are usually impersonal hulks with jungle-like atmospheres, but World House

SLEEPING BAZAAR DISTRICT

BOSPHORUS NIGHTS

If you're in İstanbul to relax rather than indulge in an orgy of sightseeing, you should consider staying in one of a growing number of glam boutique hotels in the Bosphorus suburbs. Most of these are housed in painstakingly restored *yalıs* (waterside timber mansions), have chic fit-outs and offer excellent restaurants. They're a long way from the sights of Sultanahmet and the entertainment district of Beyoğlu, but are perfect places for a romantic retreat. Our favourite is the elegant **Sumahan on the Water** (☑216-422 8000; www.sumahan.com; Kuleli Caddesi 51, Çengelköy; r €175-325, ste €225-615; ❄@🛜; ⛴15, 15F, 15P from Üsküdar), which is located on the Asian side of the strait and has a waterside terrace, an in-house bar-restaurant, a hamam and a hotel launch to transport guests across the water.

Closer to the city centre are two super-luxurious options: **Four Seasons Istanbul at the Bosphorus** (Map p250; ☑212-381 4000; www.fourseasons.com/bosphorus; Çırağan Caddesi 28; s €370-540, d €400-570, ste €600-18,000; ❄@🛜❄; ⛴Bahçeşehir University or Çırağan) is set in an Ottoman-era building right on the water and features luxe rooms, a fabulous swimming pool and a luxury spa; and **Armaggan Bosporus Suites** (Map p250; ☑212-227 8080; www.armaggan.com; Yalı Çıkmazı Sokak 5, Ortaköy; r €700-2800; ❄@🛜; ⛴Ortaköy) is an intimate boutique hotel occupying three 19th-century *yalıs* in Ortaköy.

is reasonably small and very friendly. Best of all is its location close to Beyoğlu's entertainment strips but not too far from the sights in Sultanahmet. There are large and small dorms (one shower for every six beds), but none are female-only.

★MARMARA PERA   HOTEL €€
Map p248 (🖉212-251 4646; www.themarmarahotels.com; Meşrutiyet Caddesi 1, Tepebaşı; s €109-160, d €135-199; 🏵 @ 🛜 🛋; Ⓜ Şişhane, 🚠 Karaköy, then funicular to Tünel) A great location in the midst of Beyoğlu's major entertainment enclave makes this high-rise modern hotel an excellent choice. Added extras include a health club, a tiny outdoor pool, a truly fabulous buffet breakfast spread and the Mikla (p135) rooftop bar and restaurant. Rooms with a sea view are approximately 30% more expensive.

HAS HAN GALATA   BOUTIQUE HOTEL €€
Map p248 (🖉212-251 4218; www.hahsan.com.tr; Bankalar Caddesi 7, Galata; r €150-180, ste €180-215; 🏵 🛜; Ⓜ Şişhane, 🚠 Karaköy) Located on the cosmopolitan side of the Galata Bridge, this recently opened establishment has nine well-appointed and beautifully decorated rooms and an in-house cafe. The happening neighbourhood of Karaköy is close by, and the Old City is a relatively short walk away.

RICHMOND HOTEL   HOTEL €€
Map p248 (🖉212-252 5460; www.richmondhotels.com.tr; İstiklal Caddesi 227; d €120-210, tr €180-260, ste €280-320; 🏵 @ 🛜; Ⓜ Şişhane, 🚠 Karaköy, then funicular to Tünel) Behind its 19th-century facade, the Richmond is modern, comfortable and well run. Rooms have been renovated in recent years and are a good size; light sleepers should request one at the rear as the hotel's location on ever-busy İstiklal Caddesi means that those at the front can be noisy. The Leb-i Derya bar on the 6th floor is a definite draw.

★WITT ISTANBUL
HOTEL   BOUTIQUE HOTEL €€€
Map p248 (🖉212-293 1500; www.wittistanbul.com; Defterdar Yokuşu 26, Cihangir; d ste €195-385, penthouse & superior king €385-450; 🏵 @ 🛜; Ⓜ Taksim, 🚠 Tophane) Showcasing nearly as many designer features as an is-

sue of *Wallpaper** magazine, this stylish apartment hotel in the trendy suburb of Cihangir has 18 suites with kitchenette, seating area, CD/DVD player, iPod dock, espresso machine, king-sized bed and huge bathroom. Penthouse and superior king suites have fabulous views. It's a short but steep climb from the Tophane tram stop.

VAULT KARAKÖY   BOUTIQUE HOTEL €€€
Map p248 (🖉212-244 6434; www.thehousehotel.com; Bankalar Caddesi 5, Karaköy; r €125-320, ste €210-800; 🏵 @ 🛜; Ⓜ Şişhane, 🚠 Karaköy) Han Tümertekin's US$40 million fit-out of this new hotel epitomises the modern city, being an exciting and evocative meld of old and new. Occupying a grand bank building complete with vaults (hence the name), the hotel's public areas are full of art and include a lobby restaurant and bar. There's also a summer roof terrace, a gym and a spa complete with sauna, steam room and hamam.

TOMTOM SUITES   BOUTIQUE HOTEL €€€
Map p248 (🖉212-292 4949; www.tomtomsuites.com; Tomtom Kaptan Sokak 18; ste €169-649; 🏵 @ 🛜; Ⓜ Şişhane, 🚠 Karaköy, then funicular to Tünel) We're more than happy to beat the drum about this suite hotel occupying a former Franciscan nunnery off İstiklal Caddesi. Its contemporary decor is understated but elegant, with particularly impressive bathrooms, and each suite is beautifully appointed. There's also a rooftop bar-restaurant with fantastic views

🛏 Kadıköy

HUSH MODA   HOSTEL €
Map p253 (🖉216-330 1122; www.hushhostels.com; Güneşlibahçe Sokak 50b; dm ₺35-45, d ₺120-145, without bathroom ₺90-120; 🏵 @ 🛜; 🚢 Kadıköy, Ⓜ Kadıköy) The new metro link between the Old City and Asian suburbs has made Kadıköy a viable accommodation location at last, and the Hush flashpacker operation has responded by opening two hostels here. This is the best of the two. Most private rooms have air-con (dorms don't), there's a terrace bar and guests can use the kitchen (the produce market is nearby).

Understand İstanbul

İstanbul Today

As the 21st century gets into gear, this meeting point of Europe and Asia is revelling in the unprecedented growth and prosperity it has achieved over the past decade. It's also getting larger – the official population is 14 million, but most locals think that 20 million is a more accurate estimate, leading to huge problems with urban sprawl and inadequate infrastructure.

Best in Music

Mercan Dede A major name on the international World Music scene, Dede's distinctive Sufi-electronic techno-fusion is showcased in his albums *Sufi Dreams* (1996), *Journeys of a Dervish* (1999), *Sayahatname* (2001), *Nar* (Fire; 2002), *Sufi Traveller* (2003), *Su* (Water; 2004), *Nefes* (Breath; 2006), *800* (2007) and *Dünya* (Earth; 2013).

İlhan Erşahin The Turkish-American jazz saxophonist and composer is a big name in both New York, where he resides, and İstanbul, where he and his Istanbul Sessions ensemble regularly play at the Nublu venue in Karaköy. Their two albums are *Ilhan Erşahin's Istanbul Sessions with Erik Truffaz* (2009) and *Night Rider* (2012).

Fazıl Say The internationally renowned pianist and composer has innumerable compositions and recordings to his credit, including the 2007 violin concerto *1001 Nights in the Harem* and 2010 *İstanbul Symphony*.

Sezen Aksu The queen of Turkish pop; *Öptüm* (2011) was her first international release.

Too Many Tourists?

Tourism is booming. Turkey is now the sixth-most-visited tourist destination in the world, and İstanbul is the country's number-one destination for visitors. At present, the city hosts nearly 12 million visitors per year, and while this brings prosperity, it also brings challenges. Chief among these are the detrimental effects that crowds can have on the physical condition of ancient monuments such as Aya Sofya and Topkapı Palace, which together host nearly seven million visitors per year.

Civil Unrest

When İstanbul hit the international headlines in mid-2013, it wasn't because of the tourist boom. Anti-government demonstrations had been triggered by a decision to hand over one of Beyoğlu's few public green spaces, Gezi Park near Taksim Meydanı (Taksim Sq) to developers but swiftly developed into a much larger movement protesting at what the largely secularist and left-leaning protesters saw as an increasingly autocratic style of leadership by then–Prime Minister Recep Tayyip Erdoğan and a crackdown on democratic rights including freedom of speech and the press by the ruling AKP party. Riot police brought the Gezi protests to a violent end, but anger at Mr Erdoğan and the AKP continues unabated among a vocal sector of the city's population.

Infrastructure Upgrades

Over the past two decades the constantly growing population has placed a huge strain on the city's public transport system. Fortunately, the local authorities and Ankara anticipated this problem and in 2005 commenced works on the Marmaray project, a hugely ambitious transportation infrastructure program that is ongoing. Works have included building an underwater railway link between the European and Asian suburbs, erecting a railway bridge over the Golden Horn and integrating the new railway lines with other city transport options. Construction has been slowed by constant archaeological discoveries (always a possibility in a city this ancient), but the first phase of the project opened to great fanfare at the end of 2013. The second phase, which includes railway track renewal and construction between Gebze and İbrahimağa on the Asian side of the city and between Yenikapı and Halkalı on the European side, is scheduled for completion in 2015.

Heritage Initiatives

A massive program of heritage restoration has occurred in recent years, with the main focus being on the imperial mosques. These are being magnificently restored, but we are sorry to report that the city's Byzantine building stock hasn't received the same level of care and attention. Some Byzantine buildings have been 'mosquified' (Little Aya Sofya), some have been all but destroyed (the historic land walls) and others are being subjected to restorations that can only be described as reprehensible (Church of the Monastery of Christ Pantokrator).

An Exciting Cultural Landscape

Over the past decade the city's big banks, business dynasties and universities have built and endowed an array of cutting-edge museums and cultural centres, many of which have been designed by local architectural practices with growing international reputations.

Joining relatively new and mightily impressive cultural centres such as SALT and ARTER in Beyoğlu will be the Antrepo 5 Museum of Contemporary Art, a visually arresting building in Tophane designed by high-profile local architectural firm Emre Arolat; and Koç Contemporary, a sleek building designed by UK-based Grimshaw Architects. Local culture vultures are almost beside themselves with excitement.

These and a number of other institutions (large and small, public and private) aim to nurture a new and exciting generation of Turkish arts practitioners. Complementing their exhibition, lecture and performance programs is the city's festival circuit, which is spearheaded by the İstanbul Foundation for Culture and Arts and is now one of the busiest in Europe.

And Some Dodgy Developments

The city's skyline is in many ways its signature, but in the past decade some modern – and ugly – developments have been added to it. In order to accommodate this 'urban regeneration' some residents – a good percentage of whom, critics have noted, are members of minority social groups – have been forcibly removed from their homes in inner-city suburbs including Sulukule and Tarlabaşı and relocated to purpose-built high-rise housing in outer suburbs. Local environmental and heritage activists are quick to point out that many of the developments are being built by consortia with strong ties to the ruling AKP party.

if İstanbul were 100 people

65 would live on the European side
35 would live on the Asian side

religion
(% of population)

66 Sunni Muslim

33 Alevi Muslim

1 Non-Muslim (Christian, Jewish)

population per sq km

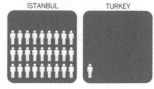

İSTANBUL   TURKEY

≈ 95 people

History

İstanbul has a history that has been turbulent and triumphant in equal measure. In its guises of Byzantium and Constantinople it was ruled by Greeks, Romans and their descendants, many of whom left their stamp on the city's built heritage. After the fall of Byzantium, it functioned as the capital of the world's most-powerful empire and benefited from the riches associated with this. Its politics have given us the descriptor 'Byzantine' and its patrons have endowed it with a legacy of buildings and artefacts that certainly brings history to life.

Byzantium

Legend tells us that the city of Byzantium was founded around 667 BC by a group of colonists from Megara, northwest of Athens. It was named after their leader, Byzas.

The new colony quickly prospered, largely due to its ability to levy tolls and harbour fees on ships passing through the Bosphorus, then as now an important waterway. A thriving marketplace was established and the inhabitants lived on traded goods and the abundant fish stocks in the surrounding waters.

In 512 BC Darius, emperor of Persia, captured the city during his campaign against the Scythians. Following the retreat of the Persians in 478 BC, the town came under the influence and protection of Athens and joined the Athenian League. Though this was a turbulent relationship, Byzantium stayed under Athenian rule until 355 BC, when it gained independence.

By the end of the Hellenistic period, Byzantium had formed an alliance with the Roman Empire. It retained its status as a free state, and kept this even after being officially incorporated into the Roman Empire in AD 79 by Vespasian. Life was relatively uneventful until the city's leaders made a big mistake: they picked the wrong side in a Roman war of succession following the death of the Emperor Pertinax in AD 193. When Septimius Severus emerged victorious over his rival Pescennius Niger, he mounted a three-year siege of the city, eventually

TIMELINE	1000 BC	667 BC	512 BC
	Thracian tribes found the settlements of Lygos and Semistra; Plinius mentions the founding of Semistra in his histories and traces of Lygos remain near Seraglio Point.	Legend tells us that Byzas, a citizen of the city of Megara, northwest of Athens, travels up the Bosphorus and founds Byzantium on the site of Lygos.	The army of the Persian emperor Darius captures the city; after the Persians' retreat in 478 BC, Byzantium chooses to join the Athenian League for protection.

massacring Byzantium's citizens, razing its walls and burning it to the ground. Ancient Byzantium was no more.

The new emperor was aware of the city's important strategic position, and soon set about rebuilding it. He pardoned the remaining citizens and built a circuit of walls enclosing a city twice the size of its predecessor. The Hippodrome was built by Severus, as was a colonnaded way that followed the present path of Divan Yolu. Severus named his new city Augusta Antonina and it was subsequently ruled by a succession of emperors, including the great Diocletian (r 284–305).

Constantinople

Diocletian had decreed that after his retirement, the government of the Roman Empire should be overseen by co-emperors Galerius in the east (Augusta Antonina) and Constantine in the west (Rome). This resulted in a civil war, which was won by Constantine in AD 324 when he defeated Licinius, Galerius' successor, at Chrysopolis (the present-day suburb of Üsküdar).

With his victory, Constantine (r 324–37) became sole emperor of a reunited empire. He also became the first Christian emperor, though he didn't formally convert until he was on his deathbed. To solidify his power he summoned the First Ecumenical Council at Nicaea (İznik) in 325, which established the precedent of the emperor's supremacy in church affairs.

Constantine also decided to move the capital of the empire to the shores of the Bosphorus, where he had forged his great victory and where the line between the Eastern and Western divisions of the Empire had previously been drawn. He built a new, wider circle of walls around the site of Byzantium and laid out a magnificent city within. The Hippodrome was extended and a forum was built on the crest of the second hill, near today's Nuruosmaniye Mosque. The city was dedicated on 11 May 330 as New Rome, but soon came to be called Constantinople.

Constantine died in 337, just seven years after the dedication of his new capital. His empire was divided up between his three sons: Constantius, Constantien and Constans. Constantinople was part of Constantius' share. His power base was greatly increased in 353 when he overthrew both of his brothers and brought the empire under his sole control.

Constantius died in 361 and was succeeded by his cousin Julian. Emperor Jovian was next, succeeded by Valens (of aqueduct fame).

The city continued to grow under the rule of the emperors. Theodosius I ('the Great'; r 378–95) had a forum built on the present site of

The name İstanbul probably derives from 'eis ten polin' (Greek for 'to the city'). Though the Turks kept the name Constantinople after the Conquest, they also used other names, including İstanbul and Dersaadet (City of Peace and/or Happiness). The city's name was officially changed to İstanbul by Atatürk in the early republican years.

335 BC	AD 79	330	380
Byzantium is granted independence but stays under the Athenian umbrella, withstanding with Athenian help a siege by Philip, father of Alexander the Great, in 340 BC.	Byzantium is officially incorporated into the Roman Empire ruled by the soldier-emperor Vespasian; it retains its status as a free state but pays high taxes to the empire.	Constantine the Great declares Byzantium the capital of the Roman Empire; the city soon becomes known as Constantinople.	Theodosius I declares Christianity the imperial religion; a year later, he summons an ecumenical council to Constantinople to define church orthodoxy.

POWERS BEHIND THE THRONE

Many powerful women have featured in İstanbul's imperial history. Our favourites are the following:

Theodora

The wife of Justinian, Theodora (500–548) was the daughter of a bear-keeper at the Hippodrome and, according to Herodotus, had been a courtesan before she married. She subsequently became extremely devout and endowed a number of churches in the city. Justinian was devoted to her and she was widely acknowledged by contemporary historians to be the true power behind the throne. During her time as consort, she established homes for ex-prostitutes, granted women more rights in divorce cases, allowed women to own and inherit property, and enacted the death penalty for rape.

Zoe

Feisty Zoe (978–1050) was 50 years old and supposedly a virgin when her dying father, Constantine VIII, insisted she marry the aged Romanus III Argyrus. Romanus had in fact been happily married for 40 years but neither Zoe nor her father were going to let that get in their way, threatening him with blinding if he didn't consent. When Constantine died, Romanus was crowned emperor and Zoe empress. Finding married life a tad dull, Zoe took as her lover the much younger Michael the Paphlagonian. After Romanus mysteriously drowned in his bath in 1034, Zoe quickly married her virile companion, who joined her on the throne as Michael IV. Eight years later, after Michael died from an illness contracted while on campaign, Zoe and her sister Theodora ruled as empresses in their own right. At the age of 64 Zoe was married again, this time to an eminent senator, Constantine IX Monomachus, who eventually outlived her.

Roxelana

The wife of Süleyman the Magnificent, Hürrem Sultan (1506–58) was more commonly known as Roxelana. She was beautiful, clever and a thoroughly nasty piece of work. Though allowed four legal wives and as many concubines as he could support by Islamic law, Süleyman was devoted to Roxelana alone and ended up marrying her. Secure in her position, she mastered the art of palace intrigue and behind-the-scenes manipulation, even convincing the sultan to have İbrahim Paşa, Süleyman's lifelong companion and devoted grand vizier, strangled when he objected to her influence. Unfortunately, she also made sure that her drunken son, Selim the Sot, would succeed to the throne by having the able heir apparent, Prince Mustafa, strangled.

Beyazıt Meydanı (Beyazıt Sq) and erected the Obelisk of Theodosius at the Hippodrome. His grandson Emperor Theodosius II (r 408–50), threatened by the forces of Attila the Hun, ordered that an even wider, more formidable circle of walls be built around the city. Encircling

524	527	548	565
Justinian, the most famous of the Byzantine emperors, marries a courtesan called Theodora, the daughter of a bear-keeper at the Hippodrome.	Justinian takes the throne and makes Theodora joint ruler; his introduction of heavy taxes leads to the Nika riots of 532 and half of the city is destroyed.	Theodora dies; during her reign she was known for granting women more rights in divorce cases, allowing women to own and inherit property, and enacting the death penalty for rape.	Justinian dies; his lasting memorial is the church of Hagia Sophia (Aya Sofya), which was to be the centre of Eastern Orthodox Christianity for many centuries.

all seven hills of the city, the walls were completed in 413, only to be brought down by a series of earthquakes in 447. They were hastily rebuilt in a mere two months – the rapid approach of Attila and the Huns acting as a powerful stimulus. The Theodosian walls successfully held out invaders for the next 757 years and still stand today, though they are in an increasingly dilapidated state of repair.

Theodosius died in 450 and was succeeded by a string of emperors, including the most famous of all Byzantine emperors, Justinian the Great. A former soldier, he and his great general Belisarius reconquered Anatolia, the Balkans, Egypt, Italy and North Africa. They also successfully put down the Nika riots of 532, killing 30,000 of the rioters in the Hippodrome in the process.

Three years before taking the throne, Justinian had married Theodora, a strong-willed former courtesan who is credited with having great influence over her husband. Together, they further embellished Constantinople with great buildings, including SS Sergius and Bacchus, now known as Küçük (Little) Aya Sofya, Hagia Eirene (Aya İrini) and Hagia Sophia (Aya Sofya), which was completed in 537.

From 565 to 1025, a succession of warrior emperors kept invaders such as the Persians and the Avars at bay. Though the foreign armies often managed to get as far as Chalcedon (the present-day suburb of Kadıköy), none were able to breach Theodosius' land walls. The Arab armies of the nascent Islamic empire tried in 669, 674, 678 and 717–18, each time in vain.

In 1071 Emperor Romanus IV Diogenes (r 1068–1071) led his army to eastern Anatolia to do battle with the Seljuk Turks, who had been forced out of Central Asia by the encroaching Mongols. However, at Manzikert (Malazgirt) the Byzantines were disastrously defeated, the emperor captured and imprisoned, and the former Byzantine heartland of Anatolia thus thrown open to Turkish invasion and settlement. Soon the Seljuks had built a thriving empire of their own in central Anatolia, with their capital first at Nicaea and later at Konya.

As Turkish power was consolidated to the east of Constantinople, the power of Venice – always a maritime and commercial rival to Constantinople – grew in the West. This coincided with the launch of the First Crusade and the arrival in Constantinople of the first of the Crusaders in 1096. Soldiers of the Second Crusade passed through the city in 1146 during the reign of Manuel I, son of John Comnenus II 'the Good' and his empress, Eirene, both of whose mosaic portraits can be seen in the gallery at Aya Sofya.

In 1204 soldiers of the Fourth Crusade led by Enrico Dandolo, Doge of Venice, attacked and ransacked the city. They then ruled it with an ally, Count Baldwin of Flanders, until 1261, when soldiers under

The Empress Theodora makes a great subject in Stella Duffy's rollicking biographical novel *Theodora: Actress. Empress. Whore.* (2010), and the palace intrigues orchestrated by Süleyman the Magnificent's consort Roxelana make for great television drama in the enormously popular prime-time Turkish show *Muhteşem Yüzyıl* (The Magnificent Century).

620	717	1204	1261
Heraclius I (r 610–41) changes the official language of the eastern empire from Latin to Greek, inaugurating what we now refer to as 'The Byzantine Empire'.	Leo III, a Syrian, becomes emperor after deposing Theodosius III; he introduces edicts against the worship of images, ushering in the age of iconoclasm.	Enrico Dandolo, Doge of Venice, leads the crusaders of the Fourth Crusade in a defeat of Constantinople; they sack the city and steal many of its treasures.	Constantinople is recaptured by Michael VIII Palaeologus, a Byzantine aristocrat in exile who had risen to become co-emperor of Nicaea; the Byzantine Empire is restored.

Michael VIII Palaeologus, a Byzantine aristocrat in exile who had risen to become co-emperor of Nicaea, successfully recaptured it. The Byzantine Empire was restored.

İstanbul

Two decades after Michael reclaimed Constantinople, a Turkish warlord named Ertuğrul died in the village of Söğüt near Nicaea. He left his son Osman, who was known as Gazi (Warrior for the Faith), a small territory. Osman's followers became known in the Empire as Osmanlıs and in the West as the Ottomans.

Osman died in 1324 and was succeeded by his son Orhan. In 1326 Orhan captured Bursa, made it his capital and took the title of sultan. A victory at Nicaea followed, after which he sent his forces further afield, conquering Ankara to the east and Thrace to the west. His son Murat I (r 1362–89) took Adrianople (Edirne) in 1371.

Murat's son Beyazıt (r 1389–1402) unsuccessfully laid siege to Constantinople in 1394, then defeated a Crusader army 100,000 strong on the Danube in 1396. Though temporarily checked by the armies of Tamerlane and a nasty war of succession between Beyazıt's four sons that was eventually won by Mehmet I (r 1413–21), the Ottomans continued to grow in power and size. By 1440 the Ottoman armies under Murat II (r 1421–51) had taken Thessalonica, unsuccessfully laid siege to Constantinople and Belgrade, and battled Christian armies for Transylvania. It was at this point in history that Mehmet II 'The Conqueror' (r 1451–81) came to power and vowed to attain the ultimate prize – Constantinople.

In four short months, Mehmet oversaw the building of Rumeli Hisarı (the great fortress on the European side of the Bosphorus) and also repaired Anadolu Hisarı, built on the Asian shore half a century earlier by his great-grandfather Beyazıt I. Together these fortresses controlled the strait's narrowest point.

The Byzantines had closed the mouth of the Golden Horn with a heavy chain to prevent Ottoman boats from sailing in and attacking the city walls on the northern side. Not to be thwarted, Mehmet marshalled his boats at a cove (where Dolmabahçe Palace now stands) and had them transported overland by night on rollers, up the valley (present site of the Hilton Hotel) and down the other side into the Golden Horn at Kasımpaşa. Catching the Byzantine defenders by surprise, he soon had the Golden Horn under control.

The last great obstacle was provided by the city's mighty walls. No matter how heavily Mehmet's cannons battered them, the Byzantines rebuilt the walls by night and, come daybreak, the impetuous young sultan would find himself back where he'd started. Finally, he received

1432	1453	1520	1556
Mehmet II, son of the Ottoman sultan Murad II, is born in Edirne; he succeeds his father as sultan twice – once in 1444 and then permanently in 1451.	Mehmet's army takes İstanbul and he assumes power in the city becoming known as Fatih, 'The Conqueror'; he dies in 1481 and is succeeded by his son Beyazıt II.	Beyazıt's grandson Süleyman, who would come to be known as 'The Magnificent', ascends to the throne and soon builds a reputation for his military conquests.	Süleyman dies while on a military campaign in Hungary; his son Selim II assumes the throne and becomes known as 'The Sot' for obvious reasons.

a proposal from a Hungarian cannon founder called Urban who had come to help the Byzantine emperor defend Christendom against the infidels. Finding that the Byzantine emperor had no money, Urban was quick to discard his religious convictions and instead offered to make Mehmet the most enormous cannon ever seen. Mehmet gladly accepted and the mighty cannon breached the western walls, allowing the Ottomans into the city. On 28 May 1453 the final attack began and by the evening of the 29th the Turks were in complete control of the city. The last Byzantine emperor, Constantine XI Palaiologos, died fighting on the walls.

Seeing himself as the successor to great emperors such as Constantine and Justinian, the 21-year-old conqueror at once began to rebuild and repopulate the city. Aya Sofya was converted to a mosque; a new mosque, the Fatih (Conqueror) Camii, was built on the fourth hill; and the Eski Saray (Old Palace) was constructed on the third hill, followed by a new palace (Topkapı) on Sarayburnu a few years later. The city walls were repaired and a new fortress, Yedikule, was built. İstanbul, as it began to be known, became the new administrative, commercial and cultural centre of the ever-growing Ottoman Empire.

Under Mehmet's rule, Greeks who had fled the city were encouraged to return and an imperial decree calling for resettlement was issued; Muslims, Jews and Christians all took up his offer and were promised the right to worship as they pleased. The Genoese, who had fought with the Byzantines, were pardoned and allowed to stay in Galata, though the fortifications that surrounded their settlement were torn down. Only Galata Tower was allowed to stand.

Mehmet died in 1481 and was succeeded by Beyazıt II (r 1481–1512), who was ousted by his son, the ruthless Selim the Grim (r 1512–20), famed for executing seven grand viziers and numerous relatives during his relatively short reign.

The building boom that Mehmet kicked off was continued by his successors, with Süleyman the Magnificent (r 1520–66) and his architect Mimar Sinan being responsible for an enormous amount of construction. The city was endowed with buildings commissioned by the sultan and his family, court and grand viziers; these include the city's largest and grandest mosque, the Süleymaniye (1550). Later sultans built mosques and a series of palaces along the Bosphorus, among them Dolmabahçe.

However, what had been the most civilised city on earth in the time of Süleyman eventually declined along with the Ottoman Empire, and by the 19th century İstanbul had lost much of its former glory. Nevertheless, it continued to be the 'Paris of the East' and, to affirm this,

Great Reads

Byzantium (Judith Herrin; 2007)

Constantinople (Philip Mansel; 1995)

Inside the Seraglio (John Freely; 1999)

Istanbul: The Imperial City (John Freely; 1996)

A Short History of Byzantium (John Julian Norwich; 1997)

Strolling through Istanbul (John Freely & Hilary Sumner-Boyd; 1972)

1574	1729	1826	1839
Selim II – known as 'The Sot' – drowns after falling in his bath while drunk and is succeeded by his son Murat III, who orders the murder of his five younger brothers to ensure his accession.	A huge fire sweeps through the city, destroying 400 houses and 140 mosques and causing 1000 deaths.	The Vakayı Hayriye, or 'Auspicious Event' is decreed under which the corrupt and powerful imperial bodyguard known as the Janissary Corps is abolished.	Mahmut II implements the Tanzimat reforms, which integrate non-Muslims and non-Turks into Ottoman society through civil liberties and regulations.

the first great international luxury express train, the famous *Orient Express,* connected İstanbul and the French capital in 1883.

The city's decline reflected that of the sultanate. The concept of democracy, imported from the West, took off in the 19th century and the sultans were forced to make concessions towards it. In 1876 Sultan Abdül Hamid II allowed the creation of an Ottoman constitution and the first-ever Ottoman parliament. However, these concessions didn't last long, with the sultan disabling the constitution in 1876 and suspending the parliament in 1878. A group of educated Turks took exception to this and established the Committee for Union and Progress (CUP), better known as the Young Turks, to fight for the reformation of the Ottoman sultanate and the introduction of democratic reform. In 1908 they forced the sultan to abdicate, reinstated the constitution and assumed governance of the empire.

One of the factors leading to the The Young Turks' decision to ally themselves with the Central Powers in WWI was their fear that the Allies (particularly Russia) coveted İstanbul. Unfortunately, the alliance led to their political demise when the Central Powers were defeated. The Young Turk leaders resigned, fled İstanbul and went into exile, leaving the city to be occupied by British, French and Italian troops placed there in accordance with the Armistice of Mudros, which ended Ottoman participation in the war. The city was returned to Ottoman rule under the 1923 Treaty of Lausanne, which defined the borders of the modern Turkish state.

Although he was instrumental in moving the capital of Turkey from İstanbul to Ankara, Atatürk loved the city and spent much of his time here. He kept a set of apartments in Dolmabahçe Palace and died there on 10 November 1938.

The post-WWI campaign by Mustafa Kemal (Atatürk) for independence and the reinstatement of Turkish territory in the Balkans was directed from Ankara. After the Republic was founded in 1923, the new government was set up in that city. Robbed of its status as the capital of a vast empire, İstanbul lost much of its wealth and atmosphere. The city's streets and neighbourhoods decayed, its infrastructure was neither maintained nor improved and little economic development occurred there for the next half-century.

The Recent Past

The weak economic position of İstanbul was reflected in the rest of the country, and this – along with some anger about Turkey's strengthening alliance with the USA – led to growing dissatisfaction with a succession of governments. There were military coups in 1960 and 1971, and the late 1960s and 1970s were characterised by left-wing activism and political violence. This reached a shocking crescendo on May Day 1977, when there was a flare-up between rival political factions at a huge demonstration in Taksim Meydanı (Taksim Sq). Security forces intervened and approximately 40 protesters were killed.

1853–56	1914	1915	1922
The Ottoman empire fights in the Crimean War against Russia; Florence Nightingale arrives at the Selimiye Army Barracks near Üsküdar to nurse the wounded.	The government allies itself with the Central Powers and joins WWI; the Bosphorus and Dardenelles are closed to shipping, leading to the Allies' decision to attack Gallipoli.	Many prominent members of the city's 164,000-strong Armenian population have their property confiscated and are deported from the city.	The Turkish Grand National Assembly abolishes the Ottoman sultanate; the last sultan, Mehmet VI, leaves the country on a British warship.

Under the presidency of economist Turgut Özal, the 1980s saw a free-market-led economic and tourism boom in Turkey and its major city. Özal's government also presided over a great increase in urbanisation, with trainloads of peasants from eastern Anatolia making their way to İstanbul in search of jobs in the booming industrial sector. The city's infrastructure couldn't cope back then and is still catching up, despite three decades of large-scale municipal works being undertaken.

The municipal elections of March 1994 were a shock to the political establishment, with the upstart religious-right Refah Partisi (Welfare Party) winning elections across the country. Its victory was seen in part as a protest vote against the corruption, ineffective policies and tedious political wrangles of the traditional parties. In İstanbul Refah was led by Recep Tayyip Erdoğan (b 1954), a proudly Islamist candidate. He vowed to modernise infrastructure and restore the city to its former glory.

In the national elections of December 1996, Refah polled more votes than any other party (23%), and eventually formed a government vowing moderation and honesty. Emboldened by political power, Prime Minister Necmettin Erbakan and other Refah politicians tested the boundaries of Turkey's traditional secularism, alarming the powerful National Security Council, the most visible symbol of the centrist military establishment's role as the caretaker of secularism and democracy.

In 1997 the council announced that Refah had flouted the constitutional ban on religion in politics and warned that the government should resign or face a military coup. Bowing to the inevitable, Erbakan did as the council wished. In İstanbul, Mayor Erdoğan was ousted by the secularist forces in the national government in late 1998.

National elections in April 1999 brought in a coalition government led by Bülent Ecevit's left-wing Democratic Left Party. After years under the conservative right of the Refah Partisi, the election result heralded a shift towards European-style social democracy.

Unfortunately for the new government, there was a spectacular collapse of the Turkish economy in 2001, leading to its electoral defeat in 2002. The victorious party was the moderate Adalet ve Kalkınma Partisi (Justice and Development Party; AKP), led by phoenix-like Recep Tayyip Erdoğan. In İstanbul, candidates from the AKP were elected into power in most municipalities, including the powerful Fatih Municipality, which includes Eminönü.

Elections in 2007 and 2011 had the same result, as did the municipal election in 2014. The result of the 2014 election was a disappointment to many secular and left-leaning İstanbullus, as well as to former AKP supporters who had changed their political allegiance as a result of the government's handling of the 2013 Gezi Park protests. These protests,

1923	1925	1934	1942
The Grand National Assembly relocates the nation's capital from İstanbul to Ankara; shortly afterward, it proclaims the Turkish Republic.	The Republican government bans Dervish orders; many of the city's historic *tekkes* (Dervish lodges) are demolished.	Women are given the vote; by 1935 4.6% of the national parliament's representatives are female.	A wealth tax is introduced on affluent citizens. Ethnic minorities are taxed at a higher rate than Muslims; many are bankrupted and forced to leave the city.

which were staged in and around Taksim Meydanı, were initially a public response to a plan to redevelop the park, on the northeastern edge of the square, but transformed into a much larger protest by İstanbullus against what they saw as an increasingly autocratic and undemocratic Turkish government. Called in to disperse the crowd, police used tear gas and water cannons, which led to violent clashes, 8000 injuries, at least four deaths and thousands of arrests.

The current AKP-endorsed mayor of İstanbul, Kadir Topbaş (b 1945) is one of Erdoğan's former advisors and a former mayor of the Beyoğlu municipality. He has been mayor since 2004.

2006	2011	2013	2014
İstanbul successfully bids to become a European Capital of Culture for 2010, and launches an ambitious program of heritage restoration and cultural development.	The ruling soft-Islamist Justice & Development Party (AKP), led by İstanbul-born Prime Minister Recep Tayyip Erdoğan, wins a third term in government.	Large demonstrations by İstanbullus protesting a plan to redevelop Gezi Park on the northeastern edge of Taksim Meydanı (Taksim Sq) are met with a violent response by the government.	Recep Tayyip Erdoğan, coming to the end of his long term as Turkey's prime minister, runs as a candidate in Turkey's presidential election and wins office.

Architecture

Architects and urban designers wanting to study the world's best practice need go no further than İstanbul. Here, delicate minarets reach towards the heavens, distinctive domes crown hills, elegant mansions adorn the water's edge and edgy art spaces claim contemporary landmark status. The skyline has the wow factor in spades and the historical layers of the built environment are both handsome and fascinating – together, they offer travellers an exhilarating architectural experience.

Byzantine Architecture

After Mehmet the Conquerer stormed into İstanbul in 1453 many churches were converted into mosques; despite the minarets, you can usually tell a church-cum-mosque by the distinctive red bricks that are characteristic of all Byzantine churches.

Above: Blue Mosque (p67)

During Justinian's reign (527–65), architects were encouraged to surpass each other's achievements when it came to utilising the domed, Roman-influenced basilica form. Aya Sofya is the supreme example of this.

Early Byzantine basilica design used rectangular external walls; inside was a centralised polygonal plan with supporting walls and a dome. Little Aya Sofya (Küçük Aya Sofya Camii), built around 530, is a good example. Later, a mixed basilica and centralised polygonal plan developed. This was the foundation for church design from the 11th century until the Conquest and many Ottoman mosques were inspired by it. The Monastery of Christ Pantokrator is a good example.

The Byzantines also had a yen for building fortifications. The greatest of these is the still-standing land wall. Constructed in the 5th century by order of Emperor Theodosius II, it was 20km long and protected the city during multiple sieges until it was finally breached in 1453.

Constantine the Great, the first Byzantine Emperor, named his city 'New Rome'. And, like Rome, it was characterised by great public works such as the stone aqueduct built by Emperor Valens between 368 and 378. The aqueduct fed a series of huge cisterns built across the city, one being the Basilica Cistern.

Like Rome, the city was built on seven hills and to a grid pattern that included ceremonial thoroughfares such as Divan Yolu and major public spaces such as the Hippodrome.

> Unfortunately, İstanbul notches up regular mentions in the World Monuments Fund's watchlist of heritage in danger. Recent entries include Haydarpaşa train station and the Church of the Monastery of Christ Pantokrator.

Ottoman Architecture

After the Conquest, the sultans wasted no time in putting their architectural stamp on the city. Mehmet didn't even wait until he had the city under his control, building the monumental Rumeli Hisarı on the Bosphorus in 1452, the year before his great victory.

Once in the city, Mehmet kicked off a centuries-long Ottoman building spree, constructing a number of buildings including a mosque on the fourth hill. After these he started work on the most-famous Ottoman building of all: Topkapı Palace.

Mehmet had a penchant for palaces, but his great-grandson, Süleyman the Magnificent, was more of a mosque man. With his favourite architect, Mimar Sinan, he built the greatest of the city's Ottoman imperial mosques. Sinan's prototype mosque form has a forecourt with a şadırvan (ablutions fountain) and domed arcades on three sides. On the fourth side is the mosque, with a two-storey porch. The main prayer hall is covered by a central dome surrounded by smaller domes and

> İstanbul's Old City is included in Unesco's World Heritage List for its 'unique integration of architectural masterpieces...and its incomparable skyline formed by the creative genius of Byzantine and Ottoman architects'.

THE GREAT SINAN

None of today's star architects come close to having the influence over a city that Mimar Koca Sinan had over Constantinople during his 50-year career.

Born in 1497, Sinan was a recruit to the devşirme, the annual intake of Christian youths into the janissaries. He became a Muslim (as all such recruits did) and eventually took up a post as a military engineer in the corps. Süleyman the Magnificent appointed him the chief of the imperial architects in 1538.

Sinan designed a total of 321 buildings, 85 of which are still standing in İstanbul. He died in 1588 and is buried in a self-designed türbe (tomb) located in one of the corners of the Süleymaniye Mosque, the building that many believe to be his greatest work.

Harem (p60), Topkapı Palace

semidomes. There was usually one minaret, though imperial mosques had more.

Each imperial mosque had a *külliye* (mosque complex) clustered around it. This was a philanthropic complex including a *medrese* (seminary), hamam, *darüşşifa* (hospital), *imaret* (soup kitchen), *kütüphane* (library), *tabhane* (inn for travelling dervishes) and cemetery with *türbes* (tombs). Over time many of these *külliyes* were demolished; fortunately, many of the buildings in the magnificent Süleymaniye and Atik Valide complexes are intact.

Later sultans continued Mehmet's palace-building craze. No palace would rival Topkapı, but Sultan Abdül Mecit I tried his best with the grandiose Dolmabahçe Palace and Abdül Aziz I built the extravagant Çırağan Palace and Beylerbeyi Palace. These and other buildings of the era have been collectively dubbed 'Turkish baroque'.

These mosques and palaces dominate the landscape and skyline of the city, but there are other quintessentially Ottoman buildings: the hamam and the Ottoman timber house. Hamams were usually built as part of a *külliye,* and provided an important point of social contact as well as facilities for ablutions. Architecturally significant hamams include the Ayasofya Hürrem Sultan Hamamı, the Çemberlitaş Hamamı, the Cağaloğlu Hamamı and the Kılıç Ali Paşa Hamamı. All are still functioning.

Wealthy Ottomans and foreign diplomats built many *yalıs* (waterside timber mansions) along the shores of the Bosphorus; city equivalents were sometimes set in a garden but were usually part of a crowded, urban streetscape. Unfortunately, not too many of these houses survive, a consequence of the fires that regularly raced through the Ottoman city.

Two family dynasties have played major roles in İstanbul's architectural scene: the Balyans, who worked in the 18th and 19th centuries, and the Tabanlıoğlus, working in the 20th and 21st centuries.

Above: Şakirin Mosque (p151)
Left: Kanyon shopping centre

Ottoman Revivalism & Modernism

In the late 19th and early 20th centuries, architects created a blend of European architecture alongside Turkish baroque, with some concessions to classic Ottoman style. This style has been dubbed 'Ottoman Revivalism' or First National Architecture.

The main proponents of this style were architects Vedat Tek (1873–1942) and Kemalettin Bey (1870–1927). Tek is best known for his Central Post Office in Sirkeci (1909) and Haydarpaşa İskelesi (Haydarpaşa Ferry Dock; 1915–17). Kemalettin Bey's Bebek Mosque (1913) and Fourth Vakıf Han (1912–26), a bank building in Eminönü that now houses the Legacy Ottoman Hotel, are his best-known works.

When Atatürk proclaimed Ankara the capital of the republic, İstanbul lost much of its glamour and investment capital. Modernism was played out on the new canvas of Ankara, while İstanbul's dalliances went little further than the İstanbul City Hall in Fatih, designed by Nevzat Erol and built in 1953; the İstanbul Hilton Hotel, designed by SOM and Sedad Hakkı Eldem and built in 1952; the Atatürk Library in Gümüşsuyu, also by Eldem; and the much-maligned Atatürk Cultural Centre by Hayati Tabanlıoğlu, built from 1956 to 1957 and currently closed for renovation.

Recent architecture in the city can hardly be called inspiring. One building of note is Kanyon, a mixed residential, office and shopping development in Levent designed by the LA-based Jerde Partnership with local architects Tabanlıoğlu Partnership. The nearby Loft Gardens residential complex and İstanbul Sapphire tower, both by Tabanlıoğlu Partnership, are also impressive. Notable contemporary religious buildings are few and far between, with one of the only exceptions being the Şakirin Mosque in Üskudar by Hüsrev Tayla and Zeynep Fadıllıoğlu.

Many art museums and cultural centres around town feature impressive new wings or inspired architectural conversions of industrial or commercial spaces. The best of these are İstanbul Modern, by Tabanlıoğlu Partnership; SALT Galata, by Mimarlar Tasarım; the Sakıp Sabancı Museum, by Savaş, Erkel and Çırakoğlu; the new İstanbul Naval Museum in Beşiktaş, by Mehmet Kütükçüoğlu; and santralistanbul in Sütluce on the Golden Horn, by Emre Arolat, Nevzat Sayın and Han Tümertekin. Emre Arolat's Eyüp Cultural Centre and Marriage Hall is also noteworthy.

At the time of writing, a number of exciting projects by high-profile international firms were on the drawing board or in the first stages of construction. These included a contemporary art museum in Beyoğlu funded by the Vehbi Koç Foundation and designed by Grimshaw; a mixed-use commercial development in Kagithane by JDS Architects; and a new Ziraat Bank Headquarters by Kohn Pedersen Fox Associates.

The city's first art nouveau building, Botter House on İstiklal Caddesi in Beyoğlu, was designed in 1900–01 by Abdül Hamid II's Italian chief palace architect, Raimondo d'Aronco.

ARCHITECTURE OTTOMAN REVIVALISM & MODERNISM

Nevzat Erol's 1953 İstanbul Belediye Sarayı (İstanbul City Hall), located opposite the Şehzade Mehmet Mosque on Şehzadebaşı Caddesi in Fatih, was the first International Style building in the city.

İstanbul on Page & Screen

Replete with colours, characters, sounds and stories, İstanbul has been inspiring writers and artists for as long as it has been seducing first-time visitors (and that's a very long time indeed). Those keen to indulge in some inspirational predeparture research should consider reading a book set in the city, or watching a film that has been shot here – there are many to choose from, both local and foreign.

İstanbul in Print

Lord Byron spent two months in Constantinople in 1810 and wrote about the city in his satiric poem *Don Juan*.

Turkey has a rich but relatively young literary tradition. Its brightest stars tend to be based in İstanbul and are greatly revered throughout the country. Fortunately, many of their works are now available in English translation.

It's not only Turks who are inspired to write about the city, though. There are a huge number of novels, travel memoirs and histories by foreign writers.

Literary Heritage

Under the sultans, literature was really a form of religious devotion. Ottoman poets, borrowing from the great Arabic and Persian traditions, wrote sensual love poems of attraction, longing, fulfilment and ecstasy in the search for union with God.

By the late 19th century the influence of Western literature began to be felt. This was the time of the Tanzimat political and social reforms initiated by Sultan Abdülmecit, and in İstanbul a literary movement was established that became known as 'Tanzimat Literature'.

This movement was responsible for the first serious attacks on the ponderous cadences of Ottoman courtly prose and poetry, but it wasn't until the foundation of the republic that the death knell of this form of literature finally rang. Atatürk decreed that the Turkish language should be purified of Arabic and Persian borrowings, and that in the future the nation's literature should be created using the new Latin-based Turkish alphabet. Major figures in the new literary movement (dubbed 'National Literature') included poet Yahya Kemal Beyatli (1884–1958) and novelist Halide Edib Adıvar (1884–1964).

Though not part of the National Literature movement, İrfan Orga (1908–70) is probably the most-famous Turkish literary figure of the 20th century. His 1950 masterpiece *Portrait of a Turkish Family* is his memoir of growing up in İstanbul at the start of the century and is among the best writing about the city ever published.

Politician, essayist and novelist Ahmet Hamdi Tanipar (1901–62) wrote *A Mind at Peace* in 1949. Set in the city at the beginning of WWII, it is beloved by many Turks. Another of his novels, *The Time Regulation Institute,* was released in an English-language edition for the first time in 2014.

Contemporary Novelists

The second half of the 20th century saw a raft of İstanbul-based writers and poets being published locally and internationally. Many were socialists, communists or outspoken critics of the government, and spent long and repeated periods in jail. The two most famous were Nâzım Hikmet (1902–63), whose masterwork is the five-volume collection of lyric and epic poetry entitled *Human Landscapes from My Country;* and Yaşar Kemal (b 1923), whose best-known work is *Mehmed, My Hawk.* Two of Kemal's novels – *The Birds Are Also Gone* and *The Sea-Crossed Fisherman* – are set in İstanbul.

High-profile writer Elif Şafak was born in Strasbourg in 1971 to Turkish parents and now divides her time between London and İstanbul. Her best-known novels are *The Flea Palace* (2002), *The Saint of Incipient Insanities* (2004), *The Bastard of Istanbul* (2006), *The Forty Rules of Love* (2010) and *Honour* (2012). Şafak's novels often address issues that are controversial in Turkey (eg honour killing, gay identity, the Armenian genocide, sex before marriage). Her most recent novel *Ustam and I* (2014) revolves around the life of the Ottoman architect Mimar Sinan. It, *The Flea Palace* and *The Bastard of Istanbul* are all set in the city.

Arrested after the 1980 military coup, left-wing activist Izzet Celasin (b 1958) spent several years in a Turkish jail before being granted political asylum in Norway. His debut novel *Black Sky, Black Sea* (2012) is a semi-autobiographical story about young activists in İstanbul during the period of political unrest in the late 1970s. The timing of the novel's release (just before the Gezi protests of 2013) made it resonate both in Turkey and overseas.

Turkish novelist, poet, songwriter and film director O Z Livaneli (b 1946) has written 15 bestsellers but only one, the acclaimed 2003 novel *Bliss* (*Mutluluk* in Turkish), is available in an English-language edition. Dealing with weighty issues such as honour killing and partially set in İstanbul, it was made into a film in 2007.

ORHAN PAMUK

When the much-fêted Orhan Pamuk (b 1952) was awarded the 2006 Nobel Prize in Literature, the international cultural sector was largely unsurprised. The writing of the İstanbul-born, now US-based, novelist had already attracted its fair share of critical accolades, including the IMPAC Dublin Literary Award, *The Independent* newspaper's Foreign Fiction Award of the Month and every local literary prize on offer.

In their citation, the Nobel judges said that in his 'quest for the melancholic soul of his native city' (ie İstanbul), Pamuk had 'discovered new symbols for the clash and interlacing of culture'. The only voices heard to criticise their judgement hailed from Turkey. Pamuk had been charged with 'insulting Turkishness' under Article 301 of the Turkish Criminal Code (the charges were dropped in early 2006), and some local commentators alleged that in his case the Nobel Prize was awarded for political (ie freedom of speech) reasons rather than purely on the merit of his literary oeuvre.

Pamuk has written eight novels to date. His first, *Cevdet Bey and His Sons* (1982), is a dynastic saga of the İstanbul bourgeoisie. It was followed by *The Silent House* (1983), *The White Castle* (1985) and *The Black Book* (1990). The latter was made into a film *(Gizli Yuz)* by director Omer Kavur in 1992. After this came *The New Life* (1995), *My Name is Red* (1998) and *Snow* (2002). His most recent novel is *The Museum of Innocence* (2009), a moving story of love and loss set in İstanbul circa 1975. In 2005 he published a memoir, *Istanbul: Memories of a City,* about the city he loves so well. His other nonfiction works are *Other Colours: Essays and a Story* (2007) and *The Naive and Sentimental Novelist* (2010).

In 2012 Pamuk opened the Museum of Innocence (p125), his conceptual art project occupying an entire house in Cihangir. This was inspired by his novel of the same name, and has proved to be a popular with locals and tourists alike.

Through Foreign Eyes

Foreign novelists have long tried to capture the magic and mystery of İstanbul in their work. One of the earliest to do so was French novelist Pierre Loti (1850–1923), whose romantic novel *Aziyadé*, written in 1879, introduced Europe to Loti's almond-eyed Turkish lover and to the mysterious and all-pervasive attractions of the city itself.

After Loti, writers such as Harold Nicolson set popular stories in the city. Nicholson's 1921 novel *Sweet Waters* is a moving love story cum political thriller set in İstanbul during the Balkan Wars. Nicholson, who was based here as a diplomat, based the novel's main character on his wife, Vita Sackville-West.

Graham Greene's 1932 thriller *Stamboul Train* focuses on a group of passengers travelling between Ostend and İstanbul on the *Orient Express*. It was filmed in 1934 as *Orient Express*.

Thriller-writer Eric Ambler used İstanbul as a setting in three highly regarded novels: *The Mask of Dimitrios* (1939), *Journey into Fear* (1940) and *The Light of Day* (1962).

Historical novels set here include *The Rage of the Vulture* (Barry Unsworth; 1982), *The Stone Woman* (Tariq Ali; 2001), *The Calligrapher's Night* (Yasmine Ghata; 2006) and *The Dark Angel* (Mika Waltari; 1952). Young readers will enjoy *The Oracle of Stamboul* (Michael David Lukas; 2011).

Although best known as Pamuk's English translator and John Freely's daughter, Maureen Freely is also a writer of fiction. In her 2007 novel *Enlightenment* she writes about truth, repression and the personal and political risks of becoming enmeshed in a foreign culture.

Travelogues

Constantinople (Edmondo De Amici; 1878)

Constantinople in 1890 (Pierre Loti; 1892)

The Innocents Abroad (Mark Twain; 1869)

The Turkish Embassy Letters (Lady Mary Wortley Montagu; 1837)

THE DARK SIDE OF THE CITY

İstanbul features as the setting for some great crime novels. If you're a fan of the genre, you may like to read the following:

The Inspector İkmen Novels Barbara Nadel investigates the city's underbelly in a suitably gripping style. Whether they're set in Balat or Beyoğlu, her books are always evocative and well researched. Start with *Belshazzar's Daughter* (1999).

The Yashim the Ottoman Investigator Novels Jason Goodwin writes historical crime novels with a protagonist who is a eunuch attached to the Ottoman court. Titles in the series include *The Janissary Tree* (2006), *An Evil Eye* (2011) and *The Baklava Club* (2014).

Murder on the Orient Express Hercule Poirot puts ze leetle grey cells to good use on the famous train in this 1934 novel by Agatha Christie. It was made into a film by Sidney Lumet in 1974 and features a few opening shots of İstanbul.

The Kamil Paşa Novels These historical crime novels by Jenny White feature a magistrate in one of the new Ottoman secular courts. Titles include *The Sultan's Seal* (2006), *The Abyssinian Proof* (2009) and *The Winter Thief* (2010).

Island Crimes Lawrence Goodman's series of comic mystery novels set on the Princes' Islands includes *Sweet Confusion on the Princes' Islands* (2005), *Sour Grapes on the Princes' Islands* (2006), *A Grain of Salt on the Princes' Islands* (2007) and *Something Bitter on the Princes' Islands* (2008).

The Hop-Çıkı-Yaya Novels Mehmet Murat Somer's series of gay crime novels feature a transvestite amateur sleuth. Titles include *The Prophet Murders* (2008), *The Kiss Murders* (2009) and *The Wig Murders* (2014).

The Kati Hirschel Murder Mysteries Written in Turkish and translated into English, these novels by Esmahan Aykol feature a German amateur sleuth who owns a bookshop in Galata. Titles include *Hotel Bosphorus* (2011) and *Baksheesh* (2013).

Alan Drew's 2008 novel *Gardens of Water* follows the lives of two families in the aftermath of the devastating earthquake that struck western Turkey (including İstanbul's outskirts) in 1999.

Joseph Kanon's 2012 thriller *Istanbul Passage* is set just after the end of WWII, when espionage is rife and Mossad is attempting to illegally transport Jewish refugees through the city en route to Palestine.

Cinema

Turks have taken to cinema-going with alacrity over recent decades, and the local industry has gone from strength to strength. Local directors, many of whom are based in İstanbul, are now fixtures on the international festival circuit.

Local Stories

Oddly enough, few masterpieces of Turkish cinema have been set in İstanbul. Acclaimed directors including Metin Erksan, Yılmaz Güney and Erdan Kıral tended to set the social-realist films they made in the 1960s, '70s' and '80s in the villages of central or eastern Anatolia.

All this started to change in the 1990s, when many critical and popular hits were set in the city. Notable among these were the films of Zeki Demirkubuz, Omer Kavur, Yeşim Ustaoğlu, Mustafa Altıoklar and Yavuz Turgul.

Contemporary directors of note include Ferzan Özpetek, who has a growing number of Turkish/Italian coproductions to his credit. His 1996 film *Hamam,* set in İstanbul, was a big hit on the international festival circuit and is particularly noteworthy for addressing the hitherto hidden issue of homosexuality in Turkish society.

Yavuz Turgul's 2005 film *Lovelorn* is the story of idealist Nazim, who returns home to İstanbul after teaching for 15 years in a remote village in eastern Turkey and starts a doomed relationship with a single mother who works in a sleazy bar. It's particularly notable for the soundtrack by Tamer Çıray, which features the voice of Aynur Doğan.

Kutluğ Ataman's 2005 film *2 Girls* and Reha Erdem's 2008 film *My Only Sunshine* are both dramas in which the city provides an evocative backdrop.

Turkish-German director Fatih Akın received rave reviews and a screenwriting prize at Cannes for his 2007 film *The Edge of Heaven,* parts of which are set in İstanbul. His 2005 documentary about the Istanbul music scene – *Crossing the Bridge: The Sound of Istanbul* – was instrumental in raising the Turkish music industry's profile internationally.

Erdem Tepegöz's bleakly realistic 2013 film *Zerre* (Particle) follows single working woman Zeynep as she searches for a job to support her mother and handicapped daughter. The film was shot in Tarlabaşı, near Beyoğlu.

Another 2013 release, Filiz Alpgezmen's *Yabancı* (Stranger), tells the story of Özgür, who was raised in Paris but returns to her parents' home town of İstanbul to bury her father, in the process discovering much about her family and herself.

Turkey's most acclaimed director, Nuri Bilge Ceylan, was awarded the 2014 Palme d'Or at Cannes for his film *Winter Sleep,* which is set in Cappadocia. At the awards ceremony, he dedicated his prize to 'all the young people of Turkey, including those who lost their lives over the past year', a clear statement of support for the Gezi protesters. Ceylan has directed three films set in İstanbul: *Distant* (2003), *Climates* (2006) and *Three Monkeys* (2008).

Through Foreign Eyes

Many of the foreign-made films set in İstanbul have been thrillers. These include James Negulesco's *The Mask of Dimitrios* (1944), based on the Eric Ambler novel; Olivier Megaton's *Taken 2* (2012); and three James Bond films: *From Russia with Love* (1974), *The World Is Not Enough* (1999) and *Skyfall* (2012).

Other films to look out for are Jacques Vierne's 1961 film *Tintin and the Golden Fleece;* Alan Parker's 1978 hit *Midnight Express;* and Jules Dassin's 1964 crime spoof *Topkapi,* which was based on Eric Ambler's novel *In the Light of Day.*

Greek director Tassos Boulmetis set part of his popular 2003 art-house film *A Touch of Spice* here.

In 2014 Australian/New Zealand actor Russell Crowe released his directorial debut, *The Water Diviner.* The film tells the story of an Australian father who makes his way to İstanbul to ascertain the fate of his three sons, all missing in action after the Battle of Gallipoli in 1915.

Clamour over Galata Tower, Aya Sofya's dome, the minarets of the Blue Mosque and the roof of Topkapı Palace while playing the popular PS3/Xbox 360 video game *Assassin's Creed: Revelations,* which is set in Constantinople in 1511.

Survival Guide

Transport

ARRIVING IN ISTANBUL

It's the national capital in all but name, so getting to İstanbul is easy. There are two international airports and three otogars (bus stations) from which national and international services arrive and depart. At the time of research international rail connections were few and far between, but this situation may change when upgrades to rail lines throughout the country are completed.

Flights, tours and rail tickets can be booked at www.lonelyplanet.com/bookings.

Air

Atatürk International Airport

The city's main airport, **Atatürk International Airport** (IST, Atatürk Havalımanı; ☑212-463 3000; www.ataturkairport.com), is located in Yeşilköy, 23km west of Sultanahmet. The international terminal (Dış Hatlar) and domestic terminal (İç Hatlar) operate at or close to capacity, which has prompted the Turkish Government to announce construction of a new, much larger, airport 50km north of the city centre. The first stage of the new airport's construction is due to be completed by 2018 but the facility won't be fully operational until 2025.

There are car-rental desks, exchange offices, stands of mobile-phone companies, a 24-hour pharmacy, ATMs and a PTT (post office) at the international arrivals area of Atatürk International Airport. There is also a **Tourist Information Desk** (☑212-465 3547; International Arrivals Hall, Atatürk International Airport; ◷9am-9pm) supplying maps and advice. A 24-hour supermarket is located on the walkway to the metro. The **left-luggage service** (☑212-465 3442; ◷24hr) charges ₺18 to ₺25 per suitcase per 24 hours; you'll find the booth to your right as you exit customs.

One annoying thing about Atatürk airport is that travellers must pay to use a trolley on either side of immigration. You can pay in lira (₺1) or euros (€1 or €2), which are refunded on return of the trolley.

TAXI

A taxi from the airport costs around ₺45 to Sultanahmet, ₺55 to Taksim Meydanı (Taksim Sq) and ₺75 to Kadıköy.

METRO & TRAM

There's an efficient metro service between the airport and Zeytinburnu, from where it's easy to connect with the tram to Sultanahmet, Eminönü and Kabataş. From Kabataş, there's a funicular to Taksim Meydanı. Note that if you are going to the airport from the city centre you should take the Bağcilar service rather than the Cevizlibağ one, which terminates before Zeytinburnu.

The metro station is on the lower ground floor beneath the international departures hall – follow the 'Metro/Subway' signs down the escalators and through the underground walkway. You'll need to purchase a *jeton* (ticket token; ₺4) or purchase and recharge an İstanbulkart (travelcard; ₺10) from the machines at the metro entrance. Services depart every six to 10 minutes from 6am until midnight. When you get off the metro, the tram platform is right in front of you. You'll need to buy another token (₺4) to pass through the turnstiles. The entire trip from the airport takes around 50 to 60 minutes to Sultanahmet, 60 to 70 minutes to Eminönü and 85 to 95 minutes to Taksim.

AIRPORT BUS

If you are staying in Beyoğlu, the **Havataş** (☑212-444 2656; http://havatas.com) airport bus from Atatürk International Airport is probably the most convenient option. This departs from outside the arrivals hall. Buses leave every 30 minutes between 4am and 1am; the trip takes between 40 minutes and one hour, depending on traffic. Tickets cost ₺10 and the bus stops in front of the Point Hotel on Cumhuriyet

Caddesi, close to Taksim Meydanı. Note that signage on the buses and at stops sometimes reads 'Havaş' rather than 'Havataş'.

A public bus service (No 96T) travels from a stop next to the Havataş buses outside the arrivals hall and travels to Taksim Meydanı (₺4, 120 minutes, six daily); check the İETT website for departure times. To travel on this bus, you must have an İstanbulkart; these are available at the machines at the metro station entrance on the lower ground floor.

HOTEL SHUTTLE

Many hotels will provide a free pick-up service from Atatürk International Airport if you stay with them for three nights or more. There are also a number of cheap (one way €5) but very slow shuttle-bus services from hotels to the airport for your return trip. Check details with your hotel.

Sabiha Gökçen International Airport

The city's second international airport, **Sabiha Gökçen International Airport** (SAW, Sabiha Gökçen Havalimanı; ☏216-588 8888;

www.sgairport.com), is at Pendik/Kurtköy on the Asian side of the city. It's popular with low-cost airlines.

There are ATMs, car-rental and accommodation-booking desks, stands of mobile-phone companies, exchange bureaux, a mini-market, a left-luggage office and a PTT in the international arrivals hall.

TAXI

Taxis from this airport to the city are expensive. To Taksim you'll be looking at around ₺100, to Sultanahmet around ₺130.

AIRPORT BUS

Havataş (☏212-444 2656; http://havatas.com) airport buses travel from the airport to Taksim Meydanı between 4am and 1am. There are also services to Kadıköy between 4.15am and 12.45am. Tickets cost ₺13 to Taksim (90 minutes) and ₺8 to Kadıköy (60 minutes). If you're heading towards the Old City from Taksim, you can take the funicular from Taksim to Kabataş (₺4) followed by the tram from Kabataş to Sultanahmet (₺4). From Kadıköy, ferries travel to Eminönü (₺4).

HOTEL SHUTTLE

Hotels rarely provide free pick-up services from Sabiha Gökçen. Shuttle-bus services from hotels to the airport for return trips cost €12 but are infrequent – check details with your hotel. The trip can take up to two hours, so allow plenty of time.

Boat

Cruise ships arrive at the **Karaköy Passenger Terminal** (Karaköy Yolcu Salonu; ☏212-249 5776), near the Galata Bridge.

Bus

The **Büyük İstanbul Otogarı** (Big İstanbul Bus Station; ☏212-658 0505; www.otogaristanbul.com) is the city's main bus station for both intercity and international routes. Often called simply 'the Otogar' (Bus Station), it's located at Esenler in the municipality of Bayrampaşa, about 10km west of Sultanahmet. The metro service from Aksaray stops here (₺4; Otogar stop) on its way to the airport; you can catch this to Zeytinburnu and then easily connect with

İSTANBULKARTS

İstanbul's public transport system is excellent, and one of its major strengths is the İstanbulkart, a rechargeable travel card similar to London's Oyster Card, Hong Kong's Octopus Card and Paris' Navigo.

İstanbulkarts are simple to operate: as you enter a bus or pass through the turnstile at a ferry dock or metro station, swipe your card for entry and the fare will automatically be deducted from your balance. The cards offer a considerable discount on fares (₺2.15 as opposed to the usual ₺4, with additional transfers within a two-hour journey window ₺1.60 for the first transfer, ₺1.50 for the second and ₺1.30 for the third). They can also be used to pay for fares for more than one traveller (one swipe per person per ride).

The cards can be purchased from machines at metro and funicular stations for a nonrefundable charge of ₺10, which includes ₺4 in credit. If you buy yours from a street kiosk near a tram or bus stop (look for an 'Akbil', 'Dolum Noktası' or 'İstanbulkart' sign), you will pay ₺8 including a plastic cover or ₺7 without. These won't include any credit.

Cards can be recharged with amounts between ₺5 and ₺150 at kiosks or at machines at ferry docks, metro and bus stations. Machines will only accept ₺5, ₺10 or ₺20 notes.

a tram (₺4) to Sultanahmet or Kabataş/Taksim. If you're going to Beyoğlu, bus 830 leaves from the centre of the otogar every 15 minutes between 5.50am and 8.45pm and takes approximately one hour to reach Taksim Meydanı. The trip costs ₺4 and is slower than the metro/tram alternative. A taxi will cost approximately ₺35 to both Sultanahmet and Taksim.

There's a second, much smaller, otogar at Alibeyköy where buses from Central Anatolia (including Ankara and Cappadocia) stop en route to Esenler. From here, passengers can take a *servis* (service bus) to Taksim; the transfer is included in the ticket cost. The only problem with this option is that service drivers rarely speak English and passengers sometimes have to wait for a *servis* – it's probably easier to go to Esenler.

The city's third otogar is on the Asian shore of the Bosphorus at Harem, south of Üsküdar and north of Haydarpaşa train station, but this will probably be decommissioned in the near future. Some bus companies have already relocated to an otogar at Ataşehir, on the Asian side at the junction of the O-2 and O-4 motorways. From Ataşehir, *servises* transfer passengers to Asian suburbs including Kadıköy and Üsküdar.

Train

At the time of research, only one international service – the daily Bosfor Ekspresi between İstanbul and Bucharest via Sofia – was operating in and out of İstanbul, departing at 10pm daily (€39 to €59 plus couchette surcharge). The service included a bus link between Sirkeci Gar (Sirkeci train station) and Çerkezköy, a two-hour drive northwest of İstanbul. The weekly Trans Aysa service to Tehran in Iran leaves from Ankara. Check **Turkish State Railways** (TCDD; www. tcdd.gov.tr) for details.

A new fast train service between Ankara and Pendik, 20km southeast of Kadıköy on the Asian side of town, commenced in July 2014. The journey takes approximately 3½ hours and ticket prices start at ₺70. Unfortunately, Pendik is difficult to access. You'll need to take a ferry to Kadıköy then the M4 metro to the end of the line at Kartal. From Kartal, bus 251 and taxis travel the last 6km to Pendik Gar. There are future plans to link Pendik with the M4 but a timetable for this has yet to be announced.

GETTING AROUND İSTANBUL

Public transport options are cheap, plentiful and efficient. This is fortunate, as traffic congestion is a growing problem and driving here can be stressful and time-consuming.

Tram

An excellent *tramvay* (tramway) service runs from Bağcılar, in the city's west, to Zeytinburnu (where it connects with the metro from the airport) and on to Sultanahmet and Eminönü. It then crosses the Galata Bridge to Karaköy (to connect with the Tünel) and Kabataş (to connect with the funicular to Taksim Meydanı). In the future, it will be extended from Kabataş to the ferry dock at Beşiktaş. A second service runs from Cevizlibağ, closer to Sultanahmet on the same line, through to Kabataş. Services run every five minutes from 6am to midnight. The fare is ₺4; *jetons* are available from machines on every tram stop and İstanbulkarts can be used.

A small antique tram travels the length of İstiklal Caddesi in Beyoğlu from a stop near Tünel Meydanı to Taksim Meydanı. Electronic tickets (₺4) can be purchased from the ticket office at the Tünel funicular, and İstanbulkarts can be used.

Ferry

The most enjoyable way to get around town is by ferry. Crossing between the Asian and European shores, up and down the Golden Horn and Bosphorus, and over to the Princes' Islands, these vessels are as efficient as they are popular with locals. Some are operated by the government-owned İstanbul Şehir Hatları; others by private companies including Dentur Avrasya. Timetables are posted at *iskelesis* (ferry docks).

On the European side, the major ferry docks are at the

FERRY TRAVEL

Ferries ply the following useful two-way routes:
- ➜ Beşiktaş–Kadıköy
- ➜ Beşiktaş–Üsküdar
- ➜ Eminönü–Anadolu Kavağı (Bosphorus Cruise)
- ➜ Eminönü–Kadıköy
- ➜ Eminönü–Üsküdar
- ➜ Emirgan–Kanlıca–Anadolu Hisarı–Bebek (weekends only)
- ➜ İstinye–Emirgan–Kanlıca–Anadolu Hisarı–Kandilli–Bebek–Arnavutköy–Çengelköy
- ➜ Kabataş–Kadıköy
- ➜ Kabataş–Kadıköy–Kınaılada–Burgazada–Heybeliada–Büyükada (Princes' Islands ferry)
- ➜ Kabataş–Üsküdar
- ➜ Karaköy–Kadıköy (some stop at Haydarpaşa)
- ➜ Karaköy–Üsküdar
- ➜ Sarıyer–Rumeli Kavağı–Anadolu Kavağı
- ➜ Üsküdar–Karaköy–Eminönü–Kasımpaşa–Hasköy–Ayvansaray–Sütlüce–Eyüp (Golden Horn Ferry)

mouth of the Golden Horn (Eminönü and Karaköy), at Beşiktaş and next to the tram stop at Kabataş, 2km past the Galata Bridge.

The ferries run to two annual timetables: winter (mid-September to May) and summer (June to mid-September). Tickets are cheap (usually Ŧ4) and it's possible to use an İstanbulkart on most routes.

There are also *deniz otobüsü* and *hızlı feribot* (seabus and fast ferry) services, but these ply routes that are of less interest to the traveller and are also more expensive than the conventional ferries. For more information, check İstanbul Deniz Otobüsleri.

Taxi

İstanbul is full of yellow taxis. Some drivers are lunatics, others are con artists; most are neither. If you're caught with the first category and you're about to go into meltdown, say *'yavaş!'* (careful/slow down!). Drivers in the second of these catego-

ries – the con artists – tend to prey on tourists. All taxis have digital meters and must run them, but some of these drivers ask for a flat fare, or pretend the meter doesn't work so they can gouge you at the end of the trip. The best way to counter this is to tell them no meter, no ride. Avoid the taxis waiting for fares near Aya Sofya Meydanı as we have received reports of rip-offs.

Taxi fares are very reasonable, and rates are the same during both day and night. It costs around Ŧ15 to travel between Beyoğlu and Sultanahmet.

Few taxis have seatbelts. If you catch a taxi over either of the Bosphorus bridges, it is your responsibility to cover the toll (Ŧ3.40). The driver will add this to your fare.

Metro

Metro service leaves every two to 10 minutes between 6am and midnight. *Jetons* cost Ŧ4 and İstanbulkarts can be used.

One line (the M1A) connects Aksaray with the airport, stopping at 15 stations including the otogar along the way. There are plans to add a link between Aksaray and Yenikapı, southwest of Sultanahmet.

Another line (the M2) connects Yenikapı with Taksim, stopping at three stations along the way: Vezneciler, near the Grand Bazaar; on the new bridge across the Golden Horn (Haliç); and at Şişhane, near Tünel Meydanı in Beyoğlu. From Taksim, another service travels northeast to Hacıosman via nine stations.

A fourth line known as the Marmaray connects Kazlıçeşme, west of the Old City, with Ayrılak Çeşmesi, on the Asian side. This travels via a tunnel under the Sea of Marmara, stopping at Yenikapı, Sirkeci and Üsküdar en route, and connecting with the M4 metro running between Kadıköy and Kartal. A small number of İstanbullus refuse to use this tunnel link, believing that safety standards were compromised during its construction so as to expedite its opening.

Funicular & Cable Car

There are two funiculars *(funiküleri)* and two cable cars *(teleferic)* in the city.

A funicular called the Tünel carries passengers between Karaköy, at the base of the Galata Bridge (Galata Köprüsü), to Tünel Meydanı. The service operates between 7am and 10.45pm and a *jeton* costs Ŧ4.

The second funicular carries passengers from Kabataş – at the end of the tramline – to Taksim Meydanı, where it connects to the metro. The service operates from 6am and midnight and a *jeton* costs Ŧ4.

A cable car runs between the waterside at Eyüp to

the Pierre Loti Café (₺3) from 8am to 11pm. Another travels between Maçka (near Taksim) downhill to the İstanbul Technical University in Taşkışla, but is of little use to travellers.

All are short trips and İstanbulkarts can be used.

Bus

The bus system in İstanbul is extremely efficient, though traffic congestion in the city means that bus trips can be very long. The introduction of Metrobüs lines (where buses are given dedicated traffic lanes) aims to relieve this problem, but these tend to service residential suburbs out of the city centre and are thus of limited benefit to travellers. The major bus stands are underneath Taksim Meydanı and at Beşiktaş, Kabataş, Eminönü, Kadıköy and Üsküdar; most services run between 6am and 11pm. Destinations and main stops on city bus routes are shown on a sign on the right (kerb) side of the bus (otobüs) or on the electronic display at its front. You must have an İstanbulkart before boarding

The most useful bus lines for travellers are those running along both sides of the Bosphorus and the Golden Horn, those in the Western Districts and those between Üsküdar and Kadıköy. Note that İstanbulkart transfer charges are slightly lower on buses than they are on trams and ferries.

Dolmuş

A dolmuş is a shared minibus; it waits at a specified departure point until it has a full complement of passengers (in Turkish, dolmuş means full), then follows a fixed route to its destination. Destinations are displayed in the window of the dolmuş. Passengers flag down the driver to get on and indicate to the driver when they want to get off, usually by saying 'inecek var!' (someone wants to get out!). Fares vary (pay on board) but are usually the same as municipal buses. Dolmuşes are almost as comfortable as taxis, run later into the night in many instances, and often ply routes that buses and other forms of transport don't service. Most travellers are unlikely to take a dolmuş during their visit to the city. The only routes they are likely to find useful are between Kadıköy and Taksim Meydanı, Kadıköy and Üsküdar, Beşiktaş and Harbiye, and along the Bosphorus shores.

Directory
A–Z

Customs Regulations

İstanbul's Atatürk International Airport uses the red and green channel system, randomly spot-checking passengers' luggage. You're allowed to import the following without paying duty:

Alcohol 1L of alcohol exceeding 22% volume, 2L of alcoholic beverages max 22% volume

Tobacco Three cartons

Food 2kg of chocolate or candy; 1kg of coffee and/or tea

Currency No limit

Perfume 600ml

Other goods No more than €1500, but this varies by nationality

Note that it's illegal to take antiquities out of the country. Check www.gumruk.gov.tr for more information.

Electricity

230V/50Hz

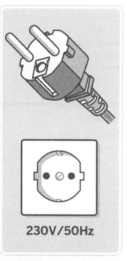

230V/50Hz

Emergency

Ambulance (112)
Fire (110)
Police (155)

Gay & Lesbian Travellers

Homosexuality isn't illegal in Turkey, but neither is it officially legal. There's a generally ambivalent attitude towards it among the general population, although there are sporadic reports of violence towards gay people and conservative İstanbullus frown upon open displays of affection between persons of the same sex.

The monthly *Time Out İstanbul* magazine includes gay and lesbian listings.

Useful websites include the following:

IstanbulGay.com Handy guide to the gay, lesbian and

PRACTICALITIES

➡ **Currency** Türk Lirası (Turkish Lira; ₺). Coins come in amounts of one, five, 10, 25 and 50 kuruş and one lira; notes in five, 10, 20, 50, 100 and 200 lira.

➡ **Smoking** Forbidden in all hotels and enclosed restaurant and bar spaces.

➡ **Tipping** Usually 10% in restaurants; round taxi fares up to the nearest lira.

transgendered scenes in the city. It includes plenty of information about gay-friendly clubs, bars and hotels.

Lambda (www.lambdaistan bul.org; 🏳️) Turkish branch of the international Gay, Lesbian, Bisexual and Transgender Liberation Group. It's based in Beyoğlu.

Pride Travel Agency (📞212-527 0671; www.travel agencyturkey.com; 4th fl, Ateş Pasaji, İncili Çavuş Sokak 15) Well-regarded gay-owned and gay-run travel agency specialising in booking accommodation and tours for gay travellers.

Trans X Turkey (www.trans xturkey.com/en) Advocacy group for Turkey's transgendered community.

Health
Food & Water
Standards of food hygiene are generally high in İstanbul, and visitors experience few food-related illnesses. To be safe, treat street food with caution and if you dine in a *lokanta* (restaurant serving ready-made food) make sure you choose dishes that look hot and freshly prepared.

Tap water in İstanbul is chlorinated, but is still not guaranteed to be safe (many locals don't drink it). Spring water is cheap and sold everywhere in 0.33L, 1.5L and 3L plastic bottles.

Vaccinations
You won't need special inoculations before entering Turkey unless you're coming from an endemic or epidemic area. However, do discuss your requirements with a doctor. Consider typhoid fever and hepatitis A and B vaccinations if you plan to travel off the beaten track in Turkey; also make sure that your tetanus/diphtheria and polio vaccinations are up to

date (boosters are necessary every 10 years).

Internet Access
As is the case elsewhere in Europe, the proliferation of personal communications devices has led to internet cafes becoming a dying breed. Wi-fi connections are ubiquitous in hotels and hostels, and common in chain cafes and fast-food joints.

In our reviews we use an @ icon to indicate accommodation that provides an internet station or laptops for guest use. A 📶 icon is included if wi-fi access is offered.

If using a local computer, you may have to use a Turkish keyboard. When doing so, be aware that Turkish has two 'i's: the familiar dotted 'i' and the less familiar dotless 'ı'. Unfortunately the one in the usual place is the dotless 'ı' on a Turkish keyboard; you will need to make sure you use the correct dotted 'i' when typing in a web or email address. To create the @ symbol, hold down the 'q' and the right-hand ALT keys at the same time.

Legal Matters
➡ The age of consent in Turkey is 18 – as is the legal age for voting, driving and drinking.

➡ Technically, you should carry your passport at all times. Many travellers choose to carry a photocopy and leave the actual document in their hotel safe.

➡ It is illegal to take antiquities out of the country.

➡ In recent years local politics has become increasingly socially conservative. This has manifested itself in a number of ways, including bans on some outdoor drinking venues in the Beyoğlu Belediyesi (Beyoğlu local government area); the closure of some Beyoğlu hotels accused of promoting immoral-

ity by allowing unmarried guests to share rooms; and police crackdowns on gay venues across the city, especially gay hamams and spas, which are regularly accused of breaching public decency laws. If you visit one of these hamams, there is a chance that you could be caught up in a police raid.

Media
There are print and online English-language editions of the daily *Hürriyet Daily News* (www.hurriyetdailynews. com), *Today's Zaman* (www. todayszaman.com) and *Daily Sabah* (www.dailysabah. com) newspapers. The *Hürriyet Daily News* is secularist, *Today's Zaman* is Islamist (it's aligned with Fethullah Gülen's Hizmet movement) and the *Daily Sabah* is unashamedly – many would say scandalously – pro-AKP. A printed English-language edition of the monthly *Time Out* İstanbul magazine is available, and there is also an online edition (www.time outistanbul.com/en/). There are printed and online editions of *The Guide İstanbul* (www.theguideistanbul. com), a listings-heavy bimonthly guide to the city.

Medical Services
Turkey doesn't have reciprocal health-care arrangements with other countries, so having travel insurance is highly advisable.

For minor problems, it's customary to ask at a chemist/pharmacy (*eczane*) for advice. Many pharmacists speak English and will prescribe treatment on the spot. Drugs requiring a prescription in Western countries are often sold over the counter (except for the most dangerous or addictive ones) and will often be cheaper, too. Make sure that you know the generic name of your medicine; the commercial name may not be the same in Turkey.

Most doctors in Turkey speak English and half of all the physicians in İstanbul are women. If a woman visits a male doctor, it's customary for her to have a companion present during any physical examination or treatment.

Though they are expensive, it's probably easiest to visit one of the private hospitals listed here if you need medical care when in İstanbul. Their standard of care is generally quite high and you will have no trouble finding staff who speak English. Both accept credit-card payments and charge around ₺250 for a standard consultation.

American Hospital (Amerikan Hastenesi; ☑212-444 3777, 212-311 2000; www. americanhospitalistanbul.org/ ENG; Güzelbahçe Sokak 20, Nişantaşı; ☉24hr emergency department; Ⓜ Osmanbey) Pediatric, dental and many other clinics.

Memorial Hospital (☑212-314 6666, 444 7888; www.me morial.com.tr/en; Piyalepaşa Bulvarı, Okmeydanı; Ⓜ Şişli) Pediatric, general medicine and dentistry clinics.

Money

We have cited prices for most hotels and organised tours in euros to reflect the reality on the ground. All other prices given are in Turkish liras (₺).

ATMs

ATMs (cashpoints) are everywhere in İstanbul. Virtually all of them offer instructions in English, French and German and will pay out Turkish liras when you insert your bank debit (cash) card. They will also pay cash advances on Visa and MasterCard. The limit on cash withdrawals is generally ₺600 to ₺800 per day, though this varies from bank to bank.

Changing Money

➡ The 24-hour *döviz bürosu*s (exchange bureaux) in the arrivals halls of the international airports usually offer competitive rates.

➡ US dollars and euros are easily changed at exchange bureaux. They are sometimes accepted in carpet shops and hotels.

➡ Turkish liras are fully convertible, so there is no black market.

Credit Cards

Most hotels, car-rental agencies, shops, pharmacies, entertainment venues and restaurants will accept Visa and MasterCard; Amex isn't as widely accepted as the others and Diner's is often not accepted. Inexpensive eateries usually accept cash only.

Opening Hours

Opening hours vary wildly across businesses and services in İstanbul. The following is a very general guide:

Post offices & banks 8.30am to 5pm Monday to Friday

Shops 9am to 6pm Monday to Saturday

Restaurants & cafes Breakfast 7.30am to 10.30am, lunch noon to 2.30pm, dinner 6.30pm to 10pm

Bars Afternoon to early morning

Nightclubs 11pm till late

Post

➡ Post offices are known as PTTs (peh-teh-teh; Posta, Telefon, Teleğraf) and have black-and-yellow signs.

➡ İstanbul's **Central Post Office** (Merkez Postane; Map p238; Büyük Postane Caddesi) is several blocks southwest of Sirkeci train station.

➡ The *yurtdışı* slot is for mail to foreign countries, *yurtiçi* is

for mail to other Turkish cities, and *şehiriçi* is for mail within İstanbul.

➡ Mail delivery is fairly reliable. For more information on PTT services go to www.ptt.gov.tr.

Public Holidays

Banks, offices and government services close for the day on the following secular public holidays:

New Year's Day 1 January

National Sovereignty & Children's Day 23 April

Labor & Solidarity Day 1 May

Commemoration of Atatürk, Youth & Sports Day 19 May

Victory Day 30 August

Republic Day 29 October

Religious festivals are celebrated according to the Muslim lunar Hejira calendar; two of these festivals (Şeker Bayramı and Kurban Bayramı) are also public holidays. Şeker Bayramı is a three-day festival at the end of Ramazan, and Kurban Bayramı, the most important religious holiday of the year, is a four-day festival whose date changes each year. During these festivals, banks and offices are closed and hotels, buses, trains and planes are heavily booked.

Though most restaurants and cafes open to serve non-Muslims during the holy month of Ramazan (called Ramadan in other countries), it's polite to avoid smoking, eating and drinking in the street during this period.

Safe Travel

Pedestrian Safety

As a pedestrian, always give way to vehicles; the sovereignty of the pedestrian is recognised in law but not out on the street. Footpaths (sidewalks) and road surfaces are often in a poorly maintained state and some shops have basements that are accessed from the footpath via steep steps without barriers – watch where you are walking!

Theft & Robbery

Theft is not generally a big problem and robbery (mugging) is comparatively rare, but don't let İstanbul's relative safety lull you. Take normal precautions. Areas to be particularly careful in include Aksaray/Laleli (the city's red-light district), the Grand Bazaar (pickpocket central) and the streets off İstiklal Caddesi in Beyoğlu.

Assault

In 2013 an American woman was murdered while exploring one of the areas around the historic city walls. Though an isolated incident, it was a reminder that not all parts of the city are safe – travellers (especially those who are solo) should be careful when exploring derelict buildings/areas and when walking around the city at night.

Telephone

If you are in European İstanbul and wish to call a number in Asian İstanbul, you must dial ⏌0, followed by ⏌216. If you are in Asian İstanbul and wish to call a number in European İstanbul, use ⏌0 followed by ⏌212. Do not use a prefix (that is, don't use the ⏌0 or ⏌212/6) if you are calling a number on the same shore.

Country code ⏌90

European İstanbul ⏌212

Asian İstanbul ⏌216

Code to make an intercity call ⏌0 + local code

International access code ⏌00

Directory inquiries ⏌118

International operator ⏌115

Mobile Phones

➡ Mobile phone reception is excellent in İstanbul.

➡ All mobile phone numbers start with a four-figure code beginning with ⏌05.

➡ There are three major networks: **Turkcell** (www.turkcell.com.tr), **Vodafone** (www.vodafone.com.tr) and **Avea** (www.avea.com.tr). Each has shops throughout the city selling prepaid SIM cards (kontürlü SIM karts) that are handy for travellers. These cost around ₺45 (including approximately ₺20 in credit) and can be recharged in amounts from ₺15 upwards.

➡ Turkey uses the standard GSM network operating on 900MHz or 1800MHz (so not all US and Canadian phones work here).

➡ To use a local SIM in a phone you've bought from home, you'll need to register the phone. This is a complicated and time-consuming procedure that involves visiting a tax office to pay a registration fee, registering at a police station and then waiting up to 30 days for your registration to be approved. It is only worth pursuing if you plan to be in the country for an extended period.

➡ If you buy a local SIM card and use it in your mobile from home without registering the phone, the network will detect and bar it within a week or two.

➡ If you purchase a phone in Turkey, you won't need to register it. Just purchase a SIM card from a Turkcell, Vodafone or Avea shop and ask the staff to organise the activation for you (you'll need to show your passport). The account should activate within a few hours.

➡ There are plenty of shops selling phones in the streets opposite the Sirkeci train station. Starting models cost around ₺100.

Time

İstanbul time is East European Time, two hours ahead of Coordinated Universal Time (UTC, alias GMT), except in the warm months, when clocks are turned ahead one hour. Daylight-saving (summer) time usually begins at 1am on the last Sunday in March and ends at 2am on the last Sunday in October.

Turks use the 24-hour clock.

Tourist Information

The **Ministry of Culture & Tourism** (www.turizm.gov.tr) currently operates four tourist information offices or booths in the city; a fifth is scheduled to open at some stage in the future inside the Atatürk Cultural Centre on Taksim Meydanı (Taksim Sq). In our experience, the Sirkeci office is the most helpful and the Sultanahmet office is the least helpful.

Tourist Office – Atatürk International Airport (⏌212-465 3547; International Arrivals Hall, Atatürk International Airport; ⏰9am-9pm)

Tourist Office – Karaköy (Map p248; Karaköy International Maritime Passenger Terminal, Kemankeş Caddesi, Karaköy; ⏰9.30am-5pm Mon-Sat; 🚋Karaköy)

Tourist Office – Sirkeci Train Station (Map p238; ⏌212-511 5888; Sirkeci Gar, Ankara Caddesi, Sirkeci; ⏰9am-6pm mid-Apr–Sep, 9am-5.30pm Oct–mid-Apr; 🚋Sirkeci)

Tourist Office – Sultanahmet (Map p240; ⏌212-518 8754; Hippodrome, Sultanahmet; ⏰9.30am-6pm mid-Apr–Sep, 9am-5.30pm Oct–mid-Apr; 🚋Sultanahmet)

Travellers with Disabilities

İstanbul can be challenging for mobility-impaired travellers. Roads are potholed and pavements are often crooked and cracked. Fortunately, the city is attempting to rectify this.

Government-run museums are free of charge for disabled visitors. Public and private museums and sights that have wheelchair access and accessible toilets include Topkapı Palace, the İstanbul Archaeology Museums, İstanbul Modern, the Pera Museum and the Rahmi M Koç Museum. The last three of these also have limited facilities to assist accessibility for vision-impaired visitors.

Airlines and most four- and five-star hotels have wheelchair access and at least one room set up for disabled guests. All public transport is free for the disabled, and the metro and tram can be accessed by people in wheelchairs.

FHS Tourism & Event (www.accessibleturkey.org) is an İstanbul-based tour agency that has a dedicated department organising accessible travel packages and tours.

Visas

At the time of research, nationals of the following countries (among others) could enter Turkey for up to three months with only a valid passport (no visa required): Denmark, Finland, France, Germany, Greece, Israel, Italy, Japan, New Zealand, Russia, Sweden and Switzerland.

Nationals of the following countries (among others) needed to obtain an electronic visa (www.evisa. gov.tr) before their visit: Australia, Canada, China, Ireland, Mexico, Netherlands, Spain, UK and USA. These visas were valid for between 30 and 180 days and for either a single entry or a multiple entry, depending on the nationality. Visa fees cost US$15 to US$60 depending on nationality.

Chinese and Indian nationals needed to 'meet certain conditions' before being granted an electronic visa.

Your passport must have at least six months' validity remaining, or you may not be admitted into Turkey. See the website of the **Ministry of Foreign Affairs** (www. mfa.gov.tr) for the latest information.

Women Travellers

Travelling in İstanbul as a female is easy and enjoyable provided you follow some simple guidelines. Tailor your behaviour and your clothing to your surrounds – outfits that are appropriate for neighbourhoods such as Beyoğlu and along the Bosphorus (skimpy tops, tight jeans etc) are not appropriate in conservative suburbs such as Üsküdar, for instance.

It's a good idea to sit in the back seat of a taxi rather than next to the driver. If approached by a Turkish man in circumstances that upset you, try saying *Ayıp!* (ah-*yuhp*), which means 'Shame on you!'

You'll have no trouble finding sanitary napkins and condoms in pharmacies and supermarkets in İstanbul; tampons can be a bit difficult to access. Bring a shawl to cover your head when visiting mosques.

Language

Turkish belongs to the Ural-Altaic language family. It's the official language of Turkey and northern Cyprus, and has approximately 70 million speakers worldwide.

Pronouncing Turkish is pretty simple for English speakers as most Turkish sounds are also found in English. If you read our coloured pronunciation guides as if they were English, you should be understood just fine. Note that the symbol ew represents the sound 'ee' pronounced with rounded lips (as in 'few'), and that the symbol uh is pronounced like the 'a' in 'ago'. The Turkish r is always rolled and v is pronounced a little softer than in English.

Word stress is quite light in Turkish – in our pronunciation guides the stressed syllables are in italics.

BASICS

Hello.
Merhaba.   mer·ha·ba

Goodbye.
Hoşçakal.   hosh·cha·kal
(said by person leaving)
Güle güle.   gew·le gew·le
(said by person staying)

Yes.
Evet.   e·vet

No.
Hayır.   ha·yuhr

Excuse me.
Bakar mısınız.   ba·kar muh·suh·nuhz

WANT MORE?

For in-depth language information and handy phrases, check out Lonely Planet's *Turkish Phrasebook*. You'll find it at **shop.lonelyplanet.com**, or you can buy Lonely Planet's iPhone phrasebooks at the Apple App Store.

Sorry.
Özür dilerim.   er·zewr dee·le·reem

Please.
Lütfen.   lewt·fen

Thank you.
Teşekkür ederim.   te·shek·kewr e·de·reem

You're welcome.
Birşey değil.   beer·shay de·eel

How are you?
Nasılsınız?   na·suhl·suh·nuhz

Fine, and you?
İyiyim, ya siz?   ee·yee·yeem ya seez

What's your name?
Adınız nedir?   a·duh·nuhz ne·deer

My name is ...
Benim adım ...   be·neem a·duhm ...

Do you speak English?
İngilizce   een·gee·leez·je
konuşuyor   ko·noo·shoo·yor
musunuz?   moo·soo·nooz

I understand.
Anlıyorum.   an·luh·yo·room

I don't understand.
Anlamıyorum.   an·la·muh·yo·room

ACCOMMODATION

Where can I find a ...?	Nerede ... bulabilirim?	ne·re·de ... boo·la·bee·lee·reem
campsite	kamp yeri	kamp ye·ree
guesthouse	misafirhane	mee·sa·feer·ha·ne
hotel	otel	o·tel
pension	pansiyon	pan·see·yon
youth hostel	gençlik hosteli	gench·leek hos·te·lee

How much is it per night/person?
Geceliği/Kişi   ge·je·lee·ee/kee·shee
başına ne kadar?   ba·shuh·na ne ka·dar

Is breakfast included?
Kahvaltı dahil mi? kah·val·*tuh* da·*heel* mee

Do you have	*... odanız*	*... o·da·nuz*
a ...?	*var mı?*	var muh
single room	*Tek kişilik*	tek kee·shee·*leek*
double room	*İki*	ee·*kee*
	kişilik	kee·shee·*leek*

air conditioning	*klima*	*klee·*ma
bathroom	*banyo*	*ban·*yo
window	*pencere*	*pen·*je·re

DIRECTIONS

Where is ...?
... nerede? *... ne·*re·de

What's the address?
Adresi nedir? ad·re·*see* ne·deer

Could you write it down, please?
Lütfen yazar lewt·fen ya·*zar*
mısınız? muh·suh·*nuhz*

Can you show me (on the map)?
Bana (haritada) ba·*na* (ha·ree·ta·*da*)
gösterebilir gers·te·re·bee·leer
misiniz? mee·seen·*neez*

It's straight ahead.
Tam karşıda. tam kar·shuh·*da*

at the traffic lights
trafik tra·*feek*
ışıklarından uh·shuhk·la·ruhn·*dan*

at the corner	*köşeden*	ker·she·*den*
behind	*arkasında*	ar·ka·suhn·*da*
far (from)	*uzak*	oo·*zak*
in front of	*önünde*	er·newn·*de*
near (to)	*yakınında*	ya·kuh·nuhn·*da*
opposite	*karşısında*	kar·shuh·suhn·*da*
Turn left.	*Sola dön.*	so·*la* dern
Turn right.	*Sağa dön.*	sa·*a* dern

EATING & DRINKING

What would you recommend?
Ne tavsiye ne tav·see·*ye*
edersiniz? e·*der*·see·neez

What's in that dish?
Bu yemekte neler var? boo ye·mek·*te* ne·ler var

I don't eat ...
... yemiyorum. *... ye·mee·yo·room

Cheers!
Şerefe! she·re·*fe*

That was delicious!
Nefisti! ne·*fees*·tee

The bill/check, please.
Hesap lütfen. he·*sap* lewt·fen

KEY PATTERNS

To get by in Turkish, mix and match these simple patterns with words of your choice:

When's (the next bus)?
(Sonraki otobüs) (son·ra·kee o·to·*bews*)
ne zaman? ne za·*man*

Where's (the market)?
(Pazar yeri) nerede? (pa·zar ye·ree) ne·re·de

Where can I (buy a ticket)?
Nereden (bilet ne·re·den (bee·*let*
alabilirim)? a·la·bee·lee·reem)

I have (a reservation).
(Rezervasyonum) (re·zer·vas·yo·*noom*)
var. var

Do you have (a map)?
(Haritanız) (ha·ree·ta·*nuhz*)
var mı? var muh

Is there (a toilet)?
(Tuvalet) var mı? (too·va·*let*) var muh

I'd like (the menu).
(Menüyü) (me·new·*yew*)
istiyorum. ees·tee·yo·room

I want to (make a call).
(Bir görüşme (beer ger·rewsh·*me*
yapmak) yap·*mak*)
istiyorum. ees·tee·yo·room

Do I have to (declare this)?
(Bunu beyan (boo·*noo* be·yan
etmem) gerekli mi? et·*mem*) ge·rek·*lee* mee

I need (assistance).
(Yardıma) (yar·duh·*ma*)
ihtiyacım var. eeh·tee·ya·*juhm* var

I'd like a table	*... bir masa*	*... beer ma·*sa
for ...	*ayırtmak*	a·*yuhrt*·mak
	istiyorum.	ees·tee·yo·room
(eight) o'clock	*Saat (sekiz)*	sa·*at* (se·*keez*)
	için	ee·*cheen*
(two) people	*(İki)*	(ee·*kee*)
	kişilik	kee·shee·*leek*

Key Words

appetisers	*mezeler*	me·ze·*ler*
bottle	*şişe*	shee·*she*
bowl	*kase*	ka·*se*
breakfast	*kahvaltı*	kah·val·*tuh*
(too) cold	*(çok) soğuk*	(chok) so·*ook*
cup	*fincan*	feen·*jan*
delicatessen	*şarküteri*	shar·kew·te·*ree*
dinner	*akşam yemeği*	ak·*sham* ye·me·ee
dish	*yemek*	ye·*mek*

food	yiyecek	yee·ye·jek
fork	çatal	cha·tal
glass	bardak	bar·dak
grocery	bakkal	bak·kal
halal	helal	he·lal
highchair	mama sandalyesi	ma·ma san·dal·ye·see
hot (warm)	sıcak	suh·jak
knife	bıçak	buh·chak
kosher	koşer	ko·sher
lunch	öğle yemeği	er·le ye·me·ee
main courses	ana yemekler	a·na ye·mek·ler
market	pazar	pa·zar
menu	yemek listesi	ye·mek lees·te·see
plate	tabak	ta·bak
restaurant	restoran	res·to·ran
spicy	acı	a·juh
spoon	kaşık	ka·shuhk
vegetarian	vejeteryan	ve·zhe·ter·yan

Meat & Fish

anchovy	hamsi	ham·see
beef	sığır eti	suh·uhr e·tee
calamari	kalamares	ka·la·ma·res
chicken	piliç/ tavuk	pee·leech/ ta·vook
fish	balık	ba·luhk
lamb	kuzu	koo·zoo
liver	ciğer	jee·er
mussels	midye	meed·ye
pork	domuz eti	do·mooz e·tee
veal	dana eti	da·na e·tee

Fruit & Vegetables

apple	elma	el·ma
apricot	kayısı	ka·yuh·suh
banana	muz	mooz
capsicum	biber	bee·ber
carrot	havuç	ha·vooch
cucumber	salatalık	sa·la·ta·luhk
fruit	meyve	may·ve
grape	üzüm	ew·zewm
melon	kavun	ka·voon
olive	zeytin	zay·teen
onion	soğan	so·an
orange	portakal	por·ta·kal

peach	şeftali	shef·ta·lee
potato	patates	pa·ta·tes
spinach	ıspanak	uhs·pa·nak
tomato	domates	do·ma·tes
watermelon	karpuz	kar·pooz

Other

bread	ekmek	ek·mek
cheese	peynir	pay·neer
egg	yumurta	yoo·moor·ta
honey	bal	bal
ice	buz	booz
pepper	kara biber	ka·ra bee·ber
rice	pirinç/ pilav	pee·reench/ pee·lav
salt	tuz	tooz
soup	çorba	chor·ba
sugar	şeker	she·ker
Turkish delight	lokum	lo·koom

Drinks

beer	bira	bee·ra
coffee	kahve	kah·ve
(orange) juice	(portakal) suyu	(por·ta·kal soo·yoo)
milk	süt	sewt
mineral water	maden suyu	ma·den soo·yoo
soft drink	alkolsüz içecek	al·kol·sewz ee·che·jek
tea	çay	chai
water	su	soo
wine	şarap	sha·rap
yoghurt	yoğurt	yo·oort

Signs	
Açık	Open
Bay	Male
Bayan	Female
Çıkışı	Exit
Giriş	Entrance
Kapalı	Closed
Sigara İçilmez	No Smoking
Tuvaletler	Toilets
Yasak	Prohibited

Question Words

How?	Nasil?	na·seel
What?	Ne?	ne
When?	Ne zaman?	ne za·man
Where?	Nerede?	ne·re·de
Which?	Hangi?	han·gee
Who?	Kim?	keem
Why?	Neden?	ne·den

EMERGENCIES

Help!
İmdat!   eem·dat

I'm lost.
Kayboldum.   kai·bol·doom

Leave me alone!
Git başımdan!   geet ba·shuhm·dan

There's been an accident.
Bir kaza oldu.   beer ka·za ol·doo

Can I use your phone?
Telefonunuzu   te·le·fo·noo·noo·zoo
kullanabilir miyim?   kool·la·na·bee·leer mee·yeem

Call a doctor!
Doktor çağırın!   dok·tor cha·uh·ruhn

Call the police!
Polis çağırın!   po·lees cha·uh·ruhn

I'm ill.
Hastayım.   has·ta·yuhm

It hurts here.
Burası ağrıyor.   boo·ra·suh a·ruh·yor

I'm allergic to (nuts).
(Çerezlere)   (che·rez·le·re)
alerjim var.   a·ler·zheem var

SHOPPING & SERVICES

I'd like to buy ...
... almak istiyorum.   ... al·mak ees·tee·yo·room

I'm just looking.
Sadece bakıyorum.   sa·de·je ba·kuh·yo·room

May I look at it?
Bakabilir miyim?   ba·ka·bee·leer mee·yeem

The quality isn't good.
Kalitesi iyi değil.   ka·lee·te·see ee·yee de·eel

How much is it?
Ne kadar?   ne ka·dar

It's too expensive.
Bu çok pahalı.   boo chok pa·ha·luh

Do you have something cheaper?
Daha ucuz birşey   da·ha oo·jooz beer·shay
var mı?   var muh

There's a mistake in the bill.
Hesapta bir   he·sap·ta beer
yanlışlık var.   yan·luhsh·luhk var

ATM	bankamatik	ban·ka·ma·teek
credit card	kredi kartı	kre·dee kar·tuh
post office	postane	pos·ta·ne
signature	imza	eem·za
tourist office	turizm bürosu	too·reezm bew·ro·soo

TIME & DATES

What time is it? Saat kaç?   sa·at kach
It's (10) o'clock. Saat (on).   sa·at (on)
Half past (10). (On) buçuk.   (on) boo·chook

in the morning	öğleden evvel	er·le·den ev·vel
in the afternoon	öğleden sonra	er·le·den son·ra
in the evening	akşam	ak·sham
yesterday	dün	dewn
today	bugün	boo·gewn
tomorrow	yarın	ya·ruhn
Monday	Pazartesi	pa·zar·te·see
Tuesday	Salı	sa·luh
Wednesday	Çarşamba	char·sham·ba
Thursday	Perşembe	per·shem·be
Friday	Cuma	joo·ma
Saturday	Cumartesi	joo·mar·te·see
Sunday	Pazar	pa·zar
January	Ocak	o·jak
February	Şubat	shoo·bat
March	Mart	mart
April	Nisan	nee·san
May	Mayıs	ma·yuhs
June	Haziran	ha·zee·ran
July	Temmuz	tem·mooz
August	Ağustos	a·oos·tos
September	Eylül	ay·lewl
October	Ekim	e·keem
November	Kasım	ka·suhm
December	Aralık	a·ra·luhk

TRANSPORT

Public Transport

At what time does the ... leave/arrive?	... ne zaman kalkacak/ varır?	... ne za·man kal·ka·jak/ va·ruhr
boat	Vapur	va·poor
bus	Otobüs	o·to·bews
plane	Uçak	oo·chak
train	Tren	tren

Numbers

1	bir	beer
2	iki	ee·kee
3	üç	ewch
4	dört	dert
5	beş	besh
6	altı	al·tuh
7	yedi	ye·dee
8	sekiz	se·keez
9	dokuz	do·kooz
10	on	on
20	yirmi	yeer·mee
30	otuz	o·tooz
40	kırk	kuhrk
50	elli	el·lee
60	altmış	alt·muhsh
70	yetmiş	et·meesh
80	seksen	sek·sen
90	doksan	dok·san
100	yüz	yewz
1000	bin	been

Does it stop at (Maltepe)?
(Maltepe'de) (mal·te·pe·de)
durur mu? doo·roor moo

What's the next stop?
Sonraki durak son·ra·kee doo·rak
hangisi? han·gee·see

Please tell me when we get to (Beşiktaş).
(Beşiktaş'a) (be·sheek·ta·sha)
vardığımızda var·duh·uh·muhz·da
lütfen bana lewt·fen ba·na
söyleyin. say·le·yeen

I'd like to get off at (Kadıköy).
(Kadıköy'de) inmek (ka·duh·kay·de) een·mek
istiyorum. ees·tee·yo·room

I'd like a ...	(Bostancı'ya)	(bos·tan·juh·ya)
ticket to	... bir bilet	... beer bee·let
(Bostancı).	lütfen.	lewt·fen
1st-class	Birinci mevki	bee·reen·jee mev·kee
2nd-class	Ikinci mevki	ee·keen·jee mev·kee
one-way	Gidiş	gee·deesh
return	Gidiş-dönüş	gee·deesh·der·newsh

first	ilk	eelk
last	son	son
next	geleçek	ge·le·jek

I'd like	... bir yer	... beer yer
a/an ... seat.	istiyorum.	ees·tee·yo·room
aisle	Koridor tarafında	ko·ree·dor ta·ra·fuhn·da
window	Cam kenarı	jam ke·na·ruh

cancelled	iptal edildi	eep·tal e·deel·dee
delayed	ertelendi	er·te·len·dee
platform	peron	pe·ron
ticket office	bilet gişesi	bee·let gee·she·see
timetable	tarife	ta·ree·fe
train station	istasyon	ees·tas·yon

Driving & Cycling

I'd like to hire a ...	Bir ... kiralamak istiyorum.	beer ... kee·ra·la·mak ees·tee·yo·room
4WD	dört çeker	dert che·ker
bicycle	bisiklet	bee·seek·let
car	araba	a·ra·ba
motorcycle	motosiklet	mo·to·seek·let

bike shop	bisikletçi	bee·seek·let·chee
child seat	çocuk koltuğu	cho·jook kol·too·oo
diesel	dizel	dee·zel
helmet	kask	kask
mechanic	araba tamircisi	a·ra·ba ta·meer·jee·see
petrol/gas	benzin	ben·zeen
service station	benzin istasyonu	ben·zeen ees·tas·yo·noo

Is this the road to (Taksim)?
(Taksim'e) giden (tak·see·me) gee·den
yol bu mu? yol boo moo

(How long) Can I park here?
Buraya (ne kadar boo·ra·ya (ne ka·dar
süre) park sew·re) park
edebilirim? e·de·bee·lee·reem

The car/motorbike has broken down (at Osmanbey).
Arabam/ a·ra·bam/
Motosikletim mo·to·seek·le·teem
(Osmanbey'de) (os·man·bay·de)
bozuldu. bo·zool·doo

I have a flat tyre.
Lastiğim patladı. las·tee·eem pat·la·duh

I've run out of petrol.
Benzinim bitti. ben·zee·neem beet·tee

GLOSSARY

Below are some useful Turkish words and abbreviations:

ada(lar) – island

arasta – row of shops near a mosque

Asya – Asian İstanbul

Avrupa – European İstanbul

bahçe(si) – garden

bey – 'Mr'; follows the name

boğaz – strait

bulvar(ı) – often abbreviated to 'bul'; boulevard or avenue

caddesi – often abbreviated to 'cad'; road

cami(i) – mosque

çarşı(sı) – market, bazaar

çay bahçesi – tea garden

çeşme – spring, fountain

deniz – sea

deniz otobüsü – catamaran; sea bus

dervish – member of the Mevlevi Muslim brotherhood

dolmuş – shared taxi (or minibus)

döviz bürosu – currency-exchange office

eczane – chemist/pharmacy

eski – old (thing, not person)

ezan – Muslim call to prayer; also *azan*

fasıl – energetic folk music played in *meyhanes* (taverns)

fayton – horse-drawn carriage

feribot – ferry

hamam(ı) – Turkish steam bath

han – traditional name for a caravanserai

hastanesi – hospital

hısar(ı) – fortress or citadel

imam – prayer leader; Muslim cleric; teacher

iskele(si) – landing place, wharf, quay

kadın – wife

kale(si) – fortress, citadel

kapı(sı) – door, gate

karagöz – shadow-puppet theatre

KDV – *katma değer vergisi*; value-added tax (VAT)

kebapçı – place selling kebaps

keyif – relaxation

kilim – pileless woven rug

konak, konağı – mansion, government headquarters

köprü – bridge

köy(ü) – village

külliye – mosque complex

kuru temizleme – dry cleaning

mahfil – high, elaborate chair

Maşallah – Wonder of God! (said in admiration or to avert the evil eye)

medrese – Islamic school of higher studies

merkez postane – central post office

meydan(ı) – public square, open place

mihrab – niche in a mosque indicating the direction of Mecca

mimber – pulpit in a mosque

minaret – mosque tower from which Muslims are called to prayer

müezzin – the official who sings the *ezan*

müze(si) – museum

nargile – water pipe

oda(sı) – room

otel(ı) – hotel

otobüs – bus

otogar – bus station

Ottoman – of or pertaining to the Ottoman Empire, which lasted from the end of the 13th century to the end of WWI

padişah – Ottoman emperor, sultan

paşa – general, governor

pazar(ı) – weekly market, bazaar

PTT – Posta, Telefon, Teleğraf; post, telephone and telegraph office

Ramazan – Islamic holy month of fasting (Ramadan)

şadırvan – fountain where Muslims perform ritual ablutions

saray(ı) – palace

sebil – fountain

şehir – city; municipal area

selamlık – public/male quarters of a traditional household

Seljuk – of or pertaining to the Seljuk Turks, who in the 11th to 13th centuries created the first Turkish state to rule Anatolia

sema – dervish ceremony

semahane – hall where whirling-dervish ceremony is performed

sokak, sokağı – often abbreviated to 'sk' or 'sok'; street or lane

Sufi – Muslim mystic, member of a mystic (dervish) brotherhood

sultan – sovereign

tarikat – a Sufic order

tavla – backgammon

TC – Türkiye Cumhuriyeti (Turkish Republic); designates an official office or organisation

tekke – dervish lodge

tramvay – tram

tuğra – sultan's monogram, imperial signature

türbe – tomb

ücretsiz servis – free service

valide sultan – queen mother

vezir – vizier (minister) in the Ottoman government

yalı – waterside timber mansion

yeni – new

yıldız – star

yol(u) – road, way

FOOD GLOSSARY

General Terms

acı – spicy
afiyet olsun – bon appétit
aile salonu – family room; for couples, families and women in a Turkish restaurant
akşam yemeği – dinner
ana yemekler – main courses
bakkal – grocery store
balık restoran – fish restaurant
bardak – glass
bıçak – knife
börekçi – place selling pastries
büfe – snack bar
buz – ice
çatal – fork
dolma – vegetables stuffed with rice and/or meat
etyemez/vejeteryan – vegetarian
fasulyecı – restaurant serving cooked beans
fincan – cup
garson – waiter/waitress
hazır yemek lokanta – casual restaurant serving ready-made food
helal – halal
hesap – the bill
içmek – drink
İngilizce menu – menu in English
kaşık – spoon
kase/tas – bowl
kahvaltı – breakfast
kebapcı – kebap restaurant
köftecı – *köfte* (meatball) restaurant
koşer – kosher
lokanta – abbreviation of *hazır yemek lokanta*
mama sandalyesi – highchair
menü – menu
meyhane – tavern
meze – small dish eaten at the start of a meal; similar to tapas

ocakbaşı – fireside kebap restaurant
öğle yemeği – lunch
pastane – cake shop
pazar – market
peçete – napkin
pidecisi – pizza restaurant
porsiyon – portion, helping
restoran – restaurant
sade – plain
şarküteri – delicatessen
şerefe! – cheers!
servis ücreti – service charge
sıcak – hot; warm
şişe – bottle
tabak – plate
uç – tip
yarım porsiyon – half *porsiyon*
yemek – eat; dish
zeytinyağlı – food cooked in olive oil

Staples

ayva – quince
bal – honey
balık – fish
beyaz peynir – salty white cheese similar to fetta
biber – bell pepper
ceviz – walnut
ciğer – liver
çilek – strawberry
çorba – soup
dana eti – veal
domates – tomato
ekmek – bread
elma – apple
enginar – artichoke
erik – plum
et – meat
et suyu – meat stock
fıstık – pistachio
hamsi – anchovy
havuç – carrot
incir – fig

ıspanak – spinach
kalamar – calamari
kalkan – turbot
kara/toz biber – black/white pepper
karpuz – watermelon
kaşar peyniri – cheddar-like sheep's milk cheese
kavun – melon
kayısı – apricot
kestane – chestnuts
kiraz – cherry
kuzu – lamb
levrek – sea bass
limon – lemon
lüfer – bluefish
mantar – mushroom
meyve – fruit
midye – mussels
muz – banana
pastırma – pressed beef preserved in garlic and spices
patates – potato
patlıcan – eggplant
peynir – cheese
pirinç/pilav – rice
portakal – orange
salata – salad
salatalık – cucumber
sebze – vegetables
şeftali – peach
şeker – sugar
sığır eti – beef
simit – sesame-encrusted bread ring
soğan – onion
tavuk/piliç – chicken
taze fasulye – green beans
tuz – salt
un – flour
uskumru – mackerel
üzüm – grape
vişne – sour cherry, morello
yumurta – egg
zeytin – olive

Popular Dishes

MEZE

acılı ezme – spicy tomato and onion paste

ançüez – salted or pickled anchovy

barbunya piliki – red-bean salad

beyaz peynir – white cheese from sheep or goat

çacık – yoghurt dip with garlic and mint

çerkez tavuğu – Circassian chicken; made with chicken, bread, walnuts, salt and garlic

enginar – cooked artichoke

fasulye pilaki – white beans cooked with tomato paste and garlic

fava salatası – mashed broad-bean salad

haydari – yoghurt dip with roasted eggplant and garlic

humus – chickpea dip with sesame oil, lemon and spices

imam bayıldı – literally 'the imam fainted'; eggplant, onion, tomato and peppers slow-cooked in olive oil

kalamar tava – fried calamari

lakerda – strongly flavoured salted kingfish salad

midye dolma – stuffed mussels

muhammara – dip of walnuts, bread, tahini, olive oil and lemon juice; also known as *acuka* or *civizli biber*

patlıcan kızartması – fried eggplants with tomatoes

piyaz – white-bean salad

Rus salatası – Russian salad

semizotu salatası – green purslane with yoghurt and garlic

sigara böreği – deep-fried cigar-shaped pastries filled with white cheese

turşu – pickled vegetables

yaprak sarma/yaprak dolması – vine leaves stuffed with rice, herbs and pine nuts

yeşil fasulye – green beans

KEBAPS (KEBABS) & KÖFTE (MEATBALLS)

Adana kebap – a spicy version of *şiş köfte*

alinazik – eggplant purée with yoghurt and ground *köfte*

beyti sarma – spicy ground meat baked in a thin layer of bread and served with yoghurt

çiğ köfte – raw ground-lamb mixed with pounded bulgur, onion, spices and pepper

döner kebap – compressed meat (usually lamb) cooked on a revolving upright skewer and thinly sliced

fıstıklı kebap – minced lamb studded with pistachios

içli köfte – meatballs rolled in bulgur and fried

İskender (Bursa) kebap – döner lamb served on crumbled pide with yoghurt, topped with tomato and butter sauces

ızgara köfte – grilled meatballs

karışık ızgara – mixed grilled lamb

kebap – meat grilled on a skewer

köfte – meatballs

patlıcan kebap – cubed or minced lamb grilled with eggplant

pirzola – lamb cutlet

şiş kebap – small pieces of lamb grilled on a skewer

şiş köfte – meatballs wrapped around a flat skewer and barbecued

tavuk şiş – small chicken pieces grilled on a skewer

testi kebap – small pieces of lamb or chicken in sauce that is slow-cooked in a sealed terracotta pot

tokat kebap – lamb cubes grilled with potato, tomato, eggplant and garlic

Urfa kebap – a mild version of the Adana kebap served with lots of onion and black pepper

Other Dishes

Arnavut çiğeri – Albanian-style spicy fried liver

balık ekmek – sandwich of grilled fish and salad

börek – sweet or savoury filled pastry

çoban salatası – salad of tomatoes, cucumber, onion and pepper

gözleme – filled savoury pancake

hünkâr beğendi – literally 'sultan's delight'; lamb or beef stew served on a mound of rich eggplant purée

iç pilav – rice with onions, nuts and currants

işkembe çorbası – tripe soup

kısır – bulgur salad

kokoreç – seasoned, grilled lamb/mutton intestines

kuru fasulye – haricot beans cooked in a spicy tomato sauce

lahmacun – thin and crispy Arabic-style pizza

mantı – Turkish ravioli stuffed with beef mince and topped with yoghurt, garlic, tomato and butter

menemen – breakfast eggs cooked with tomatoes, peppers and white cheese

mercimek çorbası – lentil soup

pide – Turkish-style pizza

su böreği – lasagne-like layered pastry laced with white cheese and parsley

sucuk – spicy beef sausage

tavuk kavurma – roast chicken

Drinks & Desserts

Amerikan kahvesi – instant coffee

aşure – dried fruit, nut and pulse pudding

ayran – drink made with yoghurt and salt

baklava – layered filo pastry with honey or sugar syrup; sometimes made with nuts

beyaz şarap – white wine
bira – beer
bitki çay – herbal tea
çay – tea
dondurma – ice-cream
elma çay – apple tea, predominantly a tourist drink
fırın sütlaç – rice pudding
helva – sweet prepared with sesame oil, cereals and honey or sugar syrup
kadayıf – dough soaked in syrup and topped with a layer of kaymak (clotted cream)
kahve – coffee
kırmızı şarap – red wine

kiraz suyu – cherry juice
kola – cola-flavoured soft drink
künefe – shredded-wheat pastry with pistachios, honey and sugar syrup
limonata – lemonade
lokum – Turkish delight
maden suyu – mineral water
mahallebi – sweet rice-flour and milk pudding
meyve suyu – fruit juice
rakı – strong aniseed-flavoured liquor
sahlep – hot drink made with crushed tapioca-root extract

şalgam suyu – sour turnip juice
şarap – wine
su – water
süt – milk
(taze) nar suyu – (fresh) pomegranate juice
(taze) portakal suyu – (fresh) orange juice
Türk kahvesi – Turkish coffee
...az şekerli – with a little sugar
...çok şekerli – with a lot of sugar
...orta şekerli – with medium sugar
...sade/şekersiz – no sugar

Behind the Scenes

SEND US YOUR FEEDBACK

We love to hear from travellers – your comments keep us on our toes and help make our books better. Our well-travelled team reads every word on what you loved or loathed about this book. Although we cannot reply individually to your submissions, we always guarantee that your feedback goes straight to the appropriate authors, in time for the next edition. Each person who sends us information is thanked in the next edition – the most useful submissions are rewarded with a selection of digital PDF chapters.

Visit **lonelyplanet.com/contact** to submit your updates and suggestions or to ask for help. Our award-winning website also features inspirational travel stories, news and discussions.

Note: We may edit, reproduce and incorporate your comments in Lonely Planet products such as guidebooks, websites and digital products, so let us know if you don't want your comments reproduced or your name acknowledged. For a copy of our privacy policy visit lonelyplanet.com/privacy.

OUR READERS

Many thanks to the travellers who used the last edition and wrote to us with helpful hints, useful advice and interesting anecdotes:

Anne Jaumees, Anne Marie Mingiardi, Astrid Joublanc, Connlaodh MacThoirealaigh, David Munday, Emilie Pause, Fernando Figueiredo, Francesca Voci, Jeff Michels, Ketan Gurjar, Kyle Hughes, Laura Seaton, Luciano Rezende, Tony Boas

AUTHOR THANKS

Virginia Maxwell

Many thanks to Pat Yale, Mehmet Umur, Emel Güntaş, Faruk Boyacı, Atilla Tuna, Tahir Karabaş, Jen Hartin, Eveline Zoutendijk, George Grundy, Barbara Nadel, Ercan Tanrıvermiş, Ann Nevans, Tina Nevans, Jennifer Gaudet, Özlem Tuna, Ansel Mullins, Ken Dakan and the many others who shared their knowledge and love of the city with me.

ACKNOWLEDGMENTS

Illustrations p52-3, p58-9 by Javier Zarracina.

Cover photograph: Golden Horn & Süleymaniye Mosque, Claudio Cassaro/4Corners.

THIS BOOK

This 8th edition of Lonely Planet's *İstanbul* guidebook was researched and written by Virginia Maxwell. The previous four editions were also written by Virginia. This guidebook was commissioned in Lonely Planet's London office, and produced by the following:

Destination Editor Jo Cooke
Coordinating Editor Kristin Odijk
Product Editor Elin Berglund
Senior Cartographer Corey Hutchison
Book Designer Virginia Moreno

Assisting Editors Melanie Dankel, Gabrielle Stefanos
Cover Researcher Naomi Parker

Thanks to Bruce Evans, Ryan Evans, Justin Flynn, Larissa Frost, Jouve India, Claire Naylor, Karyn Noble, Clifton Wilkinson, Amanda Williamson

See also separate subindexes for:

✗ **EATING P224**
🍴 **DRINKING & NIGHTLIFE P225**
☆ **ENTERTAINMENT P226**
🛍 **SHOPPING P226**
🏃 **SPORTS & ACTIVITIES P226**
🛏 **SLEEPING P226**

Index

✗ EATING

İstanbul Maps

Sights

- Beach
- Bird Sanctuary
- Buddhist
- Castle/Palace
- Christian
- Confucian
- Hindu
- Islamic
- Jain
- Jewish
- Monument
- Museum/Gallery/Historic Building
- Ruin
- Sento Hot Baths/Onsen
- Shinto
- Sikh
- Taoist
- Winery/Vineyard
- Zoo/Wildlife Sanctuary
- Other Sight

Activities, Courses & Tours

- Bodysurfing
- Diving
- Canoeing/Kayaking
- Course/Tour
- Skiing
- Snorkelling
- Surfing
- Swimming/Pool
- Walking
- Windsurfing
- Other Activity

Sleeping

- Sleeping
- Camping

Eating

- Eating

Drinking & Nightlife

- Drinking & Nightlife
- Cafe

Entertainment

- Entertainment

Shopping

- Shopping

Information

- Bank
- Embassy/Consulate
- Hospital/Medical
- Internet
- Police
- Post Office
- Telephone
- Toilet
- Tourist Information
- Other Information

Geographic

- Beach
- Hut/Shelter
- Lighthouse
- Lookout
- Mountain/Volcano
- Oasis
- Park
- Pass
- Picnic Area
- Waterfall

Population

- Capital (National)
- Capital (State/Province)
- City/Large Town
- Town/Village

Transport

- Airport
- Border crossing
- Bus
- Cable car/Funicular
- Cycling
- Ferry
- Metro station
- Monorail
- Parking
- Petrol station
- S-Bahn/Subway station
- Taxi
- T-bane/Tunnelbana station
- Train station/Railway
- Tram
- Tube station
- U-Bahn/Underground station
- Other Transport

Note: Not all symbols displayed above appear on the maps in this book

Routes

- Tollway
- Freeway
- Primary
- Secondary
- Tertiary
- Lane
- Unsealed road
- Road under construction
- Plaza/Mall
- Steps
- Tunnel
- Pedestrian overpass
- Walking Tour
- Walking Tour detour
- Path/Walking Trail

Boundaries

- International
- State/Province
- Disputed
- Regional/Suburb
- Marine Park
- Cliff
- Wall

Hydrography

- River, Creek
- Intermittent River
- Canal
- Water
- Dry/Salt/Intermittent Lake
- Reef

Areas

- Airport/Runway
- Beach/Desert
- Cemetery (Christian)
- Cemetery (Other)
- Glacier
- Mudflat
- Park/Forest
- Sight (Building)
- Sportsground
- Swamp/Mangrove

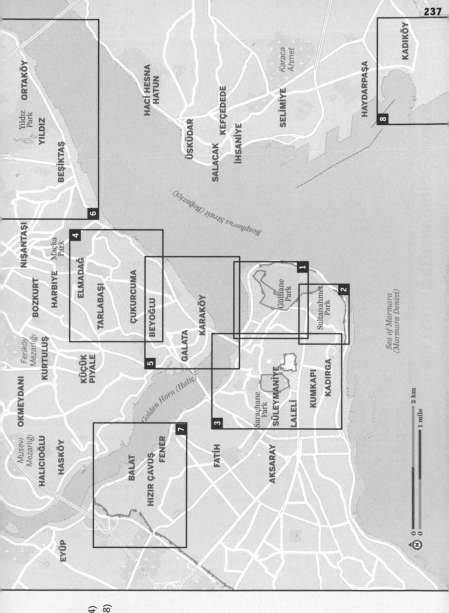

MAP INDEX

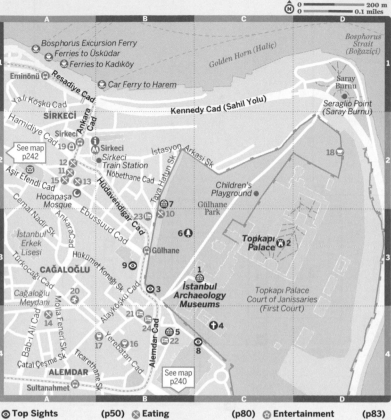

SULTANAHMET & AROUND - SOUTH *Map on p240*

SULTANAHMET & AROUND – SOUTH

Key on p239

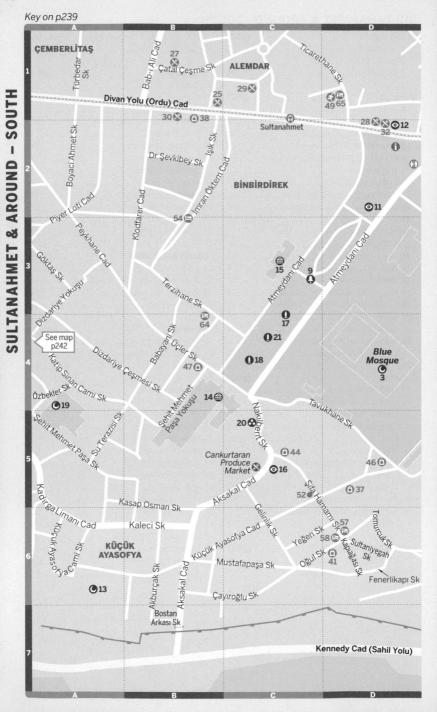

ÇEMBERLİTAŞ

Türbedar Sk

Bab-ı Ali Cad

Çatal Çeşme Sk 27

ALEMDAR

29

Ticarethane Sk

Divan Yolu (Ordu) Cad 25 49 65

30 38

Sultanahmet

28 32 12

Boyaci Ahmet Sk

Dr Şevkibey Sk

Işık Sk

İmran Öktem Cad

BİNBİRDİREK

Piyer Loti Cad

Klodfarer Cad

54

11

Peykhane Cad

Göktaş Sk

Dizdariye Yokuşu

Terzihane Sk

Atmeydanı Cad

15

9

Babayani Sk

Üçler Sk

64

Atmeydanı Cad

17

See map p242

Dizdariye Çeşmesi Sk

21

47

18

Blue Mosque
3

Katip Sinan Cami Sk

Özbekler Sk

19

Şehit Mehmet Paşa Yokuşu

14

Tavukhane Sk

Şehit Mehmet Paşa Sk

Su Terazisi Sk

20

Nakilbent Sk

Cankurtaran Produce Market

44

46

16

52

37

Kadirga Limanı Cad

Kasap Osman Sk

Kaleci Sk

Aksakal Cad

Küçük Ayasofya Cami Sk

KÜÇÜK AYASOFYA

Akburçak Sk

Aksakal Cad

Küçük Ayasofya Cad

Gelinlik Sk

Mustafapaşa Sk

Yeğen Sk

Sıfa Hamamı Sk

57

58

Oğul Sk

41

Kapıağası Sk

Sultaniyegah Sk

Tomurcuk Sk

Fenerlikapı Sk

13

Çayıroğlu Sk

Bostan Arkası Sk

Kennedy Cad (Sahil Yolu)

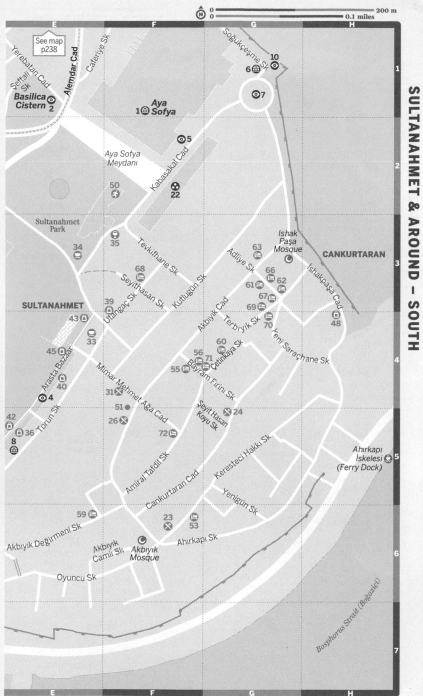

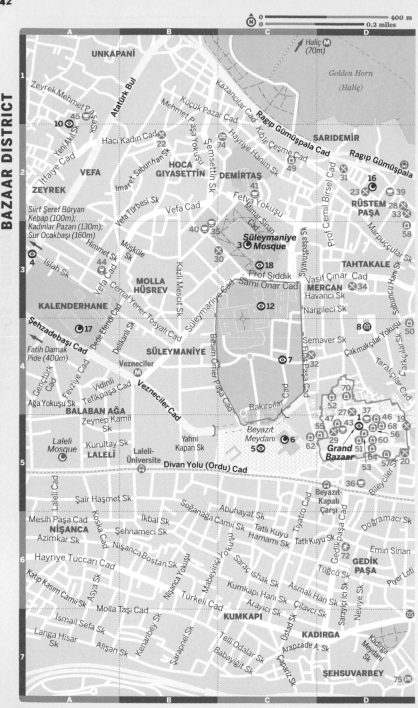

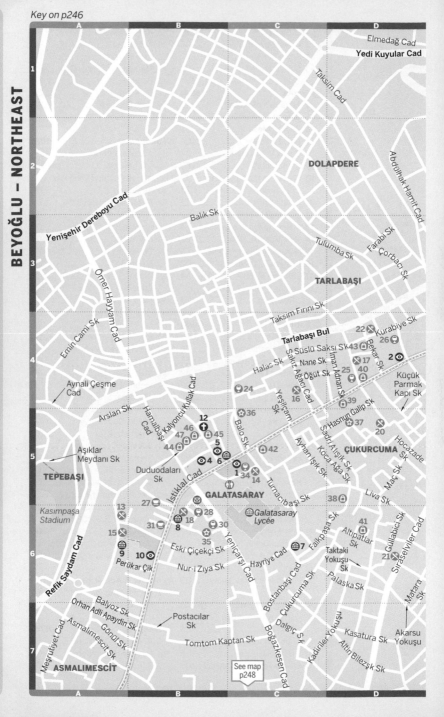

BEYOĞLU – NORTHEAST

Elmedağ Cad
Yedi Kuyular Cad

Taksim Cad

DOLAPDERE

Abdülhak Hamit Cad

Balık Sk

Yenişehir Dereboyu Cad

Tulumba Sk

Farabi Sk

Çorbacı Sk

TARLABAŞI

Ömer Hayyam Cad

Emin Cami Sk

Taksim Fırını Sk

Tarlabaşı Bul

22 Kurabiye Sk
26
Aynalı Çeşme
Cad

Halas Sk

Süslü Saksı Sk 43
Sakız Ağacı Cad
Nane Sk İman Adnan Sk 17
25 Öğüt Sk 40
2

Arslan Sk

Hamalbaşı Cad

Kalyoncu Kullak Cad

24

16

Yeşilçam Sk

39

Küçük
Parmak
Kapı Sk

Aşıklar
Meydanı Sk

36

Balo Sk

Hasnun Galip Sk

37

20

TEPEBAŞI

12
46
47 45
44 5
4 6

1 34
14

Duduodaları
Sk

İstiklal Cad

42

Sadri Alışık Sk

Koca Ağa Sk

Ayhan Işık Sk

ÇUKURCUMA

Hocazade
Sk

Maç Sk

GALATASARAY

Turnacıbaşı Sk

38

Liva Sk

Kasımpaşa
Stadium

27

13
31

18
28

30

Galatasaray
Lycée

41

Altıpatlar
Sk

Gülübcü Sk

Siraselviler Cad

15

35

Eski Çiçekçi Sk

Yeniçarşı Cad

Hayriye Cad

Bostanbaşı Cad

7

Falkpaşa Sk

21

Refik Saydam Cad

9
10

Perükar Çik

Nur-i Ziya Sk

Çukurcuma Sk

Taktaki
Yokuşu
Sk

Palaska Sk

Matara

Balyoz Sk

Orhan Adli Apaydın Sk

Gönül Sk

Postacılar
Sk

Dalgıç Sk

Kadiriler Yokuşu

Altın Bilezik Sk

Kasatura Sk

Akarsu
Yokuşu

Meşrutiyet Cad

Asmalımescit Sk

Tomtom Kaptan Sk

Boğazkesen Cad

ASMALIMESCİT

See map
p248

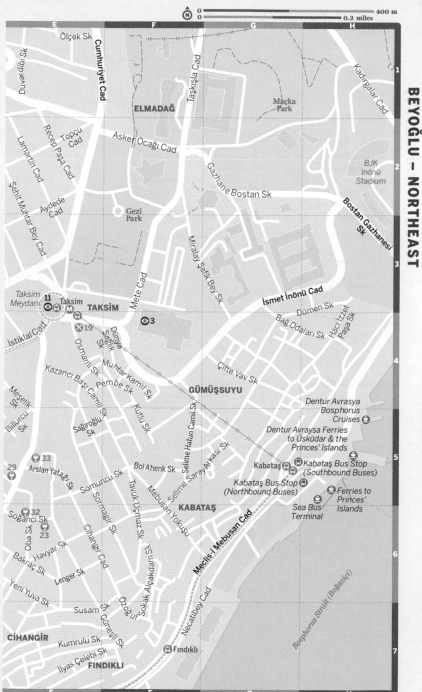

0 400 m
0 0.2 miles

Ölçek Sk
Duvardibi Sk
Cumhuriyet Cad
Taşkışla Cad
ELMADAĞ
Maçka Park
Kadırgalar Cad

Lamartin Cad
Recep Paşa Cad
Topçu Cad
Asker Ocağı Cad
Gazhane Bostan Sk
BJK İnönü Stadium

Şehit Muhtar Bey Cad
Aydede Cad
Gezi Park
Miralay Şefik Bey Sk
Bostan Gazhanesi Sk

Taksim Meydanı
Taksim
TAKSİM
3
İsmet İnönü Cad
Dümen Sk
Bağ Odaları Sk
Hacı İzzet Paşa Sk

İstiklal Cad
19
Dünya Sağlık Sk
Mete Cad
Çifte Vav Sk

Meşelik Sk
Billurcu Sk
Kazancı Başı Camii Sk
Osmanlı Sk
Muhtar Kamil Sk
Pembe Sk
GÜMÜŞSUYU
Kutlu Sk
Selime Hatun Camii Sk
Saray Arkası Sk
Dentur Avrasya Bosphorus Cruises

29
33
Arslan Yatağı Sk
Sağıroğlu Sk
Bol Ahenk Sk
Dentur Avraysa Ferries to Üsküdar & the Princes' Islands
Kabataş
Kabataş Bus Stop (Southbound Buses)

Somuncu Sk
Sormagir Sk
Tavuk Uçmaz Sk
Mebusan Yokuşu
KABATAŞ
Kabataş Bus Stop (Northbound Buses)
Ferries to Princes' Islands
Sea Bus Terminal

32
Soğancı Sk
23
Oba Sk
Çhangır Cad
Lenger Sk
Sokak Alçakdam Sk
Meclis-i Mebusan Cad

Bakraç Sk
Havyar Sk
Yeni Yuva Sk
Özoğul
Susam Sk
Güneşli Sk
Necatibey Cad
Bosphorus Strait (Boğaziçi)

CİHANGİR
Kumrulu Sk
İlyas Çelebi Sk
FINDIKLI
Fındıklı

BEYOĞLU - NORTHEAST *Map on p244*

BEYOĞLU - SOUTHWEST *Map on p248*

BEYOĞLU – SOUTHWEST

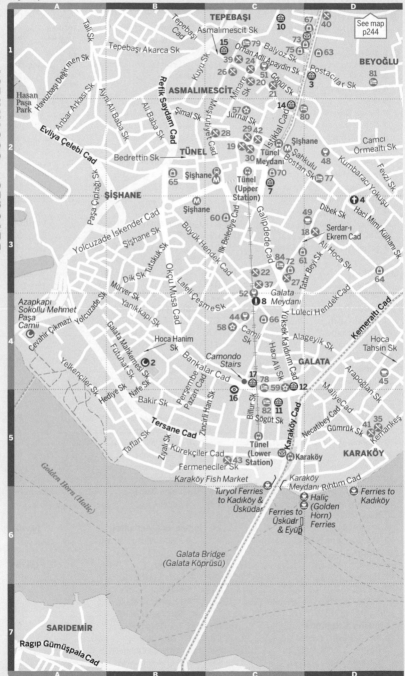

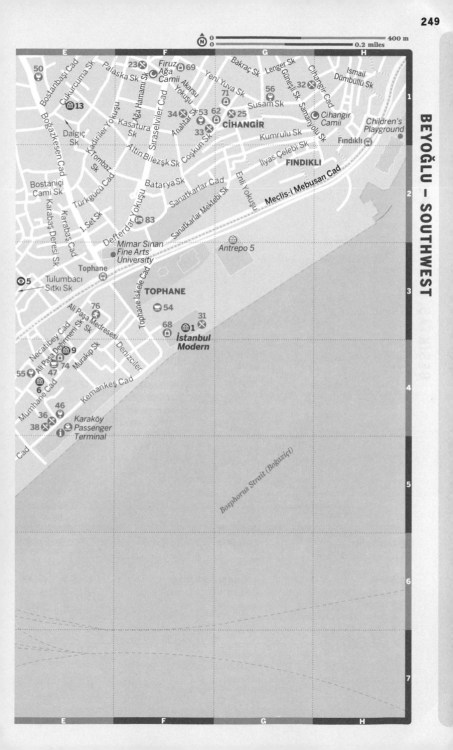

BEŞİKTAŞ, ORTAKÖY & KURUÇEŞME

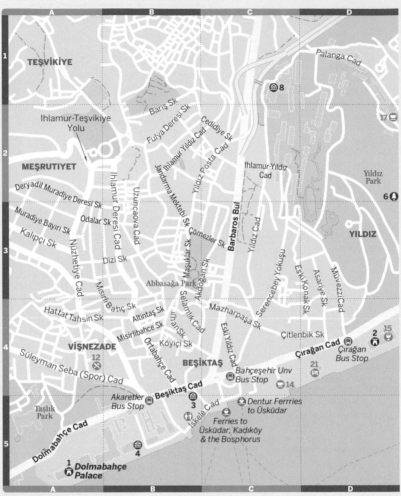

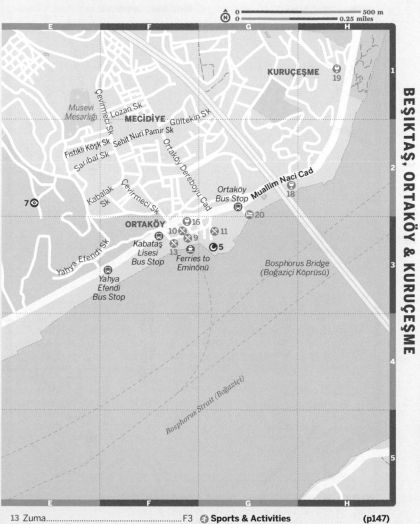

WESTERN DISTRICTS

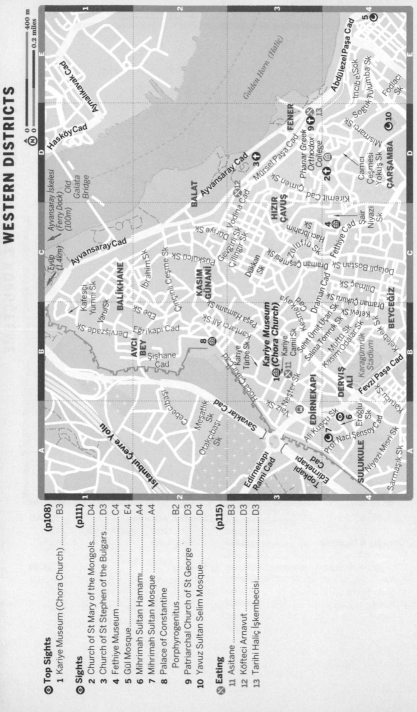

KADIKÖY

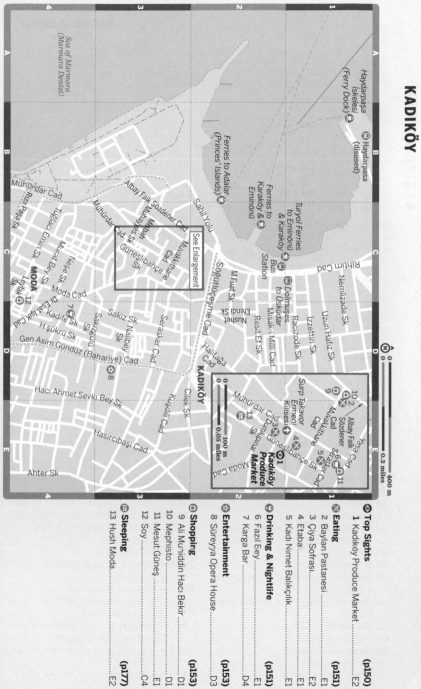

Sea of Marmara
(Marmara Denizi)

Haydarpaşa
İskelesi
(Ferry Dock)

Haydarpaşa
(disused)

Ferries to Adalar
(Princes' Islands)

Ferries to
Karaköy &
Eminönü

Turyol Ferries
to Eminönü
& Karaköy

Dolmuşes
to Üsküdar

Bus
Station

Rıhtım Cad

Nemlizade Sk

Mühürdar Cad

Albay Faik Sözdener Cad

Sahil Yolu

Muvakkithane
Cad

Güneşlibahçe
Sk

See Enlargement

Söğütlüçeşme Cad

M Fuat Sk

Nushet
Efendi Sk

Misak-ı Milli Cad

Reşit Ef Sk

Halitağa
Cad

İzzettin Sk

Uzun Hafız Sk

Racizode Sk

Tuğlacı Emin Sk

Rıza Paşa Sk

Serasker Cad

Sakız Sk

Mühürdar Cad

MODA

Neşe Sk

Murat Bey Sk

Moda Cad

Leylak
Sk

Dr Esat Işık Cad

Kadife Sk

Sakızgülü
Sk

Nailbey
Sk

Genç Asim Gündüz (Bahariye) Cad

Hacı Ahmet Şevki Bey Sk

Çilek Sk

Kuşdili Cad

Hasırcıbaşı Cad

Ahter Sk

KADIKÖY

**Kadıköy
Produce
Market**

Surp Takavor
Ermeni
Kilisesi

Mühürdar Cad

Dumlupınar
Sk

Güneşlibahçe Sk

Moda Cad

Muvakkithane
Cad

Albay Faik
Sözdener
Cad

Serasker Cad

400 m
0.2 miles

100 m
0.05 miles

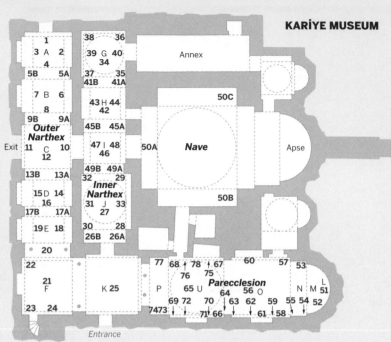

◎ Mosaics

1 The voyage of the Virgin to Bethlehem & the dream of Joseph

2 The census held for the enrolment for taxation & registration of Mary & Joseph in the presence of Cyrenius, Governor of Syria

3 Jesus going with Mary & Joseph to Jerusalem

4 Remains of mosaics – Jesus among the doctors in the temple

5A St Trachos

5B St Andronikus

6 The birth of Jesus

7 The return of the Virgin Mary with Jesus

8 The attempts of Satan to deceive Jesus

9A St Georgios

9B St Demetrius

10 Jesus & the inscription 'the dwelling-place of the living'

11 The prayer of the Virgin & the attendant angels

12 The wedding at Cana & the miracles

13A Depiction of the saints

13B Depiction of the saints

14 The Magi on their way to Jerusalem riding on horseback & the three Magi in audience with King Herod

15 Elizabeth & John the Baptist running away from a pursuing soldier

16 Remains of mosaics

17A Depiction of the saints

17B Depiction of the saints

18 The scene of King Herod's investigation & a guard standing

19 The mourning mothers

20 No mosaics left

21 A decorative medallion

22 The meeting of Jesus with the Samaritan woman at the well

23 The healing of a paralysed person by Jesus

24 King Herod giving the order for the massacre of the innocents & the execution thereof

25 Remains of mosaics

26A The healing by Jesus of a young man with an injured arm

26B The healing by Jesus of leprous man

27 Twenty-four of the early ancestors of Jesus (Genealogy of Christ)

28 The healing by Jesus of a woman asking for the restoration of her health

29 The healing by Jesus of the mother-in-law of St Peter

30 The healing by Jesus of a deaf person

31 Dispersion of good health by Jesus to the people

32 The healing by Jesus of two blind men

33 The Khalke Jesus & the praying Virgin

34 Mary and the Baby Jesus surrounded by her ancestors

35 Joachim in the mountains praying to have a child

36 No mosaics left

37 The breaking of the good news of the birth of Jesus to Mary – The Annunciation

38 The chief priest Zacchariah judging the Virgin

39 Mary & Joseph bidding each other farewell

40 The breaking of the good news of the birth of Mary to Anne

41A The meeting of Anne & Joachim

41B Joseph bringing the Virgin into his house

42 Mary in the arms of Anne & Joachim & the blessing by the priests

43 Giving of the stick with young shoots indicating Joseph as Mary's fiancé

44 The birth of the Virgin Mary

45A The first seven steps of the Virgin & below, St Peter

45B The prayer of the chief priest Zacchariah in front of the 12 sticks

46 The presentation of Mary (age three) to the temple by her parents

47 The Virgin taking the skeins of wool to weave the veil for the temple

48 Theodore Metochites presenting a small model of the church to Jesus

49A The feeding of the Virgin by an angel & below, St Peter

49B Remains of mosaics – Directives given to the Virgin at the temple

50A The Assumption of the Virgin

50B Mary and the Baby Jesus

50C Jesus in a standing posture, holding the Bible in his hand

◉ **Frescoes**

51 The Anastasis

52 The Church fathers

53 The raising (resurrection of the widow's son)

54 The healing of the daughter of Jairus

55 The Virgin Elousa

56 The Last Judgement

57 Abraham & the beggar Lazarus on his lap

58 St George

59 Rich man burning in Hell's fire

60 Those entering Heaven & the Angel Seraphim with the semi-nude good thief

61 Depiction of Andronikus II & his family & the inscription & depiction above of Makarios Tornikes & his wife Eugenia

62 The Bearing of the Ark of the Covenant

63 St Demetrius

64 St Theodore Tiro

65 Mary & child Jesus with the 12 attending angels

66 Four Gospel Writers (Hymnographers): St Cosmos

67 Four Gospel Writers (Hymnographers): St John of Damascene

68 Four Gospel Writers (Hymnographers): St Theophanes

69 Four Gospel Writers (Hymnographers): St Joseph

70 St Theodore Stratelates

71 King Solomon & the Israelites

72 Placement into the temple of the Ark of the Covenant

73 The combat of an angel with the Asurians in the outskirts of Jerusalem

74 St Procopios, St Sabas Stratelates

75 Moses in the bushes

76 Jacob's ladder & the angels

77 Aaron & his sons carrying votive offerings, in front of the altar

78 St Samonas & Guiras

Our Story

A beat-up old car, a few dollars in the pocket and a sense of adventure. In 1972 that's all Tony and Maureen Wheeler needed for the trip of a lifetime – across Europe and Asia overland to Australia. It took several months, and at the end – broke but inspired – they sat at their kitchen table writing and stapling together their first travel guide, *Across Asia on the Cheap*. Within a week they'd sold 1500 copies. Lonely Planet was born.

Today, Lonely Planet has offices in Franklin, London, Melbourne, Oakland, Beijing and Delhi, with more than 600 staff and writers. We share Tony's belief that 'a great guidebook should do three things: inform, educate and amuse'.

Our Writer

Virginia Maxwell

Although based in Australia, Virginia spends much of her year researching guidebooks in the Mediterranean region. Of these countries, Turkey is unquestionably her favourite. As well as working on the previous four editions of the *İstanbul* city guide, she is the author of Lonely Planet's *Pocket İstanbul* and the İstanbul and Thrace & Marmara chapters of Lonely Planet's *Turkey* guidebook. She also writes about the city for a host of international magazines and websites. Virginia usually travels with partner Peter and son Max, who have grown to love Turkey as much as she does.

Published by Lonely Planet Publications Pty Ltd
ABN 36 005 607 983
8th edition – February 2015
ISBN 978 1 74321 477 0
© Lonely Planet 2015   Photographs © as indicated 2015
10 9 8 7 6 5 4 3 2 1
Printed in China

Although the authors and Lonely Planet have taken all reasonable care in preparing this book, we make no warranty about the accuracy or completeness of its content and, to the maximum extent permitted, disclaim all liability arising from its use.